THE MODERN LIBRARY
of the World's Best Books

>>>

THE METROPOLITAN
OPERA GUIDE

THE METROPOLITAN

OPERA GUIDE

The Standard Repertory of The Metropolitan Opera Association, Inc.

as selected by Edward Johnson, former General Manager

BY MARY ELLIS PELTZ AND ROBERT LAWRENCE

ILLUSTRATED BY ALEXANDRE SEREBRIAKOFF

A PUBLICATION OF THE METROPOLITAN OPERA GUILD, INC.

THE MODERN LIBRARY

NEW YORK

THE MODERN LIBRARY

IS PUBLISHED BY

RANDOM HOUSE, INC.

BENNETT A. CERF · DONALD S. KLOPFER · ROBERT K. HAAS

Manufactured in the United States of America

Foreword

THE new opera audience of America extends from coast to coast, and beyond to the islands of the sea. By the magic of radio the band of opera lovers known as the Metropolitan Opera Guild has grown from a membership resident in New York City and its environs to a host of enthusiasts in forty-six states of the union and a half dozen foreign countries.

To serve these men and women it has become necessary to devise a new book on opera. Since the organization of the Metropolitan Opera Guild in 1935, a brief manual has been issued each year with a summary of opera plots and recordings, composers' biographies, book lists and other material. The current repertory of the Metropolitan Opera Association has in each case been taken as the basis of the volume.

Today we are constantly asked for further aids in the appreciation of opera. Our growing radio membership reminds us that the stage setting must remain a mystery unless we present it by word or picture. Even the entrances and exits of leading characters can only be guessed by the distant audience.

The thousands of young people who have attended the special junior performances sponsored by the Metropolitan Opera Guild wish for further direction in their study of the classic works. Cities which the Metropolitan company visits on tour desire to anticipate the experience with additional preparation. Communities which have built up local opera companies around visiting Metropolitan artists are anxious for information on which to found their own traditions. Listening groups beg for courses of study. Casual radio fans want to steep themselves in the world of opera for an hour before they tune in on the Saturday broadcasts.

The Metropolitan Opera Guide is the Opera Guild's answer to this varied and urgent demand. The close co-operation of the Metropolitan management has enabled us to provide certain details of information not otherwise available to the general public. The list of operas represents Mr. Johnson's own choice of the standard operatic repertory.

Anyone reading this book who is not already a member of the Guild will be received with cordial warmth into our fellowship. Our organization is founded on the belief that the more we know of opera the more we will enjoy it, and the deeper our enjoyment, the keener will be our desire to assume a share in the responsibility for the production of opera.

And so, whether the volume will mark your first venture across the romantic landscape which is opera—or whether we may serve you as a more intimate guide into its farthest refuge—I bid you welcome, in the name of The Metropolitan Opera Guild.

Mrs. August Belmont

Acknowledgment

THE METROPOLITAN OPERA GUILD INC. and the authors of this volume desire to acknowledge the courteous permission of the following music publishers to quote selections from the operas to which they hold the copyright: G. Ricordi & Co., Inc. for Verdi's *Falstaff* and *Otello,* Puccini's *La Bohème, Madama Butterfly, Gianni Schicchi* and *Tosca,* and Montemezzi's *L'Amore dei Tre Re;* G. Schirmer, Inc. for Massenet's *Manon* and *Thaïs,* Saint-Saëns' *Samson et Dalila,* Charpentier's *Louise* and Beethoven's *Fidelio* in the version of Artur Bodanzky; Galaxy Music Corporation for Richard Strauss' *Elektra, Der Rosenkavalier* and *Salome;* the Associated Music Publishers, Inc. for Offenbach's *Les Contes D'Hoffmann* and Humperdinck's *Hänsel und Gretel;* and Elkan-Vogel Co., Inc. for *Pelléas et Mélisande.*

Vocal scores of the following operas are published by G. Schirmer, Inc.: *Aïda, Il Barbiere di Siviglia, Carmen, Cavalleria Rusticana, Les Contes d'Hoffmann, Le Coq D'Or, Don Giovanni, Faust, Lohengrin, Lucia di Lammermoor, Die Meistersinger von Nürnberg, Mignon, I Pagliacci, Rigoletto, Roméo et Juliette, Tannhäuser, La Traviata, Il Trovatore* and *Die Walküre.*

The operas in this volume have been selected by Edward Johnson, former General Manager of The Metropolitan Opera Association, Inc., as forming the basis of the Metropolitan repertory. While the entire list does not appear in the prospectus of any one season, nor include all the current novelties and revivals at the Metropolitan Opera House, it comprises operas which have all been produced at the Metropolitan and may, in his opinion, be considered standard.

Contents

I

Opera Is Born

Opera is a plural word. The variety of its nature appears in any dictionary definition. Opera is "the musical form of drama, composed of airs, recitatives and choruses, etc., with accompaniment of orchestra, scenery, and acting." Opera has been accused by its enemies of being a hybrid. They say it is neither so good drama as a play, nor so good music as a symphony. Its supporters find virtue in its very wealth of appeal. Opera for them is the perfect blend of poetry, drama, dance and song.

The birth of opera did not mark the appearance of a new element in art, but rather a fusion of hitherto independent forces. The event occurred in the year 1600, when Peri's *Euridice,* the earliest opera extant, was performed before a public audience in Florence as part of the wedding celebrations of Henry IV of France and Marie de' Medici.

An audience of today would have found *Euridice* but meager entertainment. It was little more than a continuous recitative with occasional choral passages, accompanied by a few chords from an orchestra of harpsichord, lyre and lutes. And yet in this slender frame was contained a lofty ambition: the desire of a few gentle-men of Florence, gathered about their leader, Count Giovanni Bardi, to create a drama as vivid and expressive as that of the ancient Greeks, and to provide it with a musical accompaniment that should heighten its eloquence.

Since no trace remained of the music that had accompanied Greek tragedy, the early composers of opera had to fall back upon other traditions. For years they had listened to the polyphonic music of the church, which reached its fullest development in the work of Palestrina (1524-1594). In the very year of his death, one of their number, Orazio Vecchi, had strung together a series of madrigals, or songs written for five or six voices in the ecclesiastical manner, woven about them a secular plot, and allotted their presen-tation to costumed singers. The result, which the composer entitled *Amfiparnasso,* might have earned the name of opera but for one limitation: there was no attempt at acting, nor illusion of human drama.

Through the course of the seventeenth century, opera gradually outgrew its original aristocratic connections. Claudio Monteverde (1567-1643) was commissioned to write, as Peri had done, for the festivities of the court, and celebrated the nuptials of the son of the Duke of Mantua with his *Orfeo* (1608). Later the composer made a radical innovation, descending from Olympus to the plains of human history in his theme for *L'Incoronazione di Poppea.*

In Naples, where the natural beauty of the voice has always flourished, Alessandro Scarlatti (1659-1725) stressed the formal vocal perfection of the aria and started opera on its road toward the goal of vocal display.

Jean Baptiste Lully (1632-1687) traveled to the court of Louis XIV in the service of a French princess and developed the scenic importance of opera, a feature which was to dominate the operatic stage in that country for two hundred years. He also originated the operatic overture, developed the ballet, and first introduced brass into the opera orchestra.

Jean Philippe Rameau (1683-1764) turned to opera in middle life, and progressed beyond Lully in musical characterization, wealth of harmony and melodic expressiveness. He was so concerned with the fine points of musical theory, however, that his texts took second place, and dramatic interest suffered accordingly.

While opera was flourishing in court circles in France, it was constantly attracting a wider audience in Italy. At the end of the seventeenth century, there were no fewer than eleven opera houses in Venice alone. But the original dramatic contribution of the Florentines was neglected in favor of a new interest, a purely vocal concern which had originated in the church: the use of male singers whose soprano or alto voices had been artificially retained from boyhood. The singing voice was thus a far cry from the voice of the character represented, and the dramatic effect of opera was subordinated to a purely technical display.

Since audiences still demanded the illusion of reality, little operettas were introduced between the acts, with no relation to the opera itself. These *intermezzi*, or foster children of early opera, became in turn the parents of light opera (*opera buffa*).

A hundred years after Peri's classical work, opera had developed two main forms: recitative, either spoken or sung, by which the story was told and the action moved; and aria, which was often sung to a dozen words only, divided into their component syllables, and repeated *ad libitum* through music which was important for itself alone. Hence the use of tone, which in the days of the Greeks had arisen to make the words audible to remote listeners out-of-doors, came in itself to outweigh, and even obscure, the text.

II

Opera Faces Reality

As opera developed, it suffered the growing pains that affect all art during a period of change. Self-consciousness replaced the simplicity of the early Florentine music dramas, and a desire to make a striking impression, regardless of the means employed, crept into the music written for the lyric stage.

Great voices were the order of the day. These voices, however, did not serve the opera; on the contrary, opera was tailored to the demands of the individual singer. At the outset of the eighteenth century, the better-known Italian composers wrote music that would set off the voice in every phase of performance.

Under such conditions, opera became a series of display arias connected only by the semblance of a plot. The union of music and drama, which had originally brought opera into being, was obscured by the brilliance of vocal effect. In its very nature, an aria with a formal three-part design cannot express a great variety of mood. Yet it was this abstract type of music which dominated opera, while the unfolding of the drama was reduced to a few lines of recitative. Conventions went so far as to crystallize two different patterns of recitative: one was a brittle kind of song-speech, often unaccompanied, or punctuated by the harpsichord, called *secco* (dry); while the other—a nobler type of declamation with orchestral accompaniment—was called *stromentato* (accompanied).

This virtuoso school of opera did not confine itself to Naples, the place of its birth. At practically every royal court on the Continent, an Italian composer was in command as director of the opera house. If native musicians ever attained such a post, it was because they had studied in Italy and were intimately acquainted with the Italian language and traditions.

Christoph Willibald Gluck was one of the many German composers who wrote operas in Italian for the Northern court theatres. During his early career, he followed the Neapolitan tradition without question. It was only during his stay in Vienna, after he had reached his middle years, that he experienced a complete reorientation of viewpoint. In *Orfeo,* he took his first step toward ridding opera of its extravagances; and in the preface to his *Alceste* (1767), the composer definitely expressed his principles of music drama, which were a return to the pure ideals of the Florentine founders.

In his zeal for reform, Gluck abolished *secco* recitative as unworthy of the operatic stage. He also radically altered the aria, transforming it into a simple, almost folk-like melody, free of all vocal pyrotechnics.

Opera was facing reality. It had to reform or die. While Gluck's changes were not in themselves lasting, they paved the way for the innovations of a future generation.

GLUCK

CHRISTOPH WILLIBALD VON GLUCK was born near Neumarkt in the Upper Palatinate on July 2, 1714. After acquiring a sound musical background in Prague, he went to Vienna as private musician to Prince Lobkowitz. Like most German composers of the time, he was anxious to complete his education in Italy; and thus, he journeyed to Milan, where his first opera, *Artaserse*, was produced.

During this early period, Gluck was merely an average composer with a predilection for traveling. He voyaged to London, where he seems to have enjoyed more fame as performer on the glass harmonica than as a creative genius. Finally, in 1754, he was summoned to direct the Court Opera at Vienna. Under the influence of the great artists with whom he came in contact, headed by Raniero Calzabigi, the court poet, Gluck's ideals of operatic art began to take shape.

In 1761, the composer reached the turning point of his career with the dramatic ballet *Don Juan*, which still holds the stage today. The following year he set to music Calzabigi's libretto of *Orfeo ed Euridice*. With the success of this work, Gluck embarked on a series of operas consecrated to the reform of the musical stage: *Alceste* and *Paris ed Elena*, first performed in Vienna; then *Iphigénie en Aulide*, *Armide* and *Iphigénie en Tauride*, produced at Paris, while Gluck was in the service of the French Court.

All of these subjects were taken from history or legend. The composer invested them with a simple and moving dignity which was lacking in the stage works of his contemporaries. During his stay in Paris, Gluck's uncompromising integrity often brought him into conflict with other composers of the day. But he emerged victorious and returned laden with honors to Vienna, where he died on November 15, 1787.

ORFEO ED EURIDICE

ORFEO, *an opera in which Gluck strove for a union of music, drama and ballet, was produced at Vienna in 1762. According to a convention of the period, the libretto, although performed in an Austrian theatre, was Italian, and the title role was sung by a male alto* (castrato). *During a Paris revival of the last century, the part of Orfeo was entrusted to a contralto, a procedure which has been standard ever since.* Orfeo *first appeared at the Metropolitan in 1891 with Giulia Ravogli in the title role and her sister Sofia as Euridice. In November, 1938, it was restored to the repertory with a newly studied production and Kerstin Thorborg in the leading part.*

Characters, in order of appearance:

Orfeo: *contralto*
Amor: *soprano*
A Happy Shade: *soprano*
Euridice: *soprano*
Choruses
and
Ballets } *Attendants of Orfeo, the Furies, Blessed Spirits, Guardians of the Temple of Love.*

Time: Legendary   *Place:* Greece and the Nether World

ACT I

SCENE: THE TOMB OF EURIDICE (32 Minutes)

UNTIMELY death has claimed Euridice, wife of Orfeo. The famous minstrel has lost his power of song. All he can bring himself to utter

20

is the despairing cry: "Euridice!" But groups or youths and *Attendants*
maidens cluster about the tomb, chanting their grief. *and Orfeo*

At last, Orfeo finds words in which to express his sorrow. "My
friends," he sobs, "your lamentations only add to my distress!
Come—let us honor Euridice and scatter flowers on her grave!"

In silence, his companions celebrate the antique rites for the *Exeunt*
dead. Flowers are heaped about the tomb—torches are extinguished *Attendants*
in mourning—and the celebrants depart.

Orfeo lingers, hoping for a sign from his beloved. Vainly does he
invoke the shade of Euridice. The groves and valleys repeat his cry
in dreary echo.

Andantino

Chia - mo_il mio ben co - - si,   quan-do si mo - stra il di.
I mourn my loved one__ gone,   when__ each. day__ does__ dawn.

"Relentless gods!" exclaims the minstrel. "I must see my bride
again! Not even the gates of Hades can keep me from her!"

"Then go!" proclaims a high, clear voice. Orfeo looks up in *Enter*
astonishment and beholds Amor, the god of Love, who stands before *Amor*
him with a golden lyre.

"Descend to the underworld," the god instructs. "Let your voice
and this lyre move the rulers of the dead. You shall return leading
Euridice!"

"O command me!" begs Orfeo. "What further must I do?"

"You are not to glance at your wife before reaching the earth," *Exit*
the god warns, "or you will lose her forever!" As quickly as he *Amor*
has come, Amor disappears.

"Alas!" Orfeo laments. "What sorrow will be mine if I find
Euridice and cannot look upon her! But the gods have spoken—I
shall be brave!"

Clutching the golden lyre, Orfeo sets off amid thunder and
lightning in search of the path to Hades.

Act II

SCENE: THE GATES OF THE UNDERWORLD (14 Minutes)

THE souls of the damned are packed in a fearful barrier before *Furies*
the gates of death. Their fury, when aroused, is unbounded; while
they lie at rest, they are prey to dull despair.

Suddenly, the sound of a lyre invades the kingdom of darkness. *Enter*
Orfeo stands on a promontory, looking down into the abyss. *Orfeo*

"O Furies," he pleads, "let me pass! Have pity on me!"

"No!" they thunder.

The minstrel is undaunted by their wrath. "I know you suffer torture," he declares. "Your fate is hard—but mine, too, is past all bearing. I have lost the one I love!"

Even the dread Furies are moved by Orfeo's plea. "Open, ye gates," they command, "and grant him entrance to the realm of death!"

Gazing straight before him, the minstrel descends into the writhing mass of the damned. They leap about him with frightful gestures—but Orfeo does not waver. Guided by devotion, he passes through the flaming gates into the world beyond.

Act III

SCENE: THE ELYSIAN FIELDS (30 Minutes)

Ballet of Blessed Spirits

In the clear air of the Elysian fields a band of blessed spirits dances in delight.

Enter a Happy Shade

One of their number—a happy shade—sings of the joys of death. "Our sorrows have been forgotten," she declares. "Only tranquil thoughts remain!"

Exeunt Happy Shade and Blessed Spirits Enter Orfeo Enter Blessed Spirits and Euridice (veiled)

The blessed spirits wander to another part of the fields; and while the landscape radiates gladness even in solitude, Orfeo appears. "What pure light!" he exclaims. "What smiling meadows! Shall I indeed find my loved one here?"

"Orfeo!" calls a chorus of mysterious voices. "Euridice is near you."

A veiled figure approaches, led by the blessed spirits. It is Euridice. Striving to master the joy and anguish within him, Orfeo averts his glance. As the spirits lift the veil, he takes Euridice by the hand—and the terrible journey back to earth has begun.

Act IV

SCENE 1: A CAVERN ON THE WAY TO EARTH (20 Minutes)

ORFEO's resolve cannot much longer stand the test imposed by the gods. On their way from the kingdom of death, Euridice has been reproaching him constantly. "Why are you so indifferent?" she protests. "Alas! I was far happier in the realm of the departed!"

Enter Orfeo and Euridice

Unable to bear his wife's reproaches, he takes her in his arms. Instantly, she assumes the pallor of the dead. "Farewell!" she whispers. "Remember your Euridice!"

Euridice dies

"She is gone!" cries Orfeo. "What shall I do without her?"

Andante con moto

mf

Che fa - rò sen-za Eu - ri - di - ce,   do-ve an - drò sen-za il · mio   ben?
She is gone and gone for   e - ver,   all my   joy   a - las   is   flown.

Determined to live no longer, the minstrel raises his dagger—but a commanding voice restrains him. Amor has suddenly emerged from the clouds.

Enter Amor

"Forbear!" the god exclaims. "You have suffered enough. Euridice shall be yours!"

Euridice revives

At a sign from Amor, the stricken woman rises from the ground and embraces her husband. In deepest gratitude, Orfeo dedicates himself to the worship of the benevolent god.

SCENE 2: THE GARDENS OF THE TEMPLE OF LOVE (6 Minutes)

High in a verdant garden stands the temple of Amor. On mighty steps flanked by cypress trees, his disciples are awaiting the coming of their master. At last he arrives, leading Orfeo and Euridice.

Ballet of Guardians of Temple

At the sight of the reunited lovers, the bacchantes of the temple join in rapturous dances. And finally, as the faithful minstrel and his wife are crowned with garlands of flowers, the entire throng pays homage to the gracious Amor. "O God of Love," they fervently intone, "may you reign forever more!"

Enter Orfeo, Euridice, and Amor

III

Opera Comes of Age

IN addition to the sobriety exercised upon opera by Gluck, another influence arose in the west of Europe. A new era of enlightenment was at hand; Rousseau was preaching the significance of nature and the value of the individual man. Beaumarchais had written a comedy which glorified the *bourgeoisie* at the expense of the nobility. Inevitably, these social forces could not fail to leave their mark upon opera.

It was characteristic of the time that Wolfgang Amadeus Mozart of Vienna and Salzburg should have taken the French play of Beaumarchais, *Le Mariage de Figaro,* and set it to music in an Italian adaptation. His librettist was Lorenzo da Ponte (1749-1838), a fantastic figure even more representative of the shifting tendencies of the period than Mozart. After acquiring a certain notoriety for his own gallantries, da Ponte appropriately based his next libretto for Mozart, *Don Giovanni,* upon the amatory exploits of a Spanish grandee. His partnership with the great composer concluded in *Cosi fan tutte* (1790).

The audiences of Mozart's day had grown tired of the mythical deities who strode in constant parade across the operatic stage. In accordance with popular taste, Mozart treated life as he found it, and took full advantage of the opportunities for characterization which da Ponte offered him.

In developing new dramatic methods, Mozart continued and enlarged upon a device that Gluck had introduced—the use of the orchestra as an expressive medium. Equally at home in symphony and in opera, he developed the tonal palette of the opera orchestra sufficiently to incur the famous accusation, leveled by his rival Cimarosa, that "Mozart puts the statue in the orchestra pit and the pedestal on the stage." This stricture was not justified, as Mozart continued to write for voice in the old Neapolitan tradition of aria and recitative.

Opera had not entirely shaken off the faults of its adolescence. The artificialities of excess vocal decoration and *secco* recitative still remained; but with its new power of characterization, music for the theatre had definitely come of age.

· MOZART

WOLFGANG AMADEUS MOZART was born at Salzburg on January 27, 1756. He was educated musically by his father, Leopold, a violinist in the service of the Archbishop of Salzburg, and showed sufficient aptitude to study the harpsichord at the age of three. The following year he started to compose, and by the time he was six, he was taken with his eleven-year-old sister, Maria, on a tour of the chief European courts, where the children played duets and astonished the listeners with their precocity.

This gift of facile and yet profound musicianship was the keystone of Mozart's later career. His German heritage impelled him toward symphonic and chamber works, while visits to Italy quickened his interest in opera. The catalogue of his printed compositions includes examples of practically every branch of music. In the realm of the symphony, he brought greater suppleness to a form which Haydn had previously invested with vitality; and in opera, he led to a climax the existing Italian models, with their extensive use of aria and recitative. *Le Nozze di Figaro, Don Giovanni* and *Cosi fan tutte* were based entirely on accepted conventions, achieving their real distinction with Mozart's gifts of melody and orchestration. Of his two works for the German stage, *Die Entführung aus dem Serail* (The Abduction) was an *opera buffa*, and *Die Zauberflöte* (The Magic Flute) an allegory.

Though Mozart was recognized as a genius by the leading spirits of his time, he never prospered. Toward the end of his life, his financial situation became intolerable, and at his death on December 5, 1791, he was buried in a pauper's grave.

DON GIOVANNI

Don Giovanni, *a comedy drama in two acts, was given its world première at Prague, with Mozart conducting, in October, 1787. The work was an instantaneous success and was soon presented at Vienna (with three additional arias), where it was not so well received. Its first New York performance was promoted by the author of the libretto, Lorenzo da Ponte, who had settled in America. The cast was headed by Manuel Garcia and his daughter Maria, later known as Mme. Malibran.*

The initial appearance of Don Giovanni *at the Metropolitan Opera House took place in November, 1883.*

Characters, in order of appearance:
Leporello, servant of Don Giovanni: *bass*
Donna Anna: *soprano*
Don Giovanni: *baritone*
The Commandant: *bass*
Don Ottavio, fiancé of Donna Anna: *tenor*
Donna Elvira, a noble lady of Burgos: *soprano*
Zerlina, a peasant girl: *soprano*
Masetto, her suitor: *bass*

Time: Eighteenth Century   *Place:* Spain

Act I

SCENE 1: THE GARDENS OF THE COMMANDANT'S PALACE
(15 Minutes)

Don Giovanni, grandee of Spain, has embarked on a daring adventure. At dead of night, he has broken into the house of the

Commandant of Seville, intent upon seducing Donna Anna, the Commandant's daughter.

Leporello

All of the Don's plans have been carefully made. He has brought along a lookout—Leporello—who watches in the garden for any possible intrusion. "I never get any rest!" Leporello complains. "My pay is poor and my work is hard!"

Enter Giovanni and Anna

Suddenly, the lookout sees Don Giovanni fleeing from the palace, pursued by Donna Anna. With the utmost caution, the grandee hides his features.

Exit Anna Enter Commandant Exeunt Giovanni and Leporello Enter Anna and Ottavio

"I will find you out!" cries Donna Anna. "Whoever you are, you shall pay dearly for this!"

And now the Commandant comes running from his chamber—he has heard his daughter's cry for help. Drawing his sword, he attacks the stranger, as Donna Anna rushes for assistance. But ill fate overtakes the Commandant—he perishes, run through by Don Giovanni's blade; and the murderer escapes unharmed.

Aided by her fiancé, Don Ottavio, and a devoted band of servants, Donna Anna hastily returns. The garden is deserted; there is no trace of the assassin. Kneeling beside the body of her father, the unfortunate woman swears an oath of revenge. "Help me, Don Ottavio!" she demands. "We must pursue the criminal until we bring him to justice!" Solemnly, Don Ottavio promises to avenge the memory of Don Pedro, Commandant of Seville.

SCENE 2: A STREET (14 Minutes)

Giovanni and Leporello

Don Giovanni and Leporello are roaming the city in search of new conquests. "Ah!" murmurs the Don, with a perception heightened by experience. "I smell the aroma of womankind!" He crouches in a doorway as an elegant sedan-chair approaches.

Enter Elvira

Bidding her servants depart, a heavily veiled woman alights from the chair and paces the street in agitation. "Oh, if only I could find him again!" she exclaims. "He has left me brokenhearted!"

"It's a lady in distress," whispers the Don to Leporello. "I think I'll try to console her." With a sweeping bow, Giovanni approaches the lady—and finds, to his consternation, Donna Elvira of Burgos, whom he had jilted some time ago. This woman is a veritable Nemesis, following him everywhere. Making only the feeblest apologies, Don Giovanni dashes away, leaving Leporello in charge.

Exit Giovanni

"Why are you so angry?" Leporello bluntly demands of Donna Elvira. "You're not the first one he's tricked—nor will you be the last!"

Thumbing a bulky catalogue, Leporello continues, "Here is an exact list of Giovanni's loves. In Italy, he has had six hundred and forty. Germany is down for two hundred and thirty-one. France gave him a hundred. Turkey wasn't so good: only ninety-one. But in Spain, up to the present moment, we have recorded one thousand and three!"

Allegro

Ma - da - mi - na!   Il ca - ta - lo - go è
Pret - ty la - dy!   Here's a list I would

ques - to, del - le bel - le, che a-mo il pad - ron mi - o
show you, of the fair ones my mas - ter has court - ed

"Any type of woman appeals to him—young or old, portly or slender. It's his mission to win them all. And you, O lady, are well aware that he succeeds!"

With an ironic smile, Leporello runs off, leaving Donna Elvira to her grief.

SCENE 3: THE OPEN COUNTRY (48 Minutes)

In a grove before a rustic tavern, a crowd of peasants is dancing. They are celebrating the approaching wedding of the pretty Zerlina to her suitor, Masetto. Suddenly, Don Giovanni appears on the scene with Leporello. He is not long in taking a fancy to Zerlina and in wishing to be rid of her troublesome bridegroom. "Come!" he exclaims, "I invite all of you good people to my castle. And you, Masetto, shall be escorted by my servant, Leporello!"

Poor Masetto protests in vain. He is carried off—and Don Giovanni remains alone with Zerlina. "I mean you no harm," declares the Don. "If you wish, I may even marry you."

Zerlina, Masetto and chorus Enter Giovanni and Leporello Exeunt Masetto, Leporello and chorus

Andante

Là ci da - rem la ma - no, là mi di - rai di sì.
Give me thy hand, oh fair - est, whis - per a gen - tle "Yes".

Against her better judgment, Zerlina listens to Giovanni's pleading. She is even about to go off with him—but Fate intervenes in the person of Donna Elvira. Arriving just in time, the indignant lady snatches Zerlina away from the Don and leads her into the tavern.

Enter Elvira Exeunt Elvira and Zerlina

Enter
Ottavio
and
Anna

Baffled for the first time in his career, Giovanni faces another difficulty. He sees Don Ottavio and Donna Anna crossing the meadow. Before he can escape, they are upon him.

"Good morning, Don Giovanni," calls Ottavio amiably. And Giovanni, quick as a flash in every situation, realizes that he has not yet been recognized as the Commandant's assassin. "We are in trouble," Ottavio continues. "I wonder if you can help us."

Enter
Elvira
Exeunt
Elvira
and
Giovanni

The Don flatters Ottavio and Anna with courtliest bow. Of course he will help them! But like an avenging Fury, Donna Elvira hurries from the tavern. "Don't believe him!" she calls. "Whatever he says is a lie!" In vain does Giovanni command her to be silent. Finally, with muttered threats, he is forced to lead her away.

Donna Anna stares after him. The voice—those gestures—are terrifyingly familiar. "Don Ottavio!" she cries. "That man is the murderer of my father!"

In ringing accents, Donna Anna reminds Ottavio of his oath to avenge the memory of the Commandant. "The time has come!" she proclaims. "You must aid me!"

Exit
Anna

Overwrought with emotion, she leaves Ottavio. And the loyal fiancé, stirred by Donna Anna's grief, resolves to take action against Don Giovanni.

SCENE 4: A TERRACE BEFORE DON GIOVANNI'S CASTLE (15 Minutes)

Giovanni
and
Leporello

The setback suffered by Don Giovanni in his pursuit of Zerlina has not discouraged him. Exquisitely attired, he bids Leporello welcome all the peasants to his castle for a night of gaiety. "Let there be wine!" he cries. "Champagne shall be king!"

Exeunt
Giovanni
and
Leporello
Enter
Zerlina
and
Masetto

With a burst of laughter, he ascends the steps of the castle. For a moment, the terrace is deserted. Then Zerlina appears, trying to pacify the outraged Masetto.

"I've done nothing wrong," she pleads. "O Masetto, forgive me!"

Andante grazioso

Bat - ti   bat - ti, o bel Ma - set - to,   la   tua   po - ve - ra   Zer - li - na:
Canst thou   see   me,   un - for - giv - en,   Here   in   sor - row stand and   lan - guish?

At first, Masetto is adamant. Zerlina can go to her nobleman if she wishes! But soon, he succumbs to her pleading. "I'll hide in this arbor," he declares, "and watch you. Beware of Don Giovanni!"

By now, the terrace is quite dark. Don Giovanni stands at the foot of the steps, welcoming his guests. After everyone has entered, the Don remains—looking for Zerlina. It does not take him long to find her; and with his most persuasive charm, he attempts to draw her into the arbor.

Enter Giovanni and chorus Exit chorus

The Don is not even ruffled when Masetto emerges from the foliage. "Ah, Masetto!" he exclaims. "We were just trying to find you!" Nimbly uniting the two rustics, he leads them into the castle.

Exeunt Giovanni, Zerlina, Masetto Enter Ottavio, Elvira, Anna

No sooner has Giovanni gone inside, than his Nemesis appears on the terrace—Donna Elvira. She has joined forces with Anna and Ottavio; and all three—masked, and clothed in black—are determined to invade the ball and punish Don Giovanni.

Their way is made unexpectedly easy. Leporello, lolling on a balcony, thinks they are three gay figures in a masquerade. "Come in!" he calls. "You are welcome!"

The strangers bow and pass through the gateway. "O powers above," they murmur, "we depend on you for vengeance!"

SCENE 5: THE BALLROOM OF DON GIOVANNI'S CASTLE (7 Minutes)

Don Giovanni has spared no expense in entertaining his guests. Three orchestras, on different balconies of the ballroom, join in a lilting minuet, as servants ply the peasants with food and wine.

Giovanni, Leporello, Zerlina, Masetto and chorus

Minuetto

At the height of the gaiety, the three maskers enter the hall. Taking no part in the dance, they look on—awaiting a favorable moment to strike. And their opportunity soon arrives! Giovanni has drawn Zerlina into a secret alcove. Suddenly, the maiden's screams rise above the music. The dancers stop in confusion; battering down the door, they rescue Zerlina.

Enter Anna, Elvira and Ottavio

This time, Giovanni's glib excuses cannot save him. The crowd closes in on him; the three figures in black remove their masks. "Tremble!" they cry. But once again, boldness and luck come to the help of Don Giovanni. Brandishing his sword, he disarms Don Ottavio and forces his way to liberty, followed by the faithful Leporello.

ACT II

SCENE 1: BEFORE THE HOUSE OF ELVIRA (22 Minutes)

In the Metropolitan production of Don Giovanni, *the lament of Elvira—"Mi tradì" ("He betrayed me")—is inserted at the beginning of the second act. Traditions vary in regard to the placing of this aria. Elvira stands before her house, alone and forsaken. Hearing the sound of approaching voices, she goes within.*

Elvira
Exit

LEPORELLO is in an unusually righteous mood. Walking along the street with Giovanni, he urges his master to reform. "Give up these seductions!" he urges.

Enter
Giovanni
and
Leporello

Don Giovanni laughs. "I have a new interest," he replies. "Have you seen Elvira's fascinating servant girl?" Slipping Leporello a few coins, Giovanni decides on a plan of campaign. "You shall wear my cloak, Leporello—make love to Elvira and get her out of the way. Then her maid will be left for me!"

Enter
Elvira

Giovanni's plan works perfectly. Under cover of darkness, he calls to Elvira, who has appeared on her balcony. "O my love," he chants, "how I have wronged you! Come down and let me beg your forgiveness!"

Exeunt
Elvira
and
Leporello

Filled with a hopeless love for Don Giovanni, Elvira consents. As soon as she reaches the street, she is passionately embraced by Leporello in the gay mantle and plumed hat of the Don. He draws her into the darkened city, leaving the way clear for his master.

And now Giovanni strums a mandolin, serenading Elvira's servant girl:

Allegretto

p Deh   vie - ni al - la   fi - ne - stra,   o   mio___ te - so - ro,
From   out_ thy   case - ment   glanc - ing,   Oh smile___ up - on___ me,

Enter
Masetto
and male
chorus

For a moment the girl appears at the window—but she vanishes as a crowd of peasants enters in search of Don Giovanni. They are armed with cudgels and their leader, Masetto, carries a pistol.

Not for a moment is Giovanni afraid. He has already changed

cloaks with his servant—and now, pulling his hat over his eyes, he
pretends to be Leporello. "Are you looking for Don Giovanni?" he
asks the peasants. Giving them false directions, he scatters them
through the city—and to complete the confusion, invites Masetto
to stay.

"Show me your weapons!" Giovanni urges. With no qualms,
Masetto hands over his pistol. Utterly defenseless, he is set upon
and beaten by the Don, who escapes.

"Oh!" wails Masetto. "My head is broken!" But soon Zerlina
appears with a lantern and leads him homeward. The once faithless
girl has brought him solace.

Ve - drai, ca - ri - no, se sei buo - ni - no,
Come, shall I tell thee How what be - fell— thee

SCENE 2: A COURTYARD BEFORE THE HOUSE OF DONNA ANNA
(8 Minutes)

Groping for means of flight, Leporello has led Elvira into a
darkened courtyard. He is tired of the comedy—of Elvira's words
of love. Never again will he impersonate his master!

Suddenly, he spies a door in the courtyard wall, which, to his
complete discomfiture, is opened from the other side—and Donna
Anna appears on the threshold with Don Ottavio.

Even now, Leporello has not reached the end of his misfortunes.
Zerlina and Masetto, invading the courtyard in search of Don
Giovanni, confuse the servant with his master. Terrified, Leporello
flees for his life.

Enter
Zerlina
and
Masetto
Exit
Leporello

While Zerlina and Masetto run off in pursuit, the two noble
ladies withdraw—and only Don Ottavio is left in the dimly lighted
street. "I will bring Giovanni to justice," he vows, "and comfort
my beloved!"

Exeunt
Zerlina,
Masetto,
Anna
and
Elvira

Il mio te - so - ro in - tan - to
To my be - loved, O has - ten,

SCENE 3: A CHURCHYARD (7 Minutes)

Fugitives from the townspeople, Don Giovanni and Leporello
meet in the comparative safety of a graveyard. Exchanging cloaks,

Enter
Giovanni
and
Leporello
The Com-
mandant

they banter about their adventures. But suddenly, a hollow voice echoes through the night: "Your jests will turn to woe before morning!"

Looking about him, Giovanni perceives a huge statue. It is the likeness of the murdered Commandant of Seville!

Giovanni strikes the monument with his sword. "Give answer!" he shouts mockingly. "Will you sup with me?"

"Yes!" replies the statue, with a gruesome nod of the head.

Brimming with defiance, Giovanni goes home to prepare for his strange guest. Only Leporello, who accompanies him, feels a fore-warning of doom.

SCENE 4: A ROOM IN THE HOUSE OF DONNA ANNA (6 Minutes)

Anna
and
Ottavio

Still mourning for her father, Donna Anna keeps a lonely vigil before his portrait. Not even the pleading of her fiancé can lessen Anna's grief.

"Beloved!" Ottavio exclaims. "Forget the past—and be my wife!"

"How can I?" Anna answers. "Some day, I know, we shall be wed. But I must wait until my father has been avenged."

SCENE 5: A DINING HALL IN GIOVANNI'S PALACE (20 Minutes)

Giovanni
and
Leporello

Heedless of approaching disaster, Don Giovanni is seated at table with two charming ladies. Leporello serves them with choice deli-cacies. A private band plays Giovanni's favorite airs. Everything is going well for the Don!

Enter
Elvira

Much to his annoyance, the door is flung open and Elvira appears. "You are in danger!" she cries, "I beg you to repent!"

Exit
Elvira
Enter
Com-
mandant

Ignored by Giovanni, Elvira prepares to go. But on reaching the portal, she screams in fright and rushes away. The statue, true to its word, has come to visit Don Giovanni:

In vain does the phantom urge Giovanni to mend his ways. The statue sinks through the ground, as flames envelop the hall. From far below are heard the croaking voices of the damned. Fear grips the heart of Don Giovanni. He strives frantically to escape—but fire pursues him from every side. With a cry of despair, he is swallowed up by the forces of damnation.

Exit
Com-
mandant

EPILOGUE

Leporello, crouched beneath a table, has viewed the demise of his master. Now he runs to tell the tale to all who will listen. At once, he is surrounded by Masetto and Zerlina, Ottavio and Anna, and the lonely Donna Elvira. Stepping to the footlights, they warn the audience that a similar fate awaits all libertines.

Leporello,
Zerlina,
Masetto,
Anna,
Elvira,
Ottavio

IV

Opera Shows Off the Voice

At the opening of the last century in Italy music meant opera, and opera to the Italians meant singing above everything else. There had been no Gluck to raise a standard of emotional expressiveness, no local Mozart to demand symphonic values from the opera orchestra. Two sources of wealth, however, were at hand: the technical versatility of the natural Italian voice and the Italian gift for melody.

The so-called *opera buffa,* or popular opera using spoken recitative, had grown out of the early *intermezzi.* This informal vehicle was turned to advantage in demonstrating the talents of the performers.

The character and importance of the average opera cast was dictated by the conventional assortment of voices. Every soloist had to have his aria. Virtuosity was expressed in patter songs of the baritone and bass, as well as the flourishes and trills of the soprano. The composer was not deeply concerned with human significance. He wished to entertain his audience. His medium was a happy one: the *bel canto* that was the Italian heritage.

Typical was Cimarosa's *Secret Marriage* (1793). Later examples of the *opera buffa* style were Donizetti's *L'Elisir d'Amore* (1832) with its burlesque of the love potion of romance, and his frolicking *Don Pasquale.*

In a similar manner, the *opera seria,* or serious operatic style of the period provided a means of display for the miraculous voices that were available. When the heroine talked in her sleep as in Bellini's *La Sonnambula* (1831), or went mad as in Donizetti's *Lucia* her bravura excesses were the more credible. Bellini and Donizetti may have lacked the technical resourcefulness which was so prodigal in Rossini, but they made up for it in their glorification of the voice.

If the dramatic action was held up by this exhibitionism, the lapse did not offend the audience. In their reverence for the great singers of the day, the public accepted the inevitable conventions as so many yards of glory in the train of their favorites.

It was the singer's day; opera existed for the express purpose of showing off the voice.

ROSSINI

GIOACCHINO ROSSINI, son of the town trumpeter of Pesaro and his wife, a provincial opera singer, was born in 1792.

Young Rossini studied at the Bologna Conservatory until at eighteen, he turned to opera and composed five works in twelve months.

As musical director of the Naples Opera he was required to write two operas a year, but he did not confine himself to this number. In 1821 he visited Vienna, where his personal triumphs equaled his stage successes. Later he went to Paris to occupy the posts of Director of Italian Opera and Inspector General of Singing in France. Here he presented several successful revisions of his Italian works, and finally produced his masterpiece, *Guillaume Tell*, in French.

After the 1830 Revolution, with no inducement to add further to his list of thirty-six operas, he closed his dramatic career at the age of 38.

He continued to reap the rewards of fame as Honorary Director of the Conservatory at Bologna, where he lived in retirement. In 1853 he returned to his large circle of Parisian admirers, and died at Ruelle in 1868.

Endowed with native vivacity, he was occasionally shallow, but survives by reason of his dash and humor.

IL BARBIERE DI SIVIGLIA
(*THE BARBER OF SEVILLE*)

IL BARBIERE DI SIVIGLIA *was composed by Rossini at the age of 23 in thirteen days. The original overture has disappeared; the one now used was first composed for the opera* Elisabetta, Regina d'Inghilterra.

The libretto was written by Cesare Sterbini from the text of Beaumarchais' famous play of the same name, which had taken Paris by storm in 1775.

The opera's première was held in Rome on February 6, 1816. It reached New York three years later, and was first presented at the Metropolitan in 1883.

Characters, in order of appearance:
Count Almaviva: *tenor*
Florello, his servant: *bass*
Figaro, barber of Seville: *baritone*
Rosina: *soprano*
Dr. Bartolo, her guardian: *bass*
Basilio: *bass*
Berta, her governess: *mezzo-soprano*
Notary, officer, musicians and soldiers

Time: Seventeenth Century   *Place:* Seville, Spain

ACT I
SCENE: A SQUARE IN SEVILLE (40 Minutes)

IN a handsome house in Seville, old Dr. Bartolo guards his beautiful ward, Rosina. This young lady is beloved not only by her

39

guardian, but by the noble Count Almaviva. Just before dawn a group of musicians arrives under the direction of Florello, the Count's servant, to serenade the lady.

"Softly!" cautions Florello, as they tune their instruments, and prepare to accompany his master.

At daybreak the Count arrives to sing his *aubade:*

Ec-co ri-den-te in cie - lo
Dawn with her ro-sy man - tle

Since the lady does not appear, there is nothing for the crest-fallen Count to do but dismiss the musicians.

A vivacious tune in the orchestra heralds the approach of Figaro, barber of Seville. Almaviva withdraws to listen to the patter song with which the merry factotum describes his various activities·

"Figaro here, Figaro there, Figaro wanted everywhere."

Lar - go al fac - to - tum del - la cit - tà, lar - go
Room___ for the ci - ty's fac - to - tum, make room, straight-way

The Count realizes that here, perhaps, is the very man to serve as intermediary in his suit. He emerges from an archway and describes his predicament to Figaro: how can he gain Rosina's presence?

"What luck!" answers the barber. "In this house I am barber, surgeon, druggist and vet . . ."

As they speak, the old doctor hobbles out.

"If Don Basilio should come, have him wait," he calls, locking the door behind him. "Today I must attend to my marriage."

"Who is this Basilio?" asks the Count, as the doctor departs.

"A wretched matchmaker who has set himself up as the girl's music teacher," answers Figaro. An immediate campaign of action is necessary if the Count is to win Rosina. "How about another serenade?"

Almaviva addresses Rosina once more, announcing that his name is Lindoro. Rosina, who has been listening behind her curtain, attempts a rejoinder, but her reply is cut short. She has been interrupted from within. The Count is frantic. Figaro must help him get inside the house.

"I have it!" Figaro retorts. "A regiment arrives today. You can dress up as a soldier. If you pretend to be drunk, so much the better; the old man will believe every word you say."

They give vent to their joy at this scheme in a rollicking duet:

ACT II

SCENE: A ROOM IN THE HOUSE OF DR. BARTOLO (51 Minutes)

THE scene changes to the interior of Bartolo's house, where Rosina recalls the voice that has touched her heart.

Rosina

"I am all gentleness," she confesses ingenuously. "But when I am crossed, I become like a viper."

At the close of her monologue Figaro makes a brief visit, but rushes away as Dr. Bartolo approaches.

"Have you been talking to that wretched Figaro?" scolds the doctor.

"And why not? I like him," pertly answers Rosina, as she leaves.

Don Basilio stalks in with the news that Almaviva is in town.

"What, the impudent fellow who dares to serenade Rosina?" cries the doctor. "What can we do to stop him?"

"We must invent some scandal to blacken his reputation," answers the wily Basilio:

Enter
Figaro
Exit
Figaro
Enter
Bartolo
Exit
Rosina
Enter
Basilio

Certain of success, the conspirators go off to prepare a marriage contract for the doctor and his ward.

Figaro who has, as usual, been listening at the keyhole, warns Rosina that her guardian wishes to marry her.

"Poor simpleton!" exclaims Rosina. "But tell me, Master Figaro, who was the young man beneath my window?"

Exeunt
Bartolo,
Basilio
Enter
Figaro
Enter
Rosina

"Oh, a cousin of mine," he answers. "His name is Lindoro, and he is in love at the moment."

"What is the lady's name?"

"R-o, ro, s-i, si, n-a, na."

Exit
Figaro

When Figaro suggests that she write a line of encouragement to her suitor, Rosina is ahead of him. The letter is written already, and after a gay duet, he bears it off triumphantly.

Enter
Bartolo

Dr. Bartolo comes in full of questions. Why is her hand stained with ink? Why is a sheet missing from his papers? Why is the pen freshly cut?

Rosina's answers are at the tip of her tongue. She used the ink when she burned herself. She needed the paper for wrapping. With the pen she traced a pattern for her embroidery.

Exeunt
Bartolo
and
Rosina
Enter
Berta
Enter
Count
disguised
Enter
Bartolo
Enter
Rosina

The doctor storms in vain, and finally retreats, followed by his incorrigible ward.

A knock is heard, and Berta the maid, though slightly deaf, finally goes to answer it.

The visitor is the Count, who staggers across the room in his guise of a drunken soldier. When Dr. Bartolo returns with Rosina, the gallant farceur insists that this is the house where he has been quartered. In vain the old man protests that he is exempt from housing soldiers, in vain he orders Rosina from the room—the Count manages to slip her a note. The general excitement reaches its peak in an elaborate quintet.

Enter
Figaro
Enter
officer
and
soldiers

"Stop, what is all this?" demands Figaro, rushing in.

An officer and some soldiers are at his heels. On the complaint of Dr. Bartolo, they arrest the Count, but when he takes them aside and explains who he is, they release him, to the consternation of the entire company.

ACT III

SCENE: SAME AS ACT II (53 Minutes)

Bartolo
Enter
Count
disguised

IN the same room Dr. Bartolo is congratulating himself on having gotten rid of the soldier when a knock interrupts him. It is the Count, this time disguised as an unctuous music teacher:

Andante moderato

Pa- ce e gio-ja sia con   vo - i
Peace and joy be on this dwel-ling,

"I am a pupil of Don Basilio, who is ill," he announces craftily. "The Count Almaviva lodges at the same inn with me, and this very morning I found a letter which your ward had written him. To help you, I would be glad to ruin his reputation with Rosina."

"You're a worthy pupil of Basilio," answers Bartolo. "I will go and call my ward."

In a moment he returns with Rosina for the famous lesson scene, in which the prima donna is permitted to sing any aria she may choose, the Count pretending to accompany her at the piano. — *Enter Rosina*

"A tiresome tune," exclaims Bartolo, who proceeds to sing an aria of his own, while Figaro, who has just appeared with his shaving basin, mimics him from behind. — *Enter Figaro*

"I have come to shave you," announces the barber. "I can't put it off; my calendar is full."

"Get the towel from the shelf in the hall," says the irritable old man. "Here are the keys." Figaro skips off, and a crash is heard outside. — *Exit Figaro*

"The rascal has broken all my china!" Bartolo is frantic. If he investigates the damage, he must leave Rosina with her music teacher. Deserted for a moment, the young people exchange a hurried word of love. — *Exit Bartolo*

Figaro returns, having made good use of the delay. He has taken the balcony key from the bunch given him by Bartolo. Now he is free to go about his business. He covers the doctor's face with lather and flourishes his razor. — *Enter Figaro / Enter Bartolo*

He has only just started the operation when, to the amazement of all, Don Basilio appears. — *Enter Basilio*

"What do you mean by coming out with a fever?" asks Bartolo.

Basilio is bewildered, but a purse, passed him by the Count, is sufficient explanation, and after prolonged farewells, he takes his leave.

Moderato

mf

Buo - na se - ra, mi - o si - gno - re, Buo - na se - ra, buo - na se - ra!
Fare you well sir, pleas-ant slum - ber, Fare you well sir, pleas - ant slum -ber!

Figaro proceeds with his shaving of Bartolo, distracting his attention from the lovers. — *Exit Basilio*

"We shall come for you precisely at midnight," whispers Almaviva to Rosina. "Now that we have the keys, there is nothing to fear." — *Exeunt Rosina, Count, Figaro*

Bartolo's suspicions are aroused. He drives them all out and calls for the servant Berta. No, he will show them to the door himself. — *Enter Berta / Exit Bartolo*

Exit
Berta

"What a madhouse," sighs the governess. "Love is a crazy thing, and yet I feel it myself."

Enter
Figaro,
Count,
Rosina

As night falls a thunderstorm arises.

At last the shutters open. Figaro and the Count come through the window to fetch Rosina.

"Stand off, wretches," is her greeting. She has heard slanderous tales that Lindoro wishes to sell her to Count Almaviva.

"But I myself am Almaviva!" The Count quiets her reproaches by taking her in his arms. "Lindoro is just a name!"

Figaro interrupts their transports. "Hurry," he begs, "we may still be overheard and stopped."

Enter
Basilio
Enter
notary

To their dismay they find that the ladder is gone. What to do? While they wonder, Don Basilio appears, bringing the notary that Dr. Bartolo has ordered for his own nuptials.

"Here's a ring for you if you marry us," whispers the Count, "and a bullet in your head if you refuse." The lovers are at last united.

Enter
Bartolo
Enter
officer

Bartolo rushes in with an officer to arrest the intruders, but he is too late. Even his removal of the ladder has not stopped them. "A vain precaution," laughs Figaro. There is nothing for him to do but forgive Rosina and her wealthy husband. The opera ends in a joyous ensemble.

BELLINI

Vincenzo Bellini was born in Catania, Sicily, on November 3, 1801, and received his first musical education from his father, who was an organist. At eighteen a wealthy patron sent him to the Naples Conservatory, where he profited more from his private studies of Mozart and Paisiello than from the inadequate training of the period.

During the next fifteen years he composed ten operas, *La Sonnambula* (1831) being hailed as his first masterpiece. Within a year he composed *Norma*, which, though not warmly received at its première in Milan, had such a success with the French public that the composer was commissioned to write another work for the *Théâtre Italien* in Paris, and produced *I Puritani*, only a year before his death at the village of Puteaux, on September 23, 1835.

In spite of his sparing instrumentation, and often static harmony, Bellini survives for the sensuous warmth of his melodies, his dramatic instinct and impressive grandeur.

NORMA

NORMA, *a "lyric tragedy" now played in four acts, although originally written in two, was considered by its composer, Bellini, his greatest work. Felice Romani, who acted as librettist for seven of Bellini's ten operas, took his text from a play by Alexandre Soumet, which had been produced at the* Théâtre Français *about a year earlier.*

First performed at La Scala in Milan on December 26, 1831, Norma *reached both London and Paris in 1833. It served for the opening of the Academy of Music in 1854, and was chosen by Lilli Lehmann for her benefit performance on February 27, 1890, its first appearance at the Metropolitan. A silence of over thirty-five years was broken by its revival in 1927 with Rosa Ponselle in the title role.*

Characters, in order of appearance:
Oroveso, Arch-Druid, father of Norma: *bass*
Pollione, Roman Pro-Consul: *tenor*
Flavio, a centurion: *tenor*
Norma, High Priestess of the Druids: *soprano*
Adalgisa, a virgin of the temple: *contralto*
Clotilde, Norma's confidante: *mezzo-soprano*
Druid priests and priestesses, and virgins of the temple, Norma's two children, Gallic warriors
Time: The Roman occupation of Gaul, about 50 B.C. *Place:* Gaul

46

Act I

SCENE: THE SACRED GROVE OF THE DRUIDS (60 Minutes)

DEEP in the forest beneath a giant oak, the Druids have raised their mighty altar stone, to which a solemn procession wends its way in the darkness.

First come the warriors of Gaul. Behind them march the Druids, their robes garlanded with leaves, and finally the priests, followed by their leader, Oroveso.

"On to the hills!" commands the Arch-Druid, "and search the skies for the new moon. When first you see her, sound thrice the signal on the shield of bronze, that Norma may come and cut the sacred mistletoe."

Fervently the Druids implore their goddess Irminsul to drive the Roman legions from their land, and rouse the people with a signal that shall echo even to the city of the Caesars.

No sooner have they dispersed to watch for the propitious moon than two young Roman warriors cautiously emerge from the forest.

"The way is clear at last," whispers the Pro-Consul Pollione.

"But Norma has warned us there is death in the forest," answers Flavio.

"How that name freezes my blood!" exclaims his friend. "True I loved her once; true, she is the mother of my children; but now I love another, the innocent young Adalgisa. She too serves in the temple, like a ray of starlight in the stormy sky." Pollione goes on to tell of a vision: The maiden was kneeling beside him at the altar of Venus in Rome, when suddenly a fierce voice resounded through the temple: "Thus Norma avenges the treachery of her lover!"

As he reaches the climax of this dreadful memory, the brazen signal of the Druids echoes from the hills; the moon has risen, soon the Gauls will throng to their altar. Pollione proclaims that love will protect him from their fury:

Allegro marziale

Me pro-teg-ge! me di-fen-de un po-ter mag-gior di lo - - ro:
Love will shield, will pro-tect! yes a power, Greater far than they boast will de-fend_____:

Both Romans retire hurriedly to the forest.

The entire company of Druids now gather to the beat of a dignified march:

Allegro assai

Gallic warriors, Druids, priests Oroveso

Exeunt all Enter Pollione and Flavio

Exeunt Pollione and Flavio Enter Druids, priests, Oroveso, etc.

Enter
Norma
and
attendants
In solemn chorus they announce the arrival of Norma, her head bound with mystical verbena, in her right hand a golden sickle. Surrounded by her attendants, the priestess mounts the altar.

"Seditious voices, I hear you shout for war," she exclaims boldly. "Yet it is not at your hands that Rome will fall, but from her own vices."

She turns to cut the branches of mistletoe. Then, advancing with the moonlight full upon her, she prays for peace:

"When the moment comes," announces Norma, "I will summon you to vengeance. The time is not yet."

"Let the Pro-Consul be first to fall," shout the people.

Exeunt
Norma
and all
Druids
Enter
Adalgisa
Enter
Pollione
Norma's heart is stirred. How can she punish the man she loves?

The procession follows Norma away through the trees. For a moment the grove is deserted. Then the young Adalgisa enters, flinging herself at the foot of the altar to beg for pity and protection. When she sees that Pollione has sought her out, she begs him to withdraw, but the officer finally succeeds in persuading her to escape with him at dawn:

ACT II

SCENE: NORMA'S DWELLING (25 Minutes)

Norma
Enter
Clotilde
and
children
Exit
Clotilde
and
children
Enter
Adalgisa
A FEW agitated measures introduce a scene in front of the dwelling where Norma has concealed her two children.

As the little ones are brought in by the nurse, Clotilde, Norma shudders with fear.

"Pollione has been recalled to Rome," she tells her confidante. "What if he should desert our children? Go hide them quickly, for I hear someone approaching!"

It is Adalgisa, come to confess her weakness to the priestess. Falling on her knees at Norma's feet, she tells of her decision to abandon the temple and flee with the man she loves.

Memories of her own romance cause Norma to release Adalgisa from her vows with a gentle assurance of pardon:

Animato

Ah! si fa co - re_e ab -brac - cia mi Per - do - no_e ti com-pian - - go,
Oh! cheer thee weep not! come to my arms I par - don thee, thy sor - row chase,

"What is the name of the youth you love?" asks Norma at last.

As if in answer, Pollione stands before them. "Behold him!" answers the innocent girl.

Enter Pollione

The Roman rebukes Adalgisa for confiding in Norma, but reaps the fury of the older woman, who accuses him of betraying herself and their hapless children.

The three voices join their lamentations: Norma first points out to Adalgisa the guilt of her lover, and then showers curses on his impious love. Adalgisa, gradually aware of the depth of his deception, assures Norma that she would rather perish than take him from her side. Pollione vainly begs Norma to conceal their shame from the young girl, and insists that the power of his new love is stronger than the torment of the old.

As they conclude, a distant signal booms from the shield of bronze.

"For you it is the sound of death," cry the women to Pollione, who flees with a shout of defiance.

ACT III

SCENE: THE INTERIOR OF NORMA'S DWELLING (23 Minutes)

IN a spacious wooden hut, the children of Norma repose on their Roman couch. Norma, pale and distracted, enters with a lamp and dagger in their hand.

Norma's children Enter Norma

"They sleep," she mutters. "Better for them to die than to live as slaves in Rome." Resolutely she approaches the children—hesitates—then raises her dagger with a shriek. . . . The children awaken. Norma calls Clotilde and bids her summon Adalgisa.

"Take my children to the Roman camp," she implores the younger woman. "Befriend and protect them for Pollione's sake."

Clotilde Enter Adalgisa

"Rather let me attempt to awaken his love for you again," insists Adalgisa. "Let me bring him to your side."

Norma yields to the girl's entreaties and the two women swear eternal affection:

Mi - ra Nor - ma, ai tu - oi gin - oc - chi,
See, oh Nor - ma, low - ly kneel - ing,

Act IV

SCENE 1: A LONELY SPOT NEAR THE SACRED GROVE (9 Minutes)

Gallic warriors

THE Gallic warriors assemble near a rocky cavern to learn the news from the Arch-Druid.

Enter Oroveso

"Warriors, I bring you evil tidings!" announces Oroveso, striding into their midst. "A more cruel commander is to succeed Pollione."

A new note of resentment stirs the company. "Does Norma still counsel peace?" they demand.

"Norma has not yet spoken," he answers, "but for myself I urge that you separate, hiding your hatred under a mask of submissiveness. Then, when the great day dawns we shall more readily subdue the foe. The Tiber's yoke I hate as much as you:"

pp Ah! del Te - bro al gio - go_in de - gno
At the Ti - ber's un - wor - thy hal - ter

SCENE 2: THE TEMPLE OF IRMINSUL (31 Minutes)

Norma Enter Clotilde

Beside the altar, where hangs the sacred shield, stands Norma, joyously awaiting the return of Pollione.

Her happiness is shattered on learning from Clotilde that Adalgisa has failed to bring Pollione back. Indeed, the Roman is urging the maiden once more to break her vows, and she has retired for safety to the temple.

In a rage the priestess approaches the altar and three times strikes the sacred shield.

Enter Druids, bards, priestesses Oroveso

In answer to her signal, the people throng from every side. Druids, bards and priestesses fill the temple, the Gauls restlessly fingering their spears, Oroveso towering in their midst.

"What means your summons?" asks the priest of his daughter.

"The hour has come for war!" answers Norma.

"War!" the people echo, as Clotilde announces that the temple has been violated by a Roman intruder.

The soldiers drag in Pollione, and Oroveso offers Norma the sword with which she must slay the offender. Enter Pollione Exeunt Druids, etc.

She trembles with hesitation. "First let me question him," she begs, and the temple is cleared of all but Pollione and Norma.

"You are in my power at last," she tells him, "and I alone can set you free. Swear never to see Adalgisa again, and you shall have your liberty."

"I would rather die," he answers passionately.

"I will slay your children," she threatens, "and Adalgisa shall die in the flames."

Pollione falls weeping at her feet, and begs for the dagger to put an end to his misery.

In answer Norma summons the assembly to return to the temple. Re-enter Druids and Oroveso

"I will reveal a priestess who has broken her vows," she declares. Is Norma about to denounce Adalgisa? How can she accuse another of the crime she herself has committed? Overcome by a new spirit of renunciation, she exclaims: "It is I!"

This heroic gesture inspires in the heart of the wretched Pollione a tenderness long since dead. United in love they will perish together!

In vain Oroveso implores her to retract her confession. Instead she begs him to care for the innocent children:

Deh! non vol - er - mi 'vit - ti - me!
Oh! let them not be vic - - tims!

As the Druids cover her with a black veil, and utter their maledictions, Norma leads Pollione to the funeral pyre.

DONIZETTI

GAETANO DONIZETTI was the son of a weaver of Bergamo, Italy, where the composer was born on November 29, 1797, and died on April 8, 1848. In spite of his family's ambition that he become a lawyer, he was allowed to enter the local music school, and at seventeen to undertake more advanced studies at the Bologna Conservatory.

Paternal pressure continued, however, and Donizetti joined the army as a refuge. Called for service in Venice, he composed and produced his earliest operas in that city, gaining exemption from military duties thereby. In the course of eight years he wrote more than a score of stage works.

Donizetti's second period of composition indicated a growing originality. The success of *L'Elisir d'Amore* (1832) and *Lucia di Lammermoor* spread his fame throughout Europe, and after the censorship of *Poliuto,* he deserted Naples, where he had been appointed Director of the Conservatory, and took up his residence in Paris.

The unbroken activity responsible for his sixty-six operas was interrupted by a fatal attack of paralysis before his fiftieth year.

Donizetti's flow of graceful melody places him with Rossini and Bellini in the triumvirate leading Italian opera at the opening of the nineteenth century.

LUCIA DI LAMMERMOOR

LUCIA DI LAMMERMOOR, *Donizetti's tragic drama in three acts based on Sir Walter Scott's novel,* The Bride of Lammermoor, *was first produced at Naples in 1835. Ever popular as a vehicle for coloratura soprano,* Lucia *was the second opera to be performed during the opening season of the Metropolitan—October 24, 1883—with Marcella Sembrich singing the title role.*

Characters, in order of appearance:
Norman, captain of the guard: *tenor*
Lord Henry Ashton: *baritone*
Raymond, Lucia's tutor: *bass*
Lucia Ashton: *soprano*
Alice, her companion: *mezzo-soprano*
Edgar of Ravenswood: *tenor*
Lord Arthur Bucklaw: *tenor*
Chorus of attendants; knights and ladies

Time: About 1700   *Place:* Scotland

ACT I

SCENE: GROUNDS NEAR THE CASTLE OF RAVENSWOOD (40 Minutes)

FOR many years, Lord Henry Ashton has waged an implacable fight against the family of Ravenswood. He has broken their power, seized their ancient castle—and still he does not relent. So long as Edgar of Ravenswood survives, Lord Henry knows no peace.

Still another problem weighs heavily on the warlike noble: a hostile monarch is about to ascend the throne of Scotland. Henry is in danger of proscription unless his sister Lucia marries a man with influence at court.

Enter knights, Norman, Lord Henry and Raymond

Wandering through the grounds of Ravenswood, Lord Ashton propounds these ideas to his trusted captain, Norman. "Lucia must be forced to wed!" he declares.

Norman agrees; but Lucia's elderly tutor, Raymond, who is strolling in their company, protests vigorously. "She is still mourning for her mother," he complains. "How can she think of love or marriage at a time like this?"

"Of love?" Norman laughs ironically. "She is already in love with Edgar of Ravenswood. They meet here secretly every day!"

Norman's accusation is supported by a band of huntsmen who have just seen Edgar riding toward the castle gates. Enraged, Henry vows that he will slay the intruder.

Allegretto moderato

La pie - ta de in suo fa - vo - re Mi - ti sen - si in - van mi det - ta -
If thou plead'st for her, I scorn thee, cast thee from me, then let me warn thee

Exeunt all

No amount of persuasion by the peaceful Raymond can move Lord Ashton. The angry noble and his captain, Norman, stalk away; Raymond can only leave them to their vengeance.

Enter Lucia and Alice

The grounds are now deserted. Twilight has fallen—and Lucia appears with her companion, Alice. She is awaiting Edgar at the fountain of the Ravenswoods.

"You should not have come here," Alice declares. "Think of your brother's fury!"

"I must warn Edgar," Lucia answers. "We are both in peril!"

As Alice listens with terror, Lucia tells of an apparition she has seen near the fountain—the ghost of a murdered maiden.

"I fear for you, Lucia!" cries Alice. "Come back to the castle!"

"No," Lucia declares. "One glance from Edgar and these portents will be gone!"

Moderato

Quan - do ra - pi - to in e - sta - si del più co - cen - te ar - do - re,
Were he but here, oh ec - sta - sy, Nought should I know of sor - row,

Exit Alice Enter Edgar

Alice withdraws in anxiety; and soon Edgar arrives. "I must leave Scotland tonight, Lucia," he declares sorrowfully. "Duty calls me on a mission to France. Can we not be wed before I depart?"

"No!" she sighs. "You know my brother's hatred for your clan."

"Then take this ring," Edgar urges, "and give me a token in return. Some day, when all these feuds are ended, I shall claim you as my bride."

Moderato assai

Ver - ran - no a te sul - l'a - u - re i miei so - spi - ri ar - den - ti
When twi - light shad - ows low - er, My ar - dent pray'rs as - cend - ing

The lovers embrace in a last farewell. "Remember," Edgar declares, as he hastens away, "you have pledged your faith!"

ACT II

SCENE 1: AN APARTMENT IN THE CASTLE (14 Minutes)

LORD HENRY ASHTON is finally assured of political safety. He has arranged for Lucia to wed one of the most influential nobles in the realm—Arthur Bucklaw, who is soon to appear for the ceremony.

"And yet," Lord Henry admits to his confidant, Norman, when they confer in a chamber of the castle, "I am uneasy. What if Lucia should reject this marriage? She still thinks of Edgar."

> Lord Henry and Norman

"Do not fear," Norman answers. "We have intercepted all the letters that Edgar has sent from France. Your sister will believe him faithless."

As Norman goes off to greet the approaching bridegroom, Lucia enters, pale and grieving.

> Exit Norman Enter Lucia

"Why do you persist in these plans?" she asks her brother wearily. "You know that I have pledged my faith to Edgar."

This is the moment for which Henry has been waiting. He shows the girl a forged letter which reveals that Edgar has taken a foreign bride. "Now will you wed Lord Arthur?" he demands.

> Exit Lord Henry

Lucia's resistance is shaken; and when the loyal tutor, Raymond, advises her to yield, the girl prepares with heavy heart to obey her brother.

SCENE 2: A HALL IN THE CASTLE (19 Minutes)

To the sound of festive music and the acclaim of the wedding guests, Lord Arthur Bucklaw arrives at Lammermoor. He is at a loss to account for Lucia's strange actions—the bride weeps constantly and hardly speaks to him.

> Enter chorus, Lord Henry, Lord Arthur, Raymond, Lucia and Alice

Moderato mosso

Per te d'im-men - so giu - bi - lo tut - to s'av - vi - va in - tor - no.
Hark to the hap - py brid - al day, hence ev' - ry thought of sor - row.

The marriage contract is signed. No sooner does Lucia lay down the pen than a commotion is heard at the castle gate. Edgar has returned from France to claim his betrothed! Learning in dismay that she has wed another, he savagely denounces her:

Sextet

Larghetto

Chi mi fre - na in tal mo - men - to? chi tron - cò del - l'i - re il cor - so?
What from ven-geance yet re - strains me, words suf - fice not to up - braid thee.

"Here is your ring!" Edgar cries contemptuously, casting the token at Lucia. "You have betrayed me!"

Henry Ashton draws his sword—the guests advance threateningly on Edgar; only through the timely intervention of Raymond is an armed battle averted. As the outraged scion of Ravenswood strides from the hall, Lucia collapses.

ACT III

SCENE 1: A HALL IN LORD HENRY'S CASTLE (23 Minutes)

Chorus
Enter
and exit
Raymond
Lucia
enters

REVELRY fills the great hall of Lammermoor while the wedding guests celebrate. Their mirth ceases abruptly when Raymond appears bearing terrible news: Lucia, distracted by suffering, has slain her husband.

Soon the girl enters the hall. There is a wild, unearthly stare in her eyes:

Larghetto

"Edgar!" she sighs madly. "Edgar! We are to be wed. Can you not see the burning tapers and the guests assembled? The priest is ready! At last I am yours!"

Sinking gently into the arms of her friends, the girl is borne away.

SCENE 2: A CEMETERY (16 Minutes)

Brooding over Lucia's marriage, and ignorant of its tragic outcome, Edgar wanders among the tombs of his ancestors. In the distance he can see the gleaming lights of the castle—he imagines bitterly that Lucia is lying in her husband's arms.

"I shall die," Edgar mutters, "friendless and unwept. The grave awaits me!"

Suddenly, he perceives a group of mourners coming from the direction of Lammermoor. As they march past the cemetery, Edgar's fears increase. "Why do you lament?" he calls anxiously.

Enter chorus

"It is Lucia," answers the grief-stricken retainers. "She has lost her mind through sorrow!"

Edgar's first impulse is to rush toward the castle—to see his loved one again and make amends for the past. But old Raymond approaches and bars his way. "It is to late," proclaims the tutor. "Lucia is dead!"

Enter Raymond

"Then all on earth is over for me," Edgar cries. "Without Lucia, I cannot live!"

Moderato

p Tu che a Dio spie-gà - sti l'a -li, o bel - l'al ma in -na - mo - ra - ta.
Thou hast spread thy wings to heav-en, oh thou spir - it, pure and ten - der.

Before Raymond and the retainers are able to prevent him, Edgar has stabbed himself and fallen among the tombs of the Ravenswoods.

DON PASQUALE

DON PASQUALE, *an opera buffa in three acts, was composed by Donizetti only three years before his career was closed by paralysis. The words of the text were also provided by the composer, who based his verses on a libretto which Salvatore Cammarano had written a generation earlier for the music of Stefano Pavesi under the title* Ser Marc Antonio.

The first performance of Don Pasquale *took place at the* Théâtre des Italiens *in Paris on January 4, 1843. The opera reached New York in an English version in 1846, and was first presented at the Metropolitan in January, 1900, with Sembrich in the part of Norina.*

Characters, in order of appearance:

Don Pasquale, an old bachelor: *bass*
Dr. Malatesta, his friend: *baritone*
Ernesto, nephew of Don Pasquale: *tenor*
Norina, a young widow, betrothed to Ernesto: *soprano*
A notary: *baritone*
Valets, maids, major-domo, dressmakers, hairdresser.

Time: Early Nineteenth Century   *Place:* Rome

ACT I

SCENE 1: A ROOM IN DON PASQUALE'S HOUSE (26 Minutes)

Don
Pasquale

THE old bachelor Don Pasquale is sitting in his comfortable study with one eye on the front door and the other on his watch.

"Nine o'clock already!" he grumbles, "and not a sign of the doctor!" Pasquale is impatient to put through his intended mar-

58

riage in order to punish his rebellious nephew Ernesto, and provide
himself with another heir.

Enter
Malatesta

At last the wily Dr. Malatesta arrives, and gives an account of
the charms of the bride-to-be:

"She is as lovely as an angel," the physician says, "and of a
wealthy family." He concludes with the news that she is his own
sister.

Bel - la sic - co - me un an - ge - lo   in ter - ra pel - le - gri - no
Fair as an an - gel from the sky, bound earth-ward as a mor - tal,

"When am I to see her?" inquires Pasquale, urging the doctor
to fetch the young lady at once. Left alone, the future bridegroom
muses on the joys that are ahead of him. He is quite ready to break
the news to his nephew Ernesto, who politely approaches his uncle.

Exit
Malatesta
Enter
Ernesto

"Is it true that a couple of months ago I offered you the hand
of a rich and noble wife, together with the promise of my fortune
at my death?" asks the old man, severely.

"It is true," answers Ernesto.

"Is it true that I threatened to disinherit you and even perhaps
to marry, if you refused?"

"It is true."

"Well, then," continues Pasquale, "how about it?"

Ernesto firmly declares that his heart is pledged to Norina.

"A penniless and designing widow," shouts his uncle.

"You are wrong," insists Ernesto, "and my mind is made up."

"Then you may leave the house," is Pasquale's rejoinder, "for I
have decided to get married myself!"

Ernesto is crushed by this news. He cannot offer his beloved the
poverty that will result from his uncle's disinheritance.

So - gno so - a - ve e cas - to   de miei pri - man - ni ad - di - o.
Vi - sion so pure and so ten - der, dream of my boy-hood, I leave__ you.

One avenue of escape occurs to him. Perhaps his uncle will listen
to Dr. Malatesta, who has always proved an ally to the young.

"I have already consulted the doctor," answers Pasquale triumphantly, "and he is all for my marriage. Indeed the young lady
I am to wed is his sister!"

Ernesto is prostrated at this news. "What treachery!" he mutters to himself, "and from the man I thought my friend!"

While he curses his fate, his uncle babbles on, delighted to chastise the defiant Ernesto.

SCENE 2: NORINA'S GARDEN (15 Minutes)

Norina   The charming young widow Norina is sitting in her garden, reading a romance. She laughs at the idea that she can learn anything from the heroines of the age of chivalry:

So anchio fa vir - tù   ma - gi - ca d'un guar-do_a tem-po_e   lo - co,
The ma - gic vir - tue   of   a glance I   know on each oc - ca - sion,

Enter Malatesta   A servant brings her a letter from Ernesto which strikes terror to her gay spirits. When Dr. Malatesta arrives, she at once hands him the tragic news. Ernesto, about to be disinherited by his uncle in favor of a new bride, is leaving Rome that very day, and renouncing Norina forever.

The doctor is not at all discountenanced by this threat. He has worked out a plan to take care of the entire situation.

"I have talked Pasquale into this marriage, as you know," he tells Norina, "and told him that my sister would suit him perfectly. (He knows that I have a sister in a convent.) What we are going to do is to introduce you to the old wretch by her name. My cousin Charles will dress up like a notary and perform a mock wedding. Then once you are his wife, you can drive him to such a rage that we shall have him completely at our mercy."

The sprightly Norina welcomes this scheme with delight. She loves to act, and gaily practices the airs and graces by which she expects to bewitch Pasquale. The idea of punishing Ernesto's uncle for his cruelty to her beloved lends zest to the sport.

Meanwhile the doctor rubs his hands at the trap he has set for his victim.

ACT II

SCENE: DON PASQUALE'S DRAWING-ROOM (32 Minutes)

Ernesto   ERNESTO bewails the cruel treatment of his uncle, the loss of his beloved Norina, and the treachery of his friend the doctor. But he must not give Pasquale the satisfaction of seeing the effect of his tactics. He accordingly retires at the very moment when the old man makes his appearance, magnificent in the velvet coat and lace ruffles he has put on for his wedding day.

Exit Ernesto Enter Pasquale

"You may admit the doctor and the person with him," Pasquale instructs his servant, "but no one else." Preening himself like a peacock, he comes forward to meet the doctor, who brings in Norina heavily veiled.

Enter Malatesta and Norina

"Remember, she is fresh from the convent, and very timid!" exclaims Malatesta, warning Pasquale to remain in the background.

Norina curtseys with the most alluring shyness, and expresses her terror of strangers.

When the three of them are seated, Pasquale attempts to make polite conversation with his intended, but his usual loquaciousness gives way to embarrassment.

"What do you like to do in the evening?" he asks nervously.

"I like to sew or work in the kitchen," Norina answers, her modesty instantly winning his heart.

At length she agrees to remove her veil. Pasquale is overcome by her beauty and sends for the notary at once.

Enter servants and notary

Servants meanwhile prepare the room for the ceremony to follow, placing a large table in the center, and bringing writing materials.

The doctor dictates the terms of the contract to the alleged notary: Pasquale is to make over half his fortune to his wife, and to give her full power over the household. Eagerly the bridegroom takes up his pen to sign.

While Norina prepares to do likewise, the voice of Ernesto is heard impatiently outside.

"I wished to say good-by to my uncle, and the door is barred as if I were a thief!" he complains. Pasquale then introduces Norina as his new bride, the former Miss Malatesta, and the young man's annoyance turns into horror.

Enter Ernesto

Before Ernesto can blurt out his fears, the doctor takes him aside, and hints that the marriage is a pretense, enacted on his behalf. He must keep quiet at all costs, and add his name as witness to the marriage papers.

No sooner has the notary pronounced his clients to be man and wife than Norina drops her submissive manner. She will neither embrace her husband nor permit him to dismiss Ernesto.

"This can never be," retorts Pasquale angrily.

"Oh, yes, it can," she answers. "Now, I am mistress here." She proceeds to call the major-domo and double his wages. She then orders the purchase of ten horses and a couple of carriages, demands a score of new servants and arranges for a feast of fifty that very evening. The dressmakers and jewelers can wait until the morrow.

Pasquale ineffectually attempts to put up some defense against this tyranny, and opens a vigorous quartet by complaining that he has been made a general laughing stock.

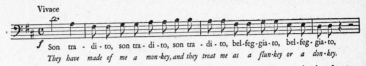

Vivace

f Son tra - di - to, son tra - di - to, son tra - di - to, bel-feg-gia-to, bel-feg-gia-to,
They have made of me a mon-key, and they treat me as a flun-key or a don-key.

Norina manages to reassure Ernesto that the farce is in fact a proof of her love for him, while Malatesta continues his adroit deception.

ACT III

SCENE 1: THE DRAWING-ROOM IN DON PASQUALE'S HOUSE, AS IN ACT II (25 Minutes)

Trades-
people

Pasquale
Enter
Norina

DON PASQUALE'S drawing-room is crowded with tradespeople bearing bonnets, shawls and laces for Norina. The old man, distracted, is sitting in front of a desk, piled high with bills. What can be done to put an end to this wild extravagance?

Norina comes in, dressed for the theatre.

"You shall not go!" cries her husband.

"Insolent fellow," she retorts, giving him a box on the ear, "take that!" Pasquale is crushed by this affront. Perhaps divorce is the only way out.

Exit
Norina
Exit
Pasquale
Enter
Malatesta
and
Ernesto

As Norina departs, she drops a letter, which Pasquale reads with growing anxiety. It is a request to meet the writer that same evening behind the garden wall. Furious at this new proof of his wife's villainy, he rushes off, sending meanwhile for Malatesta.

The doctor and Ernesto come in to discuss the next phase of their campaign. The young man is to serenade Norina in the garden, as described in the letter. When the doctor brings Pasquale to intercept them, the young suitor is to wrap his cloak about him and vanish. Ernesto promises to carry out his part of the plan and departs.

Exit
Ernesto
Enter
Pasquale

Meanwhile the doctor, genuinely sorry for Pasquale's abject condition, greets his old friend with a word of encouragement.

"It would have been a thousand times better if I had given my consent to the marriage of Norina and Ernesto, rather than face this torture," complains the wretched bridegroom. "My own wife has spent half my money, slapped my face, and is now planning to deceive me." He shows Malatesta the note announcing the rendezvous.

"There is but one thing to do," answers the doctor. "We must catch the guilty couple in the garden and take them promptly to court." In a lively duet, they rehearse their plan, each convinced that it will serve his own ends.

SCENE 2: A GARDEN NEAR DON PASQUALE'S HOUSE (11 Minutes)

Behind the garden wall, Ernesto's serenade floats through the darkness:

Ernesto off stage

Com è gen - til _____   la notte a mez-zo A · pril!
How soft the air _____   *night in A · pril is   fair.*

At length Norina, who has been listening from a little pavilion at the right of the garden, cautiously opens the gate to admit her lover. Their rapture is soon interrupted by the stealthy approach of Don Pasquale and the doctor. When her husband turns his lantern full in her face, Ernesto slips back into the house.

Enter Norina and Ernesto Enter Pasquale and Malatesta Exit Ernesto

Malatesta now plays a new trick. He informs his alleged sister that a blow is to fall. A new bride is to enter the house on the morrow. "It is Norina," he declares. "Your husband has consented that she shall marry Ernesto and assume the reins of the household."

"That wily widow!" cries Norina, with assumed disdain. "I will leave the house first myself."

Pasquale chuckles to hear such welcome news.

But I won't go until I am sure that Norina and Ernesto are genuinely married," she continues.

Malatesta agrees that this would be a good idea, and summons Ernesto from the house.

"Your uncle herewith grants you the hand of Norina and an annual income of four thousand crowns," declares the doctor to the amazed young man.

Enter Ernesto

"You had better send for Norina at once," Pasquale adds.

"But Norina is this very lady!" declares the doctor.

"But what about your sister—and the marriage ceremony?" asks the bewildered old man.

It is at last explained that everything has been a trick to prevent him from a genuine marriage by engaging him in a false one. Pasquale is soon persuaded to give his blessing to his scapegrace nephew and the clever little shrew.

V

Opera Dresses Up

SPECTACLE in opera began almost simultaneously with opera itself. The sovereigns of the seventeenth century thought nothing of lavish expenditures for mammoth settings and glittering costumes, especially if the performance in question was intended to celebrate a royal betrothal. With the gradual popularization of opera, these large-scale offerings receded into the past together with the hose and doublet of the Renaissance.

The essentially intimate atmosphere of the eighteenth century was not conducive to operatic spectacle in any form; but with the arrival of the romantic 1800's, pretentious stagecraft returned. Instead of relying on mere pageantry, the new operas fused the pomp and glory of an historical background with the somber coloring of high tragedy. In France, this type of entertainment was particularly well received, under the name of grand opera.

Halévy's *La Juive*, Auber's *Masaniello* (1828) and Hérold's *Zampa* (1831) were striking examples of the genius of native French composers in grand opera; but the trappings of splendor brought to Paris by an Italian—Spontini—in his epoch-making work, *La Vestale* (1807), found even more potent expression at the hands of another foreigner: Giacomo Meyerbeer.

The grand historical opera, as evolved by this composer, had five acts. The central personage was either a renowned hero, as John of Leyden in *Le Prophète* (1849) and Vasco da Gama in *L'Africana,* or else an entire period of history, as in *Les Huguenots* (1836), with its background of the Medicis and massacre of St. Bartholomew's Day.

Subjects of this nature demanded an elaborate scenic investiture with large choruses and masses of supernumeraries on the stage; they also provided real scope for a department of the theatre dear to French audiences since the time of Lully: the ballet. The fourth act of *L'Africana* contains a splendid example of choreography growing out of the plot, and Meyerbeer's early *Robert le Diable* (1831) is remembered for its imaginative Ballet of the Nuns.

With the increasing variety of theatrical resources at hand, operatic orchestration took on richer color. Unusual effects were often sought. Although purists of the time openly questioned the good taste of grand opera, reputable composers continued to write in this form. Rossini's *Guillaume Tell* (1829) and Verdi's *I Vespri Siciliani* (1855) were composed especially for the Paris *Opéra*.

The ultimate in spectacular opera was reached in Berlioz' *Les Troyens* (1858-63), a work in two sections, *La Prise de Troie* (The Fall of Troy) and *Les Troyens à Carthage* (The Trojans at Carthage), based on Virgil's *Aeneid*. After this, the channels of French dramatic music turned to the less extravagant *opéra comique*.

Although opera, in its evolution, has passed to other forms and styles, not every trace of the spectacular era has vanished. Works of Meyerbeer and Halévy are still included in the repertory of the Metropolitan; other composers of the period are represented at the present Paris *Opéra*, whose very architecture is an enduring monument to the spirit of historical grand opera.

HALÉVY

JACQUES FRANÇQIS HALÉVY was born in Paris on May 27, 1799, the son of a French Jewish family named Lévi. He attended the Paris *Conservatoire* and won the *Grand Prix de Rome* in 1819 with his cantata *Herminie*. Ten years later, he made his first popular success with a satirical piece called *Le Dilettante d'Avignon*. Although Halévy was esteemed by his own generation as a distinguished writer for the stage, *La Juive* alone of all his works has come down to us. The recognition that he lacks today, however, was fully accorded him in his lifetime. He received the emblem of the Legion of Honor and was admitted to the French Academy. As an educator, he also achieved renown, holding classes in composition at the Paris *Conservatoire* which were attended by such pupils as Gounod and Bizet. An influential figure in the music of his era, Halévy died at Nice, March 17, 1862.

LA JUIVE
(*THE JEWESS*)

La Juive, *an opera in five acts, now given in four, with music by Halévy and libretto by Scribe, was produced at the Paris Opéra in 1835. The first Metropolitan performance took place in 1884; and it was in* La Juive *that Enrico Caruso last appeared on the Metropolitan stage before his death in 1921.*

Characters, in order of appearance:

Ruggiero, a magistrate: *bass*
A crier: *baritone*
Rachel, a Jewess: *soprano*
Eleazar, her father: *tenor*
Cardinal Brogni: *bass*
Leopold, Prince of the Empire: *tenor*
Albert, an officer: *baritone*
Eudoxia, niece of the Emperor: *soprano*
Choir, crowd, ballet, chorus of Jews, majordomo, officer

Time: 1414   *Place:* The City of Constance

Act I

SCENE: A SQUARE IN CONSTANCE (29 Minutes)

It is a proud day for the city of Constance. The Hussite rebellion has finally been put down. Peace has returned, and the people line the streets devoutly at the approach of their magistrate, Ruggiero.
The magistrate ascends the cathedral steps and faces the crowd.

Crowd

Enter
Ruggiero
and
town
crier

"Upon this solemn day," he proclaims, "the Emperor Sigismund has issued a proclamation. Hear ye!"

A town crier in the company of Ruggiero shouts the praises of Leopold, Prince of the Empire, who has crushed the followers of the heretic John Huss. "Our danger is over," the crier announces. "The Emperor and Cardinal Brogni will both bestow their favor upon the city. In all our churches, let thanks to Heaven be rendered!"

As the crowd rejoices, the crier departs. Ruggiero is just about to follow when he hears the noise of commerce in a neighboring shop. "Who dares profane this Catholic holiday?" he demands.

Enter
Eleazar
and
Rachel

Armed guards enter the shop and bring forth Eleazar, a wealthy Jewish goldsmith. Clinging to the elderly man is his daughter Rachel. At once, the crowd surrounds them, muttering threats and insults. In the face of peril, Eleazar displays an inflexible self-control. "I have a perfect right to work today," he declares. "I am exempt from Christian laws."

Enter
Cardinal

The wrath of the populace rises still further. They are on the point of laying violent hands on the Jew and his daughter when the venerable Cardinal Brogni appears before the cathedral.

"Why this commotion?" he asks. "Whom do you lead here and what is their crime?"

"These two unbelievers have defiled our holy day!" Ruggiero declares.

The Cardinal Brogni scrutinizes both culprits and gives a sign of astonishment on seeing the elderly Jew. "We have met before!" he exclaims.

"Yes, in the city of Rome, before you entered the Church," Eleazar answers. "Well do I remember your wife and child."

The Cardinal sighs. "After I lost them, Heaven was my only refuge; now I pray constantly for the souls of men. Oh, let me intercede for you! Renounce your faith and turn to ours!"

Andantino

Si la ri - geur et la ven - gean - ce leur font ha - ir ta sain - te loi,
If cru - el scorn and ach - ing hard - ships drive them to hate thy sac - red law,

Exeunt
crowd,
Eleazar,
Rachel
and
Cardinal
Enter
Leopold

"Never!" the proud Eleazar mutters. Together with his daughter Rachel, he returns to his goldsmith's shop. Cardinal Brogni leaves for the council, and the citizens go to their homes. When the square is completely empty, a solitary figure appears. It is Prince Leopold, a hero in war and a despicable coward in daily life. Married to the

Emperor's devoted niece, Eudoxia, he seeks his pleasure elsewhere. Since his fancy has lighted on Rachel, he has assumed the disguise of a Jew to win her favor. Now, unseen by anyone, he approaches Eleazar's dwelling.

"Rachel!" he calls softly. "It is Samuel!"   *Enter Rachel*

The Jewess emerges from the shop. "How I have longed for you!" she exclaims.

Playing upon Rachel's emotions, Leopold speaks of their love— of his desire to see her again.

"Tonight!" Rachel whispers. "Come to my father's house. We are celebrating our holy feast: as a son of Israel, you will be welcome!"

Seeing the crowd return, Rachel hastens off to view the great procession that soon will begin. Finding Eleazar, she draws him to the cathedral steps—and suddenly, as they stand at their place of vantage, enjoying the spectacle, they are discovered by the cruel magistrate Ruggiero.   *Enter crowd Exit Rachel Enter Rachel Eleazar, Ruggiero and officer*

"Sacrilege!" he cries. "The threshold of our temple profaned by infidels!"

The mob takes up his cry. They seize the unfortunate Eleazar and his daughter, with the intent of plunging them in the lake of Constance. Immediately, Leopold, who has remained among the crowd, comes to the help of his beloved. Drawing his sword, he rushes toward Rachel and commands the officer of the guard to release her. Recognizing the prince, the officer obeys.

As Rachel and Eleazar are freed by the reluctant guards, they are at a loss to account for the power of their young fellow worshiper, Samuel. To avoid further trouble, they withdraw to their shop; a burst of music comes from the cathedral and the citizens of Constance kneel in prayer.   *Exeunt Rachel and Eleazar*

Act II

SCENE: THE INTERIOR OF ELEAZAR'S HOUSE (37 Minutes)

It is the eve of the Passover. Eleazar and Rachel are seated at table with their friends and kinsfolk. As Eleazar prays, the guests take up the burden of his chant. Leopold, seated among them in disguise, remains silent; he alone casts away the unleavened bread. His actions do not escape the watchful eye of Rachel.   *Eleazar, Rachel, Jews, Leopold*

The prayer is abruptly ended by a knock at the door. "Open in the name of the Emperor!" cry voices from the street. In terror, the Jews extinguish their sacred candles and hide. Rachel goes to her room, but Leopold remains at the request of Eleazar. "Samuel,"   *Exeunt Jews, Rachel* pleads the goldsmith, "you were able to help us this very day before the cathedral. Oh, help us now!"

Enter
Eudoxia
Opening the door, Eleazar does not see the persecutors whom he expects. Instead, a young and beautiful woman stands on the threshold. It is Eudoxia, the Emperor's niece. Unaware that her husband, Leopold, has already returned to Constance, she has come to the goldsmith's to buy a precious jewel in honor of his homecoming.

Leopold is actually in the room while his wife carries on negotiations with the goldsmith. Lurking in a dark corner, he cannot be detected; but he suffers a twinge of conscience as he hears the loyal Eudoxia.

"I have a wondrous chain," the goldsmith asserts. "My price is thirty thousand ducats."

"No matter!" exclaims Eudoxia. "Tonight I shall leave the chain with you; you must engrave my husband's name and mine. And tomorrow, at the banquet of victory, I shall present it to my husband as a pledge of my devotion!"

Exit
Eudoxia
Exit
Eleazar
Enter
Rachel
Eleazar escorts the princess to the door, promising to deliver the treasure. Then he retires; and Rachel steals into the deserted chamber to speak with her lover.

"I must go!" Leopold whispers. "But soon I shall return. Promise that you will meet me here alone!"

"I promise," murmurs Rachel.

Exit
Leopold
As Leopold departs, Eleazar comes from his chamber to bid the girl good night; he withdraws, and Rachel is left to herself. "I love Samuel, yet I fear him," she ponders. "Why did he cast away the unleavened bread? What mystery surrounds him? Alas, I have not the power to resist him—his destiny is linked to mine!"

Enter
Leopold
Leopold returns. In answer to the girl's troubled questions, he confesses that he is a Christian.

"But then," Rachel gasps, "we have already merited death. I have given myself to you—and the laws of our city condemn the love of a Jewess for one of Christian faith."

"We can disregard the law!" declares Leopold. "Come with me—we shall seek out a quiet retreat."

"I cannot leave my father!" Rachel exclaims, after a violent inner struggle.

"Come!" Leopold urges. "It is the moment—we must go!"

The Jewess is about to escape with her lover when the chamber door opens and Eleazar appears. "Why do you flee from me?" he demands. "Is this the way a son of Israel repays my hospitality?"

Enter Eleazar

"I am a Christian," Leopold declares. "Strike me, if you will!"

Eleazar is infuriated; but under the spell of Rachel's pleading, his wrath soon passes. "If you really love my daughter," he concedes, "you may take her for your bride."

"I cannot!" cries Leopold. Hinting that he is already wed, the prince rushes from the house, overwhelmed with shame.

Exit Leopold

As Rachel collapses, the outraged Eleazar curses the fleeing deceiver.

ACT III

SCENE: THE GARDENS OF THE EMPEROR (29 Minutes)

IN the magnificent gardens of his palace, the Emperor Sigismund is ensconced beneath a velvet canopy. Cardinal Brogni is beside him, and the wretched Leopold is seated near by with his wife Eudoxia. A celebration is being held in honor of the Prince's triumph over the Hussites. Troupes of dancers perform for the guests.

Emperor, Cardinal, Leopold, Eudoxia, chorus, ballet

Just as he has promised, Eleazar appears with the treasure. Rachel is beside him; and when she beholds Eudoxia place the golden chain about Leopold's neck, her anger is unbounded.

Enter Eleazar and Rachel

"Wait!" she cries, boldly ascending the imperial dais. "O princess, take back your token. He is not worthy of it!"

The Emperor rises from his throne; the Cardinal Brogni and Eudoxia listen in dismay to Rachel's accusation. "I yielded my honor to this man," Rachel continues. "The crime means death for *both* of us!"

Leopold can say nothing in his own defense. "An anathema upon you!" thunders the Cardinal.

So great is the wrath of the fanatical court that Eleazar, too, is condemned to die with his daughter and Leopold. As the three prisoners are led away, Eudoxia determines to save the thankless prince, even at the risk of her pride.

Act IV

SCENE 1: ANTECHAMBER TO THE COUNCIL (29 Minutes)

By permission of the Cardinal, Eudoxia has been given leave to speak to Rachel. As the Jewess is brought from her cell to the room adjoining the council chamber, the princess throws aside her imperial dignity.

Eudoxia
Enter
Rachel

"Ah, Rachel!" she pleads. 'You have the power to spare Prince Leopold. My love for him is dead; I shall never see him again—but I would lay down my life to rescue him."

"He has betrayed me," Rachel answers coldly. "He must die."

"Let him live!" begs Eudoxia. "Tell the council that he is innocent!"

Enter
Cardinal
Exeunt
Eudoxia
and
Rachel

Rachel is deeply moved by this plea. Still in love with Leopold, she decides to save his life. As the Cardinal approaches, Eudoxia quickly withdraws; and the Jewess is conducted to the council chamber.

Enter
Eleazar

"To die so young!" the Cardinal meditates, gazing after her. "And yet, she may be spared—if her father will submit to the laws of the Church." Summoning his guards, Brogni sends for Eleazar.

"Your daughter is awaiting sentence," the Cardinal declares. "You alone can save her by renouncing your faith."

"Renounce the faith of my fathers?" cries Eleazar. "Never!"

"Then you wish to die?"

"Yes," the Jew replies. "And before my death, I shall be avenged upon a Christian—upon *you!* Do you recall the day in Rome when the city was plundered? Do you recall when your palace was destroyed by flames, and your wife and child were consumed?"

"On that day," sobs the Cardinal, "I lost all that I held dear!"

"Not all!" gloats Eleazar. "Your daughter was rescued by a Jew and carried to safety."

"Eleazar!" cries the Cardinal. "Tell me where she is!"

"By what right do you ask?" the Jew demands. "You, who have persecuted me—who have scourged my race—shall never learn the secret!"

Exit
Cardinal

The Cardinal enters the council chamber in despair, and Eleazar is left alone. Tormented by doubts, he wonders if he should reveal the identity of the child he has called Rachel—if he should restore her to the Cardinal:

Ra-chel, quand du Sei-gneur la gra-ce tu-tè-lai-re
Ra-chel, when Heav-en bade me look to your pro-tec-tion

Suddenly, Eleazar hears the fanatical cries of the mob who have gathered to see him executed. "No!" he resolves. "I will consecrate Rachel to God and death!"

SCENE 2: THE EXECUTION (15 Minutes)

Soldiers, monks, members of the council and the Cardinal Brogni have assembled in a vast tent to witness the execution. The magistrate Ruggiero leads in the prisoners.

Soldiers, monks, council, Cardinal Enter Ruggiero, Eleazar and Rachel

"Hear ye!" Ruggiero proclaims. "Prince Leopold has been spared the death penalty and is banished from Constance!"

"Why must the deceiver live?" shouts Eleazar in a rage.

"I have declared him innocent," Rachel sighs. "I spared him through love."

Led by the executioner, the girl approaches the boiling cauldron. "Halt!" cries Eleazar. "My daughter, I am about to die. Do you wish to live—to renounce your faith?"

"My faith?" Rachel exclaims. "No! I would rather perish!"

Eleazar continues on the way to his doom. And now, the Cardinal rises from his place and stretches his arms imploringly toward the Jew. "On the point of death," he begs, "I beseech you to tell me—does my daughter live?"

"Yes!"

"But where? Where?"

A horrible shriek of joy rises from the crowd—Rachel has been hurled into the cauldron. "There is your daughter!" screams Eleazar. As the Cardinal falls upon his knees, the Jew goes firmly to his death.

MEYERBEER

GIACOMO MEYERBEER came of a wealthy Jewish banking family in Berlin, where he was born on September 5, 1791. A prodigy at the piano from the age of seven, he studied at Darmstadt under the Abbé Vogler.

At twenty-four, having dropped his original name of Jakob Beer, young Meyerbeer went to Venice, determined on dramatic composition. Here he fell under the influence of Rossini, and wrote in the Italian manner for nearly ten years.

A pause of six years may be explained by the reproaches of his friend Weber at his artificial style. Then, in 1826, he went to Paris and immersed himself in the study of French opera and theatre. From the successful production of *Robert le Diable* in 1831, Meyerbeer was associated with the Paris stage.

In 1842 he was called as General Music Director to Berlin, where he brought out Wagner's *Rienzi*. Meyerbeer's many premières both at the Paris *Opéra* and the *Opéra Comique*, however, drew him constantly to the French capital, where he died on May 2, 1864.

L'AFRICANA

L'AFRICANA, *an opera in five acts with a French text by Scribe, now generally given in Italian, was first produced at Paris in 1865, the year following the death of Meyerbeer, the composer. It reached the Metropolitan in 1888, and after an absence from the repertory of sixteen seasons, it was revived in 1922 with Rosa Ponselle as Selika.*

Characters, in order of appearance:
Inez, daughter of Don Diego: *soprano*
Anna, her attendant: *mezzo-soprano*
Don Diego, member of the Royal Council: *bass*
Don Pedro, President of the Council: *bass*
Grand Inquisitor: *bass*
Don Alvar, member of the Council: *tenor*
Vasco da Gama: *tenor*
Nelusko, a slave: *baritone*
Selika, a slave: *soprano*
High Priest of Brahma: *bass*
Chorus of Councilors, Inquisitors, Sailors, Indians
Time: 1497   *Place:* Portugal and India

ACT I

SCENE: THE COUNCIL CHAMBER OF THE KING OF PORTUGAL
(34 Minutes)

DRAWN by tales of the power and wealth that lay in the Indies, several Portuguese explorers of the fifteenth century tried to find a sea route connecting their mother country with the land of fabulous riches. Prominent among them was the great Bartholomeu Diaz.

In the vast council chamber at Lisbon, two women are anxiously waiting news of the Diaz expedition—Inez, daughter of the powerful Don Diego, and her maid Anna. Inez is deeply worried about her lover, Vasco da Gama, who has taken part in the venture. *[Enter Inez and Anna]*

Still another question agitates the girl. Why has her father summoned her to appear in this hall? Her fears are heightened as Don Diego finally enters with a man whom Inez dislikes—Don Pedro, unscrupulous President of the Royal Council. *[Enter Diego and Pedro]*

"My child," Don Diego exclaims, "our King has made a decision of importance concerning your future. He wishes you to marry Don Pedro."

As Inez is about to protest, Don Diego interrupts her. "I know what is in your mind; but put aside all thoughts of Vasco da Gama—we have just learned that he and all the Diaz expedition have perished!"

Inez and Anna leave the hall in despair; and the members of the council arrive. The conservatives, led by the Cardinal, are opposed to any further voyages of exploration—but the young nobles, under *[Exeunt Inez and Anna]*

Enter
Alvar,
Cardinal
and
councilors

the leadership of Don Alvar, claim that the future of their country lies in new territory.

As the Council deliberates, Don Alvar confounds his opponents with a startling announcement. "Not all of Diaz' mariners have perished," he asserts. "One survivor has actually arrived in Lisbon. He asks the honor of revealing his discoveries—Vasco da Gama."

Enter
Vasco

As Don Pedro and Don Diego exchange glances of annoyance, Vasco da Gama enters the chamber. "Noble sirs!" he exclaims. "My chief and his grave sailors were shipwrecked near the dread Cape— yet, I have charted the way and know it well. If you will give me another ship, I promise to find you the route to the Indies!"

The Cardinal, Don Diego, and the conservatives at once assert that such an expedition would be madness.

"Not madness, but wisdom," da Gama retorts. "While in Africa, I bought two captives in the slave market. Their features prove that they were born beyond the Cape, in a part of the world that we have never seen. Allow me, my lords, to exhibit these slaves; I have brought them back with me to Lisbon."

Enter
Selika
and
Nelusko
Exeunt
Selika
and
Nelusko

As the council members assent, two strange figures are brought into the hall: the dusky Selika, a young Hindu of queenly bearing, and her savage male companion, Nelusko. They firmly refuse to answer any questions; and when they are led away, the councilors prepare to vote on da Gama's plea.

Before a decision is reached, the Cardinal leads the entire assembly in prayer.

The hostile Don Pedro mounts the rostrum. "I have consulted with our members," he declares, "and we reject your insensate plan."

"Some day this assembly will regret its decision!" cries da Gama.

Wrathfully, the Cardinal and his followers rise from their places. "Imprison him!" they demand. "He has offended the Holy Inquisition!"

Vasco is led away to the dungeons of Lisbon.

ACT II

SCENE: THE PRISON OF THE INQUISITION (32 Minutes)

THE slave Selika hovers over Vasco da Gama, asleep in his cell.

Vasco
and
Selika

Andante grazioso

Fi-glio del sol, mio dol-ce_a mor, dor-mi su miei gi-noc-chi;
Lulled in my arms, thou sun's bright child, slum-ber; en-joy your sweet re-pose;

In remote Hindustan, Selika was queen; the savage Nelusko, her trusted attendant. Both were captured by Africans in a shipwreck off the Cape—and both have kept their identity a guarded secret. Now, as Selika lulls the sleeping Vasco, she sighs unhappily, for she is in love with him.

Nelusko already hates da Gama as a rival; he steals toward the sleeping man and raises his dagger. At once Selika wakens Vasco; Nelusko is obliged to retreat.

Enter Nelusko

Unaware of the danger that threatens, da Gama rises from his prison bench and unfolds a map of Africa. Tracing the southmost cape with his finger, he muses, "The passage must lie here."

Suddenly, he hears Selika's voice behind him. "That route would bring you to your death," she is saying. "You must proceed to the right, where a vast island looms in the sea. Alas, it was there that my frail bark collapsed and I was driven to the shores of Africa."

"Then the way is clear," Vasco exults. "Through your help, I shall succeed!" Joyously, he takes Selika in his arms—and at that moment, the cell door opens. Inez appears with Don Pedro just in time to witness the embrace.

Enter Inez and Pedro

Controlling her emotion, Inez hands da Gama a document. "Here is your pardon," she declares. "You are free, by order of the King . . . but I may never see you again."

"Why must you avoid me?" Vasco demands. "Are you jealous of my slave? Oh, Inez, I love you! To prove my devotion, I shall give you Selika as a handmaiden."

"And I?" cries Nelusko, who has been listening in the darkness.

"You are to follow her," Vasco answers.

Now Don Pedro brusquely speaks his mind. "We can use these slaves!" he declares. "Tomorrow, we set out for the East on a voyage of discovery."

Da Gama looks at Don Pedro in amazement. "You?" he cries. "Sailing to the East with the secret charts that I revealed to the council?"

"I have burned the charts," Pedro replies haughtily, "and I am sailing under orders of the King. Inez, let us depart!"

"Vasco!" sobs Inez. "As price of your freedom, I have wed Don Pedro. I am going with him to sea."

Vasco da Gama gazes bitterly at Inez and her treacherous husband. So deeply does he grieve that he does not notice the departure of the two slaves, who follow their new master, nor the passionate glance of farewell cast by Selika as she leaves the dungeon.

Act III

SCENE: THE DECK OF DON PEDRO'S SHIP (17 Minutes)

Pedro,
Alvar,
Inez,
Selika,
Nelusko
and
sailors

DON PEDRO has made the fatal mistake of putting his trust in Nelusko. Under the pretense that he knows the waters about the Cape, the slave has taken the wheel of Pedro's ship and is purposely steering for disaster.

The sailors have become restive; they press Nelusko for an accounting of his course. "We must beware!" he answers. "Adamastor, the monarch of tempests, is riding the sea. Unless we sail to the north, all of us will be destroyed!"

For a short time, the officers and crew are convinced of Nelusko's good faith; but their agitation rises as another ship approaches, flying the Portuguese colors. Soon, a small boat bearing Vasco da Gama rides the waves between the two vessels.

Seeing his enemy approach, Pedro orders his entire crew to go below—alone, he faces his rival. "What brings you here?" he demands angrily, as da Gama climbs to the deck.

"I have come to warn you!" Vasco answers. "This is the very place where the Diaz expedition was attacked by a thousand barks full of savage warriors!"

Ignoring Vasco's advice, Don Pedro summons his attendants. "Bind this man to the mast," he orders, "and take good aim with your muskets!"

Hearing the commotion on deck, Inez has come with Selika from her cabin. Suddenly, as the slave sees what is happening, she advances on her mistress with a dagger. "Free Vasco da Gama," she shouts to Don Pedro, "or I will kill your wife!"

To pacify the raging woman, Don Pedro orders Vasco's release. No sooner has Selika surrendered her knife than Pedro orders da Gama to be seized once more. "Lock him in the hold!" the captain orders. "And as for Selika—she shall be scourged in the presence of the crew!"

All this time, a storm has been gathering on the horizon. Now it breaks with terrible force. Wild yells are heard in the water below— the ship has been surrounded by small boats full of merciless warriors. They creep through the port-holes, pillaging the vessel and murdering the crew. In the midst of their plunder, they perceive a majestic figure on the deck, and wave their bloody knives with joy. It is Selika, their queen!

ACT IV

SCENE: INDIA, BEFORE THE TEMPLE OF BRAHMA (42 Minutes)

SELIKA is about to be crowned in the sacred temple of Brahma. Borne in triumph by a procession of priests, dancers, warriors and Amazons, she is welcomed by the High Priest of India.

"Do you swear, Selika," the Priest demands, "to maintain our laws? Do you swear that no stranger may profane the soil of Hindustan?"

Thinking of Vasco da Gama, Selika hesitates to take the oath. Nelusko, who is standing beside her, murmurs, "Oh, Queen, all of the Portuguese heroes have been slain."

Despondently, Selika enters the temple, as one of the priests whispers to Nelusko that Vasco da Gama has been found in the hold of the ship. The procession moves onward toward the shrine; the space before the temple grows silent and deserted.

Led by Hindu soldiers, Vasco appears, surveying the new terrain. Though he faces death, he rejoices that he has been able to see the land of his dreams. "At last!" he exclaims. "I claim this country for my king. It is a Paradise on earth!"

Andantino con moto

O pa - ra - di - so dal l'on - de u - sci - to,
Hail, beau - teous gar - den; a par - a - dise on earth art thou!

The solemn rites in the temple have been concluded. Selika emerges, and to her consternation, beholds Vasco da Gama in the great sacrificial square. Thoughts of the oath she has just taken arise to torture her. As Nelusko and the High Priest order the stranger to be led to his death, Selika tries a desperate solution.

"Hold!" she cries. "Vasco da Gama, whom you see before you, is *not* a stranger. When I was a slave in foreign lands, he preserved my life and honor—as reward, I married him!"

Nelusko is about to denounce Selika's lie, when the Queen turns to him with a despairing appeal. "You, Nelusko," she begs, "can vouch for the truth of this story!"

All through his wanderings with Selika, Nelusko has offered her a love that was never returned; still, he would rather die than see

[margin notes:]
Enter Selika, Nelusko, ballet and Indians
Enter High Priest

Exeunt all

Enter Vasco

Enter Selika, Nelusko, High Priest and Indians

her in distress. Sacrificing his honor, he swears that Selika speaks the truth.

"We will spare the stranger," proclaims the High Priest. "His marriage to Selika shall be consecrated at our sacred altar."

Exeunt
all but
Selika
and Vasco

The procession returns to the temple; Nelusko departs in grief; and da Gama is left alone with Selika. For the first time, he is aware of the queen's strange beauty. Taking her in his arms, he assures her of his devotion; but as a flock of dancing girls run from the temple to conduct the lovers to the altar, da Gama suddenly turns from his bride. In the distance, he has heard a wailing cry—the voice of Inez. Unable to conceal his emotion at the knowledge she is alive, he rushes in the direction of the voice. Gently the dancing girls draw him back to the temple, where the apprehensive Selika awaits him.

Voice
of Inez
(*off stage*)

Act V

SCENE: A LONELY PROMONTORY (8 Minutes)

THE fear that haunted Selika at her wedding has come true: she can never hold Vasco's love while Inez lives. In an outburst of savagery, she has even thought of slaying her rival; but abandoning the unworthy plan, the queen decides to banish Vasco from her sight and send him back to the West with Inez.

Enter
Selika

The Portuguese ship leaves the shores of India; Selika stands on a promontory overlooking the sea. Towering above her is a deadly tree—the mancanilla—whose perfume intoxicates and kills its victim.

"I feel no hatred," the queen murmurs, with a sorrowful glance at the horizon. "Only numbness and despair fill my heart!"

Breathing deeply, Selika inhales the languorous perfume. As the drug exercises its effect, she imagines that Vasco has returned to her —that he leads her once more to the altar of Brahma.

"It is he!" she cries. "He comes to me through the clouds!"

With a heart-rending cry, the queen expires, while far beyond the promontory, Vasco's ship is heading toward home.

VI

Opera Becomes Music Drama

Music drama is an art form in which music, drama, philosophy and stagecraft are presented in completely harmonious union. It was in Germany that the way was paved, over many years, for the evolution of this medium. As far back as 1695, the first German opera house had been opened at Hamburg. In contrast to the Italian court theatres, which were springing up throughout Germany and Austria, this modest structure specialized in performances of the *singspiel,* a type of work very much like the operetta of our own time.

The *singspiel* consisted of a series of set musical numbers connected by spoken dialogue. The action usually was comic in nature, although on occasion it reached tragic heights. As a whole, the form seemed to be making little headway in artistic circles until Mozart gave it his benediction. Thereafter, by reason of its simple melodies and straightforward plots, the *singspiel* served as a bridge between Gluck's early reforms and the mature innovations of Richard Wagner.

One of the most striking examples of this period of transition was Beethoven's only opera, *Fidelio* (1805) which brought a new intensity to the German lyric stage. From *Fidelio* it was but a step to the works of Carl Maria von Weber (1786-1826), who molded the elements of German melody and humor into romantic folk tales with fantastic color and technical skill. In Weber's operas, the orchestra attained great prominence, commenting upon the development of the drama by the use of leading motives—musical phrases closely identified with persons or ideas appearing in the story. *Der Freischütz* (1821) was a treatment of popular German legend, while *Euryanthe* (1823) dealt with medieval superstition and black magic.

At the start of his career, Richard Wagner was strongly under the sway of two contrasting influences. One was the ardent romanticism of Weber, flavored with the folk quality of the *singspiel;* the other, the pretentious grandeur of Meyerbeer. Indeed, Wagner's *Rienzi* (1842) nearly approximated the style of the composer of *Les Huguenots.* It was only in *Der Fliegende Holländer* that Wagner came into his own.

In his next two works—*Tannhäuser* and *Lohengrin*—Wagner retained the customary ensembles of grand opera, but made radical innovations in the music of the solo artists. There were no formal arias coming to a full conclusion. Wagner substituted what he called "the endless chain of music." In his use of the orchestra and leading motives, the composer continued what Weber had already begun.

After years of silence, Wagner emerged with a new work, *Tristan und Isolde.* Opera became music drama, with every element co-ordinated in one comprehensive art-form. It became possible, through the knowledge of leading motives—through the telling inflections of the orchestra—for a listener to detect at all times the hidden thoughts of the chief characters. Wagner had transformed the opera orchestra from a body of accompanists into a symphonic unit—his most important contribution to the evolution of opera.

Wagner followed the tragic *Tristan und Isolde* with one of the greatest comedies in the operatic repertory, *Die Meistersinger von Nürnberg.* Here, his wealth of humanity invested a comic plot with cosmic implications. In both the colossal *Ring des Nibelungen* and *Parsifal,* Wagner returned to legendary themes. Writing his own texts, he was able to achieve a complete fusion of words and tone.

Wagner's treatment of fantasy, dramatic climax, harmony, leading motives and complex orchestration has found its way into the work of almost every composer since his time.

BEETHOVEN

LUDWIG VAN BEETHOVEN was born in the town of Bonn on the Rhine, December 16, 1770. Raised and educated in this provincial city, he longed to see Vienna, the musical capital of his time. In 1787, he first obtained the means for a short visit, and five years later he was sent there, through the generosity of private patrons, for a course of study with Josef Haydn.

It was as pianist, rather than composer, that Beethoven was introduced to Vienna, although in 1797 his first published compositions attracted wide attention. In the following year, he fell victim to the deafness which pursued him for the rest of his life, and caused him to withdraw almost completely from the world.

Beethoven's fame today rests chiefly on his instrumental works. That he was also interested in the human voice is shown by the choral finale of the Ninth Symphony, his song literature and the majestic *Missa Solemnis*. The opera *Fidelio*, occurring at the same period in Beethoven's career as the *Eroica* symphony, was his only work for the stage. In its treatment of conjugal love it reflected Beethoven's ideal of opera: a union of voice and orchestra in the service of a higher morality.

During the composer's later years, his philosophic approach deepened into mysticism. When Beethoven died in Vienna, on March 26, 1827, he was still trying to find new channels of expression in music—a quest in which he unearthed the tremendous orchestral resources inherited by Richard Wagner.

FIDELIO

FIDELIO, *an opera in two acts originally known* as Leonore, *with text by Sonnleithner, was first performed at the* Theater an der Wien (*Vienna*) *in 1805. For political and musical reasons, it was not an immediate success and underwent two revisions by Beethoven, together with a change of title. In the course of these revisions, the opera acquired four overtures known as* Leonore Nos. 1, 2 and 3, *and* Fidelio. *In modern performances of the opera, according to the tradition set by Gustav Mahler, the brief* Fidelio *overture is played before the rise of the curtain and the* Leonore No. 3 *appears as a symphonic interlude during the second act.*

The Metropolitan première of Fidelio *took place in November, 1884, with Dr. Leopold Damrosch conducting. A new version of the opera by Artur Bodanzky was introduced to Metropolitan audiences in 1927. Beethoven's music remained unaltered, but much of the spoken dialogue was transformed by Mr. Bodanzky into accompanied recitative.*

Characters, in order of appearance:
Jaquino, a young turnkey: *tenor*
Marzelline, his betrothed: *soprano*
Rocco, a jailer: *bass*
Leonore (Fidelio): *soprano*
Don Pizarro, governor of the prison: *baritone*
Florestan, husband of Leonore: *tenor*
Don Fernando, Minister of Justice: *bass*
Chorus of soldiers, prisoners and townspeople
Time: Eighteenth Century   *Place:* Spain

Act I

SCENE 1: THE GATE HOUSE OF A PRISON (32 Minutes)

DON PIZARRO, a ruthless tyrant, is governor of the Spanish state prison near Seville. The prison buildings are dark and grim; but the cheerful gate house seems to belong to another world, presided over by the jailer Rocco and his attractive daughter Marzelline.

While Rocco goes about his duties in the prison, Marzelline stays at home. Young Jaquino, the turnkey, is near at hand, deluging her with questions: Why does she avoid him? Isn't she ever going to marry him?

Jaquino and Marzelline

The girl pretends to be busy with her ironing—but her mind is not on the work. She is dreaming of her father's new helper, Fidelio. "Oh, if only I were his bride!" she murmurs.

Andante con moto

O wär' ich schon mit dir ver-eint, und dürf-te Mann dich nen-nen!
Ah, 'were I now but wed with thee, Nor, long-ing, need con-ceal it!

Soon, Rocco comes in from the main building. "Where is Fidelio?" he exclaims impatiently. "It is time for him to be here!"

Enter Rocco

Even as he speaks, there is a knock at the door. Jaquino runs to open it, and the youth who is known as Fidelio stands on the threshold. In truth, Fidelio is Leonore Florestan, a lady of Seville, whose husband languishes somewhere in Spain as a political victim. Determined to find him, Leonore has disguised herself in male attire and taken the humblest position in the state prison. Now she enters the gate house, laden with provisions.

Enter Leonore

"Well done, Fidelio!" Rocco declares approvingly, as he helps Leonore lay aside the basket. With a complete lack of perception, he has already made plans for his daughter to wed this promising youth.

Leonore knows of these plans; she feels the danger she is running—but she is in no position to utter a word. Her silence is construed by Marzelline as a confession of love:

Andante sostenuto

Mir ist so wun-der-bar, es engt das Herz mir ein,
How strange a mood is mine, My heart's pent up in me,

All four characters sing the above phrase in turn (canon quartet), *each using a different text which reflects his personal emotion. Marzelline is ecstatic, Leonore worried, Rocco benevolent, and Jaquino frankly jealous of Fidelio.*

Exit Jaquino

"Oh, Master Rocco," Leonore declares, "I want so much to help you in your work. Why do you not take me with you to the subterranean vaults?"

"I have strict orders from the governor," Rocco answers. "No one may see the prisoners of state."

"Your duties are killing you!" urges Marzelline. "Surely the governor must allow you to share them with Fidelio."

"I will ask him," the jailer replies, "though I know there is one cell in this prison that none but myself may enter. A wretched fellow has been lying there for the past two years. He has little food—no light—not even a pallet of straw!"

Leonore almost cries out in despair. What if the starving prisoner should be her husband Florestan? Hiding her anguish, she exclaims, "Oh, take me with you! I have courage and will not fail."

"We shall see," Rocco declares. "First the governor will have to consent." He smiles indulgently at Marzelline and draws her to Fidelio. But Fidelio's thoughts are centered on a wretched man in a solitary dungeon, and on a plan for his rescue!

SCENE 2: THE COURTYARD OF THE PRISON (36 Minutes)

Soldiers
Enter
Don
Pizarro

An air of terror pervades the open square within the prison walls. Military commands ring through the courtyard as the soldiers assemble. Finally, the villainous governor of the prison—Don Pizarro—appears with his armed escort.

"Three sentinels on the rampart!" he orders. "Six men on the drawbridge. Let anyone approaching the moat be brought before me immediately!"

Enter
Rocco
Exit
Rocco

Seizing the dispatches which Rocco has brought him, the governor reads through them quickly. He stops in consternation—and Rocco tactfully withdraws.

"The Minister of Justice is coming to inspect the fortress," Pizarro mutters. "But he will never discover Florestan in my power —I will have the prisoner murdered before he arrives!"

Beckoning to his adjutant, the governor orders a strict watch to be kept over the road from Seville. "Captain!" he commands. "Go to the tower with a trumpeter. The minute you see a carriage escorted by cavalry, let the trumpet be blown at once!"

Allegro agitato

Ha! welch' ein Au - gen-blick! Die Ra - che werd' ich küh - len!
Ha! it is not too late! My ven - geance shall be tast - ed!

As the soldiers march from the square, Leonore appears in a doorway of the fortress and listens intently. Peering through a latticed grating, she can see Rocco crossing the yard.

"Jailer!" calls the governor. "Here is a purse of gold; there will be more if you obey me."

"What must I do?" Rocco asks.

Pizarro confronts him fiercely. "For reasons of state, one of our convicts is to die immediately. He has committed treason!"

"My lord," cries the jailer, "I am not hired to kill!"

"You are a coward!" Pizarro sneers. "If you have no courage, I'll do the deed myself. Now mind you: go to the prisoner in the vaults and dig his grave in the abandoned well. Do you understand? I will come disguised and put an end to him! Go—carry out my command!"

As the two men leave the courtyard, Leonore steps from her hiding place. "You monster!" she exclaims, staring after the cruel Don Pizarro. "Have you no pity?"

Recitative

f Ab-scheu - li - cher! wo eilst du hin?
In - fer - nal fiend! what will you do?

All that she has overheard confirms Leonore's suspicion that the solitary prisoner is Florestan, her husband. And yet she cannot be sure unless she actually descends with Rocco and sees the man. "Oh, Hope," she cries, "do not desert me! Lead me to my goal!"

For a moment, the tragic atmosphere is lifted. Leonore has gone into the garden—and the gloomy courtyard is the scene of a little comedy between Marzelline and Jaquino. As usual, the turnkey is pleading his cause with the girl.

"I won't deny that I once liked you," Marzelline answers, "but Fidelio attracts me far more."

Leonore soon returns in the company of the benevolent Rocco. "Oh, good father," she exclaims, "I have begged you so often to allow the prisoners to walk in the garden. Today, the weather is mild. Will you not grant your permission?"

"Yes, Fidelio," Rocco replies. "And now I am going to the governor to ask if you may work with me in the dungeons."

Rocco departs; unlocking the cell doors, Fidelio and Jaquino release the convicts—hopeless, dejected men who have not seen the light of day since they were first confined in Pizarro's fortress.

Exeunt
soldiers
Enter
Leonore
Enter
Rocco

Exeunt
Rocco and
Pizarro

Exit
Leonore
Enter
Marzelline
and
Jaquino

Enter
Leonore
and Rocco

Exit
Rocco
Enter
prisoners

"Oh, what joy!" sigh the unfortunate beings, as they wander into the fresh air of the garden. "Our cells have been like a tomb!"

Exeunt prisoners, Jaquino and Marzelline Enter Rocco

Marzelline and the turnkey follow them—but Leonore remains in the courtyard. At length she sees Rocco returning from the governor's house. "What news?" she cries.

"He has granted my request," answers Rocco. "You will descend with me to the depths of the prison—but not a word to anyone! We must do some digging."

Leonore trembles. "Are you afraid?" asks the jailer.

"No!" his helper exclaims. "Wherever you lead, I will follow!"

Enter Marzelline

Suddenly, Rocco looks with surprise toward the prison garden. Marzelline is running breathlessly down the steps into the courtyard. "Father!" she calls. "Take care! The governor is coming from the fortress!"

Enter Jaquino and prisoners Enter Pizarro

As Jaquino returns the convicts to their cells, Pizarro strides through the yard in a towering passion. "You fool!" he shouts at Rocco. "How dare you release these men?" In a whisper, he adds, "Be off now and clean out the cistern. There is no time to lose!"

The governor withdraws; Jaquino locks the cells, and Leonore sadly follows Rocco. Armed with tools and a lantern, she descends to the vaults of the fortress—perhaps to dig her own husband's grave.

Act II
Scene 1: a dungeon (34 Minutes)

Florestan

In the dark silence of his cell sits Florestan, haggard and in chains, thinking of Leonore:

Forgetting the grim walls about him, he imagines that his wife has come to free him. The vision passes, and the prisoner sinks back, bereft of all hope.

Enter Rocco and Leonore

The door of the dungeon swings open: Rocco and Leonore descend the stairway. As they set to work, clearing a passage to the cistern, Leonore glances at the prisoner—but in the darkness she can see nothing. Suddenly, she faints with terror as she hears the man's voice. It is Florestan!

"A drink!" he begs the jailer. "Oh, just one drop of water!"

In spite of strict orders, Rocco cannot resist the man's pleading. He gives him some wine; then resumes his digging. In a short time, the grave is ready and Rocco blows a shrill blast on his whistle. It is the signal for Don Pizarro to appear.

Enter
Pizarro

At once, the governor enters the dungeon and advances upon his victim with drawn dagger. Suddenly, the jailer's assistant steps from the shadows and bars his way.

"Go back, you insolent boy!" Pizarro roars.

Defying the governor, Leonore shields Florestan with her body. "I am his wife!" she cries.

Again Pizarro advances. Drawing a revolver, the fearless woman holds him off.

At this very moment sounds the signal that the governor has so anxiously awaited—the trumpet call from the tower. The Minister of Justice is at hand!

"God be praised!" cries Rocco. He escorts the defeated governor to the courtyard—and Leonore is left alone with her husband.

Exeunt
Rocco and
Pizarro

With overpowering emotion, the prisoner embraces his loyal wife. Guided by Leonore, Florestan ascends the stairs to freedom:

While the curtain is lowered, the orchestra plays the stirring Leonore Overture No. 3, *which includes the trumpet call heard at the climax of the prison scene.*

SCENE 2: A BASTION BEFORE THE FORTRESS (27 Minutes)

Towns-
people and
prisoners,
Don
Fernando,
Pizarro,
Marzelline,
Jaquino

Hailed by the prisoners and the people of the town, Don Fernando, Minister of Justice, has arrived to investigate conditions at the fortress. "I shall help you all," he announces, "in whatever way I can."

Immediately, Rocco pushes his way through the crowd, followed

Enter
Rocco,
Leonore
and
Florestan

by Leonore and her husband. "Then help these victims of oppression!" he pleads.

Don Fernando gazes at the prisoner in astonishment. "Florestan!" he exclaims. "You, whom I thought dead—and Leonore?"

"Allow me to explain," Pizarro interrupts; but he is silenced. "Not a word!" replies the minister. "Lead him away!"

Rocco is jubilant at this turn of affairs and his daughter Marzelline can always depend on the faithful Jaquino.

"Oh, noble wife," exclaims Don Fernando, "take the keys that unbind your husband's fetters. *You* shall free him!"

Filled with joy, Leonore liberates Florestan while the townspeople and prisoners hail her as the noblest of women.

WAGNER

RICHARD WAGNER was born at Leipzig on May 22, 1813, receiving his early education in Dresden and later at Leipzig University.

Embarking on a professional career, Wagner held the post of chorus master and then of conductor in obscure provincial theatres. These early years found him working on his first two operas, *Die Feen* and *Das Liebesverbot*. In 1837 he was appointed conductor at the relatively important opera house at Riga; but forced to flee the city two seasons later because of the debts he had accumulated, he set sail for France by way of the North Sea.

After a difficult time in Paris, where his genius went unrecognized, Wagner finally won a production for the historical opera *Rienzi* at Dresden. In 1843 he became second conductor of the Dresden Royal Opera, but after taking part in the local uprising of 1849, was forced to flee the country. In Switzerland he entered upon a new period of journalism and composition. *Tannhäuser* and *Lohengrin* had already been completed. Now Wagner bridged the gap between these transitional works and the first products of his maturity: *Tristan und Isolde* and *Der Ring des Nibelungen*.

Deeply in debt, the composer welcomed the friendship and aid that King Ludwig II of Bavaria suddenly offered him in 1864. Freed from financial worries by the King's generosity, he was enabled to complete *Die Meistersinger* and the monumental *Ring*. Enemies at the Bavarian court, however, drove him from Munich. Eventually, he took up residence in the modest town of Bayreuth, where he succeeded in building his own theatre. He spent his winters in Italy, completing his final work, *Parsifal,* at Palermo, and died in Venice on February 13, 1883.

DER FLIEGENDE HOLLÄNDER
(*THE FLYING DUTCHMAN*)

Although Der Fliegende Holländer (The Flying Dutchman) *was originally conceived as a "romantic opera," in one act, it is usually played in three. The work was completed in 1841.*

Returning to Dresden for the premiere of Rienzi, *Wagner persuaded the management to follow its success with* The Dutchman. *On January 2, 1843, the work was presented at the Dresden* Hoftheater *and given four performances. It then left the Dresden repertory for twenty-two years. In 1860, the composer applied additional touches, a few measures at the conclusion of the Overture and the final scene.*

The Flying Dutchman, *though the first Wagner opera to reach England, was not presented at the Metropolitan until November 1889.*

Characters, in order of appearance:
Daland, a Norwegian sea-captain: *bass*
The Steersman of Daland's vessel: *tenor*
Vanderdecken, The Flying Dutchman: *baritone*
Mary, Senta's nurse: *mezzo-soprano*
Senta, daughter of Daland: *soprano*
Erik, a hunter: *tenor*
Norwegian and Dutch sailors, maidens of a
Norwegian village.

Time: Eighteenth Century   *Place:* The Coast of Norway

92

The Overture

The overture, written after the rest of the opera, presents the elements of the drama to follow. A whirling tempest in the strings is three times interrupted by the thundering theme of the Flying Dutchman, condemned by the Devil for a reckless oath to sail the seas until Judgment Day, unless he find a woman faithful unto death.

As the storm dies away the gentle motive of Senta is sounded:

Again the storm beats through the full orchestra. Only at the conclusion of the Overture is it hinted that Senta may redeem the Dutchman from his cursed destiny.

Act I

SCENE: A ROCKY SHORE ON THE COAST OF NORWAY (46 Minutes)

A VIOLENT storm lashes the waves toward a cove where Daland the sea captain has been driven with his ship. Shouting at their work, the sailors furl the sails and make fast the ropes.

Daland, his sailors

The sturdy Daland meanwhile is scanning the landscape:

"We must be at Sandwike," he exclaims, "only seven miles from home, where I hoped my child Senta would be embracing me tonight!" The captain sets his steersman at watch, and as the wind has died down, returns to his cabin to sleep.

Steersman Exit Daland

To keep himself awake, the steersman sings of his sweetheart:

In spite of the wind, the young man drifts off to sleep. The sky grows darker. The storm drives a second ship to the harbor, its

Enter
Dutch
sailors

ghostly blood-red sails and black hull contrasting with the Norwegian schooner. Casting anchor with a violent crash, its spectral crew furls the sails in silence.

Enter
Dutchman

With pallid face and beard as black as his inky cloak, the captain of the second ship steps on shore. The horn theme of the prelude introduces Vanderdecken, the Flying Dutchman.

"Seven long years have passed on sea," he says wearily, "and once more I am permitted to seek salvation on land. But where is the woman who shall save me?"

Allegro molto

Wie oft in Meer - - es tief - sten Schlund stürzt'ich voll Sehn-sucht mich hin - ab,
How oft in o - cean's seeth - ing deep, death have I sought, e - ter - nal sleep.

Enter
Daland

Coming on deck, the Norwegian captain perceives the Dutch ship. He wakens the steersman, and bids him hail the strangers. After a long silence the Dutchman answers the salute, and tells them of his woeful voyage. Recounting the wealth of his cargo, Vanderdecken offers Daland a chest of treasure if he may spend one night in the Norwegian captain's home.

"Have you a daughter?" continues the Dutchman. "Give me her hand in marriage and all this booty will be yours."

The two men pledge their friendship. The wind freshens; the skies clear; the captains return to their respective ships and sail away to the joyful shouts of both crews.

ACT II

SCENE: A ROOM IN DALAND'S HOUSE (54 Minutes)

An orchestral introduction opening with the melody of the steersman's song at once establishes a cheerful mood.

Girls,
Mary,
Senta

IN a large room in Daland's house, hung with charts, fishing nets and other gear of the sea, a score of young girls work busily at their spinning wheels:

Allegretto

Summ' und brumm', du gu - tes Räd - - - - chen,
Hum, hum, hum good wheel go whirl - - - - ing,

The elderly nurse Mary rises to rebuke Senta, who alone has sat with idle hands, staring at a picture on the wall. It depicts a dark man in Spanish costume, closely resembling the Flying Dutchman.

"Her lover Erik is a hunter. If she keeps on with this fancy for the Dutchman on the wall," tease the girls, "there's no knowing what Erik will do!"

To quiet their chatter, Senta sings the ballad of the Dutchman. The girls put away their spinning wheels and gather around her.

First imitating the cries of the sailors, Senta describes the Dutchman's ghostly ship:

Trafft ihr das Schiff im Mee - re an, blut - rot die Se - gel, schwarz der Mast?
Saw ye the ship that rides the storm, blood - red the sails and black the mast?

Then she tells of the whistling wind that pursues his endless journey. "And yet he may be saved," she continues to the theme of Redemption, "if only he can find a woman who shall be faithful to him unto death."

"But where is the maiden who will save him?" ask her friends. "It is I," answers Senta ecstatically.

Her last words have been heard by the young huntsman Erik who gloomily reports that Daland has already landed. Mary hurries the girls away to meet the sailors, but Senta's suitor holds her back. He pleads that she accept his humble lot and marry her before her father can find a wealthier husband: Enter Erik
Exeunt
Mary
and girls

Mein Herz voll Treu - e ___ bis ___ zum Ster - ben,
A lov - ing heart a - - lone ___ I bring thee,

He tells her of a dream in which he has seen a stranger resembling the portrait on the wall arrive with her father, ask her hand, and take her off again on his ghostly ship.

Senta listens, entranced, and cries that she must share the Dutchman's fate.

Erik rushes off in dismay.

Senta resumes her revery. Suddenly the door opens. The Dutchman enters, escorted by Daland. Spellbound and mute, the girl

Exit Erik
Enter
Dutchman
and
Daland

Exit
Daland
compares his face with the portrait. She hardly hears her father's request to make the guest at home, nor does she notice Vander-decken's gift of pearls. Perplexed at their mysterious silence, Daland leaves his daughter with the stranger.

"My vision has come true," exclaims the Dutchman, deeply moved:

Undaunted by his warnings of impending doom if she fail, Senta swears eternal fealty to the lover of her dreams:

Enter
Daland
Daland re-enters, bestowing his good wishes on their pledge of betrothal.

ACT III

SCENE: THE HARBOR IN FRONT OF DALAND'S HOUSE (24 Minutes)

The ecstatic love theme opens the orchestral introduction, soon followed by a vigorous chantey:

Norwegian
sailors
Girls
THE Norwegian harbor is thronged with villagers, making merry in the clear summer night. Singing a gay chorus, the sailors dance about the deck of Daland's vessel while a crowd of girls brings food and drink to the Dutch crew on their unlighted ship.

Steersman
Exeunt
girls
"Better let them sleep in peace, and give us the food instead!" laugh Daland's steersman and his fellows. The girls follow their suggestion and leave them to consume the cakes and wine in the wildest hilarity.

Curious lights flicker about the Dutch ship; high waves dash against its ghostly prow. Sailors appear on the deserted deck, boasting that their rigging will last until doomsday, since the Devil himself has blessed it. *Dutch sailors*

The astonishment of the Norwegians turns to horror at these eerie words. Crossing themselves, they retreat below decks. The Dutch crew also disappears, leaving the ship as vacant as before. *Exeunt all sailors Enter Senta and Erik*

Suddenly Senta hurries out of the house, followed by the frantic Erik.

"Has this stranger bewitched you?" asks the young huntsman. "Have you forgotten the troth you plighted to me long ago?"

The Dutchman, whose arrival the young couple have not noticed, overhears Erik's last words and rushes forward with a terrible cry: "All is lost." *Dutchman*

Senta attempts to convince him of her loyalty, but he will not listen.

The Dutchman then discloses the story of his curse. "Since you did not swear your vows before God," he tells Senta, "you will not suffer eternal damnation,—but you have shattered my hopes of peace forever."

"My love is true," Senta proclaims. "I knew you from the first, and I will save you yet!"

The Dutchman rushes to his ship. At Erik's cry for help, Mary and the maidens hasten from the house and the Norwegian sailors from their vessel. With mad shouts, the Dutch sailors hoist their crimson sails. Daland with Erik and the nurse vainly attempt to hold Senta back. *Enter Mary, Daland and sailors*

The girl breaks away and rushes to an overhanging cliff. "I am faithful even unto death," she cries, and leaps into the sea.

Instantly the Dutch ship settles with all its crew. As the theme of Redemption rises to a serene cadence, the glorified forms of Senta and the Dutchman are seen above the wreck of the vessel clasped in each other's arms.

TANNHÄUSER

TANNHÄUSER, and the Contest of Song at the Wartburg, *as the full name of the music drama now reads, was first given at Dresden in 1845, with Wagner himself conducting.*

Fifteen years later Wagner revised Tannhäuser, *which was presented in March, 1861, at the Paris* Opéra. *The disastrous hostility of the members of the Jockey Club, infuriated by the fact that Wagner had put the ballet in the first act, before they had reached their seats, led to its withdrawal after two repetitions.*

Even before the Paris performance, Tannhäuser *had reached New York in its Dresden version. In 1884 it opened the period of German opera at the Metropolitan under Leopold Damrosch, and has continued to hold its place in the repertory.*

Characters, in order of appearance:

Venus: *soprano*
Tannhäuser, a minstrel knight: *tenor*
A shepherd: *soprano*
Hermann, landgrave of Thuringia: *bass*

Minstrel Knights
{
Walther von der Vogelweide: *tenor,*
Biterolf: *baritone*
Wolfram von Eschenbach: *baritone*
Heinrich der Schreiber: *tenor*
Reimar von Zweter: *bass*
}

Elisabeth, niece of the Landgrave: *soprano*
Four pages: *sopranos* and *altos*
Sirens, naiads, nymphs, bacchantes, old and young pilgrims, knights, nobles, and ladies of the Thuringian court.

Time: Early Thirteenth Century   *Place:* Near Eisenach

THE OVERTURE

The Pilgrim's Chorus at once establishes a religious mood:

It is followed by the fantastic theme of the Venusberg:

The feverish delights of the underworld are soon contrasted with the robust harmonies of Tannhäuser's Hymn to Venus:

Omitting the return to the Pilgrim's Chorus of the original version, the Overture now proceeds at once into the Bacchanale on which the curtain rises.

ACT I

SCENE 1: THE INTERIOR OF THE VENUSBERG (42 Minutes)

To the grottoes under her magic mountain, Venus, goddess of love, has lured the knight, Henry of Ofterdingen, known as Tannhäuser. Though he has been held in her domain for a year, he still kneels enthralled beside her flowery couch. A rosy light falls on the tender embraces of many languorous youths and maidens, while sleeping cupids nestle on the moss. Swarming from the background, a wild procession of fauns, satyrs, and bacchantes incite the amorous couples to more abandoned delights.

Three Graces at the side of Venus direct the cupids to aim their darts at the revelers. Gradually the dancers withdraw; only the Graces are left. The sirens' call echoes from the distance, as visions of Europa and Leda appear:

Venus
Tann-
häuser
3 Graces
Youths
and
maidens
Nymphs,
cupids
Bacchantes,
fauns,
satyrs.
Exeunt
dancers,
nymphs,
etc.

Naht euch dem Stran - - de!
Come to these bow - - ers!

The Graces depart. As if starting from a dream, Tannhäuser raises his head.

"Tell me your thoughts," asks Venus gently. "Why are you troubled?"

"I dreamed of bells," he answers sadly. "When shall I hear their peal again? When shall I see the summer grass, or hear the nightingale?"

The goddess chides him for his foolish words. Is he not now immortal? "Take up your harp," she adds, "and sing the praise of love!"

Earnestly, Tannhäuser rises to chant the hymn already quoted in the Overture, but his rapture fades into longing for release. "Too great are the joys of your love," he pleads. "Oh, goddess, set me free!"

"Traitor," cries Venus, "you despise the very love you praise!" She buries her face in her hands, then again offers him further delights.

Andante

Ge-lieb - ter, komm! sieh dort die Grot-te, von ros'-gen Düf-ten mild durch-wallt;
Be-lov - ed, come! See yon-der bow-er with ro-sy per-fumed va-pors—filled;

A second and then a third time Tannhäuser sings his sturdy hymn. He will remain her champion, but he must have his liberty. Roused to fury, Venus dismisses him with a curse. "Peace you will never find in the world! For salvation you must look to me."

"Ah, no," he answers, "my hope is not in you, but in the Virgin Mary alone!"

As Venus disappears, her kingdom melts into blackness.

SCENE 2: A VALLEY NEAR THE WARTBURG (21 Minutes)

Tann-
häuser

Shepherd

Enter old
pilgrims

Exit
shepherd
Exeunt old
pilgrims

Tannhäuser finds himself in a sunlit valley near the castle of the Wartburg. Behind him is a small shrine of the Virgin. On a cliff near by sits a young shepherd, piping to the accompaniment of sheep bells from the pasture.

A procession of hoary pilgrims now marches down the path, chanting a chorale.

"Good luck," the lad calls after them, "and pray for me in Rome!"

As the old men pass on, saluting the shrine, Tannhäuser falls on his knees. "The mercy of God be praised!" he cries. "But there will be no rest for me," he adds sadly as the pilgrims depart, "until my sins are forgiven."

The distant chiming of bells gives place to a fanfare of hunting horns. Soon the Landgrave and his minstrels emerge from the path on the left. Enter Landgrave, minstrel knights

"Who is that man at the shrine?" asks the Landgrave.

"It is Henry!" exclaims Wolfram, who first recognizes Tannhäuser, and begs his friends not to question the errant knight. Tannhäuser rises, bowing humbly to the Landgrave.

"I have wandered in a distant land," he explains. "Forgive me, and let me go my way."

His old friends urge him to return, but his resolution is broken only when Wolfram adds, "Stay—for Elisabeth!"

Spellbound, Tannhäuser repeats the name.

Wolfram hastens to tell him that his singing has won the love of Elisabeth, the Landgrave's niece, and that since his departure she has languished in retirement.

Tannhäuser begs the minstrels to lead him back to her. In a glad chorus, enlivened by the sounding of horns, the party rejoices that the days of the past have returned.

Ha, jetzt er - ken - ne ich sie wie - der
Once more I see the world be - fore me,

Act II

SCENE: THE HALL OF SONG AT THE WARTBURG (63 Minutes)

The orchestral introduction depicts Tannhäuser's happiness. A hint of warning, however, may be noted in the reappearance of the admonition given by Venus in the first scene.

The curtain rises on the great medieval hall where the minstrels are wont to engage in contests of song.

Joyfully Elisabeth greets its beloved walls: Enter Elisabeth

Dich, teu - re Hal - le, grüss ich wie - der.
Dear hall of song,___ I give thee greet - ing.

Wolfram ushers in Tannhäuser to meet her and then retires. Enter Tannhäuser

"Oh, Princess," he exclaims, "let me stay forever at your feet." Then slowly rising, he tells of his wanderings.

Innocently Elisabeth relates her own emotions: her pleasure in the songs of her childhood, the new life that his music had stirred in her, and the anguish of his sudden departure.

"Henry!" she cries, "what is it that you have done to me?"

Exit Tann-
häuser
Enter
Landgrave

"The God of Love has united us," answers Tannhäuser, joining his voice to hers in a rapturous hymn.

The Landgrave comes to welcome his niece to the hall she has so long deserted.

Enter
nobles,
ladies,
and pages

"I know the love that you feel," he says, guessing her secret affection for the knight who has returned.

Proceeding to a dais on the right, they greet a vast procession of noble guests, who enter to the strains of a majestic march:

Enter
minstrels

Trumpeters announce the arrival of the minstrels who bow to the assembly and then take their seats in the center of the hall.

The Landgrave rises. "The art of song has done as much for our land as the art of the sword," he reminds them, "so today, with our absent minstrel again in our midst, let us engage in another contest. The secret of his return may be revealed in the theme I have chosen: the praise of love." His announcement meets with universal applause.

Four pages collect small rolls of paper bearing the name of each minstrel in a golden bowl which they present to Elisabeth. She picks out a single roll, which they read, and then announce: "Wolfram of Eschenbach will begin."

Wolfram utters an austere hymn of devotion to Elisabeth, which is cordially received.

Tannhäuser, who has hitherto sat in dazed silence, now uneasily sweeps the strings of his harp, while hints of the Venusberg flutter from the orchestra. Oblivious of Elisabeth, he rejects Wolfram's chaste philosophy and declares his own impious passion as a testament to love.

Angrily Biterolf threatens to punish this insult to womanhood and the company applauds his resolve, but the Landgrave demands that he sheathe his sword.

Wolfram again sings his praise of ideal love, invoking its benign healing on the present discord.

The ecstatic Tannhäuser can only repeat the Hymn to Venus, concluding with the words: "Only those who have lain in your arms know the true meaning of love! Hasten, wretched mortals who have never tasted its delights, hasten to the Venusberg!"

In the greatest dismay the ladies leave the hall. Still lost in a trance, Tannhäuser remains standing alone at the left. Knights and minstrels group themselves about the Landgrave. With an exclamation of horror they advance with drawn swords against the miscreant, when suddenly Elisabeth, who has been standing deadly pale, rushes forward to shield him with her own body.

Exeunt ladies

"Stand back," she cries, "will you deny salvation to this man? It is I whom he has wounded, not you, and I plead for his soul."

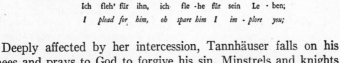

Ich fleh' für ihn, ich fle -he für sein Le - ben;
I plead for him, oh spare him I im - plore you;

Deeply affected by her intercession, Tannhäuser falls on his knees and prays to God to forgive his sin. Minstrels and knights join his supplication, softened by his evident remorse.

But the Landgrave's heart is stern. "A disgraceful crime has been committed," he declares, stepping solemnly forward. "There is only one atonement possible. On this very day a band of pious pilgrims leaves for the Holy City. Tannhäuser shall follow them to Rome."

Far in the background rises the pilgrims' chorale. A ray of hope lights Tannhäuser's face. He kisses the hem of Elisabeth's garment and then rushes away. "To Rome!"

*Exit Tann-
häuser*

"To Rome," they call after him, as the curtain falls.

INTRODUCTION TO ACT III

Tannhäuser's pilgrimage is traced by a quotation from the Pilgrim's Chorus, followed by the melody of Elisabeth's intercession, and finally by a new theme, known as Heavenly Grace:

ACT III

SCENE: A VALLEY NEAR THE WARTBURG (51 Minutes)

Elisabeth
Enter
Wolfram

THE woodland glade of the second scene is now colored with the shadowy tints of an autumn evening. At the Virgin's shrine, Elisabeth kneels prostrate in prayer. Down the path comes Wolfram.

"I knew that I should find her here," he observes, "praying for the soul of the man who has wounded her, and waiting for his return." He pauses, as the distant hymn of the returning pilgrims rises from the valley.

Enter
and
Exeunt
pilgrims

Elisabeth too has heard the chorus. Eagerly she examines the face of every man, as the procession passes. Then, she falls on her knees again in a passionate prayer to the Virgin for release:

All mächt-ge Jung-frau, hör' mein Fleh-en! Zu dir, Ge - prie - sne, ru - fe ich!
O bless - ed Vir-gin, hear my plead-ing! Thou Queen of glo - ry, grant my prayer!

Exit
Elisabeth

Vainly Wolfram urges her to let him accompany her homewards. By a gesture she assures him that she must pursue her destiny alone. As she disappears into the distance, he takes up his harp and addresses the evening star. When Elisabeth enters Heaven, it will bring her his greeting:

O du mein hold - er A - bend - stern,
O star of eve, _____ so pure, _____ so fair,

Enter
Tann-
häuser as
pilgrim

It has grown quite dark, and he does not recognize the tattered pilgrim, who, leaning on his staff, wearily approaches.

"Henry, can it be you?" asks Wolfram, starting eagerly forward. "How is it that you dare return to us?"

"Never fear, I do not seek my former comrades," retorts the knight. "Can you tell me the path to the Venusberg?"

Shocked by Tannhäuser's lack of repentance, Wolfram still proclaims pity for his friend. "Tell me," he urges, "what befell you in Rome?"

"Yearning for pardon as no pilgrim ever yearned, I sought out every hardship of the road," replies the minstrel. "I sought the sanctuary of the Holy City. I begged for absolution. The answer came from the Father himself:

> *'If you have felt this evil lust,*
> *If you have lain on Venus' breast,—*
> *As on this staff no leaf shall grow,*
> *Salvation you may never know.'*

I fell in a swoon. When I awoke it was night; I was alone; I turned and fled. Now, once more I seek for Venus!"

The darkness increases. As the sirens' call echoes in the orchestra, the goddess herself is disclosed, reclining on her couch of flowers. With the old enchantment, she beckons to her lover, offering him the raptures he once rejected. *Venus*

Tannhäuser tears himself away from the friend who would save him and resolutely approaches Venus. But Wolfram seizes him again. "An angel pleads for you in Heaven!" he exclaims: "Elisabeth!"

At that name Tannhäuser stands rooted to the spot. To the gleam of torches, minstrels and knights descend the path in a sad procession. On an open bier lies the body of Elisabeth. *Enter minstrels, knights with bier*

Tannhäuser, who has been led to the bier by Wolfram, sinks beside it on his knees, with a prayer for intercession on his dying lips. As the light of dawn floods the grove, the men extinguish their torches. The entire band of pilgrims marches in slowly, bearing a staff covered with fresh green leaves. One and all hail the miracle by which Tannhäuser's redemption is assured.

LOHENGRIN

LOHENGRIN, *an opera in three acts, was conceived by Wagner when he visited Paris in 1839. On the completion of* Tannhäuser *in 1845, he returned to the anonymous German epic of the swan knight, and sketched the text while on a holiday at Marienbad, in Bohemia. From September, 1846, to March, 1848, he composed the music.*

The opera was first performed at Weimar on August 28, 1850, under the direction of Franz Liszt. Lohengrin *reached New York in 1871, and was the occasion of the American debut of Anton Seidl at the Metropolitan in 1885. Since the first season of 1883, when it was produced in Italian, it has held the stage for more consecutive years than any other work, and is second in number of performances only to* Aïda.

Characters, in order of appearance:

The King's Herald: *baritone*
King Henry the Fowler, of Germany: *bass*
Telramund, Regent of Brabant: *baritone*
Ortrud, his consort: *soprano*
Elsa of Brabant: *soprano*
Lohengrin: *tenor*
Knights of Brabant, Thuringia and Saxony,
    maidens, noblemen, serfs and pages.

Time: Tenth Century   *Place:* Antwerp

The Prelude

The music of the prelude, which opens slowly in the highest register of the orchestra, is based upon the motive of the Grail, the holy chalice into which the Savior's blood was poured at His crucifixion:

The theme is gradually developed in descending tonalities, reaching a great climax from the full orchestra. Thus the celestial vision descends as a benediction from Heaven, to which it at length returns.

Act I

SCENE: THE BANKS OF THE SCHELDT, NEAR ANTWERP (60 Minutes)

UNDER a mighty oak tree on the left of a broad clearing, King Henry stands to address his subjects of Brabant. In the distance the river Scheldt winds across the plains toward Antwerp. About him are gathered German and Brabantian nobles, dominated by the sinister Frederic of Telramund, and his haughty consort, Ortrud.

King Henry, nobles, retainers, Ortrud Telramund

Four trumpeters silence the assembly for the King's Herald.

Herald and trumpeters

"Hear, ye princes, lords and freemen of Brabant!" cries the Herald. "King Henry has come for his lawful parley." Nobles and men-at-arms loyally greet their King.

"God bless you, my subjects," declares the sovereign, telling of the wars that have racked his kingdom. "I had come to ask your help, but I grieve to hear of strife in the province. Frederic of Telramund, you who are the soul of honor, tell me your grounds for this discord."

Telramund explains that the late Duke of Brabant made him guardian of his children Elsa and Gottfried, but that the boy had disappeared when in the care of his sister.

"I herewith accuse Elsa of the murder of her brother," he continues, "and myself lay claim to Brabant as nearest kinsman to the Duke."

The men comment on this news with awestruck tones, vowing not to sheathe their swords until judgment is pronounced. King Henry orders the Herald to summon the accused maiden and then prays humbly for wisdom.

The Herald's words have barely died away when Elsa, clad in

Enter
Elsa and
her ladies
purest white, arrives with her attendants. There sounds a theme known as her prayer for help:

"Are you Elsa of Brabant?" asks the King. "Do you accept me as your judge?" The girl, in simple dignity, bows her head.

"Do you know the charge against you? Do you admit your guilt?"

Elsa gazes sadly before her in silence, and then murmurs: "My hapless brother!"

"Come, Elsa, confide in me," begs the King, moved by her evident innocence.

Tranquilly she relates a vision that came to her in her anguish as she prayed to Heaven for help:

"A knight in shining armor approached me with words of consolation. He shall be my champion."

Elsa and Telramund formally agree to accept the results of a trial by combat. But who is to fight for Elsa?

The trumpeters blow their challenge, and the Herald summons the champion. Twice the fanfare is sounded, followed by an uneasy silence.

Elsa falls on her knees. "O Lord," she prays, "tell my knight of my great need for him!"

There is a murmuring from the river bank: "Behold," whisper the men in the background. The assembly crowds to look up stream. "A swan," they exclaim, "drawing a boat by a golden chain, and in the boat a knight in shining armor!"

Ortrud and Telramund stand transfixed with alarm. Elsa gazes rapturously into space, but turns with a joyous cry as Lohengrin in winged helmet and silver armor steps from the boat to the joyous greeting of the throng.

Enter
Lohengrin

The knight bids farewell to his swan, which swims away in silence.

Nun sei be-dankt, mein lie-ber Schwan!
Now down the stream de-part-ing float!

"How fair he is," whisper the awestruck nobles. Slowly Lohengrin advances among them and makes obeisance to the King.

"I have come as the champion of a maiden to whom cruel wrong has been done," he announces. Then, turning to Elsa, he offers his protection: "If I am victorious in this combat, will you be my wife?"

"All that I have, all that I am is yours," she answers, enthralled.

"One promise you must make me, if we are to wed," continues the knight. "Never may you ask whence I come nor who I am."

Nie sollst du mich be-fra-gen,
These quest-ions ask me nev-er,

Not satisfied with her promise, he repeats his solemn warning:

"My shield, my savior!" she exclaims, as he takes her to his breast with words of love.

After some hesitation, Telramund agrees to fight the mysterious stranger. Three Saxon nobles advance for Lohengrin and three Brabantians for Telramund, to measure off the ground. The Herald proclaims that none shall interfere, and the King prays to Heaven that truth may prevail:

Des Rei-nen Arm gieb Hel-den Kraft,
To stain-less knight give strength and might,

At length the trumpeters blow the call to arms; the King gives the signal with drawn sword. In a brief encounter Lohengrin fells Telramund, but spares his life.

While plaudits fill the air, the King presents Elsa to her deliverer, whom she addresses ecstatically:

O fänd' ich Ju-bel-wei-sen, dei-nem Ruh-me gleich,
I'd sing a song of prais-es, e-qual to thy worth,

Telramund mingles his shame with that of Ortrud. Crushed in body and spirit, he sinks in despair at her feet, unnoticed by the jubilant throng.

Act II

SCENE: EXTERIOR OF THE KING'S CASTLE (70 Minutes)

Telramund and Ortrud

DAWN has not yet brightened the courtyard of the fortress of Antwerp. On the steps of the minster the crouching figures of Telramund and Ortrud can dimly be seen. Trumpets sound distant revelry from the castle.

Telramund rises, bidding his consort follow him. Dawn must not find them in Brabant.

"I cannot go," insists Ortrud.

In an outburst of rage, Telramund denounces her: "Because of you my honor is gone. You swore that Elsa murdered her brother, and God has proclaimed your words a lie."

"Your own cowardice lost you the fight," retorts Ortrud. "A brave man would have found the stranger as weak as a child, for he owes all his strength to a magic spell. If once compelled to reveal his name and station, his power is at an end. But it is Elsa who must be lured to question him. If she fails, we can resort to force. My magic has taught me that the slightest injury will put him in our power." The prospect of vengeance unites the conspirators in a solemn invocation.

Enter Elsa

A sudden change of key heralds the appearance of Elsa on the balcony of the castle. A vision of purest white, she sings of her happiness to the night wind:

Euch Lüf-ten, die mein Kla-gen so trau-rig oft er-füllt,
Ye breez-es, who so oft-en heard tales of my dis-tress,

Exit Telramund

Ortrud sends Telramund away and piteously calls:

"Elsa, what have I done that you should spurn me? It is easy for you, who are so happy, to forget my misery!"

Exit Elsa

As Elsa retires from her balcony to come down and answer this plea, Ortrud leaps up from the steps with a wild appeal to the pagan gods, Wodan and Freia.

Escorted by two pages with candles, Elsa approaches Ortrud compassionately and begs her forgiveness.

Enter Elsa

"What fitting homage can I show you?" says the crafty Ortrud. "Let my power protect you from the magic of the strange knight!"

"Poor creature, can you never understand the joy of faith?" asks Elsa, tenderly. "I shall teach you."

As their voices blend in a duet, the dark sorceress follows her victim to the castle.

Exeunt Elsa and Ortrud

Telramund advances from his hiding place. "Thus evil enters yonder house," he observes ominously, and hides again behind a buttress of the minster.

Telramund

As daylight dawns, the reveille of the warders echoes from distant towers. Servants bring jugs and ewers to the well; retainers greet each other.

Enter retainers

The Herald with his four trumpeters proclaims the King's decree: "Frederic of Telramund is banished. The Heaven-appointed stranger, consort of the lady Elsa, has declined the dukedom, but will rule Brabant as guardian. The wedding feast we celebrate today, and tomorrow Lohengrin will lead the men to battle for the King."

Trumpeters

Four pages meanwhile appear on the balcony: "Make way for Elsa, our bride," they call.

Enter pages Enter ladies

A brilliant procession of richly clad ladies winds down the stairs of the castle:

At length Elsa enters in her magnificent bridal robe and mantle, followed by Ortrud, whose face betrays violent anger. Just as Elsa sets foot on the minster steps, Ortrud rushes forward to confront her.

Enter Elsa and ladies and Ortrud

"Back, Elsa!" she cries fiercely. "I was not born to be your menial. My own husband has been overthrown by injustice. What do you know of yours?"

"He has proved himself in combat," answers Elsa proudly.

"Why do you not question him," taunts Ortrud. "Do you fear the truth?"

Enter King, Lohengrin and nobles

At this point the King and Lohengrin, superbly clad and attended by the nobles, press their way to the scene of strife.

"My champion," cries Elsa, "protect me from this woman!"

Lohengrin motions Ortrud away and leads his bride to the minster, where another interruption forces them back in dismay. Telramund has chosen this moment to accuse the knight of sorcery, and urges the nobles to demand his name and station.

Lohengrin proudly refuses to reply, even should the King himself ask the question. "There is only one to whom I must give answer," he adds, turning to Elsa.

King and courtiers crowd about him, offering allegiance. Ortrud and Telramund seize the opportunity to whisper venomous doubts in Elsa's ear. They slink away as Lohengrin approaches.

"Elsa," he pleads, "in your hands lie all our joy and peace."

"My redeemer!" she declares. "Above the power of doubt love reigns supreme." To the pealing of the organ, they enter the minster.

ACT III

SCENE 1: THE BRIDAL CHAMBER (30 Minutes)

In a brilliant introduction the gay tumult of the wedding festivities is suggested:

Enter Elsa and ladies, Lohengrin, King and attendants

A PROCESSION of ladies escorts Elsa to her bridal chamber, the King and his nobles conducting Lohengrin to her side. Soft harmonies accompany the bridal chorus:

At length the kindly monarch withdraws, followed by his suite. Exeunt
King and
chorus
"For the first time we find ourselves alone," exclaims Lohengrin, leading his bride to a couch beside the open window.
"My heart rejoices with divine rapture," Elsa replies.

Fühl ich zu dir so süss mein Herz ent-bren-nen,
O, when I look on thee, my heart's own treas-ure,

"On your lips my name sounds so sweet that I long to speak your own," she murmurs. "Give me your confidence."

"When you vowed not to question me, I trusted you utterly," he answers gently. "Your love repays me for all the glories I have left behind."

"Then you wish to return to them?"

Vainly he implores her to be silent. In growing terror, she conjures up a vision of the swan, bringing the boat for his master. "What is your name?" she cries, "and whence do you come?"

Through the door she sees Telramund and four nobles of Brabant bursting in with drawn swords. Enter
Telramund
and nobles

"Save yourself," she shrieks, "the sword!" Exeunt
nobles
with
body

Snatching the blade from her hand, Lohengrin fells Telramund with a single blow. The four nobles sink to their knees in silence, and then bear away the body.

"Alas!" exclaims the knight. "Our joy is gone forever!" He places his fainting bride on the couch and summons her women to conduct her to the King. "There her questions will be answered," he mournfully promises.

SCENE 2: THE BANKS OF THE SCHELDT (22 Minutes)

Fanfares of trumpets herald the gathering of the nobles by the great oak tree on the river bank. With fluttering banners they assemble at dawn to greet King Henry. King,
nobles

"Would that I might find loyalty like yours in every land!" says the King. "Where is your new leader, that I may thank him?" But his brow is clouded as the four nobles carry in the corpse of Telramund. Enter 4
nobles
with
body of
Telramun

With faltering steps Elsa, pale and silent, is escorted by her ladies to a seat beside the monarch. She hardly raises her eyes to see the entry of her husband in shining armor and helmet. Enter Elsa
and
maidens
Enter
Lohengrin

The men hail him gladly, but he silences their welcome.

"I cannot lead you to battle," he tells them solemnly, "and I must ask your absolution for a crime. I slew this man in self-defense," and he uncovers the body of Telramund.

"The wife that God gave me has broken her vow," he continues sadly. "Yielding to evil counsel she has asked my name. Now I must reveal my secret to you all."

"In a distant land," he narrates, "stands the castle of Monsalvat. Here, guarded by a company of virtuous knights, is kept the Holy Grail which angels brought from Heaven. Every year a dove brings it new power to fill its votaries with faith. By its mystical nature they are strong enough to champion innocence throughout the world. But should faith be lacking, should doubt arise, they must hasten away. I have come to you from the Grail. My father Parzival rules as its monarch. His knight am I—my name is Lohengrin."

The swan is seen, drawing the boat downstream. Lohengrin turns sadly to Elsa.

"If I had remained for a single year," he tells her, "your brother would have been restored to you. If he should still return, give him my magic weapons for his defense. And now farewell."

Enter Ortrud

At this moment Ortrud exultantly appears. "Let the proud knight depart," she cries. "It was I who transformed the boy Gottfried into yonder swan! If the knight had tarried, he could have freed him from the spell."

Enter Gottfried Exit Lohengrin

Lohengrin falls on his knees in silent prayer. The swan sinks through the water, while the radiant boy Gottfried appears in its place.

Drawn by a celestial dove, the boat bears Lohengrin slowly away. The young heir advances to make obeisance to the King. Then he takes his sister in his arms as she falls lifeless to the ground with a last despairing cry: "My husband! My husband!"

TRISTAN UND ISOLDE

TRISTAN UND ISOLDE, *a music drama in three acts, was first conceived by Wagner in 1854, but it was not until the summer of 1857, which he spent near Zurich at the home of the Wesendoncks, that he composed the first drafts of the music. His source of inspiration was a passionate love for Mathilde Wesendonck. On August 6, 1859, the score was completed at Lucerne.*

This music drama was originally intended as a practicable work in contrast to the Ring, *which the composer had temporarily abandoned because of its enormous difficulties of production. Nevertheless,* Tristan *was discarded by the Court Opera in Vienna after fifty-seven rehearsals and waited until June, 1865, for its first hearing in Munich, under von Bülow. It did not achieve its American première until December 1, 1886, when it was presented at the Metropolitan under Anton Seidl.*

Characters, in order of appearance:

Isolde, an Irish Princess: *soprano*
Brangäne, her waiting woman: *mezzo-soprano*
Kurvenal, servant to Tristan: *baritone*
Tristan, nephew to the King of Cornwall: *tenor*
Melot, a knight of Cornwall: *tenor*
King Marke, king of Cornwall: *bass*
A shepherd of Brittany: *tenor*
A helmsman: *baritone*
Voice of a young sailor, other sailors, waiting women, knights, esquires and men-at-arms

Time: Legendary   *Place:* Cornwall and Brittany

THE PRELUDE

*The mood of longing is maintained throughout the prelude by a
closely woven development of leading motives. First among these
is The Confession of Love (I); the second (II), Desire:*

These themes are followed by the motive of the Glance:

*Among other motives are the Love Potion and Deliverance by
Death.*

ACT I

SCENE: THE DECK OF TRISTAN'S SHIP, AT SEA BETWEEN IRELAND AND CORNWALL (75 Minutes)

Isolde and
Brangäne

WITHIN a pavilion richly hung with tapestry lies the Irish princess Isolde, her head buried in the furs of her couch. Her companion Brangäne peers out to sea. Great curtains conceal the
afterdeck toward which steps mount in the center.

The voice of a sailor drifts from the masthead, chanting a
song of the sea to an unknown Irish maiden:

For an instant Isolde thinks it is she that he dares to address.

She rises imperiously, then turns to ask Brangäne where they are.

"With a quiet sea, we should reach Cornwall by evening," answers her maid.

"Never!" declares Isolde wildly. "My mother's witchcraft will not fail me! Let the winds rise at my bidding and destroy the ship and its company!"

In vain Brangäne attempts to comfort the princess, who left Ireland without a tear of farewell, to enter on a forced marriage with Cornwall's king.

A cry for air is Isolde's only rejoinder.

Brangäne draws the vast curtains apart. At the mainmast, sailors cluster about their ropes. On the lofty afterdeck is gathered a score of knights. In their midst stands Tristan at the helm, his trusy old servant Kurvenal at his feet. Again the sailor's song echoes from the masthead.

Curtains open Tristan, Kurvenal, knights and sailors

Isolde's eyes are fixed on Tristan as she mutters her longing for death:

"Go," she orders Brangäne, "and inform Tristan that Isolde commands his presence, though he knows neither courtesy nor care."

She watches Brangäne timidly approach the men and listens to Tristan's evasive answer: "I will wait on your mistress when I lead her to the King, my master. I do not dare leave the helm."

Brangäne repeats Isolde's curt command to Tristan. Kurvenal springs up to answer with a mocking ballad:

"When the Irish knight Morold came to levy a tax on Cornwall, all he got was a death-wound from Tristan's sword! My master is a hero."

The crew takes up the praises of their leader.

Brangäne hastens to close the curtains and soften the bitterness of her mistress' defeat. But Isolde must hear every detail of the encounter from Brangäne's own lips. At length the princess reveals the meaning of Tristan's historic offense and the secret of

Curtains close Isolde and Brangäne

her present shame, while the motive of the wounded Tristan pervades her narrative:

"A knight, wounded unto death, drifted long since in a frail boat to the Irish coast. With herbs and simples I nursed him back to health. Though he went by the name of Tantris, I soon knew him to be Tristan, the slayer of Morold, my countryman and lover. When I found a notch on his sword fitting the splinter from Morold's wound, I resolved to slay him in vengeance. But he looked up into my eyes and my heart was softened.

"This is the man who has dared to claim my hand for his old and weary kinsman, King Marke, once vassal of the Irish throne. This is the man whose life I was foolish enough to spare. A curse on his head! Death I demand for him—death for us both!"

Brangäne again attempts to soften the blow. "Sweetest lady," she says tenderly, "forget your wild fancies. How could Tristan recompense you better for your mercy than by offering you the crown of Cornwall? If so noble a knight is the liege, think how great, how powerful must be the master!"

Isolde gazes vacantly before her. In the very presence of this noble knight she must languish unloved.

"Where is the man who would not love you?" coaxes Brangäne. "And if magic powers should draw any swain from your side, remember I have your mother's subtle potions in my casket to win him back again."

"Bring me the casket," cries Isolde, darkly. Seizing a small phial from the case, she holds it aloft. "This is the draught that I shall drain: the death potion."

As the shouts of the sailors drift from the afterdeck, Kurvenal brushes aside the curtains and commands the ladies to prepare for a speedy landing.

Enter Kurvenal

Isolde conceals her emotion and addresses Kurvenal with composure: "Before your lord takes me to his master, it is fitting that he should seek forgiveness for the evil he has done me."

Exit Kurvenal

Kurvenal retires with the message, and Isolde hastens to bid Brangäne farewell. "I can trust you to prepare the poisoned cup that alone will soothe my most anguished need!" Mustering her resolution, the princess turns to address the knight, who enters with dignity:

Enter Tristan

When Isolde chides him for his lack of respect, Tristan pleads that only respect has kept him from her side. When she demands vengeance for the murder of Morold, he offers her his sword to deal him the final blow.

But Isolde will have none of the sword. Instead she demands that they drink a pledge of reconciliation. Brangäne busies herself with phial and goblet. Cries from the sailors warn them that the journey is almost over.

Tristan invokes his honor, his misery, his courage, then raises the cup to seek oblivion. Before it is drained, Isolde snatches it from his hands and swallows the drops that are left.

The two lovers stand motionless. The love potion which Brangäne has exchanged for the draught of death works its magic. A tremolo through the orchestra echoes the convulsive pangs that rack both man and woman. Finally their eyes meet:

"Tristan, my beloved traitor!" She sinks on his breast.

"Isolde, most blessed of women!" He clasps her ardently.

Brangäne wrings her hands in despair. What endless misery her deed has wrought!

Oblivious to honor and shame alike, the lovers sing rapturously of the joys of their world.

The curtains part once more, disclosing that the ship's company is making ready to disembark. *Curtains open / Enter attendants*

"Quick, bring the royal mantle," commands the waiting-woman, and, taking it from her attendants, she fastens it about the stupefied princess.

"Behold, the King!" announces the cheerful Kurvenal.

Tristan and Isolde have lost all consciousness of the situation confronting them. Faintly Isolde remembers that she had sought for death.

"What was that draught?" she murmurs.

"It was the love potion," cries Brangäne, in anguish.

Knights and seamen burst forth in acclaim, as the shores loom near the vessel, and the theme of Desire mingles with the joyous burgeoning of the sea. *Knights, sailors*

PRELUDE TO ACT II

An anguished phrase opens the introduction. It is the motive of the garish Day, enemy to all lovers:

Next sound the motives of Isolde's Impatience and Ardor, followed by the theme of Ecstasy:

ACT II

SCENE: KING MARKE'S CASTLE IN CORNWALL (57 Minutes)

Isolde, Brangäne

THE curtain rises to the sound of hunting horns. Isolde comes out to the terrace where Brangäne is watching the departure of the royal party. A single torch lights the palace steps. To the right the woods are dark.

Brangäne warns Isolde that Tristan's friend, Melot, is spying on them both, hoping to ingratiate himself with the king. This very night, the hunters are out for bigger game than she knows.

Isolde brushes aside Brangäne's fears and begs that she extinguish the torch to permit Tristan's approach.

Reproaching herself for causing all this woe, Brangäne implores her mistress to leave the torch burning.

"Foolish maid!" Isolde reassures her. "Do you not know the Love Goddess? It is she who rules the world. It is she who has planned our fate. Her realm is darkness, and on her behalf I hail the night!" With these words she dashes the torch to the

Exit Brangäne

ground, and sending Brangäne to watch from an upper tower, hastens to the summit of the terrace to wave her white scarf as a signal to the waiting Tristan.

Enter Tristan

The motive of Ecstasy rises to its highest pitch of excitement as Tristan rushes to clasp Isolde in his arms. With rapturous ejaculations they cling to each other, praising the splendor of the night, and defying the pretentious deceit of day.

At length Tristan draws Isolde to a mossy retreat at the foot of the terrace. The music ebbs to a throbbing pianissimo as they invoke the Night:

From the tower where she watches unseen floats Brangäne's warning, unheeded by the lovers. Their thoughts linger on the night of death which alone can offer them the fulfillment of their passion. In turn they sing the theme which later begins the Love Death (*Liebestod*):

Vainly Brangäne repeats her warning; the rapture of the lovers rises to a supreme cry. . . .

A shriek from the watch tower, and Kurvenal rushes in with drawn sword, calling on Tristan to save himself. King Marke with Melot and his hunting party follow, pausing in dismay as they see the lovers. Brangäne hastens to her mistress, while Tristan shields her with his cloak.

Enter Kurvenal, King Marke, Melot, Brangäne

"The last bleak day has dawned," he murmurs, as light fills the sky.

Melot turns boastfully to the King. "Was I not right? Behold the very deed on which I staked my head!"

Sorrow rather than anger moves King Marke. "Where can I look for truth, if Tristan fails me?" he cries. "Where has honor fled if there is no honor left in him?" He reveals that though Tristan brought him Isolde for Queen, he has never yet possessed his bride. "Why must I live in hell with no hope of heaven?" he asks sadly; "who will explain the mystery?"

"Oh, King," responds the knight, with compassion, "that question can never be answered." Then, turning to Isolde, "I must depart to a dark country, the abode of night itself. Will you follow me there?"

Isolde's answer echoes the voice of her lover. "I have followed you once to a foreign land. Why should I refuse this journey?"

As Tristan bends to kiss her softly on the brow, Melot starts furiously forward, drawing his sword with a cry for vengeance.

"This was my friend," exclaims Tristan bitterly, "whose own jealousy has led him to betray me!" Exposing himself to Melot's sword by dropping his guard, he sinks wounded into the arms of Kurvenal.

PRELUDE TO ACT III

A new motive—Solitude—suggests the bleakness of the scene to come, and is followed by the theme of Tristan's anguish:

ACT III

SCENE: TRISTAN'S ESTATE IN BRITTANY (57 Minutes)

Tristan and Kurvenal

WRAPPED in a cloak, and watched over by the trusty Kurvenal, the unconscious Tristan lies under an ancient linden tree. About him stand the ruined battlements of his ancestral castle of Kareol. Below, stretches a wide vista of the sea. The mournful piping of a shepherd, given to an English horn, is known as the motive of Sadness:

Shepherd

At length the old peasant peers out from behind a wall at the right. "Ho, Kurvenal!" he whispers, "is he awake? I've seen no

ship yet, but when it comes, you can be sure I'll play a happier tune."

His lament has wakened Tristan, who faintly asks where he is.

Overjoyed to hear the loved voice again, the faithful Kurvenal reassures him: "You are in your own castle, Kareol, guarded by your own vassals, warmed by the familiar sun that will speedily make you well."

"It is not so," murmurs Tristan. "I dwell in a land of oblivion, and there I must return, once Isolde shall blot out the cruel light."

"If she is alive she will come," says Kurvenal, trying to rouse his weary master. "I have sent for her."

Tristan is exalted by this news. "My truest friend!" he exclaims. "How can I thank you? I can see Isolde myself, sailing before the wind, with flags flying." His frenzy rises to fever pitch, and then falls, as the mournful melody of the shepherd echoes Kurvenal's sad news that no ship has yet been sighted.

In his delirium, Tristan recalls the potion which has caused him such torment. Again he sinks back exhausted, and the old retainer curses the enchantment which has brought this evil to pass.

Listening for his master's breath, Kurvenal hears him ask for the ship, and assures him it is on its way.

Once more Tristan relates a fevered vision of Isolde, so fair, so lovely in the repose she brings him. "Surely you can see her now," he cries, ordering his servant to the watch tower.

The shepherd pipes a joyous strain. "It is the ship," announces Kurvenal in the utmost excitement. "Her sails are full, she clears the surf, Isolde springs to land." He hastens off to meet the princess. *Exit Kurvenal*

A new frenzy seizes Tristan. Rising from his couch he clutches at his bandages. "Let the blood flow merrily to greet her, for she alone can heal my wounds."

Isolde's voice is heard from below. Tristan staggers to meet her, and dies with her name on his lips. Passionately she tries to call him back, leaning over the couch where he has fallen. *Enter Isolde, Kurvenal*

"Only one hour, and we might have died together," she pleads— but it is too late. She sinks unconscious beside him.

Hastily the shepherd calls to Kurvenal. Another ship has arrived with King Marke and his men. The Bretons barricade the gate, but Melot forces his way through, to meet death at the hand of Kurvenal. In a wild impulse, the ancient retainer sets upon Marke and his followers; then, desperately wounded, he totters toward the body of his master. *Enter Melot, King Marke and knights*

The king calls on Tristan in vain, but Brangäne, who has also *Enter Brangäne* rushed ashore from the Cornish ship, succeeds in reviving Isolde.

"Beloved mistress," she cries, "I have told the king of the love potion. When he learned the truth, he sailed in haste to find you."

Marke echoes Brangäne's story. But Isolde hears nothing. Gently she gazes at her lover: "Mild and softly he is smiling," her voice rises in the rhapsody of the Liebestod. "See how his spirit is borne to the stars, how he breathes a heavenly peace! Is it I alone who hears? Around me float waves of glistening wind. In the very breath of the spheres I shall find bliss!"

She sinks transfigured beside Tristan's body, as Marke invokes a blessing on the dead.

DIE MEISTERSINGER

THE *composition of* Die Meistersinger, *Wagner's one great comedy, covers a period of twenty-two years. He first conceived the idea in 1845, as a contrast to* Tannhäuser, *turned to it again in 1861, after temporarily abandoning the* Ring, *and completed it in 1867 at his retreat at Triebschen, near Lucerne.*

The work was first produced in Munich in 1868 under Hans von Bülow, and reached the Metropolitan in 1886.

Founded on material which Wagner studied in the old chronicles of Nuremberg, Die Meistersinger *is a glorification of the German folk, led by Hans Sachs, who was an actual member of a sixteenth-century guild known as the Mastersingers. Another member of the guild, the pedantic town clerk, Sixtus Beckmesser, was utilized by Wagner as a caricature of Hanslick, an unsympathetic critic of his own day.*

Characters, in order of appearance:

Walther von Stolzing, a young Franconian Knight: *tenor*
Eva, daughter of Veit Pogner, the goldsmith: *soprano*
Magdalene, her nurse: *mezzo-soprano*
David, apprentice to Hans Sachs: *tenor*

Veit Pogner, goldsmith: *bass* ⎫
Sixtus Beckmesser, town clerk: *baritone* ⎪
Hans Sachs, shoemaker: *bass-baritone* ⎬ Mastersingers
Kunz Vogelgesang, furrier: *tenor* ⎪
Konrad Nachtigal, bucklemaker: *bass* ⎭

Fritz Kothner, baker: *bass* ⎫
Hermann Ortel, soapmaker: *bass* ⎪
Balthazar Zorn, pewterer: *tenor* ⎪
Augustin Moser, tailor: *tenor* ⎬ Mastersingers
Ulrich Eisslinger, grocer: *tenor* ⎪
Hans Foltz, coppersmith: *bass* ⎪
Hans Schwartz, stocking weaver: *bass* ⎭

Night watchman: *bass*
People of Nuremberg, prentices, shoemakers, tailors, bakers, etc.

Time: Middle of the Sixteenth Century   *Place:* Nuremberg

ACT I

SCENE: THE INTERIOR OF ST. KATHERINE'S CHURCH (70 Minutes)
The prelude opens with the dignified theme of the Mastersingers:

soon followed by the fanfare, or Mastersingers' March, an actual melody of the period:

In a contrasting mood are heard several themes associated with the young hero. Outstanding among them is a quotation from Walther's Prize Song:

Enriched with many other references to the characters and events of the drama to follow, the music sweeps to a mighty climax based on these three motives.

THE curtain rises on the interior of St. Katherine's Church where the people are singing the last words of a chorale, to organ accompaniment, at the close of afternoon service on St. John's Eve. Against a column leans the young knight, Walther von Stolzing, trying by eager gesture to attract the attention of Eva, who with her nurse Magdalene is sitting in the last pew. Between the phrases of the chorale may be heard a lyric theme already quoted in the prelude, and associated with Walther's wooing: *(Walther, Eva, Magdalene)*

The hymn concludes and the congregation departs. Young Eva and her nurse Magdalene are among the last. *(Enter and exeunt congregation)*

"I beg you to stay," urges Walther, approaching the flaxen-haired girl. "I ask only one word from you."

Eva sends the nurse back to look for her kerchief and buckle which the girl has left behind as a ruse in order to gain a few words alone with the young man.

"Yes, or no," pleads Walther, "are you already betrothed?"

Magdalene nervously tries to lead her young charge home; but soon she is distracted by the arrival of her admirer, the apprentice David, who has come to put the sacristy in order. Together the women explain the situation to Walther. Although Eva is not already betrothed, her father, Veit Pogner, has promised to award her hand on the morrow to the man who shall win the singing contest conducted by the Mastersingers' Guild. *(Enter David)*

Eva reassures the knight, who is naturally troubled by this news. "It will be you or no one," she exclaims. Magdalene is shocked at this bold statement. Was it not yesterday that her charge met the young stranger for the first time? *(Exit David)*

David returns to plan for the coming of the Mastersingers who will soon arrive for a preliminary trial. Magdalene begs him to do his best to prepare Walther for the contest, and then persuades Eva to come home. The girl agrees, first promising to meet her suitor later in the evening. *(Enter David, Enter prentices, Exeunt Eva and Magdalene)*

The Prize Song soars from the orchestra as Walther seats himself in a great chair which the incoming prentices have drawn out from the wall at the left. Cheerfully the boys arrange the benches on the night for the Mastersingers. David directs them in assembling a small platform and hanging curtains about it.

"This is where the marker will sit," he tells Walther, "and note down every mistake you make. You are only allowed seven, so take care. Good luck to you."

The boys echo his good wishes, dancing in a gay circle about the marker's stand.

Das Blu - men-kränz-lein aus Sei - den fein, wird das dem Herr'n Ritter be - schie - den sein,
The pre - cious chap - let of sil - ken flow'rs, we hope, Sir Knight, may soon be yours,

Enter Master-singers
Enter Pogner and Beck-messer

At the entry of the Mastersingers, the prentices respectfully retire to their bench at the left.

Pogner and Beckmesser come in first, discussing the contest.

"If Eva can turn me down," complains the latter, a sly and mean-looking clerk, "what good is the trial?"

"But if you think she will, why do you enter it?" returns the goldsmith.

Walther now steps forward. "I would like to be a Mastersinger," he tells Pogner, who is no stranger to him, as they have had business dealings in the past.

Enter Sachs

The goldsmith introduces him to other members of the Guild, and tells him that he is welcome to enter the first audition. The Mastersingers are meanwhile all assembled, Hans Sachs last among them. Fritz Kothner proceeds to call the roll. The dignitaries seat themselves in the carved pews which the boys have placed on the right of the sacristy. They listen with interest while Pogner describes the contest that is to take place on the morrow, St. John's Day:

"Since we burghers are often considered close-fisted," he concludes, "I have decided to offer the best that I have as the reward. I promise to bestow all my goods on the winner, and as a crowning prize the hand of my daughter Eva—provided she is willing to accept him."

"Why not leave the choice of the winner to the people and the girl?" suggests the progressive Sachs. "Why should we always judge by our own regulations? On St. John's Day at least, it would be better to trust to the popular vote."

At this innovation the prentices clap their hands with delight, but the Mastersingers are too conservative to approve. A rising vote shows that they prefer to reserve judgment for themselves.

"Must the candidate be a bachelor?" asks Kothner.

"Or a widower!" puts in Beckmesser. "How about Sachs?"

"Eva's suitor must be younger than you or I," declares Sachs, a statement which infuriates the love-sick clerk.

Walther is now introduced by Pogner to the Masters of the Guild. In answer to their questions concerning his background he proudly praises his master, Walther von der Vogelweide. He it was whose book first opened the beauties of nature to the young man.

"I will try to sing you a mastersong," he concludes. "What I prize most in the world is at stake."

Beckmesser then goes to the marker's platform, barks out the number of errors allowed by the law, and yanks the curtains closed with crotchety satisfaction.

Kothner reads off the regulations and points Walther to the chair.

"Now, begin," calls Beckmesser, harshly.

"Now, begin," repeats Walther, musing over the words, "so cries the Spring through the forest." And he sings a rapturous improvisation based on a theme already heard in the prelude:

Meanwhile the harsh beat of chalk on slate punctuates each phrase. Walther has broken every one of the Mastersingers' rules. Beckmesser tears open the curtains: his board is completely covered. Rising in their disapproval, the Masters discuss the song.

"It may be novel, but I do not find it confused," says Sachs, with interest, "and even if it does not fit our rules, we can at least hear it to the end."

"It would be better if you gave more thought to the shoes you make," snarls Beckmesser.

Pogner himself is unable to placate the Guild. They are unanimous in their rejection of the young radical.

Exit
Walther
Exeunt
Master-
singers,
prentices
Walther in desperation continues his melody: "Over the croaking ravens and magpies," he sings, "soars a golden bird. I shall follow him where Master-crows no longer cackle, and sing my lady's praise." Haughtily quitting the room he leaves Sachs to plead his cause in vain. Only the prentices appreciate his genius.

Act II

SCENE: STREET WITH THE HOUSES OF VEIT POGNER AND HANS SACHS
(50 Minutes)

A steep lane divides two corner houses in the city of Nuremberg.
David,
prentices
On the right stands the residence of the goldsmith Pogner, shaded by a linden tree and flanked by stone seats. On the left the smaller dwelling and workshop of Sachs is overhung by an elder tree in full bloom.

David and the other prentices are closing the shutters for the
Magdalene
night. Magdalene ventures out, hoping to hear of Walther's success.

"He was rejected," sadly reports David. . . . The nurse leaves discouraged, as the boys twit the young apprentice about his sweet-
Enter
Sachs
Exeunt
prentices
heart.

Sachs, coming home down the lane, dismisses them, and orders David in to work.

Enter
Eva and
Pogner
Magdalene
Eva and Pogner return from a walk and discuss prospects for the morrow, but Magdalene contrives to get a word alone with Eva and tell her the bad news. Perhaps Sachs will help! They go into the house.

Exeunt
Pogner
Eva and
Magdalene
David brings out his master's bench and stool in front of the cobbler's shop and leaves him at work, by lamp light.

"The perfume of the elders, how sweet and soft and strong," muses Sachs, as memories of Walther's song of spring drift from the orchestra.

Enter Eva
Eva returns, breaking into his reverie. Attempting to hide her passionate interest, she manages to glean the details of Walther's trial, but cannot conceal from her shrewd old friend where her heart really lies. Though he has long loved her himself, he resolves to help her find happiness with the young knight.

Enter
Magdalene
"Why have you stayed so late?" cries Magdalene, interrupting them. "Your father has been calling you."

Sachs retires to his shop; a crack of light shows that he is still at work.

"Beckmesser plans to serenade you tonight," whispers the nurse.
"Put on my shawl and take my place at the window," begs Eva.
"I must stay here until I have talked to the man I love."

Just as Pogner calls back Magdalene, Walther arrives on the
scene. Eva greets him rapturously to the strains of her own motive:

"Come away with me," he implores her. "I may not do so well
here but in my own house at least I am a master."

The night watchman passes, sounding his horn and singing:
"Ten o'clock, lights out, praise God!"

Eva joins Magdalene within, and Walther waits for her in hiding.

Sachs, however, has overheard their plans, and when Eva comes
out, dressed in her nurse's clothes ready for the elopement, he places
his lamp so that it throws a bright stream of light across the street.

"We must hide," whispers Eva.

At that moment another interruption forces them to retreat to
the bench under the lime tree. Beckmesser has brought his lute to
serenade Eva. Strumming his accompaniment off key he is about to
sing, when Sachs, now become an ally of the lovers against the
boorish clerk, rings out a lusty ballad of his own, continuing his
work meanwhile.

"Confound the rogue," cries the furious Beckmesser.

"I'm just finishing your shoes," says Sachs, blandly, as he
hammers away.

"I wish you would help me by criticizing my song, instead,"
begs the clerk.

Sachs agrees to act as marker, provided he is allowed to pound
at each mistake.

Beckmesser starts his ridiculous serenade, while the hammer falls
so fast and furiously that soon the shoes are done:

Meanwhile the noise has aroused the neighbors. David recognizes Magdalene at the window and jealously falls on Beckmesser.

Exit
Magdalene
Enter
Walther

Enter
watchman
Exit
watchman

Enter
Beck-
messer

Enter
David

Enter
populace
and
prentices
Enter
Master-
singers
Exeunt
Sachs,
Walther,
Eva, Pog-
ner and
populace
Enter
watchman
Exit
watchman

People appear at every window in their nightdresses. The lane is thronged with prentices, journeymen, and burghers. The Mastersingers themselves join the crowd. General pandemonium is expressed in a choral fugue divided into sixteen different voice parts, based on Beckmesser's serenade.

Sachs finally draws Walther back into his own house while Pogner takes Eva home. The hubbub subsides; doors close; lights go out. Again the watchman makes his rounds, chanting his medieval call. As the bassoon refers gently to Beckmesser's serenade, the streets are flooded with midsummer moonlight and peace.

ACT III

SCENE 1: SACHS' WORKSHOP (61 Minutes)

The introduction to the third act is a musical commentary on the character of Sachs: his dual nature as cobbler and poet, and his nobility of soul. Outstanding is the theme of Renunciation:

Sachs

Enter
David

THE curtain rises on the interior of Sachs' shop. The cobbler sits in his easy chair, reading a great book in the morning sun.

David tiptoes across the room, afraid of the coming rebuke.

"Master, won't you forgive me?" he pleads penitently. "See, Magdalene has given me these goodies in a basket. She understands why I beat up the clerk."

Roused at length from his meditation, Sachs asks David to sing his verses for St. John's Day.

"Johannes—Hans," cries David impetuously. "Why, this must be your name day, too. Here, keep the flowers and ribbons for yourself."

Exit
David

Sachs sends David off to dress and returns to his philosophizing.

"The world has gone mad," he broods in a famous monologue (*Wahn! Wahn! überall Wahn!*). "Even in old Nuremberg an ignorant shoemaker may set it awry. What can I do today to guide it to a nobler end?"

Enter
Walther

Walther comes from an inner room, filled with the memory of a radiant dream which he reveals to the cobbler.

"Why not make it into a Mastersong?" suggests Sachs, and he explains how the old rules may serve the vivid inspiration of youth.

"Morning was gleaming with rosy light," sings Walther softly in the familiar melody of the Prize Song. The final verse must wait.

Sachs, who has jotted down Walther's words on a piece of paper, is deeply moved. He leads the young man out to dress for the festival.

Exeunt Sachs and Walther

First peeping cautiously through the window, Beckmesser hobbles into the workshop, lame and bruised from his encounter of the night before, but gaily clad in red and green for the contest. Finding himself alone, he investigates Sachs' table, discovers the words of the song, and thrusts them into his doublet.

Enter Beck-messer

"You sly cobbler!" he exclaims in a rage. "You are trying to get Eva for yourself. You had me beaten so that you could win the contest in my place."

"But I am not planning any courtship," insists Sachs, who comes in at the moment and finds Beckmesser.

Enter Sachs

"Is this not your writing?" retorts the furious clerk.

"Certainly, and to save you from being a thief, I will give it to you," answers Sachs.

Overcome with such generosity, Beckmesser hobbles gleefully out.

Exit Beck-messer Enter Eva

No sooner has he left than Eva enters in festal blue and white.

"My shoe is too tight," she explains as an excuse for the visit. "No," she contradicts herself, "it's too wide at the ankle." Sachs takes it to his bench.

At this moment Walther appears at the door, glorious in his knightly garb. Spellbound at the sight of Eva, he breaks into the third verse of his Prize Song.

Enter Walther

In a fit of sobbing Eva falls on Sachs' shoulder. "If my choice were free, you would be my husband," she exclaims in a burst of gratitude, while the music quotes two motives from *Tristan und Isolde*.

"My child," says Sachs gently, "I know the story of Tristan too well to wish the fate of King Marke. It is high time for the right man to claim you! But here come David and Magdalene."

Enter David and Magdalene

"A new song has been born," he continues, "and must be christened. Eva and I are the sponsors, but as no prentice can serve as a witness, I herewith raise David to the rank of journeyman," and he gives the young man a box on the ear.

Meanwhile the five characters break into the magnificent quintet which concludes the scene:

Lento

Se - lig, wie - die— Son - ne mei - nes Glück - es lacht
Daz - zling as— the— dawn that smiles up - on my glee,

SCENE 2: A MEADOW ON THE PEGNITZ (31 Minutes)

Enter
populace,
guilds, etc.

A brief orchestral interlude ushers in the final tableau: an open meadow through which the river Pegnitz winds past the city. Parties of burghers arrive in boats. A procession of the guilds marches across the stage, decked with gay banners denoting the trade of each group. As the crowd fill the benches and booths at the right, standard-bearers place flags and pennants to decorate the scene.

Enter
Master-
singers,
with
Pogner,
Sachs,
Eva, Beck-
messer

Finally heralded by trumpets, the Mastersingers march in to the opening themes of the prelude. Leading Eva and her maidens to a place of honor, they station themselves on the grandstand at the left of the stage.

As Sachs rises to address them, the company breaks into a magnificent chorale: "Awake, the day is near!" to which the historical Sachs wrote the original words.

Largo maestoso

Wach' auf! Es na - het gen den
A - wake! Draws nigh the break of

Tag, ich hör' sing-en im grün - en Hag
day. I hear up - on the haw - thorne spray

Then as master of ceremonies, Sachs calls on Beckmesser, the first contestant. Led by ribboned ushers, the clerk stumbles up to the grassy mound where each singer must stand. Minute by minute he grows more confused. His efforts to sing the song which Sachs has given him are a grotesque failure. Finally he staggers from the mound and turns on Sachs:

"Here is the man who gave me this trash," he cries, and rushes ignominiously away.

Exit Beck-
messer
Enter
Walther

"That was not my song," returns Sachs quietly. "Let me call a witness in my own defense: Sir Walther von Stolzing, who will sing it for you. It is his own."

Walther climbs the mound with firm steps, and sings his Prize Song in its complete form. People and masters unite in admiration. Eva places a wreath of laurel on his brow, and Pogner brings forward the gold chain to welcome Walther to his guild. From this reward the young knight shrinks back.

"Disparage not the masters' ways," admonishes Sachs in a final monologue dedicated to the glory of German art. Solemnly, he makes Walther a Mastersinger.

One and all repeat the final words of Sachs' speech and hail him as the hero of the city. The scene closes with an apotheosis, the populace waving their banners and kerchiefs in wild enthusiasm, the masters pledging homage to their leader. And between the young couple stands Sachs, who has found his happiness in theirs.

DER RING DES NIBELUNGEN
(*THE RING OF THE NIBELUNG*)

DER RING DES NIBELUNGEN, *Richard Wagner's music drama in the form of a trilogy and prologue, is based upon two great legendary sources: Norse mythology, and the old German epic known as the* Nibelungenlied. *From the* Nibelungenlied, *Wagner derived the story of the magic ring and its fatal connection with Siegfried the Hero; from Norse legend, he drew the gods and goddesses who people the trilogy, transforming their names and attributes into German equivalents.*

Wagner, who wrote his own texts, originally planned only one music drama on the Nibelung subject. He called the libretto Siegfrieds Tod (Siegfried's Death). *Then, thinking it desirable to explain the circumstances leading up to the tragedy, he prefaced his first drama with a second called* Der Junge Siegfried (The Young Siegfried). *Even now, Wagner felt that the story was incomplete; in the libretto of* Die Walküre (The Valkyrie), *he established the events that culminated in the birth of Siegfried, describing the hero's parents and their divine origin. Finally, in a prologue to the entire trilogy—*Das Rheingold (The Rhinegold)—*the author linked his two legendary sources, gods and Nibelungs, in a basic exposition of the drama.*

When Wagner set these texts to music, he began with Rheingold *and followed with* Walküre. *Reaching the middle of* Siegfried *(a new title in place of the earlier* Der Junge Siegfried), *he ceased all work on the* Ring *for twelve years. During this period,* Tristan und Isolde *was created, succeeded by* Die Meistersinger. *At length,*

Wagner resumed his work on Siegfried *and completed the entire* Ring *with the musical setting of* Siegfrieds Tod, *now revised and known as* Götterdämmerung (The Twilight of the Gods).

Aesthetic considerations aside, Der Ring des Nibelungen *is a stupendous achievement from the standpoint of sheer labor. Work on the text alone occupied Wagner for a period of four years (1848-1852), while the actual musical composition, including the pause of twelve years, extended from 1853 to 1874.*

At the insistence of King Ludwig II, separate performances of Rheingold *and* Walküre *were given at Munich in 1869 and 1870, before the remainder of the* Ring *had been completed. By dint of royal patronage and untold labor, Wagner at last achieved the ambition of his lifetime—the building of a festival theatre for the production of his works. It was at the Bayreuth* Festspielhaus *that* Der Ring des Nibelungen *was first given in its entirety during the summer of 1876. Although monetary difficulties caused the theatre to suspend its activities for the next few seasons, it was reopened in 1882 with the première of* Parsifal.

The first complete presentation of Der Ring des Nibelungen *in America took place at the Metropolitan Opera House during the season of 1888-89. There had been isolated performances previously of* Walküre, Siegfried *and* Götterdämmerung, *with Amalia Materna and Lilli Lehmann appearing as Brünnhilde, but none of* Rheingold.

From 1889 until the present day, the policy of offering the full Ring *cycle has been continued and expanded by the Metropolitan Opera Association.*

DAS RHEINGOLD
(*THE RHINEGOLD*)

PROLOGUE IN ONE ACT AND FOUR SCENES
Characters, in order of appearance:

Rhinemaidens
{ Woglinde: *soprano*
Wellgunde: *mezzo-soprano*
Flosshilde: *contralto*

Alberich, a dwarf of the Nibelung race: *baritone*
Fricka, wife to Wotan: *mezzo-soprano*
Wotan, ruler of the gods: *bass-baritone*
Freia, goddess of youth: *soprano*

Giants
{ Fasolt: *bass*
Fafner: *bass*

Froh, god of youth: *tenor*
Donner, god of thunder: *baritone*
Loge, god of fire: *tenor*
Mime, brother to Alberich: *tenor*
Erda, goddess of wisdom: *contralto*
Nibelung craftsmen and slaves

Before the curtain rises, an orchestral introduction evokes the atmosphere of the river Rhine:

SCENE 1: IN THE DEPTHS OF THE RHINE (23 Minutes)

Rhine-
maidens

FAR beneath the surface of the water swim three Rhinemaidens:

Tranquillo

Wei - a! Wa - ga!   Wo-ge, du Wel - le,
Vei - a! Va - ga!   Wan-der - ing wa - ters,

These maidens keep watch over a golden treasure that lies at the
bottom of the Rhine; but they guard it carelessly. Darting about
in the midst of a water game, they pay little heed to an intrusive
dwarf who creeps along the river's floor.

Enter
Alberich

Gazing lustfully at the maidens, the dwarf tries to approach
them. He is Alberich, a member of the Nibelung race that inhabits
the darkest caverns of the earth, forging precious metals. "How
you delight me!" he calls to the water sprites. "I would gladly
leave the darkness of Nibelheim for the sake of your love!"

In wanton mood, the Rhinemaidens taunt the dwarf. Every one
of the three in turn floats toward him—and as he extends his arms
to grasp them, they swim away. Alberich is crushed with misery; he
realizes that love will always be denied him.

Nevertheless, he pursues the maidens with sensual fury, clamber-
ing over the rocks in a vain effort to reach them. Unable to maintain the chase, he sinks breathlessly on the river bed. At that
moment, a soft glow is diffused through the waters of the Rhine.
It is the mysterious Rhinegold, awakening from its slumber:

Moderato

Forgetting the presence of Alberich, the three maidens join
hands and swim exultantly above the precious rock crying, "Rhinegold! Radiant treasure!"

Moderato

Rhein-gold!   Rhein-gold!
Rhine - gold!   Rhine - gold!

Fascinated, Alberich questions the maidens about the shining
rock.

"It is the Rhinegold!" they reply. "Have you indeed never heard
of it?"

"It is all-powerful!" declares the maiden Woglinde.

"It would bestow the wealth of the world upon its owner," **adds** her sister Wellgunde, "if it were forged into a ring":

The third Rhinemaiden, Flosshilde, is hesitant about discussing the gold while Alberich is near. "Be careful!" she whispers to her sisters. "The dwarf might steal our treasure."

"Impossible!" they laugh. "Only the man who renounces love may forge the gold into a magic ring—and Alberich will never turn from passion!"

The dwarf listens to their chatter. Knowing that he will always be scorned and repulsed, he springs to the summit of the golden rock. "I renounce love forever!" he screams. "And thus I seize your gold!" Wrenching the metal from its base, he plunges with it into the caverns of Nibelheim. The Rhine is plunged in darkness amid the despairing cries of the maidens.

As the orchestra begins a symphonic interlude, the murky waves of the river seem to disappear within the stage. Cloud banks arise, and when they have cleared away, the second tableau is revealed.

SCENE 2: AN OPEN SPACE ON A MOUNTAIN HEIGHT (45 Minutes)

As the rising sun casts its light upon a mountain top near the Rhine, Wotan, ruler of the gods, and Fricka, his consort, lie in slumber. Soon Fricka awakens; she gazes at a distant peak crowned with the future home of the gods—the newly built castle of Valhalla:

"Wotan!" she cries in agitation. "Arise! The castle is completed!"

The ruler of the gods opens his eyes and beholds the eternal dwelling. "The work is achieved!" he declares. "All hail, blessed abode!"

Fricka confronts him bitterly. "Yes, the work is achieved," she exclaims, "but think of the price we must pay! The giants Fafner

Exit Alberich

Wotan and Fricka

and Fasolt have built the castle. Now we must give them my own sister Freia as reward!"

"Never!" Wotan replies. "The giants shall look for other payment."

"Then shelter Freia from their wrath!" pleads Fricka. "She is coming to us even now for help!" Enter Freia

Freia, the goddess of youth and beauty, has appeared on the summit of the mountain and runs desperately toward Wotan. "Save me!" she cries. "I am pursued by the giants!"

While she speaks, the rumbling tread of Fafner and Fasolt can be heard drawing nearer. Huge, shaggy creatures, armed with tremendous clubs, they stride across the mountain top in search of their reward: Enter Fafner and Fasolt

Fasolt, the milder of the giants, approaches Wotan respectfully. "While you slumbered, O god, we toiled and labored in the building of Valhalla. The work is done. Now give us our payment!"

"I cannot give you Freia," the god answers. "Ask for some other reward and it shall be granted."

The outraged Fasolt is about to reply, but his surly brother cuts him short. "I care little for Freia," Fafner mutters, "but she tends the golden apples of youth. Once she is in our grasp, the gods will grow old and we shall inherit their power. Come, let us bear her away!"

The giants seize Freia and attempt to carry her off; but their way is barred by the sudden appearance of Froh, god of youth, and Donner, the fierce thunder god. As Donner swings his mighty hammer, Fafner and Fasolt raise their clubs. A terrible conflict is avoided only by the intervention of Wotan. Enter Froh and Donner

"Cease your quarrels!" he shouts, raising his spear. "I command you!" It is through the might of the spear that Wotan rules the world. All of his compacts are graven on the wooden shaft— if he were to break a single treaty, his power would be ended forever.

Compact

Only at the instigation of Loge, the malicious god of fire and mischief, has Wotan entered into his ruinous agreement with the giants. In urging the compact upon him, Loge glibly promised to find a substitute reward for Freia. Now Wotan is in a precarious situation, trying to withhold payment from Fafner and Fasolt, and having no alternative to offer them—for the fickle Loge has failed to appear.

Enter Loge

Suddenly, as Wotan looks anxiously toward the valley, he sees a glimmer of flame. A nimble figure, clad in fluttering garments, is leaping from rock to rock. Loge has finally arrived!

"Why have you delayed so long?" calls Wotan. "Come, name the substitute you have found for Freia!"

Loge blandly answers: "Not in the whole world have I been able to find anything to replace woman's beauty." As Wotan makes a gesture of impatience, the firegod continues, "There is only one living person who has renounced youth and beauty: Alberich the Nibelung. For the sake of power, he has robbed the Rhinemaidens of their gold—and, O Wotan, they have asked you to recover it for them."

"Why speak of the gold," Wotan exclaims angrily, "when this treaty with the giants still presses?"

Ignoring Wotan's displeasure, Loge describes the unlimited might of the Rhinegold when forged into a ring. The interest of the giants is awakened, and they offer to relinquish their claims to Freia if Wotan will grant them the treasure. At once, the god refuses. "Am I to conquer Alberich and win his gold merely to bestow it upon *you?*" he cries.

Exeunt Fafner, Fasolt and Freia

Their patience at an end, the giants bear Freia away. "We will return this evening," they proclaim. "And if the Rhinegold is not paid us as ransom, we will hold your goddess forever!"

As soon as Freia has vanished, the faces of the gods grow old and wrinkled. "Ha, the golden apples are gone!" Loge observes maliciously.

In the greatest alarm, Fricka approaches her consort. "Wotan!" she implores. "Wretched man! Behold the shame to which you have brought us!"

Wotan suddenly raises his spear in token of decision. "Come, Loge!" he commands. "We shall descend to Nibelheim and win the treasure. Freia must be ransomed!"

Exeunt Wotan and Loge

As Wotan and the firegod plunge into a steaming cavern on their descent to the home of the dwarfs, the stage is hidden by a barrier of smoke. Through an optical illusion, the entire theatre seems to be sinking into the earth. In the distance sound the anvils of the Nibelungs:

Finally, the smoke is lifted and the interior of Nibelheim is revealed.

SCENE 3: THE SUBTERRANEAN CAVERNS OF NIBELHEIM (23 Minutes)

Fear and hatred pervade the dwelling of the dwarfs. Since his seizure of the Rhinegold, melted into a ring, Alberich has become cruel and merciless, enslaving his people in a search for more treasure. Anxious to safeguard his power, he has commanded his brother Mime, a skilled smith, to forge him a magic helmet—the Tarnhelm—which can make him invisible or give him any shape he desires:

Mime has forged the Tarnhelm so successfully that he tries to keep it for himself—but Alberich has found him out and drags him savagely through the caverns. "Here, you rogue," he cries, "give me the helmet!"

Enter Mime and Alberich

Placing it upon his head, Alberich becomes invisible.

Brutally lashing the defenseless Mime, Alberich shrieks with laughter. At length, the sound of his voice grows fainter, and Mime is left alone. Cowering on the ground, the wretched dwarf looks up to see two godlike visitors descending into the cavern: Wotan and Loge.

Exit Alberich Enter Wotan and Loge

Loge immediately accosts Mime and pretends to sympathize

with him. Through adroit questioning, he finds out the extent of Alberich's power. Suddenly, Mime draws back in fear. "Beware!" he whimpers. "Alberich is returning!"

Enter
Alberich
and
Nibelungs
With the Tarnhelm on his belt, Alberich strides briskly from the glowing furnaces of the inner caverns. He wields a whip and drives a throng of frightened dwarfs before him. "There!" he shouts. "Put down the treasure! Go back to the mines and dig more gold!" Drawing the ring from his finger, he mutters a mys-
Exeunt
Mime and
Nibelungs
terious incantation. At once, the shrieking dwarfs flee in terror before the might of their master:

The presence of the two gods has not escaped Alberich. "What are you doing here?" he demands.

"We have heard of your wonderful power," Wotan replies, "and we have come to witness it."

"Then behold the golden hoard that I am gathering!" snarls the dwarf. "When my task is done, I will advance on Valhalla with my legions of darkness. As I once forswore love, *all* shall forswear it. The power of the gods will crumble into dust, for the might of the world lies in the hoard of the Nibelung:"

Wotan is about to strike the arrogant dwarf, but Loge quickly restrains him. With flattery, he placates Alberich and draws him out on the subject of the Tarnhelm. "Does the helmet really serve to transform you?" he asks with pretended awe.

"It does!" Alberich proudly exclaims.

"Could you become a dragon?"

Alberich dons the Tarnhelm. He disappears in a column of steam; and immediately, on the floor of the cavern, a great snake uncoils itself:

Feigning the greatest admiration, the gods invite Alberich to transform himself into a toad. He complies—and as Wotan pins him to the ground, Loge tears the Tarnhelm from his head. Binding the dwarf fast, the ruthless captors lead him upward to the rocky height from which they have descended.

Exeunt Wotan, Loge and Alberich

Again, the stage is hidden by a smoke screen, giving the impression of an ascent through the earth. The orchestral interlude is based mainly on the themes of Loge, the Forge, and the Giants.

SCENE 4: AN OPEN SPACE ON A MOUNTAIN HEIGHT (40 Minutes)

Driving their victim before them, Wotan and Loge emerge from the steaming caverns into the light of day, and bargain with Alberich for his freedom. As ransom, he is to surrender all the treasure of Nibelheim.

Enter Wotan, Loge and Alberich

Alberich has no choice but to acquiesce. Kissing his ring in secret command, he bids the dwarfs ascend from Nibelheim and pile the golden hoard before Wotan. As the shrinking creatures obey, Alberich hides his face—he must not be seen in the toils of bondage!

Enter Nibelungs

The treasure has been assembled; the dwarfs have returned to their cavern. "Now let me go," pleads Alberich, "and give back my helmet."

Exit Nibelungs

"That belongs to the hoard," Loge remarks, tossing the Tarnhelm among the plunder.

And still, Alberich is not released. "There is a ring on your finger that I desire," declares Wotan.

"Take my life," cries Alberich, "but not this ring!"

"Your life does not matter. *Give me the ring!*" Wotan tears the gold from Alberich—and the dwarf slumps to the ground with a terrible shriek.

Loge casually loosens Alberich's bonds. "Go back to your cavern," he laughs. "You are free."

"Free?" gasps Alberich. "Really free? Then hear my freedom's greeting: May this ring bring death to all who possess it—gnawing envy to all who do not—until it returns to the hand of the Nibelung, its rightful owner! Thus do I curse the ring:"

The dwarf rushes off; and Wotan, disregarding the curse, prepares to greet Fricka, Donner and Froh, whom he sees approaching.

Exit Alberich

Enter
Fricka,
Froh,
Donner,
Freia,
Fafner
and Fasolt

Soon Freia appears on the cliff, led by the giants. Determined to purchase her freedom, Wotan offers Fafner and Fasolt the Nibelung hoard.

"Let Freia be hidden by a wall of gold!" Fasolt replies. "When she can be seen no longer, we will accept the ransom."

The gods anxiously pile the treasure before Freia. After every nugget of the hoard has been spent, the gleaming hair of the goddess can still be seen; Loge is forced to yield the Tarnhelm. And now Fasolt discovers a small opening through which he can perceive the eyes of the goddess.

"Close the gap!" demands the surly Fafner.

"We have nothing more to give," Loge exclaims.

"Give us the ring that Wotan is wearing!" Fafner insists.

Wotan is adamant. "The ring is mine!" he declares. "I will yield it to no one."

In violent anger, the giants prepare to carry Freia away. The gods are dismayed; despite their pleading, Wotan refuses to part with the gold. Suddenly, the mountain top is plunged in darkness;

Enter Erda

a veiled figure rises from the earth. It is Erda, goddess of wisdom:

"Yield the ring, Wotan!" she warns. "You are in danger—the end of your power is in sight. Hear me: yield the ring!"

The mysterious Erda sinks back into the ground and daylight

Exit Erda
Death of
Fasolt

Exit
Fafner

returns to the mountain top. At once, Wotan carries out Erda's wishes; he hurls the ring upon the treasure. Instantly Alberich's curse takes effect. The giants quarrel over the prize and Fafner kills Fasolt. Gathering up the Tarnhelm, ring, and Nibelung hoard, Fafner trudges off as the gods look on in silence.

Thick clouds have descended on the mountain. To clear the atmosphere, Donner swings his hammer and chants an invocation to the elements:

There is a blinding flash of lightning—a roll of thunder—and the fog slowly lifts. Valhalla can be seen on its distant peak, gleaming in the late afternoon sunlight; and spanning the entire valley is a rainbow that extends as a bridge to the entrance of the castle:

Voices of
Rhine-
maidens
(*off stage*)

As Wotan takes Fricka by the arm, prepared to lead her into the new fortress, he is disturbed by the voices of the Rhinemaidens in the valley below, calling for their lost gold. "Bid them be silent!" he commands Loge.

The song of the maidens dies away; Donner, Freia and Froh follow Wotan and his consort. Only Loge remains behind, for he despises his fellow deities, and is resolved to build his own empire on the ruins of their power. With no thought of the inevitable consequence of their greed, the gods troop proudly across the rainbow bridge and enter the castle of Valhalla.

DIE WALKÜRE
(*THE VALKYRIE*)

Music Drama in Three Acts
Characters, in order of appearance:
Siegmund: *tenor*
Sieglinde: *soprano*
Hunding, Sieglinde's husband: *bass*
Wotan: *bass-baritone*
Brünnhilde, his daughter: *soprano*
Fricka: *mezzo-soprano*
8 Valkyries, sisters of Brünnhilde

THE ring of the Nibelung is now in the possession of Fafner the giant, who by means of the Tarnhelm has transformed himself into a dragon and keeps watch over the treasure in a forest cave. Eventually, through Alberich's curse, Fafner must fall. It is this impending tragedy that Wotan dreads. What if Alberich were to recapture the ring? The dwarf would lead his forces against Valhalla and annihilate the gods!

Haunted by this gnawing problem, Wotan has arrived at a decision. He cannot seek to win the gold for himself, since he has surrendered it to Fafner under the laws of compact, on which his whole system of rule is based. But he will wander on earth disguised as a mortal named Wälse (the Wolf) and create a race of independent heroes—the Wälsungs—who can gain the ring and keep it from Alberich.

At the same time, the defenses of Valhalla must be reinforced against possible invasion by the armies of Nibelheim. For such a purpose, Erda, goddess of wisdom, has borne Wotan nine valiant daughters—the Valkyries—who have been taught to stir up strife on earth, gather slain heroes on the battlefield and convey them to Valhalla, where the warriors are revived and pressed into the service of Wotan.

It is after the creation of the Wälsungs and Valkyries that the action of *Die Walküre* begins.

Act I

SCENE: THE INTERIOR OF HUNDING'S DWELLING (57 Minutes)

TORRENTS of rain are falling in the dense, lonely wood. Thunder can be heard in the distance, and echoes of Donner's invocation to the elements. The storm is subsiding:

Secure from the fury of the tempest stands an isolated house, hidden among the foliage. It is the dwelling of Hunding, a tribal chieftain. In the center of the structure rises a great ash tree. The main room seems gaunt and deserted, a flickering fire on the hearth giving the only clue to human occupancy.

Suddenly, the door of the house is flung open and a wounded man appears on the threshold. Staggering forward, he sinks on the bear rug before the hearth. "No matter who lives here," he gasps, "I must find rest!"　　　　*Enter Siegmund*

Hearing the sound of footsteps, a melancholy woman enters from an inner chamber. It is Sieglinde, who thinks her husband has returned. When she sees the exhausted stranger, she runs at once to his aid. "A draught!" begs the man, arousing Sieglinde's pity:　　*Enter Sieglinde*

Hastening to the well outside, Sieglinde returns with cooling water. As the stranger drinks, he glances at her gratefully and his eyes are filled with a portent of love.

"My weariness has left me!" he exclaims. "I am refreshed. Who are you, kindly woman?"

"This abode and I belong to Hunding," Sieglinde answers mournfully. "You are welcome to stay until my husband returns."

She offers her unknown guest another draught—this time, of honeyed mead. The stranger accepts the drink—gazes longingly at Sieglinde—and turns to depart. "Ill fate pursues me," he declares. "I must travel onward."

"Remain!" cries Sieglinde. "You cannot bring ill fate where it already dwells!"

The stranger pauses; he looks earnestly at the woman. Suddenly, the stamping of horses and the creaking noise of stable doors are heard. Hunding, the savage chieftain, has returned:

Enter Hunding

Fierce and scowling, Hunding enters the room. At once, he stares questioningly at the stranger. Since the laws of Teutonic hospitality forbid him to turn a guest away, he invites the man to stay for a single night. "My hearth is sacred to any wayfarer," he declares, adding significantly, "and may you *keep* it sacred!"

The chieftain gruffly orders Sieglinde to prepare the evening meal. Sitting at table, he continues his scrutiny of the stranger. "How closely this man resembles my wife!" he murmurs in surprise, as the orchestra sounds the motive of the Wälsung race. "The serpent's deceit glistens in both their glances!"

Mastering his astonishment, he questions the guest. "Where do you come from?" he demands. "What is your name?"

"I am called Woeful," the stranger answers. "My whole life has been filled with grief. Even as a child, I experienced misfortune. One day, when I went hunting with my father, we returned to find our home burned to the ground by envious rivals. My mother was consumed in the flames; my sister disappeared. Alone and despairing, my father and I waged constant war against our enemies."

"Where is your father now?" Sieglinde asks anxiously.

"I lost him in battle," the stranger replies. "We were separated by our foes. The only trace of him I ever found was an empty wolf skin!"

Sorrowfully, the unknown man continues his story: how he tried to save a young girl from being wed against her will—how, in protecting her, he was forced to slay her brothers. Angry kinsmen surrounded the hut—killed the bride—and wounded her champion. Deprived of his weapon, and forced to flee for his life, he made his way through the forest to the first sign of habitation—Hunding's dwelling. The orchestra intones the heroism of the Wälsungs:

When the stranger has finished his tale, Hunding rises angrily. "*I* am one of the kinsmen who were summoned too late to capture the miscreant," he declares. "And now I find him in my very house!" He advances threateningly upon the guest as if to strike him, but Sieglinde intervenes. Regaining his temper, Hunding coldly invites the man to remain for the night and accept a challenge to mortal combat in the morning. Then, bidding Sieglinde mix him a draught of wine, the chieftain makes ready to retire.

On her way to the inner chamber, Sieglinde tries to attract the stranger's glance; she points unobtrusively toward the tree in the center of the room. The significance of her gesture is lost upon the stranger, and Hunding drives her within.

The wayfarer lies uneasily beside the hearth. He is weaponless— and Hunding has challenged him to combat; he has fallen in love

Exeunt
Sieglinde
and
Hunding

with the mistress of the house—and she belongs to another. A plan for swift action gnaws at his mind; the need of a sturdy weapon drives him to a fury of despair. Dimly, he remembers that his father once promised him a sword in his hour of need. That hour has come. "Wälse!" he cries. "Wälse! Where is your sword?"

As if in answer to his plea, the fire blazes brightly in the hearth, casting its light on a flash of metal in the tree trunk. But soon the flames subside and darkness fills the room.

Enter Sieglinde

The inner door opens softly and Sieglinde steals from her chamber. "I have drugged my husband," she whispers to the stranger. "You must escape while he sleeps!"

When the guest refuses to abandon her, Sieglinde shows him a mysterious weapon that may serve as protection. Plunged to its hilt within the ash tree gleams a sword:

Sieglinde relates the history of the weapon: how at her marriage to Hunding—forced upon her by a tribe which had abducted her years before—an aged wanderer entered the room, drove the sword into the tree and then departed. All of the guests tried to draw the weapon from the trunk—none succeeded; and Sieglinde realized that only the man who might save her from Hunding could possess the sword.

Now she gazes pleadingly at the youthful stranger. "Ah, if you were the chosen one!" she exclaims.

The guest takes her in his arms—the great doors at the rear of the dwelling swing open, set in motion by a magic hand. The storm has passed; radiant moonlight fills the room; and fondly embracing Sieglinde, the stranger hails the coming of spring, symbolic of love and fulfillment.

"You are the spring!" Sieglinde declares. "How long I have waited for you to bring gladness into my life! And yet—must you be called Woeful?"

"No!" replies the stranger. "Call me what you will. My father was known as Wälse."

"Are you a Wälsung?" cries Sieglinde. "Then the sword was struck in the tree for you; and the name that I have treasured is yours: SIEGMUND!"

Siegmund mounts the table at the base of the tree and grasps the hilt of the sword. "This weapon comes in my hour of need," he exclaims, "and therefore I call it *Needful!*" With tremendous strength, he draws the blade from its resting place and waves it on high.

Exultant in the moment of his victory, Siegmund leaps to the ground. "We will go far from here," he proclaims, "into the forest —into the spring! You shall be my bride!"

"But I am your sister," cries Sieglinde.

"Then the blood of the Wälsungs will flourish!" Siegmund shouts defiantly. Pressing Sieglinde to him with the utmost fervor, he leads her from the house of Hunding into the night.

Exeunt Siegmund and Sieglinde

Act II

SCENE: A WILD, ROCKY HEIGHT (83 Minutes)

EVERYTHING has worked according to Wotan's plan. His was the magic spell that led Siegmund to the house of Hunding—that caused the fire to gleam upon the sword hilt—that opened the great doors and flooded the room with moonlight. It was he who, attired as a wanderer, had first plunged the sword into the tree. In his hands, Siegmund and Sieglinde have been mere pawns with no consciousness of right and wrong.

The perpetuation of the Wälsung race is Wotan's dearest hope. And now, poised in full armor upon a rocky height, he makes ready to defend Siegmund in the approaching combat with Hunding. Summoning his bravest daughter—the Valkyrie, Brünnhilde—he orders her to guard Siegmund with her shield.

Wotan and Brünnhilde

Motive of the Valkyries

Standing on a cliff directly above Wotan, Brünnhilde answers his command by waving her spear and intoning a weird battle cry:

Ho - jo - to - ho! ___ Ho - jo - to - ho! ___ hei - a - ha! ___ hei - a - ha! ___

Suddenly, the warrior maiden looks down into the valley and sees Fricka approaching. "Beware, father!" she calls. "Your wife is near —and in an angry mood!"

Exit
Brünnhilde
Enter
Fricka

As Brünnhilde goes off to bridle her steed, Fricka ascends the mountain and stands before Wotan. "I have heard Hunding's prayer for vengeance," she declares, "and as goddess of marriage I am bound to uphold him."

Wotan smilingly tries to placate his consort. "Give the Wälsungs your blessing!" he urges. "It is spring, and they are in love."

Fricka rebuffs him furiously. "If marriage vows mean nothing to you, then think of the laws of Nature! This incestuous pair must be punished!"

Under the force of Fricka's vehemence, Wotan begins a gradual retreat from his lighthearted assurance. "What is your wish?" he mutters.

"Renounce the Wälsung!" she cries.

Reluctantly, Wotan agrees to abandon the ill-fated hero. But even more is demanded of him by Fricka. "The Valkyrie, too, must turn from Siegmund!" she warns.

"Brünnhilde shall be free to choose," Wotan retorts.

"Not so! I know that she represents your will. Give orders that Siegmund fall!"

At this moment, Brünnhilde's joyous battle cry can be heard in the distance—she is returning to fulfill Wotan's commands. "The Valkyrie shall uphold the honor of the gods by protecting Hunding," Fricka declares. "See to it that she does not fail!"

Dei - ner ew' - gen Gat - tin hei - li - ge Eh - re be - schir - me heut' ihr Schild!
Your e - ter - nal con - sort's ho - li - est hon - our her shield will guard to - day!

Enter
Brünnhilde
Exit
Fricka

As Brünnhilde appears at the top of the rocky slope, Fricka, triumphant in her moral victory over Wotan, strides away.

Brünnhilde gazes at Wotan in alarm. Haggard and dejected, he wears an expression of terrible suffering. "O infinite shame!" he laments. "I am the unhappiest of all living!"

Casting away her spear, shield and helmet, Brünnhilde rushes to Wotan's side. "O father, confide in me!" she begs. "I am your inmost will."

Encouraged by Brünnhilde's words, Wotan relates the whole ignominious story of his greed: the theft of the Rhinegold from Alberich, the payment of the ring to the giants, the creation of the Wälsung race. "Once I craved for power," he declares. "But now I curse the work I have begun! I leave Valhalla and all its pomp to the greedy Nibelungs! There is only one fate that I await—my downfall!"

Filled with doubt and anxiety, Brünnhilde asks the god how she can help him. "Obey Fricka's command!" he answers. "Siegmund must fall!"

In vain does the Valkyrie protest this decree. "Beware!" Wotan Exit
Wotan
shouts. "If you fail me today, your punishment will be appalling! Heed my word!" The god departs, and Brünnhilde sadly gathers up her armor. "Alas, my Wälsung!" she sighs. "Even I must betray Exit
Brünnhilde
you!" Gazing toward the valley and spying the lovers in their flight from Hunding, the Valkyrie disappears within her cave.

For a moment, the rocky landscape is deserted; then Sieglinde Enter
Siegmund
and
Sieglinde
appears among the huge boulders, averting her head in shame. "Stay!" cries Siegmund, who is following close behind her. But the hysterical woman turns from him in dread. She imagines that Hunding's hounds have surrounded the mountain—that Siegmund is being torn to pieces. Trembling with fear, she sinks to the ground.

As night obscures the surrounding cliffs, Siegmund rests upon a stony seat, gently supporting the limp body of his beloved. The woman is breathing more easily; she has fallen into a deep slumber.

Soon, complete darkness envelops the height. In a sudden burst Enter
Brünnhilde
of moonlight, a solemn warrior maiden advances toward Siegmund, relentless as Fate:

It is Brünnhilde. She has come to warn the Wälsung of his approaching death:

"Who are you, O maiden?" asks the Wälsung. "Where do you lead me?"

"I appear only to the slain and those who are doomed to death," Brünnhilde replies. "Your path lies with me to Valhalla."

"And what of Sieglinde?" Siegmund demands. "Will she, too, make the journey?"

"No. Sieglinde is fated to remain on earth."

"Then greet the gods of Valhalla," exclaims the Wälsung, "and tell them I will not follow you. Rather will I destroy Sieglinde and myself!"

For the first time, Brünnhilde feels impelled to disobey Wotan's command. Confronted by human suffering, her sympathies lie entirely with Siegmund. "O Wälsung," she pleads, "trust Sieglinde to me! I will care for her after you are gone!"

Siegmund refuses. He is about to dispatch Sieglinde and himself with the sword, when Brünnhilde intervenes. "Wait!" she urges. "You shall live! I will protect you on the battlefield!"

Exit
Brünnhilde

As the Valkyrie rushes off to prepare for the combat, Siegmund bids farewell to his sleeping bride. Soon, the harsh horn call of Hunding is heard through the gathering mist. Siegmund climbs the mountain in search of his foe, and Sieglinde is left alone.

Exit
Siegmund

The woman stirs restlessly in her slumber. Suddenly, she is awakened by a blinding flash of lighting. "Siegmund!" she screams. "Where are you?" Looking upward, she beholds her lover at the summit of the mountain in deadly combat with Hunding. Beside him stands Brünnhilde, sheltering the hero with her shield. Just as the conquering Wälsung is about to slay Hunding, a reddish glow breaks through the clouds and Wotan appears. "Stand back!" he thunders. Throwing the weight of his spear upon Siegmund's sword, he shatters the blade. At once, Hunding runs his weapon through the defenseless warrior.

Enter
Siegmund,
Hunding,
Brünnhilde
Enter
Wotan

Death of
Siegmund

Swiftly escaping from the scene of the combat, Brünnhilde flees down the mountainside to Sieglinde, takes the woman in her arms and bears her away. Wotan remains, standing above the body of the fallen hero. "Go! Run to Fricka!" he calls bitterly to Hunding. "Tell her that I have upheld her honor. *Go!*" With a contemptuous wave of the hand, he strikes Hunding dead.

Exeunt
Brünnhilde
and
Sieglinde

Death of
Hunding

Silence descends upon the rocky height and suddenly the god gives vent to uncontrollable wrath. "Brünnhilde has disobeyed me!" he shouts. "She will pay dearly if I overtake her!" Amid storm and lightning, Wotan rides off in pursuit of his daughter.

Exit
Wotan

Act III

SCENE: BRÜNNHILDE'S ROCK (65 Minutes)

The prelude to the third act, based on the stirring motives of the Valkyries and the Hojotoho *is sometimes known as the Ride of the Valkyries.*

AT the very top of a lofty mountain stands an overhanging rock. It is here that the fierce band of Valkyries is accustomed to meet before returning from the battlefield to Valhalla. With dead heroes attached to their saddle bows, they ride through the air. Then, laughing stridently and shouting their *Hojotoho*, they dismount on the summit of the rock.

All of the warrior maidens have arrived—except Brünnhilde. Watching anxiously for their sister, they finally see her riding at incredible speed with a live woman on her saddle. The charger that bears her is foaming and exhausted; it sinks to earth.

Enter Valkyries

At once, the Valkyries rush to help Brünnhilde and her mortal companion. "O give me your aid!" cries the rebellious maiden. "Wotan is pursuing me!" Hastily she explains how she has disobeyed the god—protected Siegmund—rescued Sieglinde. "My steed can go no further," she declares. "One of you must lend me a charger so that I can escape!"

Enter Brünnhilde and Sieglinde

The Valkyrie who is standing on the highest point of the rock calls grimly to Brünnhilde. "Wotan is approaching from the north!"

All of Brünnhilde's pleas for a charger are in vain; not one of the other maidens will risk Wotan's displeasure. "O sisters," she begs, "will none of you help me? I must save Sieglinde from destruction!"

Sieglinde glances coldly at her deliverer. "Why did you not leave me to die with Siegmund?" she mutters. "What can life hold for me now?"

"You must live!" exclaims Brünnhilde. "You are bearing Siegmund's child!"

The woman is transported from dull despair to the most fervent hope. Imploring Brünnhilde to save her, she listens eagerly as the maiden tells her to flee toward a vast forest in the east. It is there that Fafner lies disguised as a dragon, guarding his gold; the land is perilous, but Sieglinde will be safe from Wotan's wrath, since the god shuns the neighborhood of Fafner's cave.

"Then go!" Brünnhilde commands. "Endure every hardship, for you will bear the bravest of heroes—Siegfried:"

Giving Sieglinde the fragments of Siegmund's sword which she has saved from the battlefield, Brünnhilde tells the woman to treasure them for her son. "Some day he will forge the splinters anew!" she predicts.

Sieglinde quickly takes the shattered steel and proclaims her gratitude:

Exit
Sieglinde
Enter
Wotan

The woman escapes; Brünnhilde remains hidden by her sisters; and soon, the raging Wotan appears on the rock. "Where is Brünnhilde?" he thunders. "Where is the disobedient one?"

Resolutely, Brünnhilde comes forward. "I am here, O father. Pronounce your sentence."

"You have shaped the sentence yourself!" Wotan answers. "Henceforth, you shall be banished from my sight. You are a Valkyrie no longer!"

Exeunt
Valkyries

As the maidens intercede for their sister, Wotan turns on them savagely. "Begone," he shouts, "lest all of you share her fate!" With wild cries, the Valkyries ride off into the night, abandoning their sister forever. Only Wotan remains with the condemned Brünnhilde.

In an onrush of despair, the maiden has fallen to the ground. Now she rises slowly and appeals to her father. "Have I acted so disgracefully," she asks, "that I deserve this punishment? Have I not been faithful and carried out your inmost wishes? I know that you wanted Siegmund to live!"

"You knew the struggle I endured?" Wotan demands. "You realized the sacrifice I made to placate Fricka—and yet you broke my command?"

"It was inevitable!" declares Brünnhilde. "If you had only seen Siegmund—you, too, would have been stirred! When I stood before him, compassion found a place in my heart."

"You have chosen the path of love," Wotan mutters. "Now follow it! Upon this mountain top you will be plunged in eternal sleep."

"The first mortal who passes shall awaken you and take you for wife!"

"One favor I beg!" cries Brünnhilde. "Surround the rock with fire so that none but the bravest hero can penetrate the flames!"

Wotan's anger toward Brünnhilde has passed away; he is faced only with the knowledge that he must sacrifice the daughter he loves to the inexorable laws of compact. And so, he grants her plea. "Farewell!" he exclaims. "O valiant child, I must forsake you. We can never meet again!" Taking Brünnhilde in his arms, he ends her godhood with a kiss, bears her to a rock beneath the solitary pine tree and covers her with the great shield of the Valkyries. She sinks to peaceful slumber:

Striking the rock three times with his spear, Wotan summons Loge, spirit of fire. "Only he who does not fear my spear point," declares the ruler of the gods, "shall pass through the blaze and awaken the bride."

The mountain is wrapped in magic flame:

For the last time, Wotan gazes at the slumbering Valkyrie. Then he turns from her and pursues his lonely path down the mountainside as the rock is hidden by fire.

SIEGFRIED

Music Drama in Three Acts and Four Scenes

Characters, in order of appearance:

Mime: *tenor*
Siegfried: *tenor*
The Wanderer (Wotan): *bass-baritone*
Alberich: *baritone*
Fafner: *bass*
Voice of the Forest Bird: *soprano*
Erda: *contralto*
Brünnhilde: *soprano*

ACT I

SCENE: A CAVE IN THE FOREST (76 Minutes)

IT is many years since Mime, the cringing Nibelung, has left the land of the dwarfs. Setting up his forge and anvil in the forest where Fafner lies disguised as a dragon, Mime has brooded on thoughts of revenge. He can never forget the cruel treatment shown him by his brother Alberich. Night and day, he dreams of gaining the ring for himself, conquering the Nibelung race and eventually ruling the world.

These are not idle dreams. Mime harbors the chosen instrument through which he can fulfill his plans: Siegfried the Hero. The unfortunate Sieglinde, in her flight from Wotan's wrath, made her way to the entrance of Mime's cave and begged for shelter. The dwarf took her in—helped deliver the child, Siegfried—and saw the woman die. He has raised Siegfried as his own son, hoping some day to send the hero against Fafner.

In spite of these elaborate plans, all is not going well with Mime. Bullied by Siegfried, he forges sword after sword: the youth angrily snaps the weapons into fragments. Hunched over his anvil, Mime vainly tries to fashion a blade powerful enough to resist the hero's strength. *Mime*

"Endless toil!" he mutters. "Terrible bondage! There is only one sword that the boy may not break—*Needful!* Yet I cannot forge the shattered steel!"

Suddenly, he breaks off in alarm—for he has heard the youthful tones of Siegfried ringing through the forest. Soon the hero enters Mime's cave, merrily driving a bear before him to the sound of his hunting call: *Enter Siegfried*

"Away with the brute!" Mime shrieks, running to the furthest recess of the cave.

"I'll drive him off," answers Siegfried, "if you give me the sword that you promised."

As Mime hobbles to the anvil and polishes the blade, Siegfried turns the bear into the forest. Then he takes the new sword and examines it closely. With one twist of his powerful hands, he breaks the steel into fragments. "You bungler!" he shouts at Mime.

The headstrong youth throws himself on a rug opposite the hearth, ignoring Mime's excuses. "Oh how ungrateful you are!" whines the dwarf. "I have brought you up, clothed you, fed you, given you all my wisdom—and this is my reward!"

"You have taught me many things," Siegfried answers, "but I have not yet learned to endure the sight of you! If you are so wise, then tell me—why do I always return to this cave?"

"Just as young birds fly back to their nests," the dwarf replies, "you return to your Mime! You love me as a father:"

"I am nothing to you and you know it!" exclaims the hero. "My features are as much like yours as a glittering fish resembles a toad! *Now* I realize why I have come back here—to learn from you the names of my father and mother!"

Mime maintains a stubborn silence; it is only when Siegfried seizes him by the throat that the dwarf reveals the story of Sieglinde and her tragic death in the forest.

Siegfried glances suspiciously at the dwarf. "How am I to believe your story?" he cries. "I must have proof!"

For a moment, Mime hesitates; then he limps behind the anvil and takes the shattered *Needful* from its hiding place. "Here," he declares, "is a broken sword that your mother gave me. She said your father had wielded it when he was slain."

"Today you shall forge these fragments anew!" orders Siegfried. "With this sword at my side, I will go forth into the world and seek adventure. Once the blade is finished, I'll never see you again!"

Exit Siegfried

The youth runs into the forest and Mime is left alone. "How can I keep him here?" the dwarf ponders. "How can I lead him to Fafner's lair?" And still another fear possesses Mime. "The sword! I cannot forge the fragments!"

Enter Wanderer

As he crouches near his anvil, he does not see an aged wanderer enter the cave. A broad brimmed hat hides his face in shadow and a plain blue cloak serves him as mantle. Only by his spear, which he carries as a staff, might the god perhaps be recognized. It is Wotan, wearing the garb of a mortal:

"Hail, worthy smith," he calls to Mime. "Will you grant shelter to a weary traveler?"

Mime shrinks in terror at the sound of a visitor in his lonely cave. "Who are you?" he cries. "What do you want of me?"

"I am called the Wanderer," the unbidden guest replies. "For many years I have roamed the world in search of wisdom. If you welcome me to your dwelling, I may bring you knowledge!"

"Be off!" Mime demands. "I know enough for my needs!"

Ominously, the Wanderer advances and takes his place beside the hearth. "I shall remain," he declares, "and challenge you to a battle of wits. You may ask me three questions—if I fail to answer any one of them, my head is forfeit."

In order to be rid of the stranger, Mime quizzes him on matters which are known to few men: "What races dwell in the cavernous depths—upon the earth's surface—and in the clouds?"

"The Nibelungs dwell in the depths," the Wanderer answers "The giants live upon the earth's surface, and the gods inhabit the cloud-hidden heights. All three races bow to the command of the world's mighty ruler: Wotan!"

The Wanderer strikes the ground with his spear; an eerie ray of light momentarily illumines his face—and Mime recognizes his guest. "You have answered my three questions," the dwarf whines in terror. "Now, O Wanderer, go your way!"

"By the laws of compact," replies the guest, "you, too, are bound to answer three questions. If you fail, you lose your crafty head. Now give answer! Tell me the name of the race that Wotan loves and yet treats so harshly."

"The Wälsungs!"

"And what is the name of the sword with which Siegfried will slay Fafner, the dragon?"

"*Needful!*"

"There is still another question, O dwarf. *Who will forge the fragments of the conquering sword?*"

"Alas!" cries Mime, springing up in consternation. "I do not know!"

The Wanderer rises slowly from his place at the hearth. "You have failed," he declares. "Your wager is lost. Now hear, O cleverest of dwarfs: only he who knows no fear shall forge the sword; and I leave your head to him!" Laughing scornfully, the Wanderer departs.

Exit
Wanderer

Left alone in his solitary cave, Mime is filled with terror. The dwarf imagines that he sees a huge beast crashing through the underbrush, coming toward him with gaping jaws. "Fafner!" he screams. "The dragon!" Limp with fright, he slumps behind the anvil.

Enter
Siegfried

And now Siegfried returns to the cave, expecting to find the finished sword. "Why haven't you forged the blade?" he exclaims, as the dwarf rises timidly from the ground.

"I have been thinking of you," Mime whispers. "Before you go forth into the world, there is one thing I must teach you—*fear!* It will make you cautious in the face of danger!"

In vain does Mime try to defeat the Wanderer's prophecy. Despite his harrowing description of the forest at dusk he cannot bring fear to the heart of Siegfried. When he describes the horrible dragon that lies within the wood, guarding a golden treasure, he only succeeds in awakening the youth's desire for adventure.

"I will slay this monster!" shouts Siegfried. "Now finish my sword, Mime, and you shall lead me to the dragon's lair!"

"Alas!" Mime sobs. "I cannot fuse the splinters!"

"Then give them to me!" Siegfried commands. "I shall forge the sword myself." Melting the fragments and fanning the flames, the hero sings lustily at his work:

No -thung! No - thung! Neid - li - ches Schwert! Was muss - test du zer - spring- en?
Need - ful! Need - ful! con - quer - ing sword! What blow has served to break you?

While Siegfried pours the glowing steel into a mould, Mime sits at the hearth brewing a poisonous draught. "If the hero should kill Fafner and win the golden ring," he mutters, "I'll feed him this drink. He will die—and the Nibelung treasure shall be mine!"

At last, Siegfried has fused the mighty splinters. He hammers vigorously at the blade, bringing it into final shape:

The work is done. Siegfried lifts the sword on high and, with a single blow, cleaves Mime's anvil. *Needful* has been reborn—the blade that once was shattered rises again in triumph!

Act II

SCENE: IN THE DEPTHS OF THE FOREST (68 Minutes)

GUARDING the ring of the Nibelung in the heart of a dismal forest, lurks the giant Fafner:

Molto ritenuto

Through the Tarnhelm's magic, he has become a ferocious dragon, frightening all intruders from the neighborhood of his cave; but the ring has availed him nothing—the golden hoard has brought him only anxiety.

There is one person who clings with stubborn courage to the terrifying forest: Alberich the Nibelung. Determined to regain his ring, he lingers outside the dragon's cave at dead of night. *Alberich*

Suddenly, as the dwarf is keeping his vigil, a mysterious light sweeps through the forest in the direction of Fafner's lair. "What can it mean?" Alberich ponders. "Is the dragon's slayer approaching?" The light disappears; Alberich looks intently through the darkness—and he beholds the Wanderer. *Enter Wanderer*

"Shameless thief!" he screams, recognizing Wotan. "Have you come to steal the ring again?"

"I am here to witness—not to act," the Wanderer replies.

"Well do I know your treachery!" snarls the dwarf. "But you shall not triumph this time! You have given the ring to Fafner in compact, and you cannot win it back!"

Another thought strikes the turbulent Nibelung. "What of the race of heroes that you have created?" he demands. "Are you still secretly helping them against me?"

"Not I," answers the Wanderer. "Your brother Mime leads a fearless hero to slay Fafner and win the gold!"

To convince Alberich that he has no further interest in the ring, the Wanderer strides toward the mouth of the cavern and calls, "Fafner, awaken! A hero is coming to slay you for your treasure."

The dragon yawns ponderously: "I have and I hold—let me sleep!"

Smiling at Fafner's stupid boast, the Wanderer turns again to Alberich. "I have tried to help you," he claims, "but the Fates do not will it. Now I must begone; and I warn you—beware of Mime!"

The mysterious light flashes once more through the forest as the Wanderer vanishes. Alberich slips into the obscurity of the forest. *Exit Wanderer*

Exit
Alberich

"Some day I shall see the whole race of gods meet their downfall!" he mutters.

No sooner has the dwarf crept away than the first rays of dawn begin to penetrate the gloomy forest. The mouth of Fafner's cave becomes visible amid the dense foliage. Soon a few rays of sunlight filter through the crowded branches. And now Mime appears, leading Siegfried toward the cavern. "This is the dragon's lair," he whispers. "And when you see him, you'll know the meaning of fear!"

Enter
Mime and
Siegfried

Exit
Mime

Driving Mime away, Siegfried lies beneath a spreading tree, gazing at the woods about him. From the branches above, drifts down a gay melody. Siegfried listens, enchanted by the song of a forest bird:

Allegro

Trying to imitate the songster, Siegfried cuts a reed with his sword and fashions it into a pipe. The reed is pinched and out of tune. Hoping to attract a companion by his music, the hero blows upon his hunting horn. He succeeds in his purpose—Fafner slides threateningly from his cave.

Enter
Fafner

At once, Siegfried attacks the beast. A furious battle ends in victory for the hero as he plunges his sword into the dragon's heart. "Beware, valiant youth!" groans the dying beast. "Whoever sent you against me is surely planning your death!"

Death of
Fafner

The monster perishes—another victim of Alberich's curse. Anxious to recover his sword, Siegfried draws the steel from the dragon's body and stains his hands with Fafner's blood. As he licks his fingers dry, the taste of the blood lends him a supernatural power; he can understand the language of the bird whose singing so delighted him as he lay beneath the tree.

"Siegfried!" the bird is calling. "Go into the dragon's cave. A splendid ring and helmet await you!"

Forest bird
Exit
Siegfried
Enter
Mime and
Alberich
Enter
Siegfried
Exeunt
Mime and
Alberich
Forest bird
Enter
Mime

Obeying the call, Siegfried enters the cavern. Immediately, Alberich and Mime creep from opposite sides of the forest, each intent upon ravishing the gold. Meeting in front of the cave, they quarrel furiously—but when Siegfried emerges, holding the ring and Tarnhelm, the dwarfs scurry back into the underbrush.

Again the forest bird calls to the hero: "Beware of Mime!" And now Mime approaches, bearing the poisoned drink. Through the power that the dragon's blood has given him, Siegfried can detect the malice of the dwarf's fawning speeches; he can see only

too plainly that Mime intends to murder him. Finally, seized with
loathing, he kills the dwarf and flings his body within the cave.
"Since you desired the hoard so dearly," he shouts, "you may guard
it in death!"

Death of
Mime

All of the Nibelung treasure except the Tarnhelm and ring still
lies within the cave. As a barrier against thieves, Siegfried rolls the
huge bulk of the dragon across the entrance. Then, overcome with
weariness, he lies down to rest. "I am so lonely," he sighs, appealing to the forest bird. "Is there no one on earth to serve me as
comrade?"

"A glorious bride waits for Siegfried!" the bird answers. "She
sleeps on a mountain surrounded by fire. If you break through the
flames and awaken the maiden, Brünnhilde shall be yours!"

Forest bird

Moderato

Durch-schritt' er die Brunst,   weckt' er die Braut,   Brünn-hil - de ___ wä - re dann sein.
Who fight-eth the flames,   wa-kens the maid,   Brunn-hil - de ___ wins for his own.

Transported with joy, Siegfried leaps to his feet and follows the
flight of the bird toward Brünnhilde's rock.

ACT III

SCENE 1: A WILD REGION AT THE BASE OF BRÜNNHILDE'S ROCK
(Cut 24 Minutes, Uncut 30 Minutes)

As thunder and lightning sweep through the jagged gorge below
Brünnhilde's rock, the Wanderer appears. Striding toward a cavern,
he raises his spear in command and summons Erda, goddess of
wisdom.

Enter
Wanderer

Slowly the goddess emerges from the earth, her eyes heavy with
sleep. "Who has broken my slumber?" she demands.

Enter Erda

"The Wanderer," answers her wakener. Concealing his identity,
he questions Erda about the future.

"Why do you not consult my daughter Brünnhilde?" asks Erda.
"Even while I dream, she can predict the destiny of the world."

"The Valkyrie has lost her wisdom!" the Wanderer declares.
"She boldly disobeyed Wotan—and as punishment, she has become
a mortal."

Dazed with sorrow, Erda can hardly believe the Wanderer's
story. "Brünnhilde deprived of her godhood?" she gasps. "My own
daughter punished by Wotan because she carried out his inmost

wishes? Alas, falsehood rules the world—let me descend to my slumber!"

"No!" the Wanderer proclaims. "You shall not go until you reveal how a god may avoid his downfall!"

Suddenly, Erda recognizes her visitor; she cries out in dismay—but the Wanderer silences her. "All of us are to perish," he exclaims. "You and I, and the others of our race. But I care not! Once, in my loathing, I bequeathed the world to the Nibelungs. All has been changed—and now, Siegfried and Brünnhilde shall inherit the earth and redeem it with their love."

At length, the Wanderer releases Erda from his spell. "Descend!" he commands. "Eternal sleep awaits you. Never more shall the world call upon your wisdom!"

Exit Erda

Erda sinks into the ground. The Wanderer remains in the deserted gorge, looking into the distance with interest—for he sees Siegfried approaching.

Enter Siegfried

As the god stands hidden in shadow, Siegfried enters the chasm. He has lost all trace of the forest bird and is climbing blindly toward Brünnhilde's rock. Just as the youth sets foot on the steep pathway, the Wanderer steps from his place of concealment. With fatherly interest, he questions Siegfried. "Who forged the sword you carry?" he asks.

"I did!" Siegfried proudly answers.

"But who created the mighty steel?"

The question irritates Siegfried. In his anxiety to climb the mountain and reach his goal, the youth has little time for quibbling. "Be off!" he commands.

The Wanderer's indulgence soon turns to seething anger. Unable to endure the taunts of the arrogant boy, he extends his spear and bars the way to Brünnhilde's rock. "You shall not pass!" he cries. "Once the sword that you bear was shattered by my weapon. It shall be broken again today!"

"Then I have found my father's ancient enemy!" shouts Siegfried. With one blow of his sword, he cuts the Wanderer's spear in two. There is a terrifying flash, a rumble of thunder—and then, complete silence in the gorge. His shoulders stooped in resignation, the god bends down to retrieve the fragments of his spear. "Fare onward," he mutters to the hero. "I cannot withstand you."

The Wanderer disappears. Unaware that he has destroyed the power of the gods, young Siegfried joyously sounds his hunting horn and plunges into the blazing fire that surrounds the mountain.

As steam rises from the footlights, obscuring the stage, the hero's ascent to Brünnhilde's rock is described by the orchestra in a brilliant interlude. When the smoke and fire clear away, the same tableau is revealed as was seen during the finale of Die Walküre.

SCENE 2: THE SUMMIT OF BRÜNNHILDE'S ROCK (42 Minutes)

Siegfried has arrived at the summit of the mountain. He gazes in awe at the distant peaks glistening in the sunlight. Then, glancing at the surface of the rock below, he sees a solitary pine tree—and, in its shade, a slumbering warrior covered with a mighty shield. Siegfried approaches the sleeping figure—removes the shield—and cuts the binding armor. To his amazement, the warrior is a woman, the first he has ever beheld.

He tries vainly to rouse the sleeper, but she will not answer his call. In a despairing attempt, he kneels beside the maiden and presses his lips to hers. Brünnhilde awakens to the kiss of Siegfried! At once, she opens her eyes, rises, and greets the world:

Rapturously, she welcomes the child of the Wälsungs. Wotan's prophecy has been fulfilled: a fearless hero has passed through the flaming barrier.

But soon Brünnhilde faces the realities of the life to which she has awakened. Siegfried, in a moment of passion, embraces her. Terrified, she flees from the ardent youth. "No god ever touched me!" she cries. "I was sacred to every hero in Valhalla!"

It is now that Brünnhilde realizes the full weight of her punishment. In losing her godhood, she has become a prey to mortal emotions; she cannot subdue the longing that burns within her.

(margin notes:)

Exit
Wanderer
Exit
Siegfried

Enter
Siegfried

Brünnhilde

"O Siegfried!" she pleads. "Torment me no longer. Go, and leave me in peace:"

"No, I will not leave you!" cries the hero. "You must awaken to life, to love. Be mine!"

"I have always been yours!" Brünnhilde answers with deep emotion. Yielding to Siegfried's plea, she casts aside her godhood forever, and entrusts herself to mortal love:

"Joyfully shall we live," Brünnhilde proclaims, "and joyfully shall we go down to mortal death!" As the sun blazes in splendor upon the rock where the Valkyries once met in conclave, the warrior maiden throws herself in Siegfried's arms.

GÖTTERDÄMMERUNG
(THE TWILIGHT OF THE GODS)
Music Drama in Three Acts, Five Scenes and a Prologue

Characters, in order of appearance:

The Three Norns: *contralto, mezzo and soprano*
Brünnhilde: *soprano*
Siegfried: *tenor*
Gunther, King of the Gibichungs: *baritone*
Hagen, his half-brother: *bass-baritone*
Gutrune, sister to Gunther: *soprano*
Waltraute, a Valkyrie: *mezzo-soprano*
Alberich: *baritone*

Rhinemaidens
{ Woglinde: *soprano*
{ Wellgunde: *mezzo-soprano*
{ Flosshilde: *contralto*

Gunther's vassals, Gutrune's women attendants

PROLOGUE

SCENE: BRÜNNHILDE'S ROCK (Cut 26 Minutes, Uncut 32 Minutes)

AT dead of night, while Siegfried and Brünnhilde slumber within their cave, three veiled figures linger on the Valkyries' rock, unwinding a mysterious rope. They are the Norns, daughters of Erda, who weave the destiny of the world.

Norns

171

As they spin, the Norns discuss the wrongs of mankind and the treachery of the gods; they predict the early fall of Valhalla:

Exeunt Norns

The rope of destiny is parting, severed by the curse of Alberich's ring. As the weavers cast it to the north, it breaks. With a cry of anguish, the three veiled figures sink into the earth. Never again will they read the future. Their task is ended.

Enter Siegfried and Brünnhilde

The shifting colors of dawn play upon the rock. When the sun has risen, Siegfried emerges from the cave in full armor, followed by Brünnhilde:

"Go forth into the world, O hero," the woman declares, "and win new fame. I will not try to keep you here when adventure calls. But wherever you travel, and whatever deeds you achieve, remember Brünnhilde."

"I shall never forget the oaths we have sworn," Siegfried answers. "As proof of my love, I give you this ring!"

Ecstatically, Brünnhilde places the ring of the Nibelung on her finger. In return, she presents the hero with her steed, Grane. No longer can the charger fly through the air, but it will endure every danger—even fire—for the sake of its master.

Exit Siegfried

The lovers embrace in a last farewell; and then Siegfried leads Grane down the mountainside, to venture forth into the world:

Running to the highest point on the rock, Brünnhilde gazes fondly into the valley. She hears her lover's horn call; for a moment she spies him as he descends the winding path. Then, Siegfried is lost to sight—and Brünnhilde awaits his return on the fire-girt mountain.

The curtain falls, and the orchestra plays an interlude known as "Siegfried's Rhine Journey," describing the progress of the hero as he sails the mighty river in search of adventure. As the interlude nears its close, the music becomes increasingly sinister, foreshadowing the villainy to follow.

ACT I

SCENE 1: THE HALL OF THE GIBICHUNGS (Cut 37 Minutes, Uncut 38 Minutes)

ON the banks of the Rhine stands a gloomy building dedicated to the glory of the Gibichung tribe. Rough, primitive beams overhang the inner hall; three crude chairs are set about a council table; and at the center of the table sits Gunther, king of the fierce and warlike Gibichungs:

Gunther, Gutrune and Hagen

Unable to make his own decisions, the cowardly chieftain turns for advice to his sister Gutrune, and his half-brother Hagen. Always at his side, they are with him now, engaged in weighty council.

"Tell me, Hagen," urges the king. "How goes my fame along the Rhine?"

Hagen glances sharply at Gunther and Gutrune. While they are fair and Nordic in appearance, his black hair and sallow skin stamp him of different race. A Gibichung queen, Grimhilde, was his mother; Alberich, his father. Secretly vowing to regain the ring for the Nibelung, he advises Gunther only as it serves his evil plans.

"Your fame is sullied, O King," he declares, "for you are in the prime of life, and yet unwed. Gutrune, too, must find a mate!" Drawing closer to the monarch, Hagen whispers, "I know of a bride for you. She dwells on a mountain top surrounded by fire. Brünnhilde is her name."

"May I pass through the flames and win her?" Gunther asks anxiously.

"No. Only the bravest warrior in the world—Siegfried the

Wälsung—may defy the blaze." Deliberately concealing his knowledge of Siegfried's union with Brünnhilde, Hagen weaves his intrigue still further. He relates how the hero is voyaging down the Rhine intent upon conquest—how at any moment, Siegfried will arrive at the hall of the Gibichungs. "If you were to grant him Gutrune in marriage," the schemer tells Gunther, "he would do your bidding and bring Brünnhilde to the Rhine."

"But surely," the gentle Gutrune protests, "if Siegfried is so great a hero, he must already have won the world's fairest women!"

"Have no fear," whispers Hagen. "I have a magic draught that will cause him to forget any woman he has ever known:"

As the two Gibichungs and their half-brother plot to win Siegfried's help, they suddenly hear a horn on the Rhine. The hero is at hand! Soon a skiff comes down the river bearing Siegfried and Grane. Hagen runs to the shore—signals to the Wälsung—and guides the skiff to a safe mooring at the water's edge.

Enter Siegfried

Siegfried alights and strides arrogantly into the hall. "Where is the King of the Gibichungs?" he demands. "Let him fight me or be my friend!"

Immediately, Gunther comes forward, offering his friendship—at a sign from Hagen, his sister advances with the magic drink. "Welcome, O guest," she exclaims. "Accept this draught from Gunther's sister."

Siegfried puts the cup to his lips and is conquered by the potion. Forgetting Brünnhilde, the hero awakens to the shy beauty of Gutrune. Determined to win the maiden, he is prepared to meet any price that her brother may demand.

Exit Gutrune

As Gutrune goes to her chamber, Siegfried tries to make a favorable impression on Gunther. Approaching the subject of marriage, he inquires if the king is already wed.

"No!" Gunther declares darkly. "The woman I most desire is

beyond my grasp. She lies in a circle of fire—and I cannot break through the flames!"

At the mention of the fire, Siegfried starts—a vague memory disturbs him—but as Gunther pronounces the name of Brünnhilde, forgetfulness clouds the hero's mind. "I will help you, Gunther!" he offers. "And if I succeed in bringing Brünnhilde to the Rhine, Gutrune shall be my reward!"

At the suggestion of Hagen, a plan of campaign is quickly arranged. Siegfried has never known the significance of the Tarn-helm, which lies idly attached to his belt. "The helmet can transport you to other lands," Hagen whispers. "It can make you invisible, or give you whatever shape you wish." Accordingly, Siegfried is instructed to disguise himself as Gunther and break through the flames. He will spend a single night in Brünnhilde's cave, holding the woman inviolate. Then on the morrow, he will lead her to the real Gunther and disappear. The Valkyrie will never know that she has been deceived!

To seal the bargain, Gunther and Siegfried mingle drops of their blood in a drinking horn filled with wine. They drain the contents, swearing an oath of blood-brotherhood.

"If this bond is ever broken," the allies proclaim, "if friend should ever be false to friend, the transgressor shall pay with his life! Such is the justice of expiation:"

The pact is concluded; Siegfried and the king set out for Brünn-hilde's rock, and Hagen is left alone to guard the hall. As the boat moves swiftly away, Gutrune comes from her chamber and gazes after the departing hero. Then she withdraws and Hagen takes his place on the steps of the hall amid the gathering shadows. "Siegfried brings Brünnhilde to the Rhine," he gloats, "and with her, he brings me *the ring!*"

The curtain falls in gloomy silence, unbroken save for the throbbing of the drums. During the following interlude, both themes of Siegfried are heard—the Hero and the Hunting Call—but so distorted as to hint at the young Wälsung's downfall. Finally, these phrases yield to the radiant theme of Brünnhilde, and the curtain rises.

Exeunt
Siegfried
and
Gunther
Enter
and exit
Gutrune

SCENE 2: BRÜNNHILDE'S ROCK (Cut 29 Minutes, Uncut 33 Minutes)

Brünnhilde

It is early evening. Brünnhilde sits peacefully before her cave, gazing with admiration on Siegfried's ring. Suddenly, amid the rumbling of thunder, she hears a wild shout in the distance—the voice of Waltraute, one of the bravest Valkyries. In highest excitement, Brünnhilde runs to meet her sister. "Has Wotan pardoned me?" she cries.

Enter Waltraute

Waltraute does not answer. "Then you have disobeyed our father in coming here?" Brünnhilde asks. "You have risked his punishment?"

"If only I might still fear his wrath!" Waltraute replies. "His power is broken—he is waiting for his downfall! But *you* can help us! O sister, renounce the ring! Cast it into the Rhine, and all of us will be free of its curse!"

"Never!" cries Brünnhilde. "The ring is a pledge from Siegfried. Though Valhalla crumble into ruins, I will not renounce my love!"

Exit Waltraute

Waltraute rushes off in despair, and Brünnhilde takes her place once more before the cave, musing over the golden ring. She glances at the flames that surround the rock—and to her surprise, they have flared up into a fiery torrent. Someone is ascending the mountain. "Siegfried!" she cries joyously. And then, in horror, Brünnhilde sees an utter stranger passing through the blaze.

Enter Siegfried

"Who are you?" she gasps.

"I am a Gibichung," the warrior replies, his face hidden by a mesh helmet, "and I have come to take you for wife."

"Go back!" screams Brünnhilde. "This ring will protect me!" She extends her arm threateningly—the stranger advances, and after a terrible struggle, he tears the ring from her finger. "Night is drawing near," he declares. "Show me the way to your cave!" Brokenly, Brünnhilde obeys.

Exit Brünnhilde

The stranger lingers on the threshold and raises his helmet—it is Siegfried. Drawing his sword, he swears a solemn oath to safeguard the woman for Gunther. Then, lowering the Tarnhelm, he enters the cave—the unwitting betrayer of his own bride.

Exit Siegfried

ACT II

SCENE: IN FRONT OF GUNTHER'S DWELLING (Cut 52 Minutes, Uncut 63 Minutes)

Hagen and Alberich

STILL keeping guard, Hagen crouches on the outer steps of the hall of the Gibichungs. He is sunk in slumber—and at his feet, sharply outlined by a ray of moonlight, lurks the baleful Alberich.

"Hagen, my son!" whispers the Nibelung. "There is no time to lose—we must gain the ring!"

"Fear not!" the sleeping Hagen replies. "The gold will be ours! Siegfried shall be murdered."

Alberich disappears, and dawn descends upon the Rhine. Soon, Hagen awakens, masking his treacherous thoughts, for Siegfried has suddenly appeared at the river bank. *(Exit Alberich Enter Siegfried)*

"I greet you, Hagen!" calls the hero. "Gunther has won his bride —he is bringing her down the Rhine in my ship!"

At the sound of Siegfried's voice, Gutrune runs from the hall to welcome her lover. "You passed without mishap through the flames?" she asks anxiously. *(Enter Gutrune)*

"Yes, and Brünnhilde thought I was Gunther!" laughs the hero.

"Then your task is finished!" Gutrune exclaims joyfully. "Let us prepare for our wedding!" As she draws Siegfried into the hall, Hagen climbs a lofty rock that towers above the Rhine. *(Exeunt Siegfried and Gutrune)*

The Nibelung's son puts a horn to his lips and blows a resounding signal. "Hoiho!" he shouts. "You vassals of Gunther! Assemble at once with mighty weapons! Our ruler has won a Valkyrie for wife!"

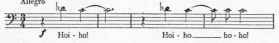

In answer to his call, armed men come swarming over the hills and line the shore. As Gunther's ship rounds a bend in the river, they strike their weapons noisily against their shields. "Hail, O Gunther!" they shout. "Hail to you and your queen!" *(Enter vassals Enter Gunther and Brünnhilde Enter Siegfried, Gutrune and women attendants)*

Acknowledging the fervent welcome, Gunther leads his bride to land. Brünnhilde's eyes are fixed on the ground; not once does she look up as another procession takes its place on the river bank— the wedding train of Siegfried and Gutrune. "I greet you, O sister!" Gunther declares gladly. "Two blessed pairs are here united: Gunther and Brünnhilde—Gutrune and Siegfried!"

On hearing Siegfried's name, Brünnhilde trembles. She looks up, astonished, and beholds the hero in the embrace of Gutrune. Overcome with dismay, she sinks toward the ground and Siegfried—

whose memory of Brünnhilde extends no further than the previous night—supports her in his arms.

Suddenly, she spies the golden ring on Siegfried's finger. "Gunther!" she cries. "You tore that ring from my hand last night; it is the pledge with which you wed me. How has it come from you to Siegfried?"

Gunther is silent; he can give no answer. And now Brünnhilde realizes that Siegfried has basely betrayed her—that it was *he* who passed through the flames, disguised as Gunther. Turning furiously to the Gibichung vassals, she points accusingly at the hero. "Bear witness, all of you!" she proclaims. "Not Gunther, but *Siegfried* is my husband. He has possessed me in the bonds of love! Where shall I look for vengeance?"

Disgraced before his entire tribe, Gunther implores Siegfried to utter some word that will refute Brünnhilde's charge. His reputation at stake, Siegfried calls for a spear on which to swear a solemn oath. "Mine be the weapon!" declares Hagen, offering the hero his spear point.

As the men solemnly form a circle, Siegfried stands in their midst. "Shining steel," he cries, clutching the weapon, "hear my oath. I swear that Brünnhilde's tale is untrue!"

Hel - le Wehr, hei - li - ge Waf - fe!
Shin - ing steel, hal - low - ed wea - pon!

Brünnhilde pushes her way among the vassals and drives Siegfried from the spear point. "Shining steel!" she exclaims. "Hallowed weapon! May you bring Siegfried to his death—for he has broken all his vows!"

Exeunt Siegfried, Gutrune, vassals and attendants Disregarding the woman's outburst, Siegfried enters the hall with Gutrune and the wedding procession. The shore becomes silent and lonely—only Brünnhilde remains, together with Hagen and the humiliated Gunther.

"Let me avenge you!" Hagen urges the woman. "If Siegfried has profaned his oaths, he must die!"

At first, Brünnhilde laughs bitterly at Hagen's offer. "One glance from the hero would be enough to destroy you!" she mutters. But then, persuaded by the schemer's wiles, she agrees to take part in a plot against Siegfried's life. "Strike at his back!" she advises Hagen. "It is his only vulnerable spot!"

Together with Gunther, the conspirators plan the manner of Siegfried's death. The hero will be slain during a hunt on the morrow. His bride, Gutrune, will never know the circumstances of his murder, thinking him the victim of a wild boar. For a moment, Gunther hesitates; because of his sister's love for the hero, he is loath to go through with the scheme. "If Siegfried dies," Hagen whispers, *"you* will gain his ring!" Swayed by greed and ambition, the cowardly king at length consents to the murder.

The river bank is again filled with people. The wedding procession has set out on its way to the hills, where the celebrants are to deck the altars of the gods with flowers. With no hint of their plans, the three conspirators join the triumphal train of Siegfried and Gutrune. Alberich's curse is again about to claim another victim!

Enter Siegfried, Gutrune, vassals and attendants

Act III

SCENE 1: A WOODED PLACE ON THE RHINE (38 Minutes)

As the late afternoon sun casts its patterns through a glen along the Rhine, three figures swim on the surface of the waters. They are the Rhinemaidens, ever mindful of their lost gold:

Rhine-maidens

Moderato

Suddenly, they hear Siegfried's hunting call. The hero, detached from the Gibichung party, is wandering through the woods. As he approaches, the Rhinemaidens call to him gaily. "We will bring you good hunting if you grant us your ring."

Enter Siegfried

Despite their utmost cajolery, they cannot induce the hero to part with his gold. Plunging into the stream, they emerge again— this time with prophecies of disaster. "Beware!" they warn. "A curse hangs upon the treasure. Unless you cast it into the Rhine, you will be slain—here and today!"

Their threats antagonize Siegfried. "I have never known the meaning of fear!" he exclaims. "If death plans to strike me, let it come!"

Despairing of further talk with the hero, the maidens swim away. Siegfried gazes after them—and he hears the harsh horn call of the Gibichungs echoing through the forest. Soon, the entire hunting party descends toward the river with the game they have captured. Lying about on the ground, the men talk of adventure.

Exeunt Rhine-maidens Enter Hagen, Gunther and vassals

"Siegfried!" calls Hagen. "I have heard it said that you understand the speech of birds."

"That was long ago," Siegfried answers. Turning to the king, who sits apart from his companions in deepest melancholy, the hero cries, "Gunther! Be of good cheer, and I will tell you the story of my youth!"

As the men gather around him, Siegfried describes his early upbringing in the forest—his cringing guardian, Mime—the forging of the sword—the battle with the dragon—and the death of the murderous dwarf. As the hero pauses in his tale, Hagen suddenly offers him a draught of wine. Unknown to Siegfried, this potion will restore the hero's memory.

Under the stimulus of the drink, Siegfried goes on with his story. While Gunther and the men listen in amazement, he relates how he climbed Brünnhilde's rock, conquered the flames, and took the warrior maiden as his bride.

Gunther rises abruptly; the men stand mute with terror. Two ravens fly over the troubled scene, winging their way across the Rhine. "Can you divine their speech, O hero?" cries Hagen. As Siegfried turns to gaze after the birds, Hagen plunges his spear in the Wälsung's back. "They have decreed your death!" he shouts.

Exit
Hagen

Death of
Siegfried

The sun has set; twilight has gathered on the hills, and Hagen strides off in the approaching darkness. With his dying breath, Siegfried calls for Brünnhilde—then, he falls back upon his shield and expires. At a command from Gunther, the vassals bear the hero's body in solemn procession to the hall of the Gibichungs.

Thick clouds arise from the Rhine, hiding the scene, and the orchestra plays the famous symphonic interlude known as Siegfried's Funeral Music.

SCENE 2: THE HALL OF THE GIBICHUNGS (Cut 25 Minutes, Uncut 43 Minutes)

Gutrune
Enter
Hagen,
Gunther
and vassals
with
Siegfried's
body

Gutrune paces apprehensively through the deserted chamber. Why has Siegfried not returned? Why has she not heard his horn? Suddenly, she perceives the red glow of torches in the distance— she listens to the strident voice of Hagen coming nearer. At last, the grim procession enters the hall with the hero's body. "Your lover has been slain," Hagen gloats, "by the tusk of a boar."

Gutrune can see that Siegfried has been murdered. Crazed with grief, she accuses her brother Gunther of the deed. "Gutrune!" the king implores. "Sister! The guilt is not mine. It was Hagen who slew your hero!"

Throwing aside all pretense, Hagen steps forward and confronts the king defiantly. "Yes, I slew Siegfried!" he exclaims. "The traitor swore falsely on my spear—and as booty, I claim his ring!"

"Away!" shouts Gunther. "The ring is mine!"

"Yours? It is the Nibelung's—*I claim it as his son!*"

Hagen rushes savagely at the king; the two men fight desperately—and Gunther falls, pierced by his half-brother's blade. As the vassals retreat in fright, Hagen stalks toward the hero's body—grasps for the ring—and suddenly retreats in terror. The corpse has raised its arm against him!

Death of Gunther

At this moment of confusion, a solemn figure appears on the threshold of the hall—Brünnhilde. Advancing slowly, she commands the vassals to pile mighty logs on the river bank as a funeral pyre for Siegfried. Too late has she learned of Hagen's treachery—that Siegfried was innocent of all broken oaths.

Enter Brünnhilde

At last, the funeral pyre stands ready. Brünnhilde draws the ring from Siegfried's finger and places it on her own. "Accursed gold!" she exclaims. "May your power soon be ended! May the Rhinemaidens claim their treasure from my ashes!"

The hero's body has been placed upon the pyre—seizing a fiery brand, Brünnhilde hurls it at the logs. As the blaze soars heavenward, she calls for her steed Grane and with a final cry of love for the slain Siegfried, mounts the charger and rides into the flames. Her sacrifice will yield atonement for the wrongs of gods and men.

Exit Brünnhilde

The hall collapses with a thunderous roar; the Rhine overflows and the Rhinemaidens swim in upon the flood, regaining their gold. "Give back the ring!" shouts Hagen, rushing madly into the waves. Seized by the maidens he is drawn to a watery doom.

Enter Rhinemaidens Exit Hagen

And now, through the ruins of the fallen hall, the proud castle of Valhalla can be seen, devoured by the flames of Siegfried's funeral pyre. Nature, in the form of flood and fire, has purified the earth—and the ring, cleansed of its curse, reposes once more in the depths of the Rhine.

PARSIFAL

PARSIFAL *received its first performance at the Bayreuth* Festspielhaus *in 1882. Because of the sacred nature of the work, Wagner called it "a stage consecrational festival play," intended for performance only at Bayreuth. In 1903, over the objections of Wagner's widow, Cosima,* Parsifal *was presented by Heinrich Conried at the Metropolitan Opera House. Frau Wagner tried to stop the production through the courts, but an injunction was not granted. More recently,* Parsifal *has become available to the great European opera houses.*

Characters, in order of appearance:

Gurnemanz, senior knight of the Grail: *bass*
Four Esquires: two *sopranos* and two *tenors*
Two solo knights of the Grail: *tenor* and *bass*
Kundry: *soprano*
Amfortas: *baritone*
Parsifal: *tenor*
Titurel: *bass*
Klingsor: *baritone*
Knights of the Grail, flower maidens, chorus of boys

Time: Middle Ages

Place: In and near the castle of Montsalvat, Spain

THE PRELUDE

The prelude to Parsifal *is based chiefly upon a long, curving phrase which is divided into three motives. The first of these motives is called the Eucharist:*

It is followed by the motive of Anguish:

and by the Lance:

The next principal motive in the prelude is the Holy Grail:

And finally, the triumphant theme of Faith:

ACT I

SCENE 1: A FOREST (62 Minutes)

ON a mountain peak in Spain stands the fortress of Mont-salvat, dedicated to the protection of the Holy Grail. The knights who guard this sacred vessel are sworn to celibacy, and only their king is allowed to have issue. Since the venerable founder of Mont-salvat—Titurel—is too old to rule any longer, his son Amfortas has taken over his duties. But Amfortas is tortured by a terrible spear wound. Weak and spiritless, he relies on the guidance of a senior knight of the chapter: the devoted Gurnemanz.

Gurnemanz and 2 esquires

Early one morning, Gurnemanz rises from his slumber in the fields. At his side are two young esquires. "Awake," exclaims the elderly knight, "and give thanks to God!" Turning toward the castle, he sees two knights coming down the hill, bound for the lake.

"How is our king?" he asks them. "Perhaps the morning bath will bring him comfort."

2 knights

The knights glance reproachfully at Gurnemanz. Surely he must know that Amfortas' wound is incurable! Plunged in sorrow, Gurnemanz admits, "Yes, all our salves are in vain! There is only one thing—one man—to help Amfortas!"

"Tell us!" urge the knights.

Enter Kundry

But Gurnemanz evades their question. "Attend to the bath!" he orders. And suddenly, the knights and esquires cry out in excitement. They have seen a wild rider hastening toward them at breathless speed. "Look!" they shout. "It is Kundry!"

Kundry has dismounted. She is a fantastic being—ageless—with dark brown skin and black, disheveled hair. When Titurel, founder of Montsalvat, built the castle, he found her sleeping in the bushes. Speaking but little, she goes on errands of mercy for the knights. On this occasion, she has traveled as far as Arabia to find a healing balsam for Amfortas. "Here!" she cries, thrusting a crystal vial toward Gurnemanz. "Take it!" Overcome with weariness, she sinks to the ground.

Enter Amfortas

She lies motionless, and a procession descends the hill—it is the ailing Amfortas, borne by his attendants. On seeing Gurnemanz, the king bids his men halt. "I have spent another night of anguish," he exclaims. "Perhaps my only release will be in death!"

Exit Amfortas

At once, Gurnemanz offers Amfortas the soothing balsam that Kundry has brought. As the king gratefully accepts it and goes off toward the lake, the young esquires turn on Kundry. "You, there!" they mutter. "Why do you lie on the ground like any beast?"

Gurnemanz quickly intervenes. "She has always helped us," he declares. "It is only when she disappears that evil falls upon our chapter."

"If she is so helpful," challenge the esquires, "why do you not send her after the king's spear?"

"That is beyond her!" cries Gurnemanz. Gloomily, he recalls the tale of Amfortas' shame: how an infidel named Klingsor had tried to gain admission into the chaste brotherhood of the Grail. In anger at being rejected, Klingsor set up a magic flower garden near the castle, where the knights of the Grail were tempted to break their vows. Finally, Amfortas himself marched against Klingsor, armed with a lance that had pierced the side of the Lord. He entered the garden—and fell prey to a woman of extraordinary beauty. As he lay in her embrace, the sacred lance was snatched away by Klingsor, who dealt the king a deadly wound. This wound has never healed, and Amfortas lives with only one hope—that he will be saved by the fulfillment of a prophecy once heard in the silence of the temple.

As Gurnemanz ends his story and the esquires gather around him, the elderly knight repeats the words of the prophecy:

"Durch Mit - leid wis.-send, der rei - ne Thor har - re sein', den ich er - kor!",
"*Made wise through pi - ty, the guile - less fool wait for him, my cho - sen tool!*"

The four young esquires softly take up the prophetic chant. But at once, their meditations are shattered. A wounded swan circles overhead, flying desperately away from the lake—and soon, it drops to earth in its flight. Wild shouts are heard in the distance; the knights come up the pathway, dragging with them a strange, defiant youth.

Enter Parsifal and knights

Gurnemanz looks sadly at the dead swan and then at the swaggering youth, who flaunts a bow and arrow. So forcibly does the knight condemn this foolhardy murder, that the youth, overcome with shame, breaks his bow and arrow, casting them away.

"Who are you?" asks Gurnemanz. "Where do you come from?"

Parsifal

To the knight's every question, the boy can give only one answer: "I know not!" And as the knight observes the youth, he ponders, "Can this be the guileless fool of Amfortas' prophecy?"

Exeunt
knights

Still glancing intently at the boy, Gurnemanz bids his fellow knights remove the body of the swan. When they have gone, the youth speaks. "I have a mother," he says. "Her name is Broken-heart. Once we lived on the edge of the forest."

Gurne-
manz,
Kundry
and
Parsifal

At once, Kundry springs up from the ground. In her travels, she has seen many things—and she knows the youth's history. "His mother tried to keep him from the world!" she exclaims. "Just before he was born, his father Gamuret was slain in battle. Lest the boy be killed as well, his mother reared him far from armor and men."

Eagerly, the youth continues Kundry's story. "Yes!" he cries. "And once I saw a band of men with shining weapons. I followed them, but I was lost. Since then, I have fought my way through the world."

"And your mother?" asks Gurnemanz. "Does she not grieve for you?"

With savage laughter, Kundry exclaims, "I rode by her hut just now. She grieves no more—his mother is dead!"

The youth springs wildly at Kundry and Gurnemanz intervenes. "What harm has she done you?" cries the knight. "Kundry never lies!"

Trembling with sorrow, the youth is about to faint. Immediately, Kundry rushes to a near-by well and brings water to revive him. As Gurnemanz thanks her, she turns gloomily toward a thicket in the forest. Sleep fills her eyes. Desperately, she tries to resist—for she knows that Klingsor the magician is casting his spell from afar. If she succumbs, she will be transformed, on awakening, into a beautiful woman to work seduction among the knights of the Grail.

Exit
Kundry

"No!" she moans. "I must not slumber!" But the spell is too strong; unseen by Gurnemanz and the strange youth, Kundry sinks down behind the thicket.

Exeunt
Parsifal
and Gurne-
manz

And now, thinks Gurnemanz, the time has come to test this youth. He will take the boy to the solemn service of the Grail. Indeed, this lad might be the guileless fool of the prophecy! Gently, Gurnemanz leads him toward the sacred hall.

Originally, moving scenery marked the progress of Gurnemanz and the youth from the meadow to the hall of the Grail. Now, however, in most opera houses, the curtains are closed while the orchestra plays a profoundly stirring interlude (The Transformation Scene) based on two leading motives. The first, indicative of Amfortas' anguish, is known as The Cry to the Saviour:

and the second suggests the chiming bells of the temple:

SCENE 2: HALL OF THE GRAIL (39 Minutes)

Within the temple is a vast semi-circular altar, where the knights assemble. Amfortas is borne to the hall on his litter; it is time for him to unveil the Grail. From a tomb-like crypt comes the voice of Titurel, father of Amfortas. Too old and feeble to join the knights in their service, he lies beneath the temple, living only through the sustenance that the Grail affords him. "Unveil the sacred vessel!" he calls.

"No!" cries Amfortas. "Leave it unrevealed!" All the terrible implications of his sin and his spear-wound rise in the presence of the chalice. But finally, at the insistence of his father, Amfortas is forced to reveal the Grail. The hall is suffused with a soft glow; the bread and wine held by the knights become the body and blood of the Redeemer. At last, the Grail is extinguished—daylight returns to hall—and Amfortas, his wound broken out anew, is borne away.

All this time, the strange youth has been watching silently. Now, as the knights depart, Gurnemanz approaches him. "Tell me," he demands. "Do you understand what you have seen?"

The youth is speechless with sorrow. He lays his hand upon his heart—and Gurnemanz, failing to understand this gesture of pity, drives him from the temple. As the knight returns and kneels before the altar, a mysterious voice from above repeats the prophecy: "Made wise through pity, the guileless fool—wait for him, my chosen one!"

Gurnemanz
and Parsifal
Enter
knights
Titurel
(*off stage*)

Amfortas

Exeunt
knights
and
Amfortas

Exit
Parsifal

Act II

THE PRELUDE

*Destructive forces are at work in the prelude to the second act.
First we hear the motive of Klingsor:*

and then, the theme of Magic Slumber, to which Kundry is prey:

As the music subsides to an ominous whisper, the curtain rises.

SCENE 1: KLINGSOR'S CASTLE (16 Minutes)

Klingsor KLINGSOR, the magician, is seated in his dark tower, about to summon Kundry from the void below. She must seduce the guileless fool!

Enter Kundry Still sleeping, Kundry rises from the depths. Heavy veils cover her body, and her face is deathly white. With a shriek, she awakens; whimpering in fear, she awaits the order of Klingsor.

"There is work to be done!" exclaims the magician. "Even now the young fool is approaching my tower. You must lead him astray!"

Exit Kundry Ineffectually, Kundry rebels. She is striving to atone for the sins of her past. But Klingsor's will prevails. As the magician peers over the battlements of his castle, watching the arrival of the guileless fool, Kundry sinks through the ground. She has already brought destruction to Amfortas—now she must corrupt the chosen redeemer!

SCENE 2: THE MAGIC GARDENS (38 Minutes)

Flower maidens and Parsifal The strange youth, in his quest for adventure, has broken into Klingsor's garden and wounded the magician's effeminate knights. As he stands surveying the scene, he is surrounded by a group of flower maidens, who sing:

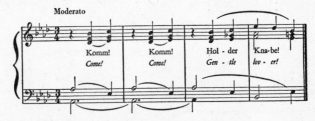

The youth resists their advances. Suddenly, from behind a hedge of the garden floats a voice of extreme beauty. It calls: "Parsifal!" And the youth recognizes the name which his mother once gave him.

At last, Kundry comes into sight, reclining on a bed of flowers. Now she is an enchantress, dazzling to behold. As the maidens disappear, Kundry beckons Parsifal to her side. In tender accents, she tells him the story of his mother, Brokenheart: how, through grief for her missing son, the woman has perished.

Enter Kundry

Exeunt flower maidens

"Alas!" cries Parsifal. "*I* have done this! *I* have caused my mother's death!"

"Acknowledge your sin," murmurs Kundry, "and grieve no more. I bring your mother's blessing—her kiss!"

The enchantress draws Parsifal toward her and holds him in a passionate embrace. But Parsifal thrusts her away. He feels the same anguish he experienced on seeing Amfortas unveil the Grail. He has learned compassion.

In vain does Kundry plead her own tragic history. "I was Herodias," she declares. "And when the Lord was on his way to the cross—*I laughed!* Now I am fated to wander until I find him again!" With all the subtle forces of seduction, Kundry urges Parsifal to redeem her. "Be mine for an hour," she cries, "and though I am rejected by God and world, I will be cleansed through you!"

Again the youth repulses her. And now, with raging fury, Kundry calls for Klingsor. "Come, help me!" she screams. "Take this fool for your victim!"

Klingsor appears on the terrace of the garden, bearing the sacred lance once stolen from Amfortas. He hurls it at Parsifal, who catches the spear in mid-air and makes the sign of the Cross. Immediately, Klingsor vanishes; the castle falls into ruins, and the magic flower garden becomes a desert. Parsifal scales the shattered walls and looks back at Kundry. "You may yet be redeemed through faith!" he declares. Then, carrying the lance, he sets off in search of Amfortas.

Enter Klingsor

Exit Klingsor

ACT III

THE PRELUDE

The chapter of knights has fallen into the deepest disgrace. No longer can Amfortas reveal the Grail. Even the faithful Gurnemanz has gone off to live as a hermit beyond the castle in solitude:

But soon there rise from the orchestra the redeeming phrases of the Prophecy and the Lance.

SCENE 1: A LANDSCAPE NEAR THE TEMPLE OF THE GRAIL
(47 Minutes)

Gurne-manz

ON a radiant afternoon in spring, Gurnemanz, now very old, is crossing the meadow in front of his hut. Suddenly, he hears unearthly groans issuing from a thicket near-by. Pushing through the underbrush, he discovers Kundry—apparently lifeless. Only after the greatest effort, is he able to revive the woman. She still wears the coarse brown garment by which Gurnemanz knows her, but her appearance has altered greatly. The wild, haunted look has left

Kundry

her; her sunburned face has grown ethereal. She murmurs, "I must serve!" and speaks no more.

Enter Parsifal

No sooner has Gurnemanz recovered from his surprise at Kundry's transformation, than a new wonder awaits him. Striding across the meadow, spear in hand, is a knight in black armor.

"Hail, O guest!" calls Gurnemanz. "Do you not know this is the realm of the Grail? Lay down your weapons—they will not serve you here!"

The unknown knight plunges his spear into the earth. Then, raising the visor of his helmet, he kneels in prayer—and Gurnemanz, overcome with emotion, recognizes the youth he expelled many years ago from the sanctuary.

"You have brought back the sacred lance!" cries the old knight, fervently.

Faint from his wanderings, Parsifal tells how he safeguarded the weapon—how, in the midst of danger, he never profaned it in battle. As he ends his tale, he asks wearily to be led to Amfortas.

"No longer can Amfortas reveal the Grail," Gurnemanz replies, "and our founder, Titurel, deprived of its light, has died."

Parsifal torments himself with a sense of guilt. Why has he not returned sooner? Overcome, he sinks upon a grassy mound—and, as in years past, the penitent Kundry tries to revive him. Gurne-

manz fetches water from the holy spring for the wanderer; and
while Kundry kneels at Parsifal's feet, anointing them with oil,
the old knight extends his arms in blessing:

Refreshed by Kundry's ministrations, Parsifal turns to Gurnemanz. "Today," he declares, "you shall proclaim me King of the
Grail."

As his first act of office, the new ruler baptizes the weeping
Kundry. Then he gazes with ecstasy upon the beauty of the
meadow.

"All nature is renewed today," explains Gurnemanz. "It is the
Good Friday spell."

"But alas!" Parsifal laments. "Should not this day be one of
grief and mourning?"

"Not so!" Gurnemanz answers. "The Saviour died on this day
that we might live; and nature rejoices."

The distant tolling of bells is heard. "Come," says the old knight.
"It is the funeral of my lord, Titurel!"

*As Gurnemanz and Parsifal solemnly march toward the hall of
the Grail, followed by Kundry, the scene again changes, as in the
first act. The pealing of bells grows louder until, as the curtains
open, we see the deserted interior of the sanctuary.*

Exeunt
Parsifal,
Gurne-
manz and
Kundry

SCENE 2: HALL OF THE GRAIL (19 Minutes)

The communion table has vanished from the altar. No longer
do the knights partake of the body and blood of Christ. And now,
the wretched Amfortas is borne into the hall, to officiate at the
rites for his father. "Reveal the Grail!" demand the knights.

Enter
knights
and
Amfortas

Brokenly, Amfortas kneels beside the body of his father and
prays for death. But the knights persist in their demand. "The
Grail!" they shout.

Amfortas refuses. Never again will he touch the chalice and
endure the pain that it causes him. Rending his garment, he cries,
"Here is my open wound. Plunge your swords into it. Kill me!"

Enter
Parsifal,
Gurne-
manz and
Kundry

At that moment, Parsifal enters the hall. "Only one weapon can end your suffering," he proclaims. "The weapon that pierced you!" Touching the lance to Amfortas' breast, he heals the deadly wound. Then he places the lance upon the altar and takes the Grail from its shrine. As he raises the sacred cup aloft, Kundry reaches out toward its radiance. Slowly, she sinks earthward, achieving her desire: a surcease from life and the promise of redemption.

A white dove descends and hovers over Parsifal. The soft light of the Grail fills the sanctuary; the prophecy has been fulfilled. The guileless fool has redeemed the brotherhood of Montsalvat!

VII

Opera Waves the Flag

In the age following the triumvirate of Rossini, Bellini and Donizetti, a new spirit permeated all phases of life in Italy. The rumblings of national revolt and liberation from the Austrian yoke made themselves felt in the music of the day. Gone were the languors of *Sonnambula* and the polished elegance of the *Barber of Seville*. Italian opera throbbed with a hot-blooded vitality.

Hardly by chance did Italian librettists of the mid-nineteenth century make crowned heads the villains of their operas; and certainly not by coincidence did these royal villains reap a swift and terrible revenge. In the midst of a stringent censorship, the theatre was the only outlet for the political emotions of a people who desperately craved freedom. The sensibilities of these audiences were particularly stirred by the music of Giuseppe Verdi. The stories of two of his operas, *Rigoletto* and *Ballo in Maschera*, were changed by the censor because of the slurs they cast upon royalty. In both cases, despite the alteration imposed by the authorities—shifting the plot to a different time and place—the audience *knew* what Verdi intended, and its patriotism was stirred to fever pitch.

Music which was created under such stress could not include subtlety as one of its attributes. The early operas of Verdi leaned heavily on thrilling episodes rather than on discriminating craftsmanship; while the vocal writing was expert, the texture of the orchestration had little life of its own.

If Verdi had been possessed only of national fervor, he would still be remembered as a composer above the average. He was endowed, however, with a capacity for development found in few other men of genius. By spending a lifetime in the cultivation of his art, he finally attained the full exercise of his powers. His skill in orchestration steadily developed until in *Aïda*, *Otello* and *Falstaff*, he set a model from which the Italian opera composers of our own generation still derive inspiration.

This marked evolution of Verdi from crude chauvinism to serene artistry was brought about by two great influences. One was Wagner, who made his innovations felt throughout Europe; and the other was the gifted Italian poet and composer Arrigo Boito (1842-1918), whose music drama *Mefistofele* (1868) made a profound impression upon Verdi.

With the development of Giuseppe Verdi, Italian opera evolved from the blood and thunder festivals of the 1840's into genuine music drama, maintaining only one important deviation from Wagnerian principles: while the orchestra was at all times important, the voice was still supreme. Vocalism, the birthright of Italian opera, has never yet been renounced.

VERDI

GIUSEPPE VERDI was born in the village of Le Roncole near Busseto on October 10, 1813, the son of an innkeeper and grocer. At ten he succeeded to the position of the village organist who had first taught him, but at eighteen was refused admission to the Milan Conservatory "on the score of the lack of musical talent."

Rigoletto, written in forty days and produced in Venice in 1851, ushered in Verdi's first period of brilliance, which included *Il Trovatore*, *La Traviata*, *Simon Boccanegra*, *La Forza del Destino* and *Don Carlos*. Gradually he turned to richer and more elaborate instrumentation and harmony which may be found in *Aïda*, *Otello* and *Falstaff*.

Verdi died in Milan in 1901, with a record of twenty-eight operas. The sensitiveness in characterization which marks his later works reflects the increased musical refinement of the nineteenth-century musical public, for which he is largely responsible.

RIGOLETTO

RIGOLETTO, *an opera in three acts, now given in four, was first performed at Venice in 1851. Verdi used the text of Piave, adapted from Victor Hugo's play,* Le Roi s'amuse. *The censorship at Venice required that the villain of the play—King Francis I—become the Duke of Mantua, and the title of the opera was changed to* Rigoletto, *the name of the Duke's court jester. It was as the Duke that Enrico Caruso made his Metropolitan debut in November, 1903.*

Characters, in order of appearance:
The Duke of Mantua: *tenor*
Borsa, a courtier: *tenor*
Countess Ceprano: *mezzo-soprano*
Count Ceprano: *bass*
Rigoletto: *baritone*
Marullo, a courtier: *bass*
Monterone: *baritone*
Sparafucile, an assassin: *bass*
Gilda, Rigoletto's daughter: *soprano*
Giovanna, her nurse: *mezzo-soprano*
A Page: *mezzo-soprano*
A Herald: *tenor*
Maddalena, Sparafucile's sister: *contralto*
Nobles and ladies of Mantua

Time: Sixteenth Century   *Place:* Mantua

ACT I

SCENE: A BALLROOM IN THE DUCAL PALACE (16 Minutes)

Duke, Borsa

THE Duke of Mantua, a corrupt prince of the Renaissance, strolls in the midst of the gay throng that fills his ballroom, bragging to the courtier Borsa of his conquests at love:

Que - sta o quel - la_____ per me pa - ri so - no a quant' al - tre
*In my heart all_____ are e - qual - ly cher-ish'd, Ev - 'ry thought_*

Countess Ceprano

In the adjoining chambers of the palace, dancers are joining in a minuet. The evening has reached the peak of its gaiety. Yet the beautiful Countess Ceprano is about to withdraw. She approaches the Duke in mute farewell.

"Cruel one!" he exclaims. "Why must you go?"

"My husband suspects us," whispers the Countess. "He insists that I leave."

Count Ceprano Enter Rigoletto

Exeunt Duke, Countess and Rigoletto Enter Marullo

Enter Duke and Rigoletto

Count Ceprano has put in a sullen appearance beside his wife. The situation is further strained by the entrance of Rigoletto, the jester. Ugly, deformed, hated by all for his lashing tongue, the fool prances forward crying, "Oho! A penny for Ceprano's thoughts! Is his Lordship displeased?"

Disregarding Ceprano's anger, the Duke of Mantua accompanies the Countess to the door. Rigoletto smirkingly follows. After the jester has left the room, his enemies voice their contempt. "I have heard," remarks a courtier named Borsa, "that the fool keeps a young mistress hidden away in town." Borsa quickly breaks off, for jester and Duke have returned, absorbed in conversation.

"I must possess her!" whispers the Duke.

"Then get rid of Ceprano," Rigoletto answers, loudly enough for the Count to overhear. "Imprison him—send him into exile—behead him!"

Ceprano is goaded to fury. "Help me punish the jester!" he whispers to Borsa and Marullo. "We'll abduct his mistress!"

Once again, the gay throng has joined in the dance. The Duke sits on his throne, watching the revelry. At his feet squats Rigoletto. Suddenly, through the corridors of the palace, there rings a shout: "I will speak to him!" The doors are burst open and Monterone, an elderly noble, forces his way into the chamber. His daughter has been seduced by the Duke.

Enter Monterone

Rigoletto seizes the occasion for a display of wit. "You are committing treason, sir," he declares, with a mocking bow. "Why this nonsense about your daughter's honor?"

"Another insult!" cries Monterone. "But your mirth will soon end. Upon you, oh, Duke of Mantua, and you, vile jester, I place a solemn malediction!"

The outraged father is led away by palace guards. As the Duke leaves the hall and the guests scatter in dismay, Rigoletto sinks beside the throne, brooding on the curse of Monterone.

Exit Duke Monterone led away

ACT II

SCENE: A STREET NEAR THE HOUSE OF RIGOLETTO (40 Minutes)

IT is late at night. The jester, returning homeward, passes through a deserted street. At the left is his modest house, with its walled-in courtyard, near the ramparts of the Ceprano palace.

Enter Rigoletto

Rigoletto walks among the deep shadows, lost in fear and despair. His worries turn to real terror when he is accosted by the sinister Sparafucile, professional assassin:

Enter Sparafucile

Andante mosso

"You need protection against your enemies," the murderer observes. "Would you have me remove them?"

"What is your price?" demands Rigoletto.

"Half before the deed is done," Sparafucile replies, "and the remainder upon completion. My sister, Maddalena, lures the victim to a tavern outside the city. I do the rest."

Rigoletto hesitates. "Perhaps I shall call upon you. Now begone!"

The assassin disappears in the shadows. "We are alike!" the jester reflects bitterly. "He strikes in the darkness—I stab by day with my poisoned wit."

Exit Sparafucile

As Rigoletto enters the courtyard of his house, his baser qualities are overshadowed by paternal love. Gilda, his daughter, whom he has brought secretly to Mantua and kept hidden for the past three months, comes running to meet him.

Enter Gilda

"Gilda!" he calls. "Have you obeyed me? Have you stayed at home?"

The girl is evasive. "Yes, father. But why this restraint? I have gone only to church."

Enter
Giovanna

"There are men in this town," mutters Rigoletto, "who would gladly separate us." Summoning Gilda's nurse, Giovanna, he makes sure that no one has visited the house.

Enter
Duke

The jester hears footsteps in the street. Fearful that his secret has been discovered, he opens the gate and peers into the darkness. Unseen by Rigoletto, the Duke slips into the courtyard and conceals himself.

Exit
Rigoletto

Apparently, the jester's fears are groundless—the street is deserted. Rigoletto fondly bids Gilda farewell. When he has gone, the girl is tormented by doubts. "Should I not have told my father, Giovanna, of the young man who followed me from church?"

Giovanna, in the pay of the Duke, replies, "There was no need for it."

"The youth was so handsome," Gilda continues. "In my dreams I have often said to him, 'I—'"

"'Love you!'" cries the Duke, stepping forward and taking Gilda in his arms.

Enter
Ceprano
and
courtiers

Gilda is about to yield, when suddenly a party of men is heard outside the courtyard. Count Ceprano and his friends have come to take revenge on Rigoletto. Knowing nothing of their plans, the Duke suspects a trap.

"I am a poor student," he hurriedly tells Gilda. "My name is Walter Maldè. And now I must go—we'll meet again!"

Exit Duke
Exit
Giovanna

Gilda embraces her lover. After he has escaped through a remote alley, the girl is left with glowing memories. "Walter Maldè," she exclaims. "Beloved name!"

Allegro moderato

Ca - ro no - me, che il mio cor fe - sti pri - mo pal - pi - tar.
Carv'd up - on my in - most heart is that name for ev - er - more.

Exit
Gilda

Slowly, with lantern in hand, she ascends the outer staircase of the house, and retires to her room. In the street below, the conspirators prepare to carry out their plot. They will achieve an even more exquisite revenge than they had hoped for—Rigoletto is returning home!

Enter
Rigoletto

As the jester approaches in the darkness, Ceprano hides and his colleague, Marullo, advances. "Good evening, Rigoletto," he calls. "There's intrigue abroad. Will you help us abduct the Countess?"

The jester's perversity rises to the surface. He eagerly consents. "Then wear this mask," Marullo orders, "and carry a ladder."

Blindfolded, Rigoletto mistakes his own house for the adjoining Ceprano palace, and places the ladder against the garden wall. The conspirators break into the courtyard and escape with Gilda. Intent upon the vicious sport, Rigoletto does not even hear his daughter's cries for help. But as an unnatural silence settles over the street, he grows restive. Tearing aside the mask, he sees the open gate. In the distance, the courtiers shout, "Victory!" Gasping with apprehension, the jester rushes to Gilda's room. Only a scarf remains, dropped by the girl in her struggle with the abductors.

Exeunt courtiers carrying Gilda

Rigoletto staggers wildly from the house. "The curse!" he cries. "It is upon me!"

ACT III

SCENE: A ROOM IN THE DUCAL PALACE (28 Minutes)

THE Duke has returned to Rigoletto's house and found Gilda gone. Despondent at his loss, he remains in seclusion. But soon, the courtiers appear and reveal their trick on Rigoletto. As a sign of their triumph, they have brought the girl to the palace. At once, the Duke rushes from the chamber, intent upon possessing Gilda.

The Duke

Enter courtiers Exit Duke

And then comes the pathetic spectacle of Rigoletto, searching for his daughter—he who has so often laughed at the misery of others. At first, the jester greets the courtiers as banteringly as ever:

Enter Rigoletto

Allegro moderato

La, ra, la ra, la ra, la ra, la ra, la ra, la ra.

Only by his roving eye, by the way he scans the room for a trace of Gilda, does he reveal his suffering.

A young page in the service of the neglected Duchess of Mantua asks for the Duke, and is told he cannot be disturbed.

Page

"Ah!" cries Rigoletto, whose suspicions have been fully aroused. "Then she must be here! The girl you have stolen *is my daughter!*"

Even his enemies are moved by the jester's grief; but they bar his way when he attempts to break into the private apartments of the Duke.

"Vile courtiers!" he shouts. "Accursed race! Give her back to me!"

At last, the inner door opens and Gilda runs to her father. Rigoletto orders the courtiers to withdraw.

Enter Gilda

Sadly, Gilda tells her father of the Duke's treachery. The jester comforts the girl and promises to take her away from Mantua. As

Exeunt courtiers

Enter
Herald and
Monterone
he speaks, a grim procession passes through the hall—Monterone is being led to prison. The aged man glances at a portrait of the Duke that hangs upon the wall.

Exeunt
Herald and
Monterone
"My curse has not reached you," he exclaims bitterly. "Live on, O Duke!" Led away by a herald, Monterone marches to the oblivion of his cell.

Only Rigoletto remains in the room with Gilda. Staring fixedly at the portrait, he cries, "You are wrong, Monterone. Not your curse, but mine will claim this villain!"

In vain does Gilda try to calm her father. Hurling her to the ground, Rigoletto shouts his hatred of the Duke. "Prepare, wretched prince! The jester's vengeance will strike like a thunderbolt from the throne of God!"

Si ven - det - ta, tre - men - da ven - det - ta,
Yes, my ___ ven - geance ___ fierce has ___ doomed thee,

Act IV

SCENE: SPARAFUCILE'S TAVERN (32 Minutes)

Enter
Rigoletto
and Gilda

RIGOLETTO has perfected his plan for revenge. On a dark night, he stands outside the lonely inn where Sparafucile, the assassin, dispatches his victims. With him is Gilda, who still loves the Duke. Forcing his daughter to look inside the tavern, Rigoletto shows her the debauched ruler of Mantua, who has just arrived incognito.

Enter
Duke

He is clamoring for wine and a bed. While waiting to be served, the Duke sings a rousing ballad about the inconstancy of women:

La don-na è mo-bi -le qual piuma al ven - to, mu-ta d'ac - cen - to e di pen - sie - ro.
Wo-man is fick - le, way-ward-ly play-ing, ne'er one way sway- ing, each whim o - bey - ing

Enter
Maddalena

Soon the object of his visit appears: Maddalena, the attractive sister of Sparafucile. The Duke has followed her to the inn, little knowing the fate that awaits him. As he makes love, Maddalena rebuffs him with professional coyness.

Quartet

Bel -la fig - lia dell' a - mo - re, schia-vo son de' vez -zi tuo - i;
Fair - est daugh-ter of the Grac - es, I, thy hum-ble slave im - plore ___ thee;

Gilda, who sees all, is grief-stricken. Rigoletto consoles her, vowing inwardly that the Duke will perish.

"Now quickly, Gilda," instructs the jester. "You'll find money and a boy's attire at home. Go at once to Verona. I shall follow."

The girl departs. Rigoletto is soon joined by Sparafucile.

Exit Gilda
Enter
Sparafucile

"Your man has arrived," declares the assassin.

"Here are twenty scudi," the jester replies. "I'll be back at midnight with more when the body is delivered to me."

A storm has arisen: sighing wind, thunder. Rigoletto goes off and Sparafucile re-enters the inn, where Maddalena is awaiting him. "The young man has gone to his room," she announces. "He is handsome, he attracts me. Why can't you spare him?"

Exeunt
Rigoletto
Maddalena
and
Sparafucile

"No!" exclaims Sparafucile. "There is only one way out—if a stranger arrives here before twelve, I'll kill him, stuff the body in a sack, and give it to the jester."

Gilda has returned in male attire to the neighborhood of the tavern, drawn by her unhappy love for the Duke. Poised on the threshold, she overhears the bloodthirsty conversation of Sparafucile and his sister. Weary of life, the girl determines to sacrifice herself for the Duke. She knocks at the door of the inn, calling, "Please give shelter to a poor traveler." The door opens; Sparafucile drags his unknown victim within, and strikes in the darkness.

Enter
Gilda

Exit Gilda
Enter
Rigoletto
Enter
Sparafucile

At midnight Rigoletto returns. True to his promise, Sparafucile appears with a sack. He offers to toss the burden in a near-by river.

"No!" Rigoletto exclaims. "This moment is for me!"

Sparafucile shrugs his shoulders, enters the tavern and bolts the door. Rigoletto remains, gloating over the sack. He is about to fling it into the stream, when suddenly he hears a familiar voice in the distance singing, "Woman is fickle!"

Exit
Sparafucile

Duke
(*off stage*)

"That voice!" he cries. "No, it cannot be. The Duke is slain."

The melody persists and a horrible presentiment seizes Rigoletto. Opening the sack, he finds the mutilated body of Gilda. She is on the verge of death, and lingers only to bid her father farewell.

Gilda

For a moment, Rigoletto stares blankly at the huddled figure. Then, with a shriek of despair, he falls upon the corpse. Monterone's curse is fulfilled.

SIMON BOCCANEGRA

SIMON BOCCANEGRA, *a melodrama in three acts and a prologue, was first produced at Venice in 1857, with only indifferent success. The story was considered too gloomy, and the plot excessively complicated. Many years later, when Verdi had acquired the creative technique of his last period, he salvaged the more satisfactory portions of the early* Simon *and added much new music that ranks with his finest pages. At the same time, the original text of F. M. Piave was revised by the librettist of* Otello *and* Falstaff: *Arrigo Boito. The opera was presented in its new form at La Scala, Milan, in 1880, with Maurel, Tamagno, and Edouard de Reszke in the leading male roles. It is this later version which first appeared at the Metropolitan in 1931, with Lawrence Tibbett, Giovanni Martinelli and Ezio Pinza.*

Characters, in order of appearance:

Paolo Albiani, a gold-spinner of Genoa: *baritone*
Pietro, Genoese commoner: *bass*
Simon Boccanegra, a corsair, later Doge of Genoa:
    baritone
Jacopo Fiesco, a Genoese nobleman, later disguised
    as Andrea: *bass*
Amelia Grimaldi (really Maria, the daughter of Boc-
    canegra): *soprano*
Gabriele Adorno, her lover: *tenor*
Amelia's maidservant: *soprano*
A captain of the guard: *tenor*
Soldiers, seamen, commoners, senators, Court of the
    Doge

Time: Fourteenth Century   *Place:* Genoa.

The Prologue
scene: a square in genoa (25 Minutes)

Genoa of the fourteenth century is torn by internal strife. Class warfare rages through the city as a new Doge is to be chosen. Two ambitious commoners—Paolo Albiani, the goldsmith, and Pietro, his accomplice, have determined to set up a puppet ruler of their own. Appealing to the prejudices of their class against the nobles, they are bound to win the election.

And now Paolo is huddled with Pietro in a great square of the city. Behind them, the cathedral of Genoa towers in the moonlight. Opposite, a huge palace stands deserted, only a dim taper burning in its windows—it is the dwelling of the hated aristocrat, Fiesco.

Paolo and Pietro

"I have a candidate!" Paolo whispers. "We shall turn the mob in favor of Simon Boccanegra. They know him for his bravery on the sea."

"And what will be our reward?" demands Pietro.

"Wealth, power and glory!"

As Pietro goes off into the town to stir the populace, Paolo gazes defiantly at the palace of the Fiescos. "Abhorred aristocrats!" he mutters. "Before long, I will be sharing your power!"

Exit Pietro

He turns quickly, on hearing someone enter the square. It is Boccanegra, a young corsair in the service of Genoa.

Enter Simon

"I greet you, friend," calls Simon. "Why have you sent for me?"

"Have you never longed for the Doge's crown?"

"You are dreaming!" laughs Boccanegra. "I cannot be tempted!"

Paolo is determined to force Simon into office through persuasion. "What of Maria Fiesco?" he asks the corsair. "Her proud father keeps you from her because you are a commoner. If you were Doge, nothing could stand in your way!"

Simon glances unhappily at the palace where his beloved Maria is held prisoner by her father. "Paolo," he exclaims, "I will join you!"

"Then go into hiding until the moment of the election!" Simon withdraws, and Paolo, with growing interest, watches a crowd of commoners approach the cathedral. Assembled by Pietro, they pledge themselves to the support of Boccanegra.

Exit Simon Enter Pietro, seamen and commoners

The crowd disperses; Paolo and Pietro go elsewhere to continue their plotting—and the gates of the Fiesco palace swing open. Like a messenger of doom, Jacopo Fiesco descends into the square.

Exeunt all Enter Fiesco

"Farewell, proud dwelling!" he exclaims. "I leave you forever!" As the wailing cry of "Miserere!" floats from the palace, the nobleman weeps. His daughter Maria is dead.

Andante sostenuto

Il la - ce - ra - to spi - ri - to del mes - to ge - ni - to - re
I am be - reft of her I love, and I must bear this an - guish!

Enter
Simon

Fiesco's sorrow turns to rage when he sees Boccanegra lingering in the square. The corsair knows nothing of Maria's death; filled with the hope of victory, Simon expects to win the girl as his bride. But as he approaches the palace, Fiesco bars his way.

For years, the nobleman has hated Simon—hated him for being a commoner, and for having been the father of Maria's natural child. Now he reviles the corsair anew.

"My lord," Simon pleads, "I beg your forgiveness! Can there never be peace between us?"

"No!" Fiesco answers gloomily. "Never—unless you yield me the daughter that Maria bore you."

"I cannot!" Simon laments. "The nurse who cared for my daughter fell ill and died—before I could reach her cottage near Pisa, my child had vanished."

"Farewell then, Simon," declares Fiesco. "We shall always be enemies!"

Despairing of further talk, Boccanegra runs to the palace door and knocks three times. There is no answer. He enters and climbs the massive staircase, as Fiesco watches below. Suddenly, Simon emerges from the building with a cry of horror—he has seen Maria's corpse.

In the distance, church bells are ringing—the city is fired with delirious excitement. "Boccanegra!" the people are calling. "Boccanegra!"

Fiesco listens with dismay. "Is this commoner to ascend the throne?" he exclaims.

Enter
Paolo,
Pietro and
people

In a rhythmic, swaying mass, the people have invaded the square. Rejoicing, they lift the reluctant Boccanegra on their shoulders. At the peak of his triumph, Simon cannot take his eyes from the palace of the Fiescos. "A tomb!" he exclaims.

"No!" shouts Paolo, who leads the noisy demonstration. "A throne!"

Act I

Scene 1: THE GRIMALDI GARDENS (31 Minutes)

TWENTY-FIVE years have elapsed since Simon Boccanegra became Doge of Genoa. Advised in all his policies by the ambitious Paolo, he has expropriated the large estates of the nobles and sent his enemies into exile.

Under such conditions, life has become intolerable for Fiesco. Vowing to overthrow the Doge, he has organized a conspiracy of his political party—the Guelphs—who meet secretly outside of Genoa. As a precautionary measure, Fiesco does not even use his own name—hatred against the nobles is so keen in Genoa that he is in danger of his life. And thus, under the pseudonym of Andrea, he lives in the Grimaldi palace overlooking the sea.

The dwelling is filled with intrigue. Even Amelia, the nominal descendant of the house, has been drawn into the web of politics. She is an orphan, found in the cloister of Pisa on the very day that the real Amelia Grimaldi died. In order to keep the estate from passing into the hands of the Doge and his favorites, Fiesco—a trusted friend of the Grimaldi family—has raised this orphan as the legitimate heiress, without revealing her identity.

Now, grown to womanhood, Amelia stands in the terraced gardens of the palace, gazing at the sea. *Amelia*

Lento assai

Co - me in quest'o - ra bru - na sor - ri - - don gli a-stri e il ma - - re!
In___ this au - ror - al hour___ How sweet - ly smiles the sea! ___

Suddenly, her young lover appears: Gabriele Adorno, a nobleman who is plotting with Andrea (Fiesco) for the overthrow of the Doge. *Enter Gabriele*

"O Gabriele, cease your intrigues!" Amelia pleads. "I am afraid. The city is full of spies—you may be imprisoned at any moment!"

Even as Amelia speaks, she breaks off nervously—for she sees a mysterious shadow hovering near the garden wall. Her terror increases when her maid appears with the news that the Doge is in the palace. *Enter maid-servant Exit maid-servant*

"The Doge?" exclaims Gabriele.

"Yes," Amelia replies nervously. "He comes to sue for my hand in behalf of his favorite, Paolo."

"Then we must wed at once!" Gabriele declares. "I'll go to your guardian, Andrea, and ask his consent."

Amelia hastens into the palace, and Gabriele anxiously seeks out Andrea. He has no trouble in obtaining the guardian's blessing, although the elderly man reveals that Amelia is not a true Grimaldi. *Enter Fiesco Exeunt Gabriele and Fiesco Enter Simon and Paolo*

"No matter!" cries Gabriele. "I love her!"

A flourish of trumpets is heard; the two conspirators withdraw. Soon the Doge appears, vigorous and hardy—but his hair is gray, and his face lined with sorrow.

Enter
Amelia
Exit
Paolo

As Amelia advances to meet him, Simon turns to his followers. "You may go now," he orders. "Paolo, we leave within the hour." The attendants depart, Paolo gazing lustfully at the Grimaldi heiress.

"I have come on an important mission," the Doge tells Amelia. "Your noble house must be reconciled to the state of Genoa. Thus I have brought a pardon for your brothers in exile. And, O noble lady—why hide yourself in this lonely palace? Have you never cared for the delights of love?"

Disarmed by the Doge's kindly manner, Amelia resolves to seek his protection. "I know, my lord," she declares, "that you are here in behalf of Paolo, who craves my inheritance. But to you alone, I must confess: I am not Grimaldi's daughter."

The Doge looks at her in astonishment. "Then who are you? Speak!"

"I have no family. My earliest memories are of a cottage on the seacoast near Pisa, where a kindly nurse watched over me. Often, she showed me the picture of my mother. But alas, my nurse lies buried!"

Simon is filled with hope at these words. "Did a seafaring man ever visit your house?" he whispers. "And was your nurse's name Giovanna?"

"Yes," Amelia answers in surprise.

"And this picture—is it not that of your mother?" Taking a medallion from his bosom, he gives it to the girl.

"Wait!" Amelia exclaims. "Here is my locket—the two portraits are alike!"

"Maria!" cries the Doge. "My own child!"

Tenderly, Simon embraces the girl and describes the happy future that lies in store for both of them. Obliged to depart, he bids Amelia farewell with the precious word: "Daughter!"

SCENE 2: THE COUNCIL CHAMBER (22 Minutes)

Nobles,
com-
moners,
Simon,

The Doge has abruptly broken off all negotiations in behalf of Paolo. "Amelia Grimaldi is not for you!" Simon tells the courtier.

Paolo grows bitterly resentful. He has put Simon on the throne to do his bidding—and now this ex-corsair has turned against him.

Together with his accomplice, Pietro, Paolo decides there is only Paolo and Pietro one course open—to abduct Amelia. While they blandly attend a meeting in the council hall of Genoa, their hirelings snatch the girl from the Grimaldi gardens and carry her to the house of Lorenzino, the money lender.

Suddenly, as the council is in session, a riotous noise is heard from the street. "Death to the Doge!" voices are shouting. The din of fighting becomes more terrifying—the populace is marching on the council chamber.

Simon fearlessly rises from his throne and mounts the balcony of the palace. Looking down into the square below, he sees Gabriele Adorno battling a mob of commoners. At the side of Adorno fights an elderly noble whom Simon does not recognize.

Paolo, too, has left his place and gone to look into the square. On seeing Gabriele, he turns deathly pale. Has the theft of Amelia been discovered? Has Adorno come to claim revenge? He is about to slink from the room when Simon Boccanegra fixes him with an imperious glance.

"Consuls of the sea!" commands the Doge. "Keep to the doors. Whoever flees admits he is a traitor!"

Paolo stops short in embarrassment and returns to his chair. "Let the gates be opened to the mob!" the Doge continues. "Tell them I am not afraid!"

In answer to his order, the consuls unlock the doors. At once, Enter Gabriele, Fiesco and people the people of Genoa come streaming into the chamber. "Vengeance!" they shout. "We want the blood of Adorno!"

"Be silent!" the Doge commands. "Gabriele Adorno, why are you accused? What have you done?"

"I have killed Lorenzino!" Gabriele answers defiantly. "He abducted Amelia Grimaldi—and before he died, he whispered that a man of rank and power had urged him to the crime."

Simon looks at the young nobleman in consternation. "Tell me the name!" he orders.

"You need not worry," Adorno sneers. "Lorenzino died before he could reveal your secret."

"What do you mean?" shouts the Doge in terrible anger.

"I mean that you were her abductor!" cries Gabriele. "Infamous pirate—prepare for death!" The nobleman raises his sword and is Enter Amelia about to plunge it in Simon's breast, when Amelia appears and rushes between them.

"Stop!" she screams. Gabriele is disarmed. "O Sire," pleads Amelia, "spare Adorno's life!"

"No man shall touch him!" the Doge replies. "He may keep his sword—but this night he must stay as prisoner. . . . Now, O maiden, tell me the name of your abductor."

"He is in this chamber," Amelia answers. "He hears me; his fear betrays him."

"His name!" demands the Doge.

"He is a noble!" shout the commoners.

"A churl!" retort the aristocrats.

All the members of the chamber draw their swords—a bloody battle seems likely. "Put down your weapons!" cries Simon. "You are all sons of Genoa!"

Andante mosso

Ple - be!   Pa - tri - zii!   Po - po - lo   dal - la   fe - ro - ce   sto - ria!
No - bles!   Ye - peo - ple!   Fra - tri - cides!   Sons   of   a   venge - ful   ci - ty!

Impressed by their ruler's words, the mob that crowds the chamber becomes strangely quiet. "Paolo!" the Doge calls sternly.

"Yes, my lord," answers the schemer.

"Paolo, I have need of your help. In you is vested the honor of the people. There is a scoundrel within these walls who is guilty of the crime against Amelia. May justice fall upon the rogue! *May he be cursed!*"

Gazing steadily at Paolo, the Doge commands: "Repeat the curse with me!"

Exit
Paolo

Sick with fright and horror, Paolo forces out the words: *"May he be cursed!"* He rushes from the hall—the people disperse— Gabriele and his accomplice Andrea are led to prison—and the Doge stands in the center of the mighty chamber, holding his daughter in his arms.

Act II
SCENE: THE DOGE'S CHAMBERS (29 Minutes)

Enter
Paolo
Enter
Fiesco and
Gabriele

UNMASKED by the Doge—an outcast from the Senate—Paolo has decided to flee from Genoa. But before the moment of his flight, he will have revenge on Simon! Stealing into the Doge's chamber, he pours a phial of poison in the drinking bowl that stands on Simon's desk. Then, to make doubly sure that his enemy will not escape him, he orders Pietro to lead Gabriele and Fiesco from their cells.

Exit
Fiesco

In vain does Paolo persuade Fiesco to assassinate the Doge. Refusing any part of the plan, the elderly aristocrat returns to his cell. Gabriele is about to follow, but Paolo detains him. "Listen!" the schemer whispers. "Do you know that Amelia is here in the palace? And that she is signaled for the Doge's shameful pleasure?"

Before Gabriele can answer, Paolo dashes from the room and locks the door. Escape is impossible for the young noble. As he remains in the chamber and broods on Paolo's words, Adorno's anger rises to a frenzied pitch. "Boccanegra slew my father," he exclaims, "and now this pirate proposes to rob me of my love. He shall die!" Exit
Paolo

Largo

Cie - lo pie - to - so, ren - di - la, ren - di - la a que - sto co - re.
Hea - ven, O guard my love, I pray, shel - ter her and bring her back to me.

Suddenly, Amelia enters the gallery and starts back in alarm on seeing Gabriele. "Who opened your prison door?" she demands. Enter
Amelia

"And you?" cries Gabriele. "Have you come to gratify Simon's pleasure?"

"He loves me," Amelia exclaims. "But, O Gabriele, believe me— I am yours!"

The girl can speak no further. A flourish of trumpets has been sounded, announcing the approach of the Doge. "You must hide!" she whispers. Just as she secretes Adorno in an alcove, Simon enters the room. Exit
Gabriele
Enter
Simon

Wearied by the events of the day, the Doge still notices that his daughter has been weeping "Why are you sad?" he asks gently. "Are you concealing something from me?"

Amelia gravely confesses. "I am in love with your foe, Gabriele Adorno."

"Adorno!" the Doge exclaims. "It was he who stirred the Guelphs against me. I have written his name on the death list."

So stirringly does Amelia plead the cause of her lover that Simon finally relents. "Go now, my daughter," he asks. "I must await the coming of dawn."

Fearing for the Doge's life—and yet unwilling to betray Adorno— Amelia begs Simon to let her remain. "Go," he answers wearily. "I wish it."

Amelia leaves the chamber; the Doge, overcome with fatigue, pours the poisoned liquid from the drinking bowl. He tastes it— and as he swallows, he remarks sadly, "Even clear water is bitter to the lips of him that rules!" Exit
Amelia

Soon, he falls asleep. Gabriele, who has seen everything but over-heard none of the conversation, approaches the Doge and lifts his dagger. On the point of striking, he is restrained by Amelia, who has quickly returned. Enter
Gabriele
Enter
Amelia

"Why do you protect this man?" Adorno demands.

As the lovers speak in an excited whisper, the Doge awakens and sees Gabriele's knife. "Strike, if you wish!" he cries. "You have already stolen all I have in the world: my daughter!"

In abject humility, Gabriele kneels before the Doge and asks forgiveness. The Doge hesitates—finally he extends his hand.

And now, threatening voices are heard outside the palace. The Guelphs have risen and are invading Simon's stronghold, resolved to slay him. "Go, join your people," the Doge counsels Gabriele.

"Never!" Adorno exclaims. "I'll wield my sword with yours!"

Drawing their blades, Simon and Gabriele rush to defend the gateway of the palace. Through love of Amelia, noble and commoner have been united.

Act III

SCENE: INTERIOR OF THE DUCAL PALACE (27 Minutes)

Enter Fiesco and captain
Exit captain

THE rebellion of the Guelphs has been completely crushed. Joyous at the final restoration of peace, Genoa is lighted as for a festival— and in his mercy, Simon has spared most of the rebel leaders. Even the active spearhead of the movement, whom the Doge knows as Andrea, has been given his liberty.

"O wretched day!" Fiesco exclaims, when he is set free by the guard. "All my plans have come to naught!"

Enter Paolo

As the noble stands morosely in a gallery of the palace, he sees the traitorous Paolo being led to execution. The schemer has been found in the ranks of the Guelphs, and is to die by order of Simon.

"I am condemned," cries the villain, "but Boccanegra will follow me in death. I have poisoned him!"

Exit Paolo
Enter captain

"Base scoundrel!" Fiesco murmurs. As Paolo is dragged away, shrieking defiantly, Fiesco withdraws into the shadows. A captain is approaching, preceded by a trumpeter, and the elderly noble watches them from behind the throne.

Solemnly, the captain ascends the balcony of the palace. "Ye townsfolk!" he calls. "It is the Doge's will that all your festive lights be dimmed, and that no one offend with clamorous joy the memory of the fallen heroes."

Exit captain
Enter Simon

As the captain and trumpeter leave the hall, gloom falls upon the city. One by one, the lights are extinguished. And now Simon appears, groping his way through the darkened hall. His temples throb —his veins are ablaze. Clutching the arm of the ducal chair, he sinks down to rest. "Ah!" he sighs. "For a breath of air—for a cooling breeze! O glorious sea, why were you not the corsair's tomb?"

"It would have been better so!" declares a voice from behind the throne.

Alarmed, the Doge looks about him—he calls the guard—but there is no answer. Fiesco, his ancient foe, advances triumphantly. "Your hour has come, Simon!" he exclaims.

Largo

Del-le fa-ci fes-tan-ti al bar-lu-me ci fre ar-ca-ne, fu-ne-bri ve-dra-i.
Where the torch-es are gleam-ing in glor-y, now a sin-is-ter gloom slow-ly falls.

"Fiesco!" cries the Doge. "Is it you? Then peace can finally reign between us. You once swore to befriend me if I ever restored to you the child of Maria. I have found her—as Amelia Grimaldi."

"Alas!" Fiesco laments. "If only I could befriend you now! Simon, you have been poisoned!"

"I know it well!" whispers Simon. "I can feel the hold of death upon me!" Fighting for his last measure of strength, he strives to sit upright on his throne as the courtiers enter the chamber. The marriage of Amelia and Gabriele has just been celebrated; the couple have come to ask the blessing of the Doge.

Enter Amelia, Gabriele and courtiers

"Andrea!" exclaims Amelia in surprise, as she sees the Guelph in converse with Simon, his hated enemy.

"This is Jacopo Fiesco," Simon murmurs. "O daughter, behold your grandsire!"

"Then these feuds are at an end!"

"Yes," gasps the Doge, "everything has an end. I am dying. Fiesco, mark my words and follow my decree. I bequeath my ducal crown to Gabriele Adorno!" Breathing the name of his daughter, Simon expires.

With genuine grief for the man whose friendship he knew too late, Fiesco ascends the balcony of the palace. "People of Genoa!" he calls. "Hail your new sovereign—Gabriele Adorno!"

"No!" shout indignant voices from the square. "Boccanegra!"

"He is dead," Fiesco sighs, as the bells of the city toll mournfully. "Peace be upon his soul!"

IL TROVATORE
(*THE TROUBADOUR*)

IL TROVATORE, *an opera in four acts with libretto by Cammanaro,
made its debut at the* Teatro Apollo (*Rome*) *in January, 1853. Since
that time, Verdi's melodrama has been among the most frequently
performed Italian works. The first Metropolitan presentation took
place during the house's opening season—1883.*

Characters, in order of appearance:
Ferrando, a captain of the guard: *bass*
Leonora, a noble lady of Aragon: *soprano*
Inez, her attendant: *soprano*
The Count di Luna: *baritone*
Manrico, a troubadour: *tenor*
Azucena, a gypsy: *mezzo-soprano*
Ruiz, a friend to Manrico: *tenor*
Servants and soldiers of the Count di Luna, gypsies,
followers of Manrico

Time: Fifteenth Century   *Place:* Biscay and Aragon

ACT I—*The Duel*

SCENE 1: A VESTIBULE IN THE PALACE OF ALIAFERIA (10 Minutes)
*A twice repeated drum roll, followed by a burst of trumpets, sets
a chivalric mood for the opening scene:*

Allegro assai sostenuto

212

It is nearly midnight. Servants and soldiers of the Count di Luna are lolling in a hall of the palace, overcome with drowsiness. Only Ferrando, the captain of the guard, keeps watch. "Bestir yourselves!" he warns the servants. "The Count may be here at any moment."

Ferrando and servants

At once, the attendants shake off their lethargy. They gossip of their master—how every night he keeps watch beneath the window of the beautiful Leonora—and how he has been driven to jealousy by an unknown troubadour who serenades the lady.

But their conversation wanes and sleep again fills their eyes. "Keep us awake, Ferrando!" they urge. "Tell us a story—perhaps the old tale about the Count's ill-fated brother."

Ferrando gladly obliges. "Once there was a gypsy," he relates, "who broke into our palace. She invaded the room of young Garzia di Luna, the Count's brother, and bewitched him. Luckily, she was caught—but from that day on, the child's health began to fail.

"The gypsy hag was put to death—and even then, our misfortunes did not end! Her fierce daughter abducted Garzia and burned him at the very stake where the mother had perished."

By now, the servants and soldiers of di Luna are thoroughly roused. "Has the daughter never been captured?" they demand.

"No!" Ferrando answers. "We have sought her for years. I would know her at once if I saw her—but our search has been vain!"

The darkness of the night and the gloom of Ferrando's tale have begun to affect the nerves of the soldiers. As the clock strikes twelve, they cry out in fright and bolt the castle doors. "Heaven guard us against the powers of evil!"

SCENE 2: THE GARDENS OF THE PALACE (17 Minutes)

The Queen of Aragon is in residence at the palace of Aliaferia, awaiting the outcome of the civil war that has torn Spain asunder. Brother has been fighting against brother—Aragon against Biscay.

In the service of the Queen is a noble lady named Leonora. Accompanied by her companion, Inez, she has stolen from the palace—and now she appears in the garden, intent upon meeting the troubadour who serenades her nightly.

Leonora and Inez

Exit Inez

"Leonora!" begs her companion. "You are foolhardy! Forget this stranger!"

"I cannot!" Leonora answers. "I love him!"

Di ta - le_a-mor, che dir . . . . . si
The love my heart o'er flow . . . . . . ing

Exit
Leonora
Enter
Count
di Luna

Awaiting the song of the unknown knight, she goes within. The garden is deserted; and soon the Count di Luna makes his way through the foliage. He is madly in love with Leonora, and will stop at nothing to win her as his bride.

For a moment, he gazes at the lighted window of her chamber. But his reverie is broken by the sound of a harp. "Ah!" he exclaims in anger. "The troubadour!"

Manrico
(*off stage*)

And now a melancholy voice rises through the night.

De - ser - to   sul - - la   ter - - ra
Naught   up - on   earth_____ is   left_____   me

Enter
Leonora
Enter
Manrico

Leonora hears it and rushes from her room. The moon has gone behind the clouds—the garden is veiled in darkness—and mistaking the Count for her lover, Leonora embraces him. Then, to her consternation, the real troubadour appears.

At once, the stranger is challenged by the Count. "Who *are* you? I demand to know!"

Raising his visor, the troubadour reveals that he is Manrico, an enemy knight in the service of Biscay. As the Count grows ever more insulting, Manrico draws his sword.

In vain does Leonora try to separate the rivals. All of her pleading is useless. Crossing their blades, Count and troubadour engage in mortal combat.

ACT II—*The Gypsy*

SCENE 1: IN THE MOUNTAINS OF BISCAY (22 Minutes)

Gypsies,
Manrico
and
Azucena

MANRICO has conquered in the duel—and spared his rival's life. But the Count di Luna knows no gratitude. He has sent his troops in pursuit of the troubadour, attacked him and left him for dead on the battlefield at Pelila. Rescued by the gypsy woman who reared him from earliest childhood—Azucena—Manrico has been recuperating in the mountains of Biscay.

Now he lies among Azucena's people, listening to their songs and watching them at work with their anvils:

Azucena sits apart from the rest, gazing into the embers of a great fire. Her mind is dwelling on the day—many years ago—when her mother was burned at the stake by the house of di Luna. As the gypsies cease their chorus, Azucena sings a chant of revenge; in a vision, she sees before her the raging fire that consumed her mother's body.

Stri - de   la   vam . . . pa!
Fierce flames are   soar . . . . ing!

It is time for the gypsy band to be off. Azucena does not even notice their departure—she is still thinking of her mother, and murmuring the plea for vengeance that the hag had uttered before she perished.

Manrico remains behind with Azucena. He has been raised in the belief that he is her son—and now he begs her to reveal the secret that he knows is preying on her mind.

"When my mother was slain," she answers, "I stole the child of the di Lunas in revenge; I meant to burn him alive! But alas—as the blaze arose, and the vision of my mother came before me, I lost my mind. Instead of young Garzia, I hurled *my own child* into the flames!"

"Then tell me!" cries Manrico. "Am I not your son?"

Azucena glares at him fiercely. Having revealed too much, she takes refuge in a lie. "Of course you are my son! Did I not rescue you from the battlefield at Pelila? Have I not always shown you the greatest devotion?"

At that moment, a horn sounds from the valley below. It is Ruiz, friend of Manrico, who arrives bearing a letter. "Our army has taken the fortress of Castellor," Manrico reads, "and the Prince has ordered that you come at once to assume command." Suddenly, the troubadour cries out in despair as he reaches the end of the letter. "Leonora thinks I have been killed in battle! Tonight she enters a convent!"

Seizing his helmet and sword, Manrico makes ready to depart. Azucena vainly tries to hold him back—for she has a premonition of disaster. Indeed, the wild creature loves the troubadour, even though he stems from the hated family of di Luna.

"I cannot stay!" Manrico declares. "O mother, farewell!" Rushing down the mountain side, he leaves on his errand of bravery.

Exeunt
gypsies

Enter Ruiz

Exit Ruiz

Exit
Manrico

SCENE 2: THE CLOISTER OF A CONVENT NEAR CASTELLOR
(18 Minutes)

Count di Luna, Ferrando and attendants

The Count di Luna has been informed of Leonora's plan to withdraw from the world. Determined to prevent it, he hides within the cloister, accompanied by Ferrando and a band of followers. "No, Leonora!" he cries, as he awaits the coming of the noble lady. "The convent is not for you. I swear you shall be mine!"

Il ba‑len del suo sor‑ri‑so d'u‑na stel‑la vin‑ce‑il rag‑gio!
In the light of her sweet glances, Joy— ce‑les‑tial beam‑eth up‑on— me;

Enter Leonora and Inez

And soon Leonora approaches, with her devoted attendant Inez. "All is over for me," she sighs. "Manrico is dead; the Church has become my only refuge." Taking leave of Inez, she is about to enter the convent when the Count di Luna and his men boldly seize her. At this crucial moment, the troubadour arrives with the soldiers of Biscay. Tearing Leonora from the arms of the Count, he bears her away to safety as the rival bands turn the peaceful cloister into a bloody battlefield.

Enter Manrico and followers

ACT III—*The Gypsy's Son*

SCENE 1: A CAMP NEAR CASTELLOR (10 Minutes)

Soldiers' chorus Exeunt soldiers Count di Luna

IT is to the fortress of Castellor that Manrico has taken Leonora. Even here, the lovers are in danger. Enemy forces lurk outside the walls; and in a field near by, the Count di Luna has pitched his tent.

"She is there!" exclaims the Count, as he gazes at the battlements of the fortress. "There—within my rival's arms! O Leonora!"

Enter Ferrando, Azucena and soldiers

His thoughts are broken off by a violent commotion in the camp. Azucena has been caught prowling about, and the loyal Ferrando has brought her before the Count for judgment. As the old retainer looks closely at the gypsy, he gives a shout of surprise. "That woman!" he cries. "Though years have passed, I remember her. She is the murderess of Garzia di Luna!"

"Lead her off!" commands the Count. "She shall be executed!"

In greatest agitation, Azucena breathes the name of Manrico. "My son!" she implores. "Come to my aid! Free me from these tyrants!"

It is a joyful moment for the Count. "So you are the mother of Manrico!" he gloats, as the gypsy is dragged away. "Through you, I'll have revenge!"

SCENE 2: A HALL ADJOINING THE CHAPEL OF CASTELLOR (8 Minutes)

In the midst of battle, Manrico and Leonora are to be wed at Castellor. Gloomy portents mar their joy—it is most likely that the fortress will be taken by the foe. But, forgetting their danger, the lovers prepare to enter the chapel. *(Manrico and Leonora)*

Suddenly, Ruiz appears. "Manrico!" he shouts. "Your mother has been captured. They will burn her at the stake!" *(Enter Ruiz)*

Casting everything aside—his impending marriage, even his personal safety—the troubadour vows that he will rescue Azucena. "Tremble, you tyrants!" he exclaims. "My mother shall be saved!" *(Exeunt Ruiz and Leonora)*

Ruiz and the other followers of Manrico have gathered in a loyal band. "Lead us on!" they urge. Brandishing their weapons, the soldiers of Biscay set off on their heroic mission to free Azucena. *(Enter Ruiz and soldiers)*

Act IV—*The Torture*

SCENE 1: A WING OF THE PALACE OF ALIAFERIA (19 Minutes)

MANRICO has failed in his sortie and been taken captive by di Luna. Now he languishes in a dark tower of the Count's palace.

At dead of night, a solitary torch can be seen in the courtyard below. It is Leonora! Guided by the faithful Ruiz, she has escaped from Castellor and comes to linger near her doomed lover. She shudders as she hears the rites for the dead being chanted. And when the troubadour's voice floats from the tower in a song of gloom and misery, Leonora's despair is unbounded. *(Enter Leonora and Ruiz Exit Ruiz)* *(Manrico and chorus (invisible))*

Just then, the Count di Luna emerges from the palace, on his way to see the doomed man in the tower. Leonora hovers in the shadow, reaching a terrible decision. Finally, she reveals herself to the Count. "Release Manrico," she offers, "and I am yours." *(Enter Count di Luna)*

The embittered Count does not readily agree, but soon he is won over. "There is only one condition," Leonora declares. "You must allow me to enter Manrico's cell and set him free. After that, you may take me."

"I promise," exclaims the Count. Filled with joy at possessing

Leonora, he does not see her open the ring that she is wearing—nor does he observe that she has swallowed poison. "Let us go in!" he cries triumphantly. "At last you shall be mine!"

SCENE 2: A DUNGEON (17 Minutes)

Manrico and Azucena

Azucena has been thrust into the same dungeon with Manrico. Suffering has unhinged her mind—and, to comfort her, Manrico murmurs that he is taking her back to freedom in the mountains of Biscay.

Ai no - stri mon - ti ri - tor - ne - re - mo,
Back to our moun - tains thou yet shalt take me,

Lulled by this false picture of the future, Azucena falls asleep. Immediately, the cell door is opened, and Leonora appears. "Hurry!" she whispers. "You are free. Make your escape!"

Enter Leonora

Manrico stares at her in amazement. "Who has sent you?" he demands. "How have you obtained my freedom?"

When Leonora does not answer, the troubadour breaks out in cruel reproaches. "You have sold yourself!" he exclaims. "Begone!"

Leonora falters—she sinks to the ground—and Manrico realizes the price she has paid to save him. "I am dying!" she whispers. "O Manrico, farewell!"

Death of Leonora Enter Count di Luna Exit Manrico

As the troubadour gazes at the body of his loved one, a sinister figure appears in the doorway of the cell. It is the Count di Luna, with his attendants. "Lead that man to the scaffold!" he commands.

The Count's orders are carried out. And now he rouses Azucena, forcing her to the window in fiendish joy. "Look!" he cries. "Your son has perished!"

A gleam of wild triumph lights the face of Azucena. "My son?" she laughs madly. "No! *He was your brother!*" Turning away from the wretched Count, she stares into space. "O Mother!" she calls. "Mother—you are avenged!"

LA TRAVIATA

La Traviata (The Strayed One) *was composed by Giuseppe Verdi as an opera in three acts, and first performed in Venice, March 6, 1853. Since its contemporary setting provoked antagonism, it was later set and costumed in the period of Louis XIV, but has now been returned to its original mid-nineteenth century period. It reached New York as early as 1856, was presented four times during the opening season of the Metropolitan, in 1883-84, and since 1893-94 has been omitted during three seasons only. It is now played as four acts.*

The libretto is by Francesco Maria Piave, whom Verdi commissioned to prepare it for the lyric stage in 1852, after he had seen the play La Dame aux Camélias. *This drama, known today as* Camille, *was adopted by Alexandre Dumas the younger from his novel of the same name, a work which had had an enormous vogue ever since its first appearance in 1848. Its heroine, known in the opera as Violetta Valery, and in the play as Marguerite Gautier, was drawn by Dumas from life: the original was a young and fashionable courtesan by the name of Alphonsine Plessis, who died of consumption in 1847 at the age of twenty-three, and is buried in the Montmartre Cemetery in Paris.*

Characters, in order of appearance:
Violetta Valery: *soprano*
Flora Bervoix: *mezzo-soprano*
Marquis d'Obigny: *bass*
Baron Douphol: *bass*
Dr. Grenvil: *bass*

Gastone, Vct. de Letorieres: *tenor*
Alfredo Germont: *tenor*
Annina, Violetta's maid: *mezzo-soprano*
Giorgio Germont: *baritone*
Chorus of guests of Violetta and Flora,
    servants, maskers dressed as mata-
    dors and picadors, ballet of gypsies,
    etc.

Time: About 1850   *Place:* Paris and Vicinity

ACT I

SCENE: VIOLETTA'S DRAWING-ROOM, PARIS (31 Minutes)

In two contrasting themes, the brief prelude at once suggests the two chief characteristics of Violetta Valery: the tragic implications of her malady:

and her absorbing passion for her lover, Alfredo:

THE curtain rises on a Paris drawing room where Violetta is receiving her friends. At the back of the stage, doors open into adjoining salons. On the left a large mantelpiece is hung with a mirror; in front of it stands a sofa on which Violetta is seated. She is a delicate woman, adorned with many jewels, and dressed in the crinolines of the '50's. Toward the center, tables are laid for a number of guests.

Violetta, Flora, d'Obigny, Douphol

Groups of the brilliant assembly are tempted to dance by the sparkling music, while others sing in praise of pleasure.

Flora Bervoix, one of Violetta's pleasure-loving friends, stands near the hostess with a Marquis.

"You really enjoy all this gaiety?" Flora asks her.

"Yes," she answers with a fling of her thin hand. "Pleasure is the only drug for my ills!"

Enter Gastone and Alfredo

While the servants prepare the supper table, Gastone comes in with his friend Alfredo Germont, whom he introduces to Violetta. The stranger cannot take his eyes from her.

"This young man worships you," Gastone adds, bending toward

Violetta with a whisper. "All through your illness he came every day to ask for you."

"Is it true?" She turns to Alfredo. "Then I thank you." She laughs at the thought that he is in love with her, although her friend, Baron Douphol, already glowers with jealousy at the newcomer.

The company calls on Alfredo for a toast, and he sings the spirited Brindisi:

Li · bia · · mo, li · bia · mo ne lie · · ti ca · · li · ci
Fill high!____ till with wine ev · 'ry gob · · let brim · · · ming.

Violetta smiles at his gallantry, and the throng joins in the chorus. As it closes, strains of another waltz are heard in the neighboring salon. Violetta suggests that her guests go to dance. Then suddenly she falls back on the sofa.

"Leave me," she protests, as they crowd around her. "I shall join you in a moment." Alfredo alone remains, unnoticed, watching her examine her pallid face in the mirror. Then she sees him, and turns.

"This sort of life will kill you," he urges. "If you were only mine, how tenderly I would care for you!"

She still cannot believe he is serious.

"For a whole year I have loved you," he continues, as the waltz echoes from the distance, and then, as the rhythm grows slower and more serious, he describes his ecstasy:

Di quel · l'a · mor, quel · l'a · mor · · ch'è pal · pi · to
Ah this is love, this ec · sta · tic sen · sa · tion.

"No . . . no. It is not possible . . . I must be frank with you," Violetta answers him. "If you feel this way, you must leave me—you will easily forget me.

"At least you must not speak to me of love," she goes on. Then, taking a flower from her dress and giving it to him, she adds, "Bring it back to me when it is faded."

Alfredo kisses her hand and leaves.

The other guests come back from their dancing. "It is almost dawn," they exclaim, and make their farewells.

Violetta is left alone. For the first time she feels herself moved by words of love. Can this be the hero of her dreams?

Exeunt
Flora,
Douphol,
d'Obigny,
Gastone,
guests

Exit
Alfredo
Re-enter
guests
Exeunt
guests

Ah for-s'è lui che l'an-i-ma
Can it be he whose im-age fair

She repeats Alfredo's own description of the passion that has seized him, and then remains silent for a moment in reverie. But she must shake off this folly. She flings herself into another brilliant aria in praise of liberty and pleasure:

Sem-pre li-be-ra deg-g'i-o fol-leg-gia-re di gio-ja_in gio-ja,
Free as air I long to flit and flut-ter on from pleas-ure to pleas-ure.

From beneath the balcony outside her window floats up the echo of Alfredo's ecstatic song.

ACT II

SCENE: GARDEN OF VIOLETTA'S COUNTRY PLACE NEAR PARIS
(33 Minutes)

FOR three months Violetta and Alfredo have been living quietly at a villa in Auteuil, near Paris.

Enter Alfredo

Dressed for the hunt, Alfredo comes in, rejoicing in the peace of their life together:

De' miei bol-len-ti spi-ri-ti
Far from the world of fa-shion

Exit Alfredo Enter Violetta and Annina Exit Annina Enter Germont

A moment after his departure, Violetta enters asking her maid Annina where Alfredo has gone.

"Strange," she exclaims, "you say he is off to Paris till evening?" Then casually she tosses aside an invitation from Flora Bervoix which has been handed her.

A visitor is admitted. Violetta, who is expecting her man of business, is astounded to hear the stranger introduce himself as Alfredo's father.

"My son is on his way to ruin," Germont announces. "Already he is arranging to give you all his possessions."

"I would not let him," answers Violetta proudly, and she shows him the papers she has prepared for the sale of her jewels. "I love Alfredo—and God has blotted out my sins with my repentance."

"In your hands lies the happiness of both my children," explains Germont. "My innocent daughter cannot marry, until you set Alfredo free and release my family from this disgrace."

"You do not know how I love him," Violetta pleads.

Germont is moved by her evident sincerity. "He may grow tired of you," he adds with a note of compassion. "What then?"

Their voices join in lamentation. At length Violetta makes her choice. She will sacrifice herself:

Andantino

Di - te al - la gio - vi - ne si bel - la e pu - ra,
Go tell your daugh - ter, young, fair and cher - ished,

"Heaven will reward you," declares the grateful father, as he goes to seek his son.

Exit Germont

Violetta sits at her table, picks up Flora's invitation, and dashes off an acceptance. Then, as she tries to write Alfredo, he suddenly appears.

Enter Alfredo

He is disturbed by the news that his father is about to visit them, but hopeful that the sight of her will win his favor.

"No, no, he must not see me," declares Violetta excitedly. But her protests soon give way to the cry of yearning which was heard in the prelude. "Say that you love me as I love you, and then— farewell!"

Exit Violetta

Alfredo is alone when a messenger brings him Violetta's letter. He reads of her decision to return to her old life. With an anguished cry he falls into the arms of his father, who has just reappeared.

Enter Germont

Germont tries to comfort him with memories of his happy childhood in Provence:

Andante

Di Pro - ven - za il mar, il suol chi dal cor ti can - cel - lò?
Who has ban - ished from your heart all the love you had for home?

The father's tender entreaties are in vain. Alfredo, who has found Flora's note on the table, glances angrily at its contents, and rushes off for revenge on the woman who has abandoned him.

Exeunt Alfredo and Germont

ACT III

SCENE: THE TERRACE OF FLORA'S VILLA (22 Minutes)

FLORA BERVOIX' terrace is crowded with guests. "I have invited Alfredo and Violetta," announces the hostess, as her friends swarm to greet her.

Flora, d'Obigny and guests

"Haven't you heard the news?" asks the Marquis d'Obigny. "They have separated."

A chorus of gypsies, hired by Flora to entertain the company, mingles with the guests, reading their palms.

Enter gypsies

Enter bull-
fighters
and
Gastone
Enter
Alfredo
Enter
Violetta
and
Douphol

They are followed by a group of maskers in the costume of Spanish bullfighters.

No sooner are the guests unmasked and settled at the gaming tables, when Alfredo strides in and recklessly sits down to play.

Violetta enters on the arm of Baron Douphol.

"Young Germont is here," whispers her new protector, with a grim threat in his voice. "Not a single word to him, remember."

The gaiety continues at high tension. Alfredo wins every hand he plays. The Baron challenges him to a match, but again Alfredo is successful. Supper is announced; the players stop their game.

"I'll take my revenge another time," says the Baron.

Exeunt all
Re-enter
Violetta
and
Alfredo

"I shall be at your service," retorts Alfredo. Both men follow the company to supper.

Violetta returns alone in the greatest alarm. She has sent for Alfredo to warn him that the Baron is about to challenge him to a duel. He must escape!

"I will go if you will follow me," Alfredo answers, passionately.

"I have sworn never to see you," she explains.

"And who dared ask you? Baron Douphol?"

With a supreme effort, Violetta conceals the truth and murmurs: "Yes."

Re-enter
company

Alfredo wrathfully summons Flora and her guests from the supper room.

"Here is the girl who spent all her wealth on me," he cries in his rage. "I call you to witness that I pay back the debt here and now." He hurls a purse at Violetta's feet.

Enter
Germont

The elder Germont, who has followed Alfredo to the *soirée,* makes his appearance, heaping reproaches on his son for his insulting conduct. Alfredo is overcome with remorse. An impressive ensemble concludes the act, Violetta declaring that love has prompted her sacrifice:

Largo

p Al-fre-do, Al-fre-do,
O Al-fred, Al-fred,

Act IV

SCENE: VIOLETTA'S BEDROOM (30 Minutes)

A brief orchestral introduction reminds us of Violetta's malady by the tenuous theme that opened the prelude to the first act.

Violetta
and
Annina

IN a modest apartment in Paris, Violetta has found a retreat. The curtains, half drawn about her bed, disclose the fact that she is still sleeping. The maid Annina is drowsing in a chair near-by.

Waking, Violetta asks for daylight. Annina opens the shutters and sees Dr. Grenvil in the street below. She helps her mistress rise, and the doctor enters in time to lead the invalid's feeble steps to the sofa. Enter doctor

"Courage," he says gently, "you will be better soon."

But Violetta sees through his kindly falsehoods. Exit doctor

The doctor departs, whispering to Annina that the end is only a few hours away; Violetta sends her maid to distribute alms to the poor. Exit Annina

To the melody of Alfredo's love song, she reads a letter from the elder Germont. The duel has taken place; the Baron was wounded. Alfredo has learned of her sacrifice and is returning to beg her forgiveness.

"I have waited, but still he does not come," she says, picking up her mirror to see the ravages made by her illness, and then bids farewell to the smiling daydreams of the past:

A chorus of revelers from the Paris Carnival sings gaily off stage. Annina returns with good news. Alfredo rushes into the room and takes Violetta in his arms. Nothing can separate them now. Enter Annina Enter Alfredo

After a rapturous duet, Alfredo begs her to leave Paris with him. Surely a happy future awaits them under sunny skies!

As soon as Violetta tries to rise, however, she totters with weakness, and sinks exhausted in a chair. Vainly she attempts to dress. Alfredo, terrified, sends Annina out to call the doctor. Exit Annina

"If your coming cannot save me," whispers the dying woman to her lover, "no power on earth can do so." Rising feverishly to her feet, Violetta appeals to God not to let her die so young.

Then she sinks again onto the sofa.

"Alas," she murmurs to Alfredo's father, who comes at last to take her to his heart as a daughter, "you are too late." She calls Alfredo and gives him a little miniature of herself. If ever he marries, he is to give it to his wife, and say that she is praying for them both in Heaven. Enter Germont

Annina returns with the doctor. Enter Annina and doctor

"Strange," exclaims Violetta, "I feel a new strength, it is life returning." A last rapturous cry, and she falls back on the sofa, dead.

UN BALLO IN MASCHERA
(*A MASKED BALL*)

UN BALLO IN MASCHERA, *an opera in three acts, now given in four, was first presented at Rome in 1859. The text by Somma originally concerned itself with King Gustavus III, who loved the wife of his best friend and was consequently slain. To please the censors, the locale was shifted from Sweden to Massachusetts, and the licentious Gustavus became Richard, colonial governor for the English Crown. In modern performances of the opera, any period or locale may be employed at the discretion of the producer. The première of* Un Ballo in Maschera *at the Metropolitan Opera House took place in 1889.*

Characters, in order of appearance:

Samuel ⎫
Thomas ⎭ conspirators: *bass*
Oscar, a page: *soprano*
Richard, the governor: *tenor*
Renato, his best friend: *baritone*
A judge: *tenor*
Ulrica, an astrologer: *contralto*
Sylvan, a sailor: *bass*
A servant: *tenor*
Amelia, wife of Renato: *soprano*
Courtiers, conspirators, townspeople, sailors, maskers

Time: Eighteenth Century   *Place:* Massachusetts

ACT I

SCENE: A HALL IN THE HOUSE OF THE GOVERNOR (17 Minutes)

IN the colonial administration of Richard, governor of Massachusetts, a band of malcontents is at work. They comprise a small minority—for Richard is loved by his people—but they are under the dangerous leadership of Samuel and Thomas, two fanatics who have sworn to assassinate Richard.

When the governor enters his audience chamber, this group feigns friendship. Richard absent-mindedly greets them and scans a list that his page Oscar has given him.

"These are the guests you have asked to the ball," Oscar explains.

As Richard glances through the invitations, he seems strangely preoccupied; he has noticed the name of Amelia—the wife of his devoted secretary, Renato. "This will be a chance to see her again!" he reflects.

The assemblage takes its leave. And now, as Richard puts aside the list of guests, he sees Renato standing before him.

"Your Grace," Renato declares. "I have come to warn you of a plot against your life."

Richard waves aside his friend's warning and prepares for the business of the day. First among his callers is a judge who hands him several dispatches.

"Why this order?" frowns the governor. "On whose authority have you exiled the negress Ulrica?"

"She is a sorceress!" the judge replies. "The worst scoundrels of our colony frequent her den!"

Young Oscar, the page of the governor, has been standing by. Now he boldly interrupts. "Ulrica is a sage," he claims, "gifted in the lore of the stars! I pray you, my lord, acquit this woman!"

Richard does not answer directly. "Call in the courtiers!" he orders. As Oscar and Renato summon the attendants, the governor smiles knowingly. He will use the sorceress as the pretext for an amusing adventure.

"My friends," he announces, "you are invited to join me today at the den of Ulrica. I shall be there in disguise."

"Beware!" whispers Renato. "Someone may attempt your life!"

Silencing his zealous secretary, Richard continues, "I shall meet all of you at three o'clock."

As the courtiers file out of the chamber, Samuel, Thomas and the conspirators exchange glances. "Perhaps our chance will come today!" they mutter.

Enter Samuel, Thomas and conspirators
Enter Oscar and courtiers
Enter Richard

Exeunt all but Richard
Enter Renato

Enter Oscar and judge

Enter Samuel, Thomas, conspirators and courtiers

Act II

SCENE: THE ABODE OF THE ASTROLOGER (29 Minutes)

Ulrica and townspeople

WHILE a gaping crowd fills Ulrica's den, hopeful of learning the future, the sorceress bends over her cauldron and moans a weird incantation:

Re—— dell' a - bis - so af-fret - ta - ti; pre - ci - —— pi - ta per l'e - tra,
King—— of the shades, I sum-mon thee, cleave through—— the earth's dark cen - tre.

Enter Richard

Suddenly, a stranger forces his way into the shadowy room—it is Richard, disguised as a sailor. As he stands in the darkness, he overhears a mariner named Sylvan asking Ulrica for her counsel.

Sylvan

"I have served the governor for fifteen years," the mariner protests, "and not once have I been rewarded. O sorceress, will recognition never be mine?"

At once, Richard steals forward, slipping money and an order of promotion into the seaman's pocket. Then, he retires into the shadow and looks on with interest as Sylvan discovers the reward.

"Ulrica!" the mariner cries. "Your prophecy has come true!"

Enter and exit servant Exeunt Sylvan and people Enter Amelia

There is a sharp rap at the door. A servant whispers a message to Ulrica—softly, but still audibly enough for Richard to overhear: Amelia, his beloved, is waiting to see the sorceress!

"Go, all of you!" Ulrica shouts. "I must consult the oracle!"

As the bystanders leave the den, Richard remains in an obscure corner. Soon a veiled woman enters, greatly agitated. It is Amelia!

"I have come to ask your help!" Amelia exclaims. "I am devoted to my husband—and against my will, I love another."

"You shall forget this man!" the sorceress predicts. "There is a magic herb that will pluck the infection from your heart—it must be gathered at midnight beyond the city wall, in the shadow of the gibbet."

"I will go tonight!" Amelia answers.

Exit Amelia Enter Oscar, Samuel, Thomas, courtiers and people

As the woman leaves, Richard vows that he will follow her. Before he can plan further, Ulrica has opened the door of her den and the prying onlookers have returned. This time, they are joined by Oscar, Samuel, Thomas and all the colonial officers.

Richard steps from his hiding place. "O prophetess," he calls, "I am a humble sailor. Will you reveal my fortune?"

Ulrica looks at him darkly. "You are soon to die—and by the hand of a friend!"

The conspirators fear their plot has been discovered. "Continue!" the governor insists. "Who shall be the murderer?"

"The man who first shakes hands with you today!"

Richard extends his hand to the bystanders. Not one of them will touch it. Suddenly, he spies Renato crossing the threshold. The governor hurries toward his secretary and grasps him by the hand. "Your oracle has lied," he shouts to Ulrica. "This man is my closest comrade!" *Enter Renato*

As he speaks, fervent shouts are heard outside the den. Sylvan, the mariner, has returned with his friends. "There is our governor!" he cries, penetrating Richard's sailor disguise. "Let us acclaim him!"

Richard throws the sorceress a purse and departs in triumph— but the implacable Samuel and Thomas remain behind, plotting his downfall.

ACT III

SCENE: A FIELD NEAR BOSTON (31 Minutes)

GUIDED only by a ray of moonlight, Amelia has reached the dread place of execution outside the city. A distant clock strikes twelve. With trembling hands, Amelia searches for the magic herb—and suddenly, she cries out in horror. A stranger is crossing the field! Powerless to flee she awaits him. It is Richard. *Enter Amelia* *Enter Richard*

"Why have you followed me?" she exclaims. "Have you no pity? Think of my husband—your friend—whom we are both betraying!"

"Think of ourselves!" pleads the governor. "Amelia—I love you!"

Amelia's resolve crumbles before Richard's pleading. "I, too, am in love!" she sighs.

Moderato

Oh qual so - a - ve bri - vi - do l'ac - ce - so pet - to ir - ro - ra!
Like dew thy words fall on my heart, a - glow with love's fond pas - sion!

The moonlight has been growing clearer; and now it reveals an officer standing near the gibbet—Renato! Unaware that the woman with the governor is his own wife, he has come to warn Richard of certain danger. As he approaches, Amelia covers her face with a heavy veil. *Enter Renato*

"Richard!" calls the trusted secretary. "You must flee—your

enemies have set a trap for you. Take the other path back to the city—and I will protect your lady."

"Give me your solemn promise," Richard demands, "that you will escort this woman without lifting her veil or seeking to know who she is—and that upon arriving in the town, you will let her go her way."

"I promise!" swears Renato.

Exit Richard Enter Samuel, Thomas and conspirators

As approaching footsteps are heard, Richard takes flight. Soon, the murderous band led by Samuel and Thomas appears in the dreary field. Enraged at missing their prey, they advance upon Renato and tear the veil from his companion. When Amelia is disclosed, cowering beneath her cloak, the conspirators burst into mocking laughter.

"Well!" they exclaim. "So Renato courts his own wife by moonlight!"

"Enough!" cries Renato. "You men shall hear from me tomorrow."

"As friend or enemy?" demand the conspirators.

"As friend!"

The intriguers turn away and descend the hill that leads to town, still laughing mockingly. Renato faces his humiliated wife. "Come!" he declares in a choking voice. "I shall take you to the city."

Act IV

SCENE 1: A ROOM IN RENATO'S HOUSE (24 Minutes)

Enter Renato and Amelia

THE love that Renato bears his wife has turned to violent hatred. Resolved to avenge his honor, he bids her prepare for death.

"I have done no wrong," pleads Amelia. "It was for your sake that I went to the field at midnight! I was trying to crush my love for Richard!"

Renato does not listen to her. Taking up his sword, he mutters, "I have waited long enough. You must die!"

"One favor I beg!" Amelia cries. "Before you sentence me, let me see my child once more!"

"Go!" Renato answers bitterly. "Embrace the child—and may his innocence remind you of your guilt!"

Exit Amelia

After Amelia has left the chamber, her husband turns sorrowfully to a picture that hangs on the wall—it is the portrait of Richard. "My best friend!" he sighs. "*You* have betrayed me! *You* have driven peace and love from my heart for evermore!"

Andante sostenuto

E - ri tu che mac - chia - vi quell a - - - ni - ma,
And would you thus have sul - lied a soul ___ so pure

As Renato broods on vengeance, Thomas and Samuel appear in answer to his summons of the night before.

"I have proofs of your treachery against the governor!" Renato informs them. "I know you are plotting his death—and yet, I have decided to join you!"

The conspirators are wary; they suspect a trap until Renato offers his own child as pledge of his sincerity. "Let us choose lots," he exclaims, "to see which of us shall slay the governor!"

As the men are about to draw, the doors of the room are flung open, and Amelia appears. "It is the page Oscar," she tells her husband nervously. "He has arrived with an invitation from the governor."

"Let him wait!" shouts Renato. "You shall stay and help us. There are three names in that urn—choose one of them!"

Surmising her husband's purpose, but helpless to interfere, Amelia draws a slip of paper. The name inscribed is Renato's!

"At last!" cries the raging husband. "The task belongs to me! Now you may admit the governor's messenger."

Immediately, the foppish Oscar enters, bearing an invitation to the masked ball:

Enter Samuel and Thomas

Enter Amelia

Enter Oscar

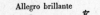

Allegro brillante

Ah! Di che ful - gor che mu - si - che, e - sul - te - ran le so - - glie,
Ah! what daz-zling light, what mu - sic bright in___ yon halls will be reign - ing!

"Tell your master that Amelia and I accept!" Renato declares savagely.

As the page withdraws, the conspirators whisper their final plans. They will be dressed in blue and red—and their watchword will be *Death!*

SCENE 2: A BALLROOM IN THE GOVERNOR'S MANSION (22 Minutes)

Richard has fallen prey to conscience. Deciding to resist further temptation, he has arranged to send Renato and Amelia back to England, with promise of a promotion for the loyal secretary.

The governor has also been greatly disturbed by a letter warning him not to attend the masked ball. Reasoning that he would be

Richard,
Renato,
Amelia,
Oscar,
Samuel,
Thomas,
conspir-
ators and
courtiers

marked as a coward if he absented himself, he determines to appear.

In the midst of the brilliant party, he is confronted by a masked woman. "Flee at once," she whispers, "or you will be stabbed!"

"Then it was you who sent me the warning letter?" the governor demands. "I know—you are Amelia!"

As they are speaking, a figure in red and blue steals behind them and plunges a knife in Richard's back. The murderer immediately discards his weapon and joins the throng of maskers—but he is caught through the vigilance of Oscar, the page.

Infuriated, the guests tear the mask from Renato and are about to kill him, when the dying Richard intervenes. "Spare him!" he orders. "Hear me, Renato, for the last time. Your wife is innocent. I loved her—but she has not betrayed you!" Feebly, Richard reaches for a paper which he has already signed, ordering Renato and his wife to England. "Here," he gasps. "Go in peace—you shall not be punished!"

As the governor dies, Thomas, Samuel and their accomplices are jubilant—but Renato is a broken man, haunted by the friendship he has shattered.

LA FORZA DEL DESTINO
(*THE FORCE OF DESTINY*)

LA FORZA DEL DESTINO, *an opera in four acts and seven scenes with text by F. M. Piave, was first produced at St. Petersburg in 1862. Its Metropolitan première took place on November 15, 1918, with Rosa Ponselle making her operatic debut as Leonora, and Caruso singing the role of Don Alvaro.*

Characters, in order of appearance:

The Marquis of Calatrava: *bass*
Leonora: *soprano*
Curra, her servant: *mezzo-soprano*
Don Alvaro: *tenor*
The Alcade: *bass*
Don Carlo di Vargas, Leonora's brother: *baritone*
Trabuco, a muleteer: *tenor*
Preziosilla, a young gypsy: *mezzo-soprano*
Melitone, a friar: *bass*
Padre Guardiano: *bass*
A Surgeon: *tenor*
Servants of the Marquis, peasants, pilgrims, friars, soldiers, vivandières

Time: Eighteenth Century   *Place:* Spain and Italy

ACT I

The overture to Forza del Destino *begins with three sustained notes, symbolic of the force of destiny. Then there appears the agitated theme of the heroine Leonora:*

233

Allegro agitato

In most presentations of the opera, as at the Metropolitan, the overture is played not before the rise of the curtain, but as an interlude between the two scenes of the first act.

SCENE 1: A DRAWING ROOM IN SEVILLE (20 Minutes)

DON ALVARO, a Peruvian of Inca blood, is in love with Leonora di Vargas. Leonora has returned his love and accepted his offer of marriage—but her father, the Marquis of Calatrava, has intervened. He despises Alvaro as a half-caste and orders Leonora never to see the man again.

Marquis,
Leonora,
Curra
Exit
Marquis

Outwardly, Leonora accepts her father's decree; she kisses the Marquis tenderly as he bids her good night. Yet, no sooner has he gone from the room than she feverishly packs her belongings. Alvaro is due at midnight, to bear her away.

The clock strikes twelve. "He will be here!" predicts Curra, Leonora's maid. And soon, the trampling of horses is heard outside in the garden. Alvaro vaults the balcony and enters Leonora's chamber.

Enter
Alvaro

"Come!" he exclaims. "I have arranged everything. A priest is waiting for us. There is no time to lose!"

Enter
Marquis

Just as they are about to escape by the balcony, the door of the room is forced open—and the Marquis stands on the threshold. Two of his servants advance upon Alvaro; the Peruvian draws a revolver and defends himself. "I yield only to you, Marquis of Calatrava!" he declares. "Your daughter is innocent." As a token of surrender, he throws away his pistol; the weapon discharges, fatally wounding the Marquis.

"Help!" gasps the nobleman. "I am dying!" With his final breath, he curses Leonora while Alvaro drags the girl to the balcony. There is no refuge for the lovers but flight.

SCENE 2: TAVERN IN THE VILLAGE OF HORNACHUELOS (16 Minutes)

The
Alcade,
Don Carlo,
Trabuco,
Preziosilla

A throng of people fills the yard of the village tavern: travelers, villagers, mule-drivers. Apart from the rest sits a student, sinister in attitude and dress. Vainly he tries to share in the mirth around him —to take part in the merry songs of the wandering gypsy girl, Preziosilla.

The melancholy man is Don Carlo di Vargas, brother of Leonora. Determined to avenge his father's death, he has relentlessly pursued his sister and her lover. From information gleaned in Seville, he knows that Leonora and Alvaro somehow lost each other on the night of the tragedy—that Alvaro has gone to America, and Leonora has disappeared.

Disguised as a student, Don Carlo has never abandoned the search for his sister. Even now, he questions with intense curiosity a muleteer named Trabuco who has recently arrived at the inn. Did not Trabuco escort a mysterious young traveler dressed as a pilgrim? Might this pilgrim possibly be a woman in disguise? The muleteer refuses to answer.

In truth, the mysterious traveler is Leonora. Clad in male attire, she has paused at the inn on her way to a sanctuary. As a sacred procession passes the tavern, Leonora appears on a covered balcony and kneels in prayer. Then, avoiding detection, she returns to her room in the hope that her brother will soon travel onward.

Enter Leonora, pilgrims
Exeunt Leonora and pilgrims

It is growing late. The gypsy Preziosilla sets off again on her wanderings; the villagers go to their beds, and Don Carlo, unsuccessful in his quest, retires to dream of future vengeance.

Act II

SCENE: A CHURCH IN SPAIN (35 Minutes)

At dead of night, Leonora—still in male attire—reaches a church on the side of a lonely mountain. Anxiously, she rings the bell at the gate.

Enter Leonora

A peevish friar named Melitone answers her call. At first he is inclined to drive the stranger away; but sensing an urgent need, he fetches the Abbot—Padre Guardiano.

Enter Melitone
Enter Guardiano

As the Abbot dismisses Melitone, he turns compassionately to the visitor. "We are alone," he declares. "You may reveal the secret that has brought you here."

Exit Melitone

"I am a woman," the stranger exclaims. "Leonora di Vargas!"

Telling the Abbot her story, Leonora begs for his protection. She wishes to become a penitent—to live among the mountains, communing with God.

"It were better to enter a cloister," Guardiano suggests. "The life of a hermit is wretched indeed!"

"Then you send me away?" cries Leonora. "You reject me in the shadow of the Cross?"

Stirred by the woman's devoutness, Guardiano decides to help her. "There is a cave near our church," he declares, "where you can take refuge. I alone shall know your identity; every seven days, I shall leave food. No living soul will ever see you again!"

Enter
Melitone
and friars

With great solemnity, Guardiano summons the friars of the monastery. The church doors open; the organ is heard within, and the monks appear with lighted tapers. Keeping strictest secrecy, the Abbot has already clothed Leonora in a friar's hood, so that none may look upon her.

"Brothers!" he exclaims. "A lonely soul has asked for shelter in the hermitage among the rocks. Let none of you approach the place! If anyone seeks to discover the name or the story of this penitent, a curse shall be upon him!"

Surrounded by the monks, Leonora kneels gratefully at the shrine of the Madonna:

Adagio

La Ver - gi - ne de - gli An - ge - li mi co - pra del suo man - to;
The saints and ho - ly guard - ians will hear me and pro - tect me;

Exit
Leonora

Then, with her friar's hood drawn closely about her, the unknown penitent sets off for her place of refuge.

Act III

SCENE 1: A BATTLEFIELD IN ITALY (26 Minutes)

EVER since the fatal tragedy in Seville, Don Alvaro has wandered unhappily through the world. Amid the confusion that followed the death of the Marquis of Calatrava, he was separated from Leonora. Now, having lost all trace of her, he believes her dead.

Enter
Alvaro

In search of forgetfulness, Alvaro has gone to Italy, fighting on the side of the native troops against the Germans—but the memory of his loved one cannot be driven from his mind. He lingers on a deserted battlefield at night, thinking of Leonora:

Andantino sostenuto

O tu che in se - no_a-gl'an - ge - li e - ter - na - men - te pu - ra.
O saint-ed soul in rest a - bove, with an - gels thou art dwell - ing.

Enter
Don Carlo

Suddenly, he hears voices raised in quarrel. Rushing into a neighboring thicket, he rescues a noble officer who has been set upon by evil companions. The officer is Don Carlo di Vargas, still traveling under an assumed name. He has never given up the pursuit of Leonora and her lover.

Exeunt
Alvaro
and Carlo

Alvaro, too, is in disguise—and since the two men have never met before, they do not realize the enmity that stands between them. As Don Carlo thanks his rescuer, a call to arms is heard in the distance. Swearing unbroken friendship, both officers rush off to battle.

Enter
Alvaro
and Carlo

The Italian army is victorious—the German onslaught repulsed; but Alvaro has been wounded. Borne from the field on a stretcher, he thinks he is on the point of death.

"No!" exclaims Don Carlo, who has remained by his side. "You shall live! And for your bravery, you shall win the order of Calatrava!"

As he hears the Di Vargas title, with all the wretched memories it conveys, Alvaro shudders. His revulsion does not escape Don Carlo.

Rising feebly on his stretcher, Alvaro begs the attendants to leave him with his fellow officer. When the soldiers have gone, the dying man makes a singular request. He gives Don Carlo the key to a secret packet, and begs him to destroy a letter that is hidden within.

Carlo gives his promise. Breathing more easily, Alvaro is carried off to undergo the surgeon's knife.

Exit
Alvaro

And now a violent conflict rages in the mind of Don Carlo di Vargas. He already suspects that the wounded man may be Alvaro. Ought he open the letter and make certain? After a protracted struggle, he decides to carry out his oath and destroy the document. But suddenly, in the very packet where the letter is concealed, he discovers a faded portrait of Leonora.

At that moment, the regimental surgeon appears. "Your friend is saved," he calls.

Enter
surgeon
Exit
surgeon

Don Carlo utters a shout of savage joy. "Then he shall live to face my revenge!"

SCENE 2: AN ENCAMPMENT (15 Minutes)

It is sunrise in the Italian camp. Soldiers emerge from the tents, cleaning their muskets and swords. Vivandières sell bread and wine. Everywhere are signs of bustling activity.

Soldiers

In the midst of the merriment, the peevish friar Melitone appears upon the scene. He has come from Spain to attend the needs of the soldiers. Instead of being free to go about his duties, he is abused by the recruits and forced to join their carousal.

Enter
Melitone

Enter Preziosilla

Another familiar figure has entered the camp: Preziosilla, the gypsy. As Melitone clamors against the iniquities of the soldiers, she saves him from their wrath. "Let him alone!" she cries. "Why make war upon a friar when all the glories of real combat are at hand?"

Seizing a drum, Preziosilla beats out martial rhythms, and sings a song of victory: "Rataplan! Rataplan! The enemy yields before us!"

The entire camp, in a frenzy of patriotism, takes up her cry. Drums are sounded—trumpets are blown—and the soldiers prepare for battle.

ACT IV
SCENE 1: INTERIOR OF THE MONASTERY (11 Minutes)

DON ALVARO, resolved to end his days as a monk, has entered the very church where Leonora was once received by Padre Guardiano. Unaware of the penitent who dwells among the rocks near by, Alvaro has taken the vows of a friar and is living peacefully within the monastery.

Enter Carlo

The force of destiny is at work. One morning, a threatening stranger appears at the gates of the church and demands admission. It is Don Carlo di Vargas, who has finally traced Alvaro to this place of refuge. Scorning further pretense, he reveals his name and identity.

Enter Alvaro

In answer to Don Carlo's summons, Alvaro meets him in the courtyard. "I have two sabers here!" exclaims the pursuer. "You may have your choice—and we shall fight to the death!"

"Your threats are in vain," Alvaro answers. "I shall not fight— my monastic vows forbid it."

Le mi - naccie i fieri ac - cen - ti por - tin seco in preda i ven - ti.
All your threats and all your fu - ry can - not stir me now to com - bat.

Infuriated, Don Carlo strikes the friar. "You coward!" he cries. "Are you afraid to take up weapons?"

Faced with dishonor, Alvaro snatches a saber from the vengeful Carlo. The men rush off to a deserted spot behind the church where only death can end their combat.

SCENE 2: A VALLEY (16 Minutes)

Enter Leonora

For many years, Leonora has lived in solitude; and yet, she has not found repose. "Oh Lord," she prays, emerging from her cave, "bring peace to my heart. I still love Alvaro. I can never forget him!"

Pa - ce,   pa - ce,   pa - ce,   mio Dio,   pace,   mio Di - o!

Par-don,   par - don,   peace, oh   I   pray you!   grant   me peace, O   Lord!

Suddenly, the penitent hears the clashing of swords near at hand. Frightened, she hurries to her grotto and barricades the opening.

Exit
Leonora

The harsh voice of Don Carlo is heard among the rocks. "Help!" he moans. "Help! I have fallen!" Alvaro appears, desperately seeking a priest for his wounded enemy. Running to the hermitage, he beats upon the entrance and begs the occupant to help him.

Enter
Alvaro

"I cannot!" the recluse calls from within. In terror, she rings a bell to summon Padre Guardiano.

Again, Alvaro tries to force the entrance. "Come!" he cries. "There is a dying man outside!"

Leonora steps from the cave—and sees Alvaro. In the terrible emotion of the moment, the friar recoils from the woman he loves. "Away from me!" he sobs. "My hands are stained with your brother's blood!"

Enter
Leonora

Immediately, the penitent runs behind the rocks, bringing aid to Don Carlo—and Alvaro hears a deathly shriek. Padre Guardiano appears on the slope with Leonora hanging limply in his arms. At the very moment of death, the vengeful Di Vargas has mortally wounded his sister.

Exit
Leonora
Re-enter
with
Guardiano

Destiny has closed in upon the lovers. As Leonora expires and Padre Guardiano raises his arms in blessing, the wretched Alvaro resigns himself to a life of never ending misery.

AÏDA

AÏDA, *an opera in four acts by Giuseppe Verdi, was commissioned by the Khedive of Egypt to commemorate the opening of the Suez Canal at the new opera house at Cairo, where it was first performed on Christmas Eve, 1871. A sketch of the story had been drafted by Mariette Bey, a French employee in the Louvre's department of Egyptian antiquities. From this text Camille du Locle prepared a libretto in French prose under the eye of the composer. The final version in Italian verse was made by Antonio Ghislanzoni.*

Aïda *was first presented in Italy, at La Scala, in Milan, where Verdi conducted it in 1872. In November, 1873, it reached the United States, and in 1886 was given its first performance at the Metropolitan, where it has continued as the most frequently presented work in the repertory.*

Characters, in order of appearance:

Ramfis, high priest of Isis: *bass*
Radames, captain of the Egyptian guard: *tenor*
Amneris, daughter of the King of Egypt: *mezzo-soprano*
Aïda, an Ethiopian slave: *soprano*
King of Egypt: *bass*
Messenger: *tenor*
Amonasro, King of Ethiopia, father of Aïda: *baritone*
Priests, priestesses, soldiers, ministers, Ethiopian slaves,
prisoners, and Egyptians.

Time: The Reign of the Pharaohs   *Place:* Memphis and Thebes

240

The orchestral introduction at once outlines the struggle between love and duty that is to beset the hero, Radames. The soft, pleading motive of Aïda is first heard:

It is followed by a solemn subject identified with the priests of Egypt, who guard the glory of the nation:

As the Aïda theme returns, the curtain rises.

ACT I

SCENE 1: GRAND HALL IN THE PALACE OF PHARAOH AT MEMPHIS
(28 Minutes)

AMONG the colonnades of the palace at Memphis, Radames, the young captain of the guard, is talking with Ramfis, the high priest. | *Radames. Ramfis*

"Yes," Ramfis is saying, "I have heard that the Ethiopians are again threatening Thebes. Isis has decreed the choice of a young and dauntless leader. I must announce him to the king."

As the priest departs, Radames muses on his future: "What if I were chosen! I could return crowned with laurels to my beloved Aïda:" | *Exit Ramfis*

Radames is so absorbed in his reverie that he does not see Amneris, the king's daughter, who has entered and is watching him closely. Her first words show her suspicions. She adores him; but fears he prefers another. | *Enter Amneris*

"What makes you look so joyful? It is a lucky woman who can make you so happy!"

Radames tells her of his ambitions, wondering if she has guessed that he is in love with her slave, Aïda. In the orchestra is heard the motive of her jealousy:

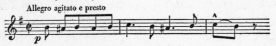

Heralded by the theme we have heard in the prelude, Aïda joins her mistress, terrified by the rumors of war. Amneris, pretending to proffer friendship, seeks to discover if her slave is indeed her rival. Does she too love Radames?

In an impressive trio, the three characters express their secret thoughts: Aïda her hapless love, Amneris her jealousy, and Radames his fear that the princess will wreck his plans.

The King of Egypt enters with a great procession of guards and ministers. A messenger is summoned.

"The Ethiopians have invaded our land and are marching on Thebes," is his report. "A fierce chieftain is leading them: Amonasro, their king."

Aïda stifles a cry. She alone knows the bitter truth: Amonasro is her father.

As the crowd cries for war, the King announces that Isis has indicated Radames as commander of the Egyptians and orders him to receive the sacred armor at the Temple of Vulcan. Amneris hands him the royal standard.

"Return victorious!" cries the princess. Aïda and the entire chorus repeat her exhortation.

Left alone, Aïda reproaches herself for her impious words: "I have wished my lover to return victorious over my father and brothers, who are fighting to restore me to my country. O gods, have pity on my suffering," she prays, "and let me die:"

Nu - mi, pie - tà del mio sof - frir! Spe - me non v'ha pel mio do - lor ·
Mer - ci - - ful gods! look from on high! Pit - y these tears hope - less - ly shed

SCENE 2: THE TEMPLE OF PHTHÀ (10 Minutes)

The temple at Memphis is lit by mysterious light. Fumes of incense arise from golden tripods about the central altar where the priest Ramfis awaits the coming of Radames. The voice of the priestess is heard, invoking almighty Phthà:

Pos - - sen - te, pos - sen - te   Fthà,
Al - - might - y, al - might - y   Pthà,

Ramfis and his priests join their chant, and the women circle the scene in a mystic dance.

Radames enters unarmed, and approaches the altar where a

silver veil is placed on his head and a sword is given him by the priest. A triumphant shout rings through the temple.

Act II

Scene 1: Amneris' Room (17 Minutes)

In her luxurious apartments, slaves array Amneris for the triumphal feast as the princess longs for the return of Radames:

Amneris
Ballet
of Moors

Ah! vie - - - ni,   vie-ni,a-mor mio, m'i - neb - bria,
Ah! come,   love, come love, with rap - ture   fill me,

A group of little Moors entertain their mistress with a weird dance. At the arrival of Aïda, Amneris dismisses her attendants. Once more she will try to probe the secret of her slave.

Enter
Aïda

"I am your friend," she declares. "Ask of me what you will."

"How can I be happy so far from home," laments Aïda, "when I cannot know the fate of my father and brothers?"

"Time will heal your wounds," replies the princess, "and love is stronger still."

Much moved, Aïda sings of love's joys and sorrows. Amneris is sure she has guessed the truth. She will inflict a final test. She tells Aïda that Radames has been killed in battle.

"I shall weep forever," moans Aïda.

In her rage, Amneris throws aside her pretense. "I have found you out!" she cries. "Radames is alive, and your rival for his affections is myself, the daughter of the Pharaohs!"

As the hymn of triumph echoes through the chamber, and the cruel princess reiterates her threats of vengeance, Aïda turns again to the gods for pity.

Scene 2: Thebes of the Hundred Gates (23 Minutes)

The great entrance to the city of Thebes is thronged with people, as a mighty procession passes the temple of Ammon and crowds about the throne. The King enters, followed by his vast retinue, and takes his seat. Amneris, surrounded by Aïda and other slaves, places herself at his side.

King,
Amneris,
Aïda
chorus

The victorious troops of Egypt defile past the monarch while trumpeters sound the familiar march:

Soldiers

Banners, sacred vessels and images of the gods are carried into the city, while dancing girls bring the spoils of the conquered.

Ballet

Radames

At the height of the excitement, Radames arrives in a magnificent chariot. The King comes down to embrace him, and Amneris crowns him with laurel. Whatever he asks will be freely granted.

"Let the captives be summoned," is Radames' first request.

Ethiopian prisoners, Amonasro

The wretched Ethiopians stagger forward in their chains. Among them Aïda is amazed to find her father Amonasro. He embraces her tenderly but whispers that she must not disclose his rank.

"The king of our people is slain," he announces craftily. "We are conquered, O ruler of Egypt, and you are supreme. Have pity on us!"

Aïda and all her countrymen join Amonasro's plea, but the priests of Ramfis oppose them bitterly. At length Radames reminds the King of his promise.

"I ask life and liberty for the Ethiopians."

Ramfis suggests a compromise: Amonasro shall remain a hostage. "I yield to your counsel," returns the King. "To celebrate the peace I will bestow on Radames the hand of my daughter Amneris."

The chorus cheers as the King descends from his throne and Amneris proudly follows him, escorted by her future consort. Aïda is left weeping in the arms of her father.

ACT III

SCENE: THE BANKS OF THE NILE (32 Minutes)

Enter Ramfis and Amneris Exeunt Ramfis and Amneris Enter Aïda

THE moon shines brightly on the banks of the Nile, whose murmur is suggested in a brief prelude. From the temple of Isis comes the faint chant of the priests. A boat draws up to the shore. Ramfis leads Amneris toward the temple, followed by her maidens. She is to spend her bridal eve in prayer.

No sooner have they left than Aïda enters heavily veiled. She has come for a secret tryst with Radames. Sadly she sings the distant beauties of her native land:

Enter Amonasro

As she waits for her lover, she hears footsteps. It is her father, who aware of her misery, has made a plan for their salvation. In turn they sing of the valleys of home, laid waste by the enemy:

Then Amonasro unfolds his plan. The Ethiopians are preparing
to strike again. All they need to know is which road the Egyptians
will take against them. This Aïda is to learn from Radames.

"You ask me to betray the man I love?" answers the wretched
girl. "I cannot."

Amonasro reminds Aïda of the pillage of her country. "You are
no daughter of mine," he rages, "but only the slave of the Pharaohs."

As she kneels beside him in submission his wrath subsides.

"Have courage," he whispers, "here is Radames. I will hide and
listen."

Radames enters with a cry of rapture at beholding Aïda:

Aïda refuses to believe in his love. He is to wed Amneris. Even
if his devotion is sincere, how are they to escape the vengeance of
the princess and the wrath of the priests?

"When I have led the army to victory once more, I will ask for
your hand as a reward from the King."

Aïda is unconvinced. The only solution that she can see is flight.
She describes the beauties of the land which awaits them. Eventually he yields. They will flee together.

But she has not fulfilled her mission. "By what path shall we
avoid the soldiers?" she asks him.

"By the path they take tomorrow," he answers, "the gorges of
Napata."

Amonasro springs from his hiding place and cries: "There will
I place my soldiers, I, King of Ethiopia."

Horrified that he has been tricked into an act of treachery,
Radames protests against Amonasro's suggestion that all three of
them flee together.

At this moment Amneris appears on the temple steps with a
cry of "Traitor!"

Ramfis orders out the guards. Aïda and her father escape into
the night, but Radames gives himself up to the high priest.

Exit
Amonasro
Enter
Radames

Enter
Amonasro

Enter
Amneris,
Ramfis
and
guards
Exeunt
Aïda and
Amonasro

ACT IV

SCENE 1: THE JUDGMENT HALL (31 Minutes)

Amneris

PRINCESS AMNERIS crouches in misery beside the portal of the subterranean hall of justice, waiting for Radames to be escorted from his prison. He may be a traitor, but she still loves him and wishes to save him.

Enter Radames and guards

Radames is led in by his guards. "Save yourself," she begs him, "and plead your innocence." But Radames has no wish to live without his Aïda.

Exeunt Radames and guards Enter and exeunt Ramfis, priests and Radames (silent) Priests off stage Re-enter priests Exeunt priests

"She is still alive," says Amneris, bitterly, "though after her father was slain, she disappeared. If you swear to renounce her I will save you."

"Never," answers Radames, and the guards lead him away.

Amneris is left alone with her jealousy and remorse. She watches the priests cross the hall on their way to the judgment chamber. Soon Radames is led to join them. The implacable theme that was heard in the prelude resounds from the depths. She listens for the verdict:

"He is silent," cries Ramfis.

"He is a traitor," echo the priests, "he shall be buried alive."

The procession returns from the crypt. Amneris vainly hurls her curses after them.

SCENE 2: THE TEMPLE OF PHTHÀ (11 Minutes)

The stage is divided in two levels. Above is the temple of Vulcan, glittering with gold. Steps lead below to a gloomy vault, supported

Radames

by huge statues of Osiris, where Radames waits his death. Two priests lower the fatal stone over his head.

Aïda, off stage priests and priestesses

Suddenly he hears a groan in the darkness. It is Aïda, who has hidden herself in order to die with him. The weird chant of the priestesses interrupts the stillness. Radames makes one last vain effort to displace the stone. With peaceful resignation, the two lovers bid farewell to earth:

O ter - ra ad - dio ad - di - o val - le di pian - ti,
Fare-well, oh earth, fare - well thou vale —— of sor - row,

Amneris

Amneris appears in the temple above and throws herself on the stone that seals the vault. As Radames and Aïda die in each other's arms in the darkness below, she prays to Isis for peace, while the priests again invoke almighty Phthà.

OTELLO

OTELLO, *a four act opera representative of Verdi's later style, first appeared at* La Scala, Milan, *in 1887. The libretto was adapted by Arrigo Boito from Shakespeare's tragedy of the Moor of Venice. Highly successful in Italy, the opera reached the Metropolitan Opera House in March, 1891, with Francesco Tamagno, who had created the title role at* La Scala, *making his American debut. Four seasons later, Victor Maurel, the original Iago, joined with Tamagno in several Metropolitan performances of the work. After vanishing from the repertory for many years, Otello was restored in 1937, with Giovanni Martinelli as the jealous Moor and Lawrence Tibbett as Iago.*

Characters, in order of appearance:

Montano, former governor of Cyprus: *bass*
Cassio, Otello's lieutenant: *tenor*
Iago, Otello's ensign: *baritone*
Roderigo, a Venetian gentleman: *tenor*
Otello, Moor of Venice: *tenor*
Desdemona, his bride: *soprano*
Emilia, her companion: *mezzo-soprano*
Lodovico, ambassador of Venice: *bass*
Natives of Cyprus, attendants

Time: Fifteenth Century   *Place:* Cyprus

ACT I
SCENE: OUTSIDE THE CASTLE OF CYPRUS (33 Minutes)

Chorus

Montano, Roderigo, Cassio and Iago

Enter Otello

IN the midst of a raging storm, the fleets of Venice and the Ottoman Empire are engaged in a grim battle for supremacy. Trade routes—the fate of eastern Europe—hang in the balance. With the island of Cyprus as a base of operations, the Venetian government has sent its bravest general—the Moor, Otello—against the Turks. He is at once commander of the fleet and governor of the island.

"God preserve him!" pray the natives of Cyprus as they line the windy shore, watching the battle.

Everywhere, there is a spirit of doubt and uncertainty as to the day's outcome. On the ramparts of the castle stands the former governor, Montano, looking anxiously to sea. Leaning against the adjoining bastions are two Venetian officers: Cassio, Otello's lieutenant, and Iago, the Moor's ensign.

Iago is the only man in Cyprus who secretly hopes for Otello's defeat. He has an insatiable ambition that will destroy anything in its path—and Otello has unwittingly offended him by appointing Cassio as first regimental officer. Stung by hatred and envy, Iago has determined to undo Otello and Cassio.

For the moment, Otello is supreme. He has conquered, and there is a deafening shout of "Victory!" as his vessel comes to shore. "We have won!" he proclaims. "Ours and Heaven's be the glory!"

Maestoso

E - sul - ta - te!   L'or - go - glio mu - sul - ma - no se - pol-to_è in mar,
Hear glad ti - dings!   Our wars are done. The   o - cean has whelmed the Turks.

Exit Otello Exeunt Montano and Cassio

As soon as the Moor has gone into the castle, Iago's plotting begins. Montano, Cassio, and the soldiers have dispersed—the people of Cyprus are busy building a bonfire of victory. And now Iago lingers by the sea-walk in the company of a young weakling named Roderigo. The youth is desperately in love with Desdemona, Otello's bride. He would give anything to possess her! Iago subtly works upon his passion—lies to him—tells him that Cassio has the same desires. "We must be rid of this fellow," he warns Roderigo. "I'll make him drunk—you provoke him to a fight. Otello will surely dismiss him from the service—and you will have Desdemona!"

Enter Cassio

Iago's plan works even more smoothly than expected. "Cassio!" he calls, as the lieutenant comes from the castle. "Let us drink to the wedding of Otello and Desdemona!"

"Thank you, no," Cassio replies. "I drink but poorly!"

"Come on!" urges Iago. "We have triumphed in battle. Let us be merry!" Raising his glass, he shouts a diabolical song in praise of wine—and Cassio soon falls victim to his spell.

Montano has again appeared on the rampart—it is time for the changing of the guard. "Go to your post!" he orders Cassio. But Cassio, under the influence of drink, has become noisy and abusive. It is an easy matter for Roderigo, prompted by Iago, to pick a quarrel with him. The two men fight—Montano intervenes—and Cassio, by now bereft of all reasoning power, turns on his superior officer. Roderigo slips away and rings the alarm bell. All of Cyprus is awakened! *(Enter Montano)*

A shout of anger issues from the castle doorway. There stands Otello, roused from his bridal couch. "What has caused this uproar?" he demands. *(Enter Otello)*

A quick investigation establishes Cassio's guilt. "Go," thunders the Moor, "and never more be lieutenant of mine!" As the wounded Montano is led away and the natives return to their homes, Otello entrusts Iago with the task of restoring quiet to the island. *(Exeunt all but Otello)*

The shore is deserted, and the Moor is about to enter the castle—but his bride has appeared in the gateway. "Desdemona!" he exclaims. *(Enter Desdemona)*

The wind and storm have ceased—the stars have emerged overhead. And now Otello draws Desdemona to a bench overlooking the sea. "My happiness is too full!" he declares. "Misgiving stirs within me!"

Gently, he kisses his bride:

They gaze once again at the heavens—and as Venus stands high in the firmament, they turn toward the castle and their chamber.

Act II

Scene: A Room in the Castle (36 Minutes)

Iago and Cassio

IAGO is not satisfied with Cassio's demotion. He wants to ruin the former lieutenant completely. And he sets about his purpose by playing the friend. "All you have to do," he tells Cassio, "is to seek the favor of Desdemona. She will intercede for you and help restore your rank."

Exit Cassio

As the deposed officer sets off to take this advice, Iago stares cynically after him. "Go on!" he mutters. "Step into the trap! I feel no remorse for your undoing. *Evil is my Credo!*"

Allegro sostenuto

Enter Otello

Simultaneously, Iago begins to plant the seeds of jealousy in the mind of Otello. Through every kind of insinuation, he intimates that Desdemona is in love with Cassio:

Moderato

È u - n'i - dra fo - sca, li - vi - da,
It is the green - eyed mon - ster;

Desdemona and chorus (off stage)

Trying to forget these innuendoes, Otello gazes into the castle garden. There, in the shade of a tree, is the lovely Desdemona surrounded by a band of adoring children. "Iago!" he exclaims. "How could such a bride be unfaithful!" But the jealousy that Iago has planted is taking effect. When Desdemona appears in the audience chamber to plead for Cassio, the Moor rebuffs her rudely. An icy sweat assails him in an agony of suspicion.

Enter Desdemona and Emilia

"My husband!" cries Desdemona. "Let me help you!" She raises her handkerchief to his brow—but Otello drives her away. And now Iago perpetrates a new piece of villainy. Motioning to his wife Emilia, who is Desdemona's companion, he bids her retrieve the handkerchief that her mistress has dropped. The two women leave the chamber, and Iago secretes the precious token in his pocket.

Exeunt Desdemona and Emilia

Slowly, Otello's morale is cracking under the ensign's treachery. He bids farewell to peace of mind:

Allegro assai sostenuto

O - ra,e per sem - pre ad - dio san - te me - mo - rie
And now for - e - ver fare - well, thou tran - quil mind——

For the last time a need for proof stirs within him. "You may be lying," he shouts, seizing Iago by the throat. "What evidence have you that Desdemona is unfaithful?"

"A handkerchief," Iago calmly announces. "One that you gave her. It lies in Cassio's lodgings."

This is the final blow. In an outburst of fury, Otello swears revenge on his bride and Cassio. "Wait for me!" Iago exclaims. "I, too, will uphold Otello's honor!" Both men solemnly kneel and vow, by all that is sacred, to restore the Moor's good name:

Molto sostenuto

Act III

SCENE: THE GREAT HALL OF THE CASTLE (37 Minutes)

OTELLO and Iago are now constant companions. Sunk in brooding, the Moor pays little attention to the announcement of his herald that Lodovico, the Venetian ambassador, is approaching. He is too absorbed in thoughts of Desdemona and her guilt. *(Enter and exit Herald. Otello and Iago. Exit Iago)*

Suddenly, Desdemona enters the hall. "My lord," she pleads, "I have come to ask you once more to forgive Cassio." *(Enter Desdemona)*

"The handkerchief!" roars Otello. "Where is the handkerchief I gave you?"

Desdemona cannot reply; as she retreats in confusion, Otello drives her from the hall. "Why," he gasps, "have *I* been chosen to suffer these torments? What have I done to merit them?" *(Exit Desdemona)*

As Otello's grief reaches terrible proportions, Iago appears in the doorway with Cassio. Signing to the Moor to hide, the villain gaily discusses with the fallen lieutenant a mysterious handkerchief that Cassio has found the night before in his lodging: *(Enter Iago. Enter Cassio)*

Allegro brillante

Ques-ta è una ra • gna do-ve il tuo cuor ___ ca-sca, si la-gna, s'im-pi-glia e muor
This is a spi • der's web,where thy poor heart ___ is caught and lan-gui-shes, ne-ver to part

Otello, out of earshot, can only see the damning evidence. Now there is no doubt that his wife is guilty! When the trumpets are sounded and the Venetian ambassador enters with all the dignitaries of Cyprus, Otello has already embarked on an irrevocable course. Desdemona must die! *(Enter Lodovico, Roderigo, Desdemona Emilia and chorus)*

The arrival of the ambassador deals Iago's intrigue a stunning blow: by decree of the Doge, Otello has been recalled to Venice—and Cassio is to govern Cyprus in his place. But Iago thinks rapidly Accosting the weakling Roderigo, who has entered the castle with the other nobles, he whispers, "You must act! If Cassio rules Desdemona will leave the island with Otello, and you'll never possess her. Yet, if Cassio should be slain—" Under Iago's influence Roderigo has no alternative but to murder.

Exeunt all but Otello and Iago

Otello has been thoroughly humiliated by the message of recall; a jealous madness and resentment against the world are rising within him. "Leave me, all of you!" he screams. The crowd disperses and Otello, seized with a convulsion, writhes in torment on the ground. Only Iago remains, watching his victim with malevolent curiosity. As he hears the people of Cyprus shouting, "Long live the lion of Venice," Iago laughs derisively and points to the prostrate figure of the Moor. *"There,"* he exclaims, "lies your lion!"

ACT IV

SCENE: DESDEMONA'S BEDCHAMBER (30 Minutes)

Desdemona and Emilia

DESDEMONA, attended by Emilia, is about to retire. Her thoughts have turned to tragedy—she meditates on a familiar song, "Willow Willow," symbolic of unrequited love and early death:

Piangea— can-tan-do nel l'er-ma lan-da,— pian-gea la me - sta.
The poor— soul sat pi - ning, a-lone and lone-ly— there on the lone-ly strand.

The wind howls outside the window and a storm beats against the castle. Suddenly, as if seized by a dreadful portent, Desdemona embraces her companion in a last farewell.

Exit Emilia

Emilia has gone; the noise of the storm has ceased, and Desdemona kneels to chant her Ave Maria:

Pre - ga per chi a-do - ran-do a te, si pro - stra
Ah, pray for her who lies in pray'r be - fore thee

When she has finished her devotions, she extinguishes her candle and goes to bed. With an almost imperceptible movement, the chamber door opens and Otello appears, sword in hand. Gently he kisses his sleeping bride, and at his third kiss she awakens.

Enter Otello

"Prepare for death," the Moor whispers. "You have been unfaithful."

In vain does Desdemona protest her innocence. Ignoring her cry for mercy, Otello smothers her until the breath has left her body. Immediately, there is a pounding at the door. It is Emilia, who forces her way into the room.

Recoiling at the sight she beholds, the woman runs to summon the guard. And then she recalls the treachery of her husband, Iago—the episode of the handkerchief. "Desdemona was never false!" she exclaims to Otello. "It was Iago who deceived you!"

Denounced by Emilia before all the officers of Cyprus, Iago offers no defense. His plans to seize power on the island have failed; his protégé Roderigo has been slain in attempting to waylay Cassio. Now, with a last hope of escape, the villainous ensign rushes off, pursued by the guard.

All is over for the Moor of Venice. He is a virtual prisoner, forced to surrender his sword. "Farewell, glory!" he cries. "Otello's profession is gone!" Drawing a dagger from his cloak, he stabs himself and sinks beside the body of his wife. For the last time, he kisses her—then lapses into the sleep of death.

Enter Emilia
Enter Lodovico, Cassio, Montano, and Iago

Exit Iago

FALSTAFF

FALSTAFF, *a lyric comedy in three acts and six scenes, with text by Boito, was the last work that Verdi wrote for the stage. Its première took place at* La Scala, *Milan, on February 9, 1893, in the presence of the eighty-year-old composer. Shortly afterward, the comedy reached the Metropolitan Opera House (February, 1894), with Victor Maurel in the title role. During the Metropolitan performances of 1909, under the direction of Toscanini, Antonio Scotti sang the fat knight, as he did again in 1924, when Lawrence Tibbett made his first great success as Ford. Falstaff's most recent revival at the Metropolitan has taken place during the season of 1938-39, with Mr. Tibbett assuming the title role and John Brownlee singing the part of Ford.*

Characters, in order of appearance:

Dr. Caius, a physician: *tenor*
Sir John Falstaff: *baritone*
Followers of Falstaff { Bardolph: *tenor*
Pistol: *bass*
Mistress Ford (Alice): *soprano*
Anne, her daughter: *soprano*
Mistress Page (Meg): *mezzo-soprano*
Dame Quickly: *contralto*
Fenton, a young gentleman: *tenor*
Ford, a wealthy burgher: *baritone*
Host of the Garter Inn: *mute*

Burghers and street folk, Ford's servants,
maskers as elves and witches

Time: Fifteenth Century   *Place:* Windsor

Act I

SCENE 1: INTERIOR OF THE GARTER INN (17 Minutes)

SIR JOHN FALSTAFF, gentleman and knave extraordinary, is taking his ease under the spacious vaulting of the Garter Inn. Reclining in a great oaken chair, he makes no move as Dr. Caius, physician of Windsor town, storms into the room and accuses him of robbery:

Falstaff,
Bardolph
and Pistol
Enter
Dr. Caius

"Villain!" cries the doctor. "You've invaded my house! You've ridden my favorite horse to death! I demand satisfaction!"

"I have done all that you mention," Falstaff calmly replies.

Unable to contend with the fat knight, Dr. Caius looks sharply at Falstaff's two accomplices, Bardolph and Pistol. "You scoundrels picked my pockets last night," he shouts, "when I consented to drink with you!"

"Depart and drink no more!" chants Falstaff sanctimoniously. As the doctor goes off in a fury, Bardolph and Pistol follow him to the door, singing a sardonic "Amen!"

Exit
Dr. Caius

"Bardolph," Falstaff commands, "bring me my purse!" As the red-nosed Bardolph rummages through the purse and produces only a few pennies, Sir John knits his brows. Finally, an idea for a new source of revenue occurs to him.

"There is a man in Windsor town named Ford," he whispers to his accomplices. "I have never seen him, but they say he is rich. And his wife, fair Alice, is known to me indeed! If I were to win her and find the way to her husband's purse strings—all our problems would be ended!"

Taking a sealed letter from the table, he hands it to Bardolph. "Here," he commands, "convey this to my lovely Alice."

And now Sir John produces another letter, destined for an equally wealthy lady. "This is for my darling Meg—Mistress Page," he explains. "Pistol, you will be the bearer."

For the first time in his long association with Sir John, Pistol rebels. Bardolph, too, joins in this unexpected show of defiance. "Think of our honor!" they protest.

Giving the letters to little Robin who sweeps the tavern floor and bidding him deliver them to the two ladies, Falstaff turns angrily on his rebellious partners. "You speak of honor!" he snorts. "Can honor ever fill your stomach? No!"

Può l'o - no - re ____ ri - em - pir - vi la pan - cia? No.
Say can ho - nour ____ fill a paunch that is emp - ty? No.

Exeunt
Bardolph
and Pistol

Carried away by his own eloquence, Falstaff rises from his chair and snatches a broom. "Begone!" he cries. "I dismiss you both from my service!" Wielding the broom like an instrument of vengeance, he drives Bardolph and Pistol from the Garter Inn.

SCENE 2: A GARDEN (16 Minutes)

Unfortunately for Falstaff's plan, Mistress Ford and Mistress Page are the best of friends. They have received Sir John's expressions of love at the same time and have hastened to compare notes.

The two women are soon joined by Anne, Alice's daughter, and by the rotund Dame Quickly. Gathering in the garden of Alice' spacious home, they resolve to punish the fat knight and play a trick that will make him repent his indiscretion.

Enter
Alice,
Meg,
Dame
Quickly
and Anne
Exeunt
women
Enter
Ford,
Bardolph,
Pistol,
Dr. Caius
and
Fenton

No sooner have the women gone inside the house than Alice' husband, Master Ford, appears in the garden. Under normal circumstaces, he is prone to anger if anyone so much as looks at his wife. But now, he is at the height of a jealous fury. Bardolph and Pistol, hoping to atone for their past misdeeds, have told him of their master's infatuation for Alice. Accompanied by the two knaves, Ford is pacing the grounds of his house, trying to devise a solution that will avenge him on Falstaff. Dr. Caius, who already has good reason to hate the paunchy knight, has joined the company, and Fenton, a young gentleman, has also put in an appearance.

Exeunt
all but
Fenton
Enter
Anne

As the men go off to perfect a plot, only Fenton remains in the garden. He has come through no fervent friendship for Ford, but because he is anxious to see Ford's daughter, Anne, with whom he is in love. Suddenly, he spies her coming from the house.

"Anne!" he calls. "Two kisses before I go!"

Allegretto moderato

Boc - ca ba - cia - ta non per - de ven - tu - ra.
Kis -sing is fraught___ with an ex - qui - site plea - sure!

Their embrace is interrupted by the return of the three women who have contrived a plan to shame Falstaff: Dame Quickly will visit him at the Garter Inn—invite him to Alice's home—and then, he will be confronted by the recipient of his other love note: Mistress Page.

The men, too, have returned, although they do not see the women at the end of the garden. They have decided that Bardolph and Pistol will go to Falstaff and ask him to receive a wealthy stranger named Brook. In reality, the stranger will be Ford, whom Falstaff has never seen. Ford will encourage the knight to woo Mistress Alice—and when Falstaff is discovered in his courtship, revenge will be forthcoming.

As the men set out, the four women remain behind. "We'll puff the fat knight up," they predict ominously, "and then we'll explode him!"

Exit Fenton Enter Alice, Meg, Dame Quickly Enter men

Exeunt men

ACT II

SCENE 1: THE INTERIOR OF THE GARTER INN (24 Minutes)

FALSTAFF is still stretched in his chair, drinking a bottle of sack. He does not stir when Bardolph and Pistol enter the room and beat their breasts penitently. "Rascals come back to vice like cats to the cream jug!" he remarks.

"Master, there is a lady here to see you," the knaves announce. "Admit her!" orders Falstaff.

And now, the mischievous Dame Quickly enters and makes a sweeping bow:

Falstaff Enter Bardolph and Pistol Exeunt Bardolph and Pistol Enter Dame Quickly

Assai moderato

Re - ve - ren - za!
Sir, fair gree - ting!

"O Sir," she exclaims. "If only you knew how poor Alice Ford sighs for you! She has sent me to tell you that her husband is away every afternoon from two until three. Will you not come to see her?"

"Tell her that I await the hour with loving impatience," the fat knight proclaims.

"And Mistress Page, too, languishes for your favors."

At once, Falstaff loses his complacency and sits bolt upright in his chair. "These two ladies know nothing of each other's love affairs?" he inquires anxiously.

"Of course not, your Grace!" replies Dame Quickly. "I shall give them both your greeting." Bowing ironically, she leaves the chamber. Sir John is mightily pleased. Everything is going as he wishes:

Exit Dame Quickly

Enter Bardolph

Suddenly, Bardolph enters and announces a stranger—one Master Brook—who would speak with Falstaff. As an earnest of his good faith, the man has sent Sir John a demijohn of wine.

Exit Bardolph Enter Ford

"Ask him in!" exclaims the knight. "He is surely welcome!"

Falstaff gazes expectantly at the door, and the stranger appears. It is Ford, under the guise of Master Brook.

"Greetings, Sir John!" he exclaims. "I have come to you with a problem. Accept this bag of gold, I pray, and offer me your help."

As Falstaff stares with mounting interest at the man called Brook, the stranger continues, "I am in love with Alice Ford. She has constantly refused me, claiming faithfulness to her husband. If *you* were to break down her scruples, perhaps there would be a chance for me!"

"Nothing easier!" Falstaff replies. "Her husband is away every day from two until three. If you'll wait a moment, I'll put on gayer clothes and set out right now!"

Exit Falstaff

As Falstaff goes inside to dress, Ford looks after him with horror:

Enter Falstaff

All through his married life, he has been obsessed with fear of being made a cuckold—the bane of Elizabethan existence! Now, believing his wife is actually unfaithful, he suffers deadly anguish. "I will have revenge," he vows.

At this moment, Falstaff returns, wearing his gaudiest attire. "I am ready, Master Brook," the knight calls gaily. "Let us start!"

SCENE 2: A ROOM IN FORD'S HOUSE (19 Minutes)

In a flutter of excitement, Alice, Meg, Dame Quickly and Anne prepare to receive Sir John Falstaff. Their plot against the knight is to be carried out in the main room of the house, which fronts on the river Thames; they have decided to frighten the knight, hide him in a laundry basket, and toss him into the water below. Alice, Meg, Dame Quickly and Anne

As the basket is brought in and all the details arranged, Alice glances keenly at her daughter. "What is wrong, Anne?" she demands. "Why are you so melancholy?"

"I am in love with Fenton," Anne exclaims, "and father insists that I marry old Dr. Caius."

"Think nothing of it!" Alice answers. Turning to Meg and Dame Quickly, she bids them put the finishing touches to the fat knight's reception.

Suddenly, they hear Falstaff approaching. The women rush away, and only Alice remains, playing her lute. Exeunt all but Alice Enter Falstaff

"At last I've caught you!" chuckles Falstaff, as he swaggers into the room.

Surprised by Alice's reticence, he plies her with compliments and extravagant phrases. "As for myself," he adds discreetly, "you must know that I was not always a stout man. Once, years ago, I was as light as a feather!"

Allegro con brio

Quand'e-ro pag-gio del Du-ca di Norfolck, e-ro sot-ti-le, sot-ti-le, sot-ti-le.
When I was page to the Duke of Norfolk's Grace, slen-der of fig-ure and come-ly of face,—

Just as the knight is attempting to embrace his fair Alice, Dame Quickly rushes into the chamber. "Mistress Ford!" she cries. "Mistress Page is at the door—she is shouting that she must see you!" Enter Dame Quickly Enter Meg

While Falstaff beats a hasty retreat behind a screen, Meg enters the room in great agitation. She had intended to frighten Falstaff with a fabricated story of Ford's approach—but now, unfortunately, Ford is really approaching!

In a moment, the jealous husband appears, trailed by Fenton, Dr. Caius, Bardolph and Pistol. "Where is your lover?" he cries, glancing furiously at his wife. When Alice does not answer, he rummages through the soiled linen in the laundry basket—but he finds nothing. Enter Ford, Fenton, Dr.Caius, Bardolph, Pistol and neighbors

"Bolt all the gates!" Ford commands. "We'll search the house!"

As the irate man and his followers set off on their quest, Falstaff runs from his hiding place and begs Alice to save him. At once, the women conceal him in the laundry basket. Exeunt men Enter Anne

Enter
men

Finding no quarry in the other rooms, Ford returns savagely to his wife's chamber and renews the search. Suddenly, he hears a noise behind the screen. Throwing it aside, he finds his daughter Anne in the arms of Fenton. "Leave my house at once!" he orders Fenton. "My daughter shall marry Dr. Caius!"

Exit
Falstaff

Alice decides that her husband has been tortured enough. Ringing a bell, she summons the servants and bids them cast the laundry basket and its contents into the river. Staggering under the burden, the servants carry out her command.

Mistress Ford draws her husband to the window. Much to his surprise and joy he sees Falstaff tumbling into the Thames—and as the neighbors shout their approval, Ford embraces his faithful wife.

ACT III

SCENE 1: A STREET IN FRONT OF THE GARTER INN (17 Minutes)

Falstaff

THOROUGHLY soaked by his bath in the river, Falstaff sits at a table before the Garter Inn, drying his garments and cursing the world in general. "Host!" he cries. "A beaker of mulled sherry!"

Enter
and Exit
Host

As the slovenly innkeeper shuffles off to fetch the wine, Sir John resumes his misanthropic train of thought. "What a wicked world!" he mutters.

The host returns with the sherry, and Sir John decides to drown his sorrows. "Good wine dispels the vapors of melancholy," he reflects, as a series of trills rises from the orchestra.

Enter
Dame
Quickly

Falstaff suddenly gulps his drink and stares in astonishment—Dame Quickly has appeared with a letter.

"Forgive us!" she pleads. "Alice is heartbroken—your drenching was all a mistake on the part of the servants!"

Falstaff is sufficiently vain to be fooled again. As he reads the amorous note that Dame Quickly bears him, Alice herself steals down the street and looks on in sly amusement.

"You must meet Mistress Ford this very night at twelve!" Dame Quickly declares. "She will be waiting near the great oak in Windsor Forest—the very tree where Herne the Hunter hanged himself. To ward off all intruders, you shall appear disguised as Herne's ghost!"

Exeunt
Falstaff
and
Quickly
Enter
Alice,
Anne,
Meg,
Ford and
Dr. Caius

"Come inside," Falstaff whispers to Dame Quickly. "We can talk more freely there." As the fat knight and his lady enter the tavern, Alice draws closer to the inn. She is accompanied by her husband, her daughter, Mistress Page and Dr. Caius.

"We'll trap him beautifully!" she exclaims. "At midnight, when he reaches the oak, we shall be masked. Anne will be Queen of the

Fairies—Meg will be a woodland nymph—and Dame Quickly an enchantress. I'll have a group of boys and girls dressed as sprites. They'll mock the knight and they'll pinch him until he begs for mercy!"

Twilight soon descends upon the street; the women hurry off to arrange the masque. Only Dr. Caius lingers in front of the inn with Alice's husband.

Exeunt Alice, Anne, Meg

"I promise," Ford declares, "that my daughter Anne shall be yours. During the merrymaking tonight lead her before me—and I will bless you both as man and wife!"

Exeunt Ford and Dr. Caius

Ford and Caius confidently saunter away; but Dame Quickly, coming from the inn, has overheard their plot. Smiling to herself, she goes off to warn young Anne.

Enter and Exit Dame Quickly

SCENE 2: WINDSOR FOREST (30 Minutes)

It is just before the midnight hour. Fenton is the first to arrive at Herne's oak. As he dreams tenderly of his beloved Anne, the girl herself appears; but the lovers are parted by Alice, Meg and Dame Quickly, who come scurrying through the forest.

Enter Fenton Enter Anne Enter Alice, Meg and Dame Quickly

"Here!" Alice commands. "Fenton, you are to wear this disguise—and ask no questions!"

The women have conceived the idea of dressing the youth in the same outfit as Dr. Caius, in order to spoil Ford's carefully laid plans. Now that their preparations are finished, they run off—for they hear Falstaff approaching.

Exeunt all Enter Falstaff

Soon the fat knight appears, dressed as Herne, the legendary huntsman. Just as he enters, a distant clock strikes midnight. Alice emerges from among the trees.

Enter Alice

No sooner does Falstaff attempt to embrace her when Meg scampers through the forest crying, "Alice, beware! The witches are coming!"

Enter Meg

The two women run away, leaving Falstaff in confusion. And soon the voice of Anne is heard, calling the elves of Windsor Forest:

Exeunt Alice and Meg

Enter
Anne,
ballet and
chorus
Enter
all the
principals

Amid a throng of witches, goblins and specters, Anne appears dressed as the Fairy Queen. Little children, disguised as imps, pinch Falstaff until he screams for mercy. Still, the fat knight's punishment is not over. In company with Ford and Dr. Caius, the truculent Bardolph and Pistol enter, disguised as avenging spirits. Wielding a broomstick, they thrash Falstaff thoroughly.

At the height of the tumult, Bardolph's cloak slips off, and Falstaff recognizes his tormentor. Suddenly, the knight realizes that the entire midnight revel is only a trick—that he has been shamed before all of Windsor. Having no other choice, he promises to mend his ways with such good humor that even the jealous Ford forgives him.

And now, to the accompaniment of a lantern procession, two masked figures come through the forest. One of them is Dr. Caius; the other, heavily veiled in white, is attired as Queen of the Fairies.

"May this young couple be happily united," Ford proclaims. "Let us cast away our disguises!" Dr. Caius ecstatically removes his mask. As he turns to kiss his bride, he recoils in confusion. Anne has eluded him, and the substitute Queen of the Fairies is none other than the red-nosed Bardolph.

Following the example set by Falstaff, Ford accepts this defeat with good grace; he blesses the marriage of his daughter to Fenton. Filled with the liveliest spirits, all the Windsor townspeople in the forest shout for joy. Anne embraces Fenton; Ford kisses his wife, forswearing jealousy for all time—and Falstaff, a reformed but happy man, induces the whole assemblage to join him in praise of mirth:

Tut-to nel mon-do è bur-la. L'uom___ è na-to bur-lo-ne, bur-lo-ne, bur-lo-ne.
Jest-ing is man's vo-ca-tion, Wise___ is he who is jol-ly, is jol-ly, is jol-ly.

VIII

Opera Takes It Personally

WHILE Halévy and Meyerbeer were crowding four or five acts with the pomp and circumstance of grand opera, François Adrien Boieldieu (1775-1834) and Daniel François Auber (1782-1871) turned for their subjects to the gentler intrigues of the village green. They carried the tradition of the *opéra comique* to such a point of sentimentality that it only remained for Jacques Offenbach to reduce them to a caricature in his witty farces.

Today neither type of opera is often heard. The modern audience finds one too pompous and the other too pretty for pleasure. But midway between them another style arose: the lyric opera which is still the basis of the French repertory.

Grand opera traditions lent dignity to the new works, from Gounod's *Faust* to Saint-Saëns' *Samson et Dalila*. Processions still marched through the finales. Historic subjects were still invoked.

The essential novelty of French lyric opera was first of all the importance of human passion, no longer merely a motivating factor, but now the subject of the action, as in Bizet's *Carmen*. The subject material was of distinct literary importance. The composers went to Goethe (Thomas' *Mignon*); Shakespeare (Gounod's *Roméo et Juliette*); Anatole France (Massenet's *Thaïs*) and other masters.

In many of the works the melodic features were outstanding. Delibes' *Lakmé* required as accomplished a coloratura soprano as Donizetti's *Lucia* of forty-eight years before. The title role of Massenet's *Manon* lay within the repertory of a lyric soprano, but several of its passages demanded coloratura range and flexibility.

The continuous popularity of the French lyric repertory is due less to these embellishments than to the intense personal relationships and strongly marked personalities of the operas. Most of them are known by the name of the heroine. Many are remembered for the temperament of the artists associated with them. Though the vocal assignments of these works were not exacting, the roles demanded convincing interpreters.

The influence of Wagner on his French contemporaries was more obvious to the critics of the time than it is today. The use of a few thematic characterizations with later references scattered through the score for purposes of association cannot be compared with the leading motives of Wagner. The French opera orchestra was asked to play an occasional introduction or *intermezzo* of deeper atmospheric significance than it had in the preceding generation, but in no such heroic mold as the Wagnerian preludes.

Like Wagner, Bizet chose a variety of characteristic rhythms to sharpen his musical portraiture. Massenet attempted the continuous melody of the Wagnerian line. But the essence of their school was not epic but lyric; not thematic, but melodic; not heroic but purely and passionately personal.

GOUNOD

CHARLES FRANÇOIS GOUNOD was born at Paris on June 17, 1818, and like most of his musical contemporaries, attended classes at the Paris *Conservatoire*. At the age of nineteen, he won the *Grand Prix de Rome*, being strongly influenced during his stay in the ancient city by its ecclesiastical atmosphere. This reverence for the music of the church persisted throughout his lifetime, finding reflection in many of the choruses of *Faust* and in the character of Friar Laurence, which dominates the third act of *Roméo et Juliette*.

Gounod's first stage piece, *Sapho*, was performed at the Paris *Opéra* in 1851. Thereafter, the composer found an outlet for his works at the *Théâtre Lyrique*, which presented his farce after Molière's play *Le Médecin Malgré Lui* in 1858 and his opera *Faust* during the following year. With the addition of several incidental ballets, *Faust* was later mounted at the Paris *Opéra*.

Roméo et Juliette found Gounod continuing to write for the *Théâtre Lyrique*. In the final period of his life, the composer worked increasingly at religious music until his death at Saint-Cloud on October 17, 1893.

FAUST

FAUST, *a grand opera in five acts now presented in four, was given for the first time at the* Théâtre Lyrique, *Paris, in 1859. Based by the librettists Barbier and Carré on the great medieval legend which Goethe immortalized in his play, it won a large public at its first hearing and was subsequently revised (1869) to fit the policies of the Paris* Opéra, *where it has been a favorite ever since.* Faust *was the work chosen to open the Metropolitan Opera House on October 22, 1883. Christine Nilsson, who had taken part in the Paris revival of 1869, again sang the music of Marguerite.*

Characters, in order of appearance:

Faust: *tenor*
Mephistopheles: *bass-baritone*
Wagner: *baritone*
Valentin: *baritone*
Siebel: *mezzo-soprano*
Marguerite: *soprano*
Martha: *contralto*
Townspeople, soldiers, students,
    chorus of demons, priests,
    chorus of angels.

Time: Sixteenth Century   *Place:* Germany

Act I

scene 1: faust's study (23 Minutes)

Steeped in the monastic ideals of the Middle Ages, the philosopher Faust has acquired knowledge at the expense of youth and love. Tired and old—brooding on thoughts of death—he sits in his lonely study. From outside his window come the songs of the workers in the fields. Their cheerful melodies increase his bitterness.

"May all human pleasure be accursed!" he exclaims. "Away with faith! O Satan, angel of evil, appear to me now!"

"I am here!" thunders a voice in the darkness of the study. Trembling with fright, Faust beholds Mephistopheles standing before him.

"Why are you surprised?" demands the Devil. "Is it my attire that upsets you? I travel like any nobleman, with plume in my cap and cloak on my shoulder!"

"Begone!" Faust mutters, fearing to look upon his visitor.

"What!" cries Mephistopheles. "You summon me from afar and then tell me to go? Remember—I can bring you gold—power— glory!"

"I want none of these," Faust answers wearily. "I crave only youth!"

"Very well!" laughs the Devil. "You shall have it—and my fee is small. On earth, I will be your servant; below, you shall wait on *me!*"

Thrusting a document at Faust, Mephistopheles bids him sign; Faust hesitates. "Are you afraid?" cries the Devil. "Behold the delights that await you!" With a wave of his hand, the archfiend conjures up the vision of a young girl at her spinning wheel— Marguerite. At once, Faust signs the compact.

"Here, O master," whispers the Fiend. "Drain this goblet!"

As the philosopher swallows the potion, all signs of age disappear from his face and figure. He stands erect, attired in splendid doublet and hose with a sword at his side. "Come!" urges Mephistopheles. "We must go forth into the world!"

Guided by his infernal ally, Faust rushes from the study to embark on a life of pleasure.

(Left margin:)
Faust
Towns-
people
(*invisible*)

Mephi-
stopheles

SCENE 2: THE KERMESSE (25 Minutes)

The great market place of the city is filled with soldiers and merrymakers. Soon the troops will be setting off to the war, and hope of a speedy victory pervades the town. Soldiers, townspeople

Only one melancholy figure appears in the square—the soldier Valentin, brother of Marguerite. He has come to drink with his friends Wagner and Siebel; but he is unmoved by the gaiety about him. "I am worried," he exclaims to his comrades. "Who shall look after my sister when I have left for the wars?" Enter Valentin

Andante

A - vant de quit - ter ces lieux, Sol na - tal de mes a - ïeux,
E - ven brav - est heart may swell In the mo - ment of fare - well.

"I will protect her!" vows the young boy Siebel. Siebel

"We shall all watch over her!" the townspeople declare.

The devoted Wagner tries to banish Valentin's gloom. "Let us drink!" he shouts. "And I'll entertain you with a song: Wagner

'A rat who was born a coward and was ugly too,
Once sat in the Abbot's cellar 'neath a barrel new' . . ."

Suddenly, Wagner breaks off. He is interrupted by a mysterious nobleman who seems to have emerged from nowhere. "May I join your party?" asks the unbidden guest. "I'll regale you with a song of my own—one better than yours!" Enter Mephistopheles

Allegro

Le veau d'or___ est tou - jours de - bout
Clear the way___ for the Calf of Gold!

The townspeople glance suspiciously at the noble. What irreligious words are these that he sings in praise of Mammon and the calf of gold? As they appraise him with growing curiosity, the stranger utters a few magic phrases and produces wine for the whole company. "To Marguerite!" he cries ironically, raising his glass.

Valentin draws his sword. "Be silent," shouts the soldier, "or I'll have your life!" Looking down, he discovers to his amazement that his blade is broken. Only then do the bystanders realize they are in the presence of the Devil. But Valentin grasps the crossed hilt of

Exeunt
all but
Mephi-
stopheles

Enter
Faust

Enter
towns-
people
and ballet

Enter
Siebel
Exit
Siebel
Enter
Marguerite

Exit
Marguerite

his sword and raises it in defiance. The populace, following his example, makes the sign of the cross. Powerless against the holy symbol, Mephistopheles is forced to let them escape. "We shall meet again!" he calls threateningly.

And now Faust crosses the market place in search of his ally. "When shall I see Marguerite?" he demands.

"She will soon be here," answers Mephistopheles. "But I warn you—she is difficult!"

The townspeople have begun to stream back to the square. Dancers appear, gaily keeping time to a waltz:

Much to his annoyance, Mephistopheles spies the lovesick Siebel among the crowd. The youth secretly adores Marguerite, and may cause trouble. "Aha, my young friend," exclaims the Devil, advancing on the boy, "so you are here again!" As Siebel runs off in terror, Marguerite crosses the square on her way from church.

Resolutely, Faust approaches the maiden. "Forgive me," he declares. "May I guide you homeward?"

"I need no escort," Marguerite replies timidly. As she walks onward, Faust looks after her with passion. "I love her!" he cries.

Dancers fill the square and the merry cries of the townspeople ring through the city. Faust goes off with his evil tutor, Mephistopheles. He must win Marguerite!

Act II

SCENE: THE GARDEN OF MARGUERITE'S HOUSE (48 Minutes)

Siebel

Exit
Siebel
Enter
Faust and
Mephi-
stopheles
Exit
Mephi-
stopheles

SIEBEL has been frightened by the satanic stranger—but not discouraged. Having sworn an oath to watch over Marguerite, the boy lingers near her house, to see that no harm befalls her. He enters the deserted garden and leaves a bouquet of flowers as a token of his love:

No sooner has Siebel departed, than Faust and Mephistopheles arrive. "Flowers!" mocks the Devil, as he notes the modest bouquet on the doorstep. "Wait! I shall bring a more persuasive gift!" He runs off, and Faust is left alone in contemplation of Marguerite's humble dwelling:

Larghetto

Sa - lut! de - meu - re chaste et pure!
All hail, thou dwell - ing pure and low - ly

Mephistopheles returns with a casket of jewels. "I warrant these will outshine young Siebel's message of love!" he declares.

As the conspirators hear Marguerite approach, they hide. The girl passes through the garden, dreaming of the youth who accosted her on the way from church. "If only I knew his name!" she murmurs.

The maiden sets her spinning wheel in motion and hums an old ballad as she works:

Moderato

Il é - tait un Roi de Thulé,
Reign'd a king in Thu - le of old,

At last, she rises restlessly and goes toward the house. There, on her doorstep, waits the bouquet of Siebel; and beneath it, a jewel box. Raising the lid, Marguerite cries out in delight:

Allegretto

Ah! _____ Je ris __ de me voir si belle en ce mi - roir!
Ah! _____ the joy __ past compare these jew - els bright to wear!

A mirror lies within the casket. Marguerite adorns herself with precious gems, pausing to admire their effect. Suddenly, she hears someone coming from behind the house. It is Aunt Martha, a middle-aged lady of uncertain principles.

"Gracious!" Martha cheerfully exclaims. "Who gave you all those gems?"

The woman's prattle is cut short by the appearance of two strangers. Marguerite cannot repress her excitement as she recognizes the youth from the market place. His sinister companion is not known to her.

With a courtly bow, the man addresses Martha. "Madame Schwertlein? I have come with tragic news. Your husband is dead —and leaves you nothing but good wishes!"

Martha swoons—but recovers in time to ogle the gallant stranger. As twilight falls, she invites him into a recess of the garden. Instead of following, he discourteously vanishes, with Martha in full pursuit.

Enter Mephistopheles
Exeunt Faust and Mephistopheles
Enter Marguerite

Enter Martha

Enter Faust and Mephistopheles

Exeunt Martha and Mephistopheles

Faust is left with his beloved. "You are lonely," he declares.

"My mother is dead," answers Marguerite, "and my brother gone to war."

Exeunt
Faust and
Marguerite
Enter
Mephi-
stopheles
Faust offers the girl his arm and they stroll among the deepening shadows. The watchful Mephistopheles appears, staring sardonically after the lovers. Satisfied with the effect of his jewels, the Arch-fiend commands the flowers of night to breathe upon the passion of Marguerite.

Exit
Mephi-
stopheles
Enter
Faust and
Marguerite
Exit
Marguerite
Enter
Mephi-
stopheles
Enter
Marguerite
Hearing the lovers return, he conceals himself. And now Marguerite, fearful of the longing that consumes her, begs Faust to leave. "Tomorrow," she promises, "I shall see you again!" Filled with the joy of being loved, she goes into the house and Faust turns to depart.

Immediately, Mephistopheles appears in the darkness and confronts his pupil: "Don't you realize, Dr. Faust, that the girl is yours?" With a scornful smile, he directs the attention of Faust to an upper story of the dwelling. Marguerite has taken her place at the window and is gazing at the stars. "He loves me!" she exclaims.

Aflame with passion, Faust climbs into Marguerite's chamber; and as the maiden sinks in his arms, the laughter of Mephistopheles rises from below.

ACT III

SCENE 1: A CHURCH (9 Minutes)

MARGUERITE has yielded—and Faust has deserted her. Now the wretched maiden, filled with fear for her salvation, enters the church to pray.

Enter
Marguerite

"O Lord, who givest ear to all repentance," she pleads, "have pity on my suffering!"

Mephi-
stopheles
(invisible)
Suddenly, a terrible voice sounds through the dimly lighted arches. "No!" it cries. "You shall pray no more! You shall not be forgiven!"

Appalled, the maiden crouches on the ground. "What voice

ascends from the shadow?" she gasps. "Alas, what doom is upon me?"

The muffled tones of the organ can be heard in the distance, and the chanting of the priests. "Ah!" moans the girl. "I am stifling!"

Chorus of priests (*invisible*)

Once more, the awful voice rises from the shadows: "Farewell, nights of love! Marguerite—*your soul is damned!*" A tomb opens and the Archfiend appears. With a shriek of despair, the girl falls prostrate in the deserted nave.

Enter Mephistopheles

SCENE 2: A PUBLIC SQUARE (21 Minutes)

The city is alive with excitement—the soldiers are returning from the wars. Singing lustily, the troops march to the square and disperse:

Enter soldiers

Tempo marziale

Gloire im - mor - tel - le de nos a - ïeux,   Sois nous fi - dè - le, Mourons comme eux!
Glo - ry and love to the men of old!—   Their sons may co - py their vir - tue bold!—

Among them is Valentin, eager to see his sister once more. "Siebel!" he calls, noticing the boy among the throng. "Come celebrate with me!"

Exeunt soldiers Enter Valentin and Siebel

Siebel turns gloomily away. "What is wrong?" Valentin demands. His anxiety aroused, the soldier rushes homeward as Siebel goes off in the twilight.

Exit Valentin and Siebel

And now the sinister figures of Mephistopheles and his pupil invade the square. Actuated by a genuine love for Marguerite, Faust has returned; but he brings only disaster in his wake.

Enter Faust and Mephistopheles

"First we must arouse your loved one!" Mephistopheles declares. "Trust to me!" Strumming a guitar, he intones a mocking serenade that ends in brutal laughter:

Allegretto

Vous qui fai - tes l'en - dor - mi -   e, N'en - ten - dez vous pas,——
Ca - ta - ri - na, while you sham a - sleep, you con - trive to hear,——

The door of the house opens and instead of Marguerite, Valentin appears. "Stay close to me!" the Devil whispers to Faust. "I'll take care of the soldier!"

Enter Valentin

Valentin has already learned of his sister's betrayal; now, finding her betrayer, he challenges Faust to a duel. Conquered by the satanic art of his opponent, the soldier falls, mortally wounded, and Faust escapes with Mephistopheles.

Exeunt Faust and Mephistopheles

Soon, the square is filled with friends of the dying Valentin.

Enter
towns-
people,
Siebel,
Martha
and
Marguerite

Siebel and Martha come to his aid. Marguerite runs anxiously through the crowd.

"Begone!" cries the soldier as his sister approaches. "Marguerite, I have been slain by your lover. Though God above may forgive you, I curse you with my dying breath!"

Valentin slumps to the ground. As his comrades kneel in prayer, Marguerite staggers toward the house, sobbing hysterically. Madness is already upon her.

Act IV

SCENE: MARGUERITE'S PRISON CELL (12 Minutes)

Marguerite
Enter
Faust and
Mephi-
stopheles
Exit
Mephi-
stopheles

THE wretched girl has slain the child she bore to Faust. Cast into prison, she is waiting to be led to the scaffold.

Faust has returned to save his beloved. Together with Mephistopheles, he has slipped past the jailor and entered the cell. Mephistopheles departs—and Faust gazes with horror at the demented creature lying on the pallet. "Marguerite!" he cries.

The girl awakens. She murmurs vaguely of the past—of their meeting at the Kermesse—of their tryst in the garden.

"Come with me!" pleads Faust. "We must escape."

Enter
Mephi-
stopheles

Suddenly, Mephistopheles appears at the prison door. "Hurry," he exclaims, "or all will be lost!"

Marguerite rises and stands transfixed. She recognizes the terrible voice, the blazing eye. "The Fiend!" she screams. "Why is he here?"

"For the last time," Faust begs her, "will you come with me?"

The haunted expression vanishes from the countenance of Marguerite. Kneeling in prayer, she invokes the help of God:

Moderato maestoso

An - ges purs, an - ges ra - di - eux,— Por-tez mon âme au sein des cieux!—
An-gels pure, an-gels— of light,— Bear ye my soul to heav'n so bright!—

Death of
Marguerite
Chorus of
angels
(invisible)
Exeunt
Faust and
Mephi-
stopheles

"Marguerite!" Faust implores. "We must be gone!"

"Then go!" shrieks the maiden. "I abhor your sight!" With a terrible cry, she expires.

"Her soul is mine!" Mephistopheles exults.

"No!" answers a chorus of celestial voices. "She is redeemed!"

The Archfiend, retreating in dismay, drags Faust with him into the fiery pit while Marguerite is borne aloft to Heaven by the angelic host.

ROMÉO ET JULIETTE

ROMÉO ET JULIETTE, *an opera in five acts and six scenes, with a libretto based by Barbier and Carré on Shakespeare's tragedy, was composed by Charles François Gounod at the age of seventy, eight years after he had completed* Faust. *A hundred consecutive performances at the* Théâtre Lyrique, *in Paris, where it was originally presented in 1867, were followed by a revival at the* Opéra Comique *in 1873. The work entered the repertory of the* Grand Opéra *in 1888.*

The part of Juliette was created for the Metropolitan in 1891 by Emma Eames, who had studied it with the composer. Since that year it has been presented during each of twenty-eight Metropolitan seasons.

Characters, in order of appearance:
Tybalt, nephew to Count Capulet: *tenor*
Count Paris: *baritone*
Count Capulet: *bass*
Juliette, his daughter: *soprano*
Mercutio: *baritone*
Gertrude, Juliette's nurse: *mezzo-soprano*
Roméo, a Montague: *tenor*
Gregorio, a Capulet retainer: *baritone*
Friar Laurence: *bass*
Stefano, page to Roméo: *mezzo-soprano*
Duke of Verona: *bass*
Benvolio, a Montague retainer: *tenor*

Time: Fourteenth Century   *Place:* Verona

PROLOGUE (6 Minutes)

A brief orchestral introduction sounds a somber martial theme followed by a vigorous fugato.

The curtain rises, disclosing the entire cast assembled on the darkened stage. In a brief commentary on the feud between the Capulets and Montagues of Verona, they chant of the tragic love of Roméo and Juliette:

ACT I

SCENE: BALLROOM OF THE CAPULETS, VERONA (30 Minutes)

Guests

COUNT CAPULET is giving a masquerade in honor of his young daughter, Juliette. To a spirited waltz measure the guests express their delight.

Enter Tybalt and Paris

"How do you like the party?" asks Tybalt, the host's nephew, of his friend, Count Paris. "You haven't seen the prize yet, though I understand she is destined for you."

Enter Capulet and Juliette Exeunt all Enter Roméo, Mercutio, and friends (*masked*) and Gregorio

"I am sure I shall love her," answers Paris, as the elderly Capulet makes his formal entry, his daughter Juliette on his arm.

"Welcome!" exclaims the host, introducing his daughter to the admiring guests.

When the room is finally cleared, Mercutio and Roméo, son of the house of Montague, enter with a few companions, all wearing masks.

"No one must know us here," warns Roméo prudently, though the foolhardy Mercutio hints that it would be easy to fight their way out of any trouble with the quarrelsome Capulets.

Roméo is uneasy. He has had a premonition of ill. Mercutio suggests that Mab, Queen of the Fairies, is responsible:

Enter Juliette and nurse

Suddenly, as his friends twit him about a former sweetheart, Roméo catches sight of Juliette.

"Never have I seen beauty before," he murmurs passionately, while the friends laugh at his change of fancy.

They draw aside to watch the approach of Juliette with her old
nurse. "I wish to live in the dreams of my youth," exclaims the
girl, to the swirling rhythm of the famous waltz:

A Capulet retainer, Gregorio, summons the nurse Gertrude to
supper, leaving Roméo free to address Juliette.

Hardly has he stolen his first kiss, when Tybalt interrupts their
duet, recognizes Roméo as his mortal enemy, and vows his death.
The young Montague, appalled to find that he has fallen in love
with the daughter of the Capulets, goes off to summon his friends,
leaving Juliette terrified. As Roméo reappears with Mercutio, and
Paris arrives to encourage Tybalt, a fight grows imminent. At the
hospitable overtures of Count Capulet, however, the young men
grudgingly sheathe their swords.

Exeunt Gregorio and Gertrude, Mercutio and friends Enter Tybalt Enter Mercutio and Paris Enter Capulet

Act II

SCENE: THE GARDEN OF THE CAPULETS (23 Minutes)

THROUGH the shadows of Count Capulet's moonlit garden, Roméo
braves his way, hoping to see Juliette once more. In the distance
he hears the voices of Mercutio and his other friends, calling him
away. Unheeding, he turns to the balcony where a sudden light
appears at Juliette's window. He sings an ardent serenade:

Enter Roméo

Sadly Juliette appears on the balcony. "Wherefore art thou
Roméo?" she sighs. "Deny the name, or I'll forswear my own."

The lovers are interrupted for a moment by Gregorio and a
group of Capulet servants who come looking for a page of the
Montagues supposedly hiding within the palace grounds. The nurse
Gertrude promises them her help, and finding Juliette, chides her
for being up so late, and leads her off to bed.

Roméo now emerges from his hiding place to hear Juliette again
calling him from the balcony: "If you wish to marry me, I will give
you all my life, but if you jest—then never see me more." With
her hand reaching down to his, the lovers bid each other farewell
until the morrow.

Enter Juliette

Gertrude

Exit
Juliette
At the repeated summons of her nurse, Juliette retires to her
room, leaving Roméo to wish her sweet dreams and smiling sleep

ACT III
SCENE 1: FRIAR LAURENCE'S CELL (9 Minutes)

Friar
Laurence,
Roméo
Enter
Juliette
and
Gertrude
DAWN is breaking when Roméo hastens to meet Juliette in Friar
Laurence's bleak cell. In spite of their family feud, the ancient
monk promises to unite the lovers. Kneeling before him, with the
nurse Gertrude for witness, they pledge their marriage vows under
his solemn blessing:

Dieu,___ qui fis l'homme à ton i - ma - ge,
Thou,___ who mad'st man in thine own im - age,

SCENE 2: A STREET (20 Minutes)

Stefano
Roméo's page Stefano seeks his master near the palace of the
Capulets, and sings an impudent song which rouses the household:

Que fais- tu, blan- che tour- te - rel - le,
Dain -ty dove, wherefore art thou ly - ing,

Enter
Gregorio
Enter
Mercutio
Enter
Tybalt
Enter
Roméo
Angry at the noise that has wakened him, Gregorio rushes out to
put an end to the impertinence with his sword. Mercutio finds them
fencing and blames the Capulet retainer for drawing on a mere
boy. At this Tybalt breaks in, engaging Mercutio until Roméo
arrives in time to separate them. Even the insults of Capulet's
nephew cannot, however, persuade Roméo to fight. He will not
take offense at any kinsman of his beloved. Only when Mercutio
resumes the quarrel and is desperately wounded by Tybalt, does
Roméo fling his scruples aside and avenge the murder of his friend.

Enter
crowd
Enter
Capulet
Enter
Duke
Meanwhile a crowd of both factions has gathered, shouting curses
at each other. Count Capulet himself emerges from his palace in
time to see Tybalt fall before Roméo's sword. Cries of vengeance
rise on all sides. The Duke of Verona makes an impressive entrance,
demands an oath of fealty, and banishes the wretched Roméo.

ACT IV
SCENE: JULIETTE'S CHAMBER (19 Minutes)

Juliette
Enter
Roméo
AT the risk of death Roméo has made his way to his bride's chamber,
where she readily forgives him the murder of her cousin Tybalt.
Together their voices rise in farewell:

Nuit d'hym-é - né - e!—
Night love in - vi - ted!—

"Listen!" says Roméo sadly. "The song of the lark reminds us that day has come."

"No," Juliette assures him, "it is the sweet nightingale, singing of love." Tearing herself from his embrace, she urges him to go.

Exit Roméo Enter nurse, Capulet and Friar Laurence

Hardly is she alone before the nurse comes in with the news that Count Capulet and Friar Laurence are at the door.

"Let sorrow be turned to joy," announces her father. "In accordance with Tybalt's dying request, you will prepare to wed Count Paris!" He departs, leaving the friar to instruct Juliette further.

Exit Capulet

"It is better to die than to accept this miserable fate," exclaims Juliette desperately, begging the aged priest to help her. The kind old man is prepared to come to her aid.

"Drink this potion," he answers gently. "It will cause you to fall into a deep sleep like unto death. When you wake on the morrow, I shall bring your husband to take you away."

Act V
scene: the tomb of juliette (18 Minutes)

A brief orchestral interlude reflects the peace of the tomb where Juliette lies on her snowy bier. Awed by the darkness and silence of the dim arches, Roméo enters, hailing the radiant beauty of his bride.

Juliette (asleep) Enter Roméo

Unaware that it is a trance which gives her the semblance of death, he lifts a phial of poison in frenzy to his lips, and drinks to his beloved. He has barely swallowed the draught, when she awakens, bewildered, and joins him in a hymn of exaltation.

Dieu de bon-té! —
Fa - ther of love! —

Their joy is short lived. He tells her of the poison which even now is numbing his limbs. Faintly he reminds her of the lark whose song she mistook for the nightingale.

"The moment is sweet," answers Juliette, tenderly. She too will seek the solace of death. Stabbing herself with a dagger that she has concealed, she joins him in a last plea for the pardon of Heaven. The lovers die peacefully in each other's arms.

THOMAS

AMBROISE THOMAS was born at Metz on August 15, 1811, and studied composition at the Paris *Conservatoire*. He tried for the *Prix de Rome* and won it, in 1832, with his cantata *Hermann et Ketty*. At the start of his formal career, Thomas wrote many ballets for the Paris *Opéra*, but after 1840 he turned almost exclusively to the more intimate *Opéra Comique*, achieving his greatest success with *Mignon*. Still harboring a desire to be represented on the stage of the larger theatre, he produced *Hamlet* at the *Opéra* in 1868. Three years later, he succeeded Auber as director of the *Conservatoire*. After winning the recognition of his country as commander of the Legion of Honor and member of the Academy, Thomas died at Paris on February 12, 1896.

MIGNON

MIGNON *received its première at the Paris* Opéra Comique *in November, 1866. Adapted from Goethe's* Wilhelm Meister, *it was expressly composed by Thomas as a vehicle for Mme. Galli-Marié, a celebrated mezzo-soprano with limited vocal range. These exist, however, later variations, which have enabled the role to be sung, if desired, by lyric soprano. Mignon was first presented at the Metropolitan Opera House in 1883.*

Characters, in order of appearance:

Lothario, an aged harper: *bass-baritone*
Philine, an actress: *soprano*
Laërte, her companion: *tenor*
Jarno, a gypsy leader: *bass*
Mignon: *mezzo-soprano*
Wilhelm Meister, a burgher of Vienna: *tenor*
Frédéric: *mezzo-soprano*
Antonio, a servant: *bass*
Chorus of townsfolk, travelers, nobles, and
   Italian peasants (unseen)

Time: Eighteenth Century   *Place:* Germany and Italy

ACT I

SCENE: THE COURTYARD OF AN INN (55 Minutes)

A MOTLEY crowd has gathered in the yard of a German wayside tavern: townsfolk and travelers—a troupe of gypsies—and a band of actors, headed by the dazzling coquette, Philine, and her friend Laërte.

Chorus,
Lothario,
Philine,
Laërte

Only the old minstrel Lothario strikes a somber note amid the gaiety of the scene. Distracted by misfortune, he is ever roaming in search of his vanished daughter, Sperata. And he trembles with anger when he sees a young member of the gypsy band—the same age as his daughter might have been—bullied into performing for the tavern guests.

"Come, Mignon," shouts the leader of the gypsies, spreading a carpet on the ground and loading it with eggs, "dance for us!"

Enter
Jarno

A frightened young girl comes forward and stares at the faces of the crowd. "No!" she exclaims. "I will not dance!"

Enter
Mignon

The leader raises his stick; he is about to strike the girl when his hand is stayed by a guest at the tavern—young Wilhelm Meister of Vienna.

Enter
Wilhelm

"Let her go!" Wilhelm commands, threatening the gypsy with a revolver.

At once the leader obeys. The incident at an end, the spectators have all gone off—except the actress, Philine. She has determined to make Wilhelm's acquaintance.

Exeunt
Jarno and
Mignon
Exeunt
chorus

Philine's design is quickly accomplished. First she sends her companion, the cynical Laërte, to engage the stranger in conversation. Then she appears quite casually, obtains an introduction, and

Exeunt
Philine
and
Laërte
Enter
Mignon

retreats into the tavern with Laërte before Wilhelm has seen too much of her.

As Wilhelm is left alone, he notices someone shyly watching him. It is the girl he befriended. "What is your name?" he asks.

"They call me Mignon."

"Who are your parents? Where do you come from?"

"I have only one memory," the child answers. Dreamily, Mignon muses of a land with citron trees, golden oranges and azure skies. It is the land of her parents.

She recollects a marble palace with pillared walls—a clear, shining lake. "Alas!" she exclaims. "Why may I not return to that happy shore? It is *there* I would live and die!"

Andantino

Con - nais tu le___ pa - ys   où fleu - rit l'o - ran - ger?___
Dost___ thou know that___ fair land   where the cit - rons bloom?___

Enter
Jarno
Exeunt
Jarno and
Wilhelm
Enter
Lothario

And now the leader of the gypsies comes to take Mignon away. "Wait!" Wilhelm declares impetuously. "I will buy her freedom!"

"Am I free?" cries the girl in delight. "Free?" She laughs joyfully as old Lothario returns to the courtyard. "O you who have also helped me," she exclaims, "come, join in my happiness!"

"I cannot stay!" the melancholy harper answers. "I must fare onward with the swallows!"

Andantino con moto

Lé - gè - res hi - ron - del - les,   Oi - seaux bé - nis de Dieu!
Ye swal - lows light - ly fly - ing,   and pois - ing high in air!

Exeunt
Lothario
and
Mignon
Enter
Philine
and
Frédéric
Enter
Wilhelm

Enter
Laërte

Suddenly, tinkling laughter issues from the tavern. "It is that woman again!" whispers Mignon, her jealousy of Philine already rising. "Come, Lothario, let us avoid her!"

As the two wandering creatures take refuge behind the inn, Philine emerges with another suitor—the jealous Frédéric. Laughing heartlessly, the actress beckons to Wilhelm Meister, who has just finished with the gypsy leader.

"I should like you and Frédéric to meet," the actress declares.

As both admirers confront each other with hostile glances, Laërte comes bustling from the tavern. "Philine!" he calls. "The Baron has invited us to perform at his castle!"

"Splendid!" Philine answers. "We shall play 'A Midsummer Night's Dream.' And you, my dear Wilhelm Meister, are welcome to join us."

As Frédéric goes off in a jealous fury, Wilhelm decides to accept Philine's offer. A serious question remains for him: what can he possibly do with the young girl whose freedom he has purchased? "Take me with you!" Mignon pleads. "I shall dress as a page and wear your livery."

At first Wilhelm demurs. But when old Lothario invites the girl to share the hardships of the open road, the young man determines to protect her. "No!" he declares. "You must come with me, Mignon!"

As the comedians leave for the Baron's castle, Wilhelm and Mignon follow them. An atmosphere of gladness reigns in the wayside tavern; only Lothario sets off sorrowfully on his lonely path.

Act II
SCENE 1: A DRESSING ROOM (30 Minutes)

THE gay Philine is already established at the Baron's castle. Preparing for the gala performance, she sits at her dressing table exchanging banter with Laërte.

There is a knock at the door, and Wilhelm Meister appears. Entranced by Philine's beauty, he ignores the devoted Mignon, who accompanies him in a page-boy livery.

"Won't you come in?" Philine calls patronizingly to Mignon. "Perhaps you will perform your dance of the eggs for us?"

"There's a storm brewing!" snorts Laërte. "I'd better go!"

As the comedian makes his escape, Philine becomes increasingly capricious. Unhappily Mignon curls up before the fireplace and pretends to be asleep.

"You really must meet the Baron!" Philine suddenly exclaims. "Come, give me your arm!" The giddy actress propels Wilhelm from the chamber, and Mignon is left alone.

With feminine curiosity, the girl approaches the dressing table and inspects Philine's cosmetics. Applying them, she utters naïve exclamations of pleasure as she sees herself in the mirror.

By now, Mignon is thoroughly elated. Resolved on a further campaign of investigation, she disappears within Philine's wardrobe.

The chamber is not empty for long. With a crashing sound, young Frédéric clumsily forces the window and makes his entrance. "So this is where my uncle, the Baron, has lodged Philine!" he exclaims.

Allegretto

Me voi - ci dans son bou - doir, et je sens mon coeur, je sens mon coeur battre d'es - poir.
Here I am in her bou - doir, and I feel my heart, I feel my heart beat high with hope!

Enter
Wilhelm

Hearing footsteps, Frédéric hides—and to his intense annoyance, Wilhelm appears. "What are you doing here?" cries the young hothead.

"I might ask the same of you," Wilhelm replies.

Enter
Mignon

In a violent temper, Frédéric draws his sword. As Wilhelm defends himself, the wardrobe door flies open and Mignon appears, dressed in Philine's finery.

Exit
Frédéric

Bursting into scornful laughter at the sight of her, Frédéric drops his sword and leaves the chamber. "Mignon! Why have you done this?" Wilhelm demands. "I see it was wrong to take you with me. We must part!"

"I shall go, if you wish," murmurs Mignon, "but do not provide for me! I can wear my gypsy clothes again; I can earn my bread by dancing."

Enter
Philine
and
Frédéric

Weeping bitterly, she is about to leave when the chamber door opens and Philine appears with Frédéric.

Savagely ripping the lace from her garment, Mignon rushes into the wardrobe. "Why, I believe she's jealous of me!" Philine declares.

Enter
Laërte
Exit
Philine,
Laërte,
Wilhelm
and
Frédéric

For the first time, Wilhelm begins to think of Mignon as a woman. "Jealous?" he wonders. But his thoughts are cut short by the arrival of the boisterous Laërte.

"Come, Philine!" shouts the comedian. "Everything's ready!"

The actress departs with her suitors; and soon Mignon runs from the wardrobe, dressed in the gypsy clothes which she wore when Wilhelm found her. "Ah!" she cries, shaking her fist at the empty room. "How I hate that Philine!"

SCENE 2: THE PARK OF THE CASTLE (22 Minutes)

Enter
Mignon

Inside a brightly lighted pavilion, the band of actors are playing "A Midsummer Night's Dream"; and in the deserted garden wanders Mignon, filled with a terrible longing for Wilhelm. The applause of the audience within—their gay laughter—complete the girl's unhappiness.

Enter
Lothario

She is about to cast herself into the waters of a near-by pond when, suddenly, she hears the sound of a harp. It is Lothario, still searching for his lost child, Sperata! Mignon turns to him and confides her sorrow.

Exit
Mignon

"Do you hear the applause inside?" cries the girl. "They are shouting *her* name—Philine! Oh why does not a bolt of lightning fall from heaven and set this castle on fire?" In a burst of despair, Mignon rushes away.

"Fire?" repeats the half-crazed minstrel. "Fire?" Slowly, he moves toward the castle and disappears.

Exit
Lotharo

The great doors of the pavilion have been flung open; the performance is ended. And now Philine, escorted by her admirers, descends into the garden. Still clad in the glittering costume of Titania, she receives the homage of the entire court with a dashing polonaise:

Enter
Philine,
Frédéric
and
chorus

Tempo di polacca

Je suis Ti-ta-ni-a la blon - de, je— suis Ti-ta-ni-a, fil-le— de l'air!
I am Ti-ta-ni-a the fai - ry queen, I— am Ti-ta-ni-a, daugh-ter gay of air!

Only one of Philine's entourage is missing: Wilhelm Meister! Remorseful at having dismissed Mignon, he has gone to look for the girl. At last, he enters the garden disconsolately—she cannot be found.

Enter
Wilhelm

But soon Mignon appears, and with her is Lothario. "I have avenged you!" he whispers. "The palace is on fire!"

Enter
Mignon
and
Lothario

"Ah!" cries Philine, spying the unhappy girl. "So you have come back? Will you fetch a bouquet that your master gave me? I've left it on the stage."

Philine is cruel, but not heartless. Desiring only to wound Mignon's pride, she knows nothing of the raging fire within the hall. Nevertheless, Mignon, with full knowledge of her peril, obeys the order.

Exit
Mignon

A moment later, there is a shattering of glass; flames leap from the pavilion. Breathless with fear, Laërte comes running from the grand salon. "The stage is destroyed!" he cries.

Enter
Laërte
Exit
Wilhelm
Enter
Wilhelm
and
Mignon

At this moment, Wilhelm realizes acutely how much Mignon means to him. Risking his life, he rushes into the burning building and bears the girl to safety. It is she that he loves—not Philine!

ACT III

SCENE: THE GALLERY OF AN ITALIAN PALACE (34 Minutes)

IN the hope of restoring Mignon to health after her harrowing experience, Wilhelm has taken her to the lakes of northern Italy and rented the palace of the Cipriani. Old Lothario, deeply attached to the child, has gone with them.

Italian
peasants
(invisible)

Once arrived at the palace, the harper acts even more strangely than before. The halls and galleries seem familiar to him; he vanishes through a secret door that has not been used in years. Wilhelm stares after the old man in perplexity—and then he thinks of the

Lothario
Enter
Wilhelm
Exit
Lothario

sleeping Mignon. "May the sunshine gladden her despairing heart!" he prays:

Andantino

O ____ prin - temps, don - ne lui ta gout - te de____ ro - sé - e!
Balm - y Spring, on__ her heart let fall__ thy dew__ re - stor - ing!

Enter Mignon

Mignon has risen from her slumber. Clothed in flowing white, she enters the gallery of the palace. At first, she looks about her in wonder. The landscape—the orange trees and azure skies—surely she knows them! Then she listens to Wilhelm's words of love.

Philine (invisible)

Vibrant with joy, she sinks in his arms—and suddenly in the distance, she hears the voice of Philine, brazenly trolling her polonaise.

"Again that woman!" she cries. Wilhelm can hardly convince the excited Mignon that he has avoided Philine—that the actress has followed him.

Enter Lothario

The lovers' quarrel is cut short by an amazing apparition. Lothario, the ragged, unkempt harper, has come through the secret door dressed in splendid raiment. "I greet you both!" he declares. "Welcome to my house and home!"

As Wilhelm and Mignon gaze at him in surprise, Lothario offers the girl a precious casket. "Within," he explains, "you will find a shawl, a bracelet and a prayerbook. They belonged to my daughter Sperata. This was our home!"

Mignon examines the objects with increasing emotion. She opens the prayer book—she reads aloud—and then, letting the book slip from her hands, she completes the prayer by memory. At once, drawn by a mysterious impulse, she rushes to the next room and returns, crying out, "I have seen it—the portrait of my mother!"

"Sperata!" weeps Lothario. "My daughter!"

By the same uncanny stroke of fate, the veil of the past has been lifted for father and child. As Wilhelm and Mignon fondly embrace, Lothario bestows his paternal blessing.

BIZET

GEORGES BIZET, born on October 25, 1838, entered the Conservatory of his native Paris at the age of nine. Before he was twenty he had won the prize for opera buffa with *Le Docteur Miracle* and the *Grand Prix de Rome* with *Clovis et Clotilde*. Four more operas were produced, but failed of popular approval. With the incidental music to Daudet's play, *L'Arlésienne*, later changed into a Suite, the tide turned, but the composer was still obliged to earn his scanty livelihood by the arrangement of popular tunes. He died only three months after the production of *Carmen*, unaware of its ultimate success.

His colorful characterizations, especially in exotic scenes, and his intensity in imaginative delineation, won recognition from Liszt, and are now responsible for his unflagging popularity today.

CARMEN

CARMEN, *a lyric drama in four acts by Georges Bizet, was founded on the short novel of Prosper Merimée by its librettists, Meilhac and Halévy. First performed in Paris, March 3rd, 1875, with Galli-Marié in the title role, it did not meet with immediate success, since its stark tragedy offended the sensibilities of the French public. By the time that it reached London and New York (1878) it had, however, begun to enjoy the world-wide popularity it has since maintained.*

Characters, in order of appearance:

Morales, an officer: *baritone*
Micaela, a peasant girl: *soprano*
Don José, a corporal of dragoons: *tenor*
Zuniga, captain of dragoons: *bass*
Carmen, a cigarette girl and gypsy: *mezzo-soprano*

Gypsies, friends of Carmen { Frasquita: *soprano*
Mercedes: *contraloto*

Escamillo, a toreador: *baritone*

Smugglers { El Remendado: *tenor*
El Dancaïro: *baritone*

Innkeeper, guide, officers, dragoons, gypsies, boys, cigarette
girls, smugglers, etc.

Time: About 1820   *Place:* Seville and neighboring mountains

PRELUDE

The first notes of the full orchestra suggest a cheerful, almost military mood. After a brief contrasting theme of a gentle pastoral character, there is a return to the opening fortissimo, which diminishes to a hint of the Toreador Song to come. More shrill trillings from the flutes reach a sudden conclusion, and then is heard the mysterious motive of Fate from woodwind, trumpets and 'cellos:

Andante moderato

On this foreboding of the tragedy to come, the prelude concludes.

ACT I
SCENE: A SQUARE AT SEVILLE (44 Minutes)

Soldiers,
Morales

THE curtain rises on a bustling square in Seville. On the right stands the gate of the tobacco factory. A bridge, approached by winding steps, crosses the back of the stage. At the left a dozen dragoons are lounging in front of their guardhouse, smoking, while passers-by throng the scene.

Enter
Micaela

The officer Morales, who like his companions has been commenting on the crowd, notices a shy young girl, who seems to seek someone, and yet lacks the courage to ask help.

He approaches her gallantly.

"I am looking for a corporal called Don José," she says. "Do you know him?"

He tells her that José will come on duty when the guard is changed, and suggests that she wait; but she is too prudent to accept his invitation, and runs across the bridge.

Exit
Micaela

A distant trumpet call prefaces a military march and heralds the changing of the guard. A squad of street urchins are at their heels. As the companies meet, Morales tells Don José of the young girl with the blue dress and long braids who has been asking for him.

Enter
José,
Zuniga
and
chorus
of boys

"It must be Micaela," says José.

A second trumpet announces the retreat of Morales' company. Alone with his captain, Zuniga, Don José submits to a bit of teasing on his pretty visitor.

"The factory girls may please your taste," retorts the corporal, "I love Micaela."

The factory bell rings the noon-day hour. The girls saunter out, blowing rings of smoke from their cigarettes, but the youths shout, "We don't see Carmen."

Enter girls

As the orchestra plays the Fate motive in a new, dazzling rhythm, Carmen darts into the square with the dark insolent beauty of a gypsy, an acacia flower in her mouth. Mocking the advances of the young men who crowd about her, she sings the haunting Habanera:

Enter
Carmen

Allegretto

L'a-mour est un oi-seau re - belle
Love is like a -ny wood-bird wild

As she sings, she watches Don José who is sitting quietly, mending a chain, apparently unaware of her presence. All the other young people have joined in the chorus.

The 'cellos sound the Fate motive. Carmen, piqued by José's indifference, tosses the blood-red flower in his face, and runs off with a mocking laugh to the factory.

Exit
Carmen

The bell has called the cigarette girls back to work. Don José is left alone. The perfume of the flower is subtle; the girl has cast her spell. He picks up the blossom and hides it in his uniform.

Exeunt
Girls

A moment later José hears the clear call of Micaela and joyfully greets his childhood sweetheart. She has brought him a letter from his mother in their far-off village, and her loving kiss.

Enter
Micaela

Allegretto moderato

Et— tu lui di-ras que sa mè-re son-ge nuit et jour— à l'ab-sent.—
Tell— him that his moth-er is lone-ly, pray-ing night and day—for her son.—

Exit
Micaela

She runs off before he can open the letter.

"Do not fear, mother," he murmurs as he reads her message, "I will do as you ask. I love Micaela and I will marry her in spite of the witch's flowers."

Enter
girls
Enter
Zuniga
and
Carmen

Cries of "Help, help!" are heard from the factory, as the girls come running out to tell of a fight that has started. Carmen has stabbed another girl.

Captain Zuniga sends Don José to look into the affair and a minute later he returns with Carmen, in defiant mood. "Tra la la la," she jeers at the officer. "Cut me, burn me, I'll say not a word."

"If you take that tone, you can sing your song in jail!" the captain retorts, leaving her bound in the charge of José.

Swinging her skirts, though her hands are tied to the chair behind her, Carmen sings the Seguidilla, tempting José with the pleasures of Lillas Pastia's tavern if only he will free her.

The charm is too strong for the well-meaning dragoon. He cuts the cord and promises to meet her at the inn.

Exit
Carmen

When the soldiers return to lead her off, she pushes José down the steps and makes her escape. Since it is clear that he is to blame, José is arrested by Zuniga and led away under guard.

Act II

SCENE: THE INN OF LILLAS PASTIA (38 Minutes)

In a brief prelude the orchestra plays a Spanish march, the song of Don José's regiment, the Dragoons of Alcala.

Gypsies,
Carmen,
Frasquita,
Mercedes
and
officers

THE curtain rises to show the courtyard of the dimly lighted tavern of Lillas Pastia. Gypsies are dancing and playing the guitar. Carmen, in a magnificent Spanish shawl, is gossiping with her friends Frasquita and Mercedes and a group of officers who are off duty. The three girls join the dance.

Pastia must close the inn for the night, and Zuniga begs Carmen to go home with him.

"You are not annoyed with me?" he asks. "Your soldier boy is free." As the group breaks up they see the gleam of a torch-light procession nearing the inn yard.

"It's Escamillo, the great toreador of Granada," says Zuniga.

The bullfighter swaggers in, dressed in the short, embroidered jacket and heavy cape of his craft, a crowd of admirers at his heels. They drink his health. *Enter Escamillo*

In answer he sings the famous Toreador Song, describing the adventures of the bull ring:

Throughout the song Carmen has not taken her eyes from Escamillo, who now asks her name: "When next I face danger, I would like to say it over as a charm."

She tells him.

"And if I were to say that I love you?" *Exeunt Escamillo and officers*

"I would tell you to keep away."

Undiscouraged, Escamillo departs with Zuniga and the officers, leaving Carmen with Frasquita and Mercedes. She claps her hands and two rough-looking men emerge from an inner room of the tavern. They are the smugglers Remendado and Dancaïro for whom Carmen and her friends have often worked. *Enter Remendado and Dancaïro*

The men urge the three girls to join them on an expedition in the mountains that very night.

"I can't go," answers Carmen. "I am in love."

As they beg her to change her mind, the voice of Don José is heard outside, singing his regimental song, "The Dragoon of Alcala." Perhaps she can persuade him to join them.

They leave her alone to greet her lover. She takes up her castanets and dances about the chair where he has seated himself, singing: *Exeunt smugglers Enter José*

A distant trumpet call interrupts them. Recognizing the sound of retreat at his barracks, José starts to leave. Carmen, furious, hurls his cap and saber after him.

"It is wrong of you to mock me," protests José. "You must listen." He shows her the wilted flower he has kept in his uniform throughout his days in prison:

Andantino

f La fleur que tu m'a-vais je - té - e, dans ma pri-son___ m'é-tait res - té - e,
This flow-er that you threw to me,___ I kept it still, while in the jail,___

"No," insists Carmen, "if you loved me, you would follow me to the freedom of the mountains."

Allegretto moderato

f Là - bas, là - bas dans la mon- tagne, ___
A - way, a - way to yon - der moun - tain!

"To desert my flag is infamy," José hesitates.

"Then go back to your barracks!" retorts Carmen, in her wounded pride. "I despise you!"

Enter
Zuniga

They are about to leave each other when Zuniga returns to see if Carmen has decided to accept his invitation. He taunts her for preferring a common corporal when she could have himself, a captain. Then he orders José back to the barracks.

"I will not go," cries the young dragoon, desperate with jealousy.

The two men draw their swords. The gypsies rush in to separate them.

"And now will you join us?" Carmen asks José. As a deserter, he has no other choice. He will follow the outlaws!

Act III

SCENE: IN THE MOUNTAINS (37 Minutes)

The woodwinds and harp play a lyric prelude, and the curtain rises on a wild and rocky height, where the smugglers pick their

Gypsies

way from the valley below to a stealthy march from the orchestra. DANCAÏRO suggests that the party set down the bales and boxes while he sends scouts to see if the coast is clear. The gypsies huddle in their cloaks on the ground.

José

Don José is not happy and gazes down the valley where his mother lives, still trusting in his honor.

Carmen

"If our life does not suit you," taunts Carmen, "why not return to her?"

At the talk of separation, José fingers his knife.

"You may kill me," answers Carmen, "but what of that?"

Frasquita
Mercedes

She goes over to watch the gay card game which Frasquita and Mercedes are playing to test their fortunes.

Allegretto con moto

Par - lez en - core, par - lez— mes — bel - les
My pret - ty toys, now here— you're — ly - ing

Carmen spreads her blanket and deals out her own pack. A dozen times it repeats the same signal: death.

Dancaïro returns and announces that the coast is clear. Three custom guards watch the pass, but Carmen and her friends are sent to wheedle safe passage from them. Don José retires to guard the goods that are left. *Exeunt gypsies and José*

Enter Micaela

At this moment Micaela, shivering in her blue cape, appears with a single guide whom she dismisses when she learns that José is near-by.

She prays for strength to carry out his mother's wishes:

Andante molto

Je dis que rien ne m'é-pou-van-te je dis hé-las! que je ré-ponds de moi:
I say that no·thing shall de - ter me, I say a - las! I'm strong to play my part;

Rising from her prayer, Micaela sees José on a cliff above her and hails him, but he does not hear her.

A shot is the only answer to her call. *Enter Escamillo*

As she hides herself in terror, Escamillo climbs jauntily through the pass, glancing cheerfully at the bullet hole in his hat. *Enter José*

"Who are you?" demands José, rushing after him.

"Escamillo, toreador of Granada. I've come to look for my gypsy girl. Her name is Carmen and the last I knew she was in love with a soldier—but her affairs don't last six months."

Both men draw their daggers. The duel is stopped by Carmen, aided by the incoming gypsies, who hold back José. *Enter Carmen and gypsies*

"Before I bid you farewell, I invite you all to the bull ring at Seville," declares Escamillo, retiring. "Anyone who loves me will come." *Exit Escamillo*

Remendado has discovered Micaela in her hiding-place and now escorts her to José.

"Your mother is weeping for you," she tells him sadly, "have pity and come home with me."

"Go along with her," puts in Carmen, "our life doesn't suit you."

Enraged at her indifference, José insists on remaining.

"But your mother is dying," pleads Micaela.

Escamillo
(*off stage*)

As he departs with her, the voice of Escamillo is heard in the distance, singing the Toreador Song. Carmen flings her pack of cards to the wind. She will laugh at Fate and live for Escamillo!

Act IV

SCENE: ENTRANCE TO THE PLAZA DE TOROS (26 Minutes)

Chorus,
ballet
Enter
Carmen,
Escamillo

A THRONG of street vendors crowd the great square in front of the arena in Seville and chatter of their oranges and programs and cigarettes. Dancers flash brilliant shawls to music which has been taken from Bizet's *Arlésienne* and *Pearlfisher Suites*. The populace cries welcome to the band. The bullfighters follow in a gay procession with the officers of the city. A shout arises from the crowd. It is for Escamillo, favorite of the day, and by his side in the open carriage sits Carmen, gorgeous in a shining jeweled dress and shawl.

Exeunt
Escamillo
Frasquita,
Mercedes

Escamillo tenderly helps Carmen to the ground. Assured of her affection, Escamillo enters the arena.

Enter
José

Frasquita and Mercedes warn Carmen not to remain there alone. Don José is at liberty and has been reported lurking in the crowd.

As Carmen waits, her desolate lover appears from an archway.

"I do not threaten you," he tells her, "but I beg you, I implore you. Let us begin another life, far from here."

"It is impossible," she answers, "all is over between us."

As he pleads, Escamillo's triumph echoes from the arena.

Don José is maddened by the success of his rival, and the pleasure which it gives Carmen. Furious, he draws his dagger.

"On your guard, Toreador," sings the chorus outside. "A dark eye is watching you and love awaits."

José plunges his knife. Carmen screams and falls.

"You may arrest me," cries José to the incoming crowd. "I have killed her," and then, throwing himself beside the body, he sobs, "O my Carmen, my adored Carmen!"

SAINT-SAËNS

CAMILLE SAINT-SAËNS was born on October 9, 1835, of a prosperous Norman family then resident in Paris. Making his debut as a pianist at the age of eleven, he entered the *Conservatoire* two years later, winning the first prize as an organist, though twice failing to achieve the *Prix de Rome*.

For nearly twenty years Saint-Saëns served as organist at the Church of the Madeleine. Founding the National Society of Music to encourage French composers, he received the highest awards of the Legion of Honor, and was admitted to the French Academy. Twice he visited the United States.

His phenomenal technique as an executant won admiration from Wagner whom he revered until, as an octogenarian, he succumbed to the prejudices of the Great War and reversed his earlier position. He died in 1920.

Giving his attention to all forms and styles of music, Saint-Saëns is as well known for his copious orchestral compositions as for his fourteen operas. Of these *Samson et Dalila* has held the stage for its masterly workmanship and theatrical effectiveness. A writer of distinction on scientific as well as musical subjects, Saint-Saëns represents the best intelligence and urbanity of the last quarter of the nineteenth century.

SAMSON ET DALILA

SAMSON ET DALILA, *an opera in three acts and four scenes, was first produced on December 2, 1877, in Weimar, under the direction of Liszt. It waited for thirteen years to reach France, the native country of its composer, Camille Saint-Saëns, since his musical theories were at that time considered too radical, even too Wagnerian, for the French public.*

Introduced to the Paris Théâtre Lyrique de L'Eden *in 1890, after an initial French production at Rouen, it was first presented to the United States two years later in concert form. In the spring of 1895* Samson *first appeared on the Metropolitan stage. Its libretto, written by Ferdinand Lemaire, a cousin of the composer, is based on the story outlined in the Book of Judges.*

Characters, in order of appearance:
Samson, leader of the Israelites: *tenor*
Abimelech, satrap of Gaza: *bass*
The high priest of Dagon: *baritone*
Two Philistines: *tenor* and *bass*
A Philistine messenger: *tenor*
An old Hebrew: *bass*
Dalila, priestess of Dagon: *mezzo-soprano*
A child
Hebrews, Philistines, dancers, attendants on Dalila

Time: 1136 B.C.   *Place:* Gaza

ACT I

SCENE: A PUBLIC PLACE IN GAZA (46 Minutes)

After a few orchestral measures, the voice of an invisible chorus is heard in supplication to the Lord of Israel.

Hebrews and Samson

IT is night, but the great portico of the heathen temple of Dagon can be seen, towering on the left above the houses of Gaza. A company of Hebrews, men and women, crowd around their leader Samson.

"We have seen our cities sacked and our altars profaned," they cry in deepest distress; "Lord of Israel, hast thou forgotten the promises made to our forefathers!"

Samson rallies their failing courage with prophetic words: "The hour of your freedom is at hand," he exclaims. "The Lord will arm you with invincible weapons and help you to burst your chains."

Piu lento

Discouragement gives place to hope. "Jehovah will lead us to victory," shout the people.

Enter Abimelech

Their hymn is interrupted by the satrap Abimelech, who strides

into their midst with an escort of Philistine soldiers at his heels. Philistine
soldiers
"This god of yours is deaf to your cries," he proclaims with a sneer.
"He is powerless before the greatest of all gods—Dagon the
mighty."

"The hour is at hand!" answers the Hebrew leader, while his
people echo his final invocation:

Allegro

Is - ra - ël! romps ta chaîne, O peu - ple, lè - ve toi!
Is - ra - el! break thy chain, O peo - ple, now a - rise!

Snatching the sword which Abimelech has already raised against
him, Samson strikes at his enemy with a mortal blow.

The Philistine soldiers scatter in confusion. Samson retreats with Exeunt
Samson
and
Hebrews
Enter
High
Priest
his followers. The gates of the temple are flung open. Surrounded
by his guard, the high priest of Dagon rapidly descends the steps.

"The slaves of Israel have slain the prince Abimelech," he cries.
"Have you let every one of them escape?"

Two of the Philistines try to excuse their cowardice, but are
roundly rebuked by the high priest. A messenger brings news that Enter
messenger
Samson and his followers are destroying the harvest.

"Let us flee from this danger and abandon the city," is the verdict Exeunt
Philistines
and Priest
with
Abimelech's
body
of the Philistines. In spite of the adjurations of their leader they
depart, carrying off the body of the satrap to a safer spot.

As day dawns, Samson and his companions venture back to the
scene of their first victory, and raise a hymn of joy and gratitude. Enter
Samson
and
Hebrews
Enter
Dalila and
maidens

Hardly have they concluded, when the doors of the temple are
again opened, and a group of Philistine maidens comes forth, bearing
garlands of flowers for the conquering Hebrews. The priestess
Dalila stands in their midst, glittering with golden ornaments.

"I come to celebrate the fame of my beloved hero," she says,
tempting Samson with the promise of her caresses, and bidding him
renew his visits of long ago to her abode in the valley of Sorek.

An old Hebrew warns him against her treacherous charms, and Old
Hebrew
Samson himself prays for strength to withstand temptation, but the
enchantment of Dalila is irresistible.

The women of the temple dance voluptuously about the Hebrew
warriors, and Dalila sings of the intoxication of the spring:

Andante

Prin - temps qui com - mence, Por - tant l'es - pé - ran - ce,
When hope - ful - ness ho - vers In dreams of the lov - er,

In vain the ancient Hebrew repeats his warning. The charms of the Philistine woman have worked their spell, and Samson is profoundly stirred.

ACT II

SCENE: DALILA'S DWELLING IN THE VALLEY OF SOREK (39 Minutes)

THE undulating phrases of the prelude suggest the tranquil spring evening in which Dalila awaits Samson. Lost in a reverie, she sits among the verdant tropical foliage that surrounds her house.

The priestess invokes the power of love to conquer her victim and satisfy the demands of her gods:

Moderato

A - mour! viens ai - der ma fai - bles - - se! '
O love, come and strength - en my weak - - ness!

Distant lightning adds to the drama of the situation, and illumines the entrance of the high priest who has come to assure himself of Dalila's help.

"The Hebrew slaves are masters of the city," he announces. "With such a leader as Samson, their power is invincible. You alone can accomplish his downfall and learn the secret of his strength. All the wealth of Dagon's shrine is yours if you succeed."

"I hate him as much as you," answers Dalila. "In the past he has rejected my embraces and left me at the call of battle. But tonight I have new weapons. He will not resist my tears."

The high priest departs, telling her that the destiny of the Philistines is in her hands. Leaning against the pillars of her dwelling, Dalila awaits Samson.

In the inky blackness of the night, the Hebrew gropes his way to the house of the priestess.

"Beloved, I have waited long," exclaims Dalila, as he approaches with hesitant steps. Then, since he seems less ardent than of old, she asks why he turns away from her caresses.

"I am but the slave of God's holy will," he answers. "At His command we must break the sweet bonds of our love, for He has chosen me to lead His people to victory."

"What is the glory of Israel to me?" she asks, weeping. "The victory of your people means the end of my happiness. A god that is stronger than yours speaks through my words; the god of love itself."

The effect of Dalila's desolate reproaches is to arouse the passion which Samson had thought under control. "So great is my love," he tells her, "that it defies my God!"

Confident of her success, Dalila pours out the joy of her heart in a rapturous strain:

Andantino

Mon coeur s'ouvre à ta voix
My heart, at thy sweet voice

To accomplish her mission, the priestess requires more than an assurance of love. As a challenge to Samson's affection, she demands the secret of his strength.

A distant storm grows nearer. "It is the wrath of God!" cries the Hebrew.

"Let us defy it together!" is her bold answer.

Just as the storm breaks, Dalila rushes away from him into the house, a final desperate gesture. A moment's hesitation, and she has won. Samson follows her. Exit
Dalila
Exit
Samson
Enter
Philistine
soldiers

Hardly has he left when a brigade of Philistine soldiers creeps out of the forest and encircles the house. A terrific clap of thunder resounds in the darkness.

"Help, help!" cries Dalila, appearing on her terrace. The soldiers burst in to seize her victim. Enter
Dalila
Exeunt
soldiers

Act III

SCENE 1: THE PRISON AT GAZA (8 Minutes)

BLINDED and fettered, his locks shorn and his head bent, the wretched Samson turns the mighty millstone to grind the corn of his Philistine captors. The reproaches of his comrades echo from neighboring cells, adding new pangs to his remorse. Samson

"Lord, have pity on my weakness," he prays, "be merciful to thy afflicted people. In lowliest submission I bless the hand that strikes and acknowledge my fault. Save thy people from the wrath of the enemy: such is my humble petition!"

A prison guard comes in to lead Samson away. Enter
guard

SCENE 2: THE INTERIOR OF THE TEMPLE OF DAGON (24 Minutes)

Although the morning is still early, the temple of Dagon is already thronged with worshipers. Near the sacrificial table the high priest has gathered the princes of the Philistines. Between two vast columns at the center of the edifice stands a statue of the Fish God. Dalila enters with her suite of maidens crowned with garlands of flowers and bearing golden cups of wine. High
Priest,
Philistines,
Dalila and
maidens

Ballet

"Though dawn is on the hills, let us put aside the woes of day and continue our revels," is the burden of their hymn. It is followed by a bacchanalian dance:

Allegro moderato

Enter Samson and boy

A sudden pause falls on the pagan revels. Led by a little boy, the blind Samson enters the assembly, his ragged garments contrasting with the gorgeous robes of his captors.

"Hail, judge of Israel," cries the high priest, with bitter irony; "a toast to the beauty of your mistress!"

Dalila adds her torturing recollections of the caresses with which she bought Samson's secret.

"Come, sing the old love songs again," continues the priest, "and if Jehovah restores your sight, I will promise to serve him!"

Samson prays for a miracle, to silence the taunts of the impious heathen. "Give me my old power if only for an instant," he cries, "that thy glory may be avenged!"

His words are lost in the tumultuous ritual that follows. Libations of wine are poured on the sacrificial fire. Dalila and the high priest lead the congregation in a hymn to Dagon the mighty.

At length Samson is commanded to offer his oblation to the infidel deity.

"Guide my feet toward the pillars," he whispers to the child who leads him. Then, as the chant of the multitude reaches its climax, he prays once more for the old strength. Standing between the mighty columns, he heaves their massive weight apart.

A shriek arises from the Philistines as the columns are shattered with a crashing roar. The roof of the temple falls on Samson and his enemies alike. Jehovah has triumphed.

OFFENBACH

JACQUES OFFENBACH was born in Cologne on June 21, 1819, the son of a Jewish cantor named Eberscht. As a child he studied the 'cello in defiance of his parents, but was permitted to enter the Paris *Conservatoire* at the age of fourteen. He soon found a place in the orchestra of the *Opéra Comique*, where he was often penalized for such tricks as imitating a bagpipe, or playing alternate notes with his neighbor. This flair for comedy served him in good stead later in his career, when he won recognition for the hilarious gaiety of *Orphée aux Enfers, La Grande Duchesse, La Belle Helène,* and numerous other works for the light opera stage.

At thirty he became conductor at the *Théâtre Français,* writing music for the intermissions, and also starting to compose his own operettas. At the Exposition of 1855 he rented a tiny theatre which he called the *Bouffes Parisiennes.* He soon became a naturalized Frenchman, and later took over the management of the *Gaité Lyrique.*

His operettas, burlesque and pantomimes give a brilliant picture of French life under the Second Empire, and reflect the urbanity, triviality and dashing wit of the composer. Although for years the rage of Paris, Offenbach was always improvident and in 1877 went on tour in America to retrieve his fortunes.

He did not live to witness the success of his greatest work, *Les Contes d'Hoffmann,* but died in Paris on October 5, 1880.

LES CONTES D'HOFFMANN
(*THE TALES OF HOFFMANN*)

LES CONTES D'HOFFMANN, *a fantastic opera originally written in four acts, but now played in three acts with a Prologue and Epilogue, was first presented at the* Opéra Comique *in Paris, on February 10, 1881, four months after the death of its composer, Jacques Offenbach. It was first produced by the Metropolitan Opera Company in 1913 and has subsequently appeared in the repertory during ten different seasons.*

The libretto of the work was constructed by Jules Barbier after a comedy played in 1851 from several of the bizarre tales of E. T. A. Hoffmann, a German writer (1776-1822) whose literary influence extended far beyond the poets and musicians of his time.

A medley of tragedy and farce, Les Contes d'Hoffmann *combines German romanticism and French irony.*

Characters, in order of appearance:

Lindorf, a councilor of Nuremberg: *baritone* *
Andrès, a servant: *tenor* †
Hermann, a student: *baritone*
Luther, an innkeeper: *bass*
Nathaniel, a student: *tenor*
Hoffmann, a poet: *tenor*
Nicklausse, his friend: *mezzo-soprano*
Spalanzani, an inventor: *tenor*
Cochenille, his servant: *tenor* †
Coppélius, rival to Spalanzani: *baritone* *
Olympia, a mechanical doll: *soprano* ‡
Giulietta, a courtesan: *soprano* ‡
Schlemil, her lover: *bass*
Pitichinaccio, another admirer: *tenor* †
Dapertutto, a magician: *baritone* *
Antonia, a singer: *soprano* ‡
Crespel, a councilor of Munich, her father: *baritone*
Franz, his servant: *tenor* †
Dr. Miracle: *baritone* *
Voice of Antonia's mother: *mezzo-soprano*
Stella, an opera singer: *soprano* ‡
Students, guests of Spalanzani and Giulietta, etc.

Time: Nineteenth Century   *Place:* Nuremberg, Venice, Munich

* † ‡ The characters marked by any one of these symbols are often played by the same singer.

PROLOGUE

SCENE: LUTHER'S TAVERN (21 Minutes)

AFTER a brief prelude, the curtain rises on Luther's tavern in Nuremberg. Casks and bottles line the walls; tables and benches are scattered about.

The evil councilor Lindorf beckons the stammering servant Andrès to follow him into the tavern. The theme that heralds his entrance reappears to characterize each of the three manifestations of Hoffmann's evil genius that follow:

Enter Lindorf and Andrès

"Are you the servant of Stella, the opera singer?" asks Lindorf. "I'll wager you are delivering a letter for her at this moment. How much will you take for it?" The councilor buys the letter for forty thalers, then finds it is addressed to his rival, the young poet Hoffmann, and contains the key to Stella's box. Gloating over his prize, he waits in a corner for his unsuspecting victim.

A score of gay students have meanwhile invaded the tavern and call for beer and wine. Just as two of their number, Nathaniel and Hermann, grow impatient for the arrival of Hoffmann, he enters from the neighboring opera house with his young friend Nicklausse. He is soon persuaded to sing a spirited ballad:

Enter students
Enter Hoffmann and Nicklausse

Il è-tait un-e fois à la cour d'Eis-en-ach!
O once_ at the court of *Ei-sen-ach!

But Hoffmann's thoughts stray from the hideous dwarf Kleinzach, the hero of his song, to the face of a woman he has loved. Though he forces himself to return to the ballad, he is in no mood for jesting. He calls for the punch bowl to be lighted.

"Come and drink with me," Hoffmann urges Lindorf. "I bear you no grudge even though you are at the bottom of all my troubles. If I play at cards, if I drink, if I love, you are my evil genius."

"So you are in love," insinuates the wily councilor.

"Yes," returns Hoffmann, "I love Stella, three women in one: artist, young girl and courtesan."

Enter
Luther

Luther brings in the news that the curtain of the opera house is about to rise, but all the company prefer to wait and hear the tales of Hoffmann's loves.

"The first," exclaims the young poet, "was Olympia!"

Act I

SCENE: THE CABINET OF THE INVENTOR SPALANZANI (34 Minutes)

Enter
Spalanzani
and
Cochenille

A RICHLY furnished room is hung with heavy portieres which curtain off a long gallery at the rear and recesses at the sides. From one of these alcoves comes the inventor Spalanzani, rubbing his hands in satisfaction at the popularity of his child, the beautiful Olympia.

"A good thing that Coppélius isn't here!" he exclaims. "Or he would claim to be her father."

Enter
Hoffmann
Exeunt
Spalanzani
and
Cochenille

Seeking to be accepted by Spalanzani as a pupil, Hoffmann modestly applies for admission, and the inventor goes off with his servant Cochenille to order champagne and light the candles. He has invited guests to witness a demonstration of his skill.

Enter
Nicklausse

Left alone, Hoffmann discovers the sleeping Olympia in an alcove, and falls rapturously in love with her.

The more sensible Nicklausse joins him, but is unable to persuade him that it might be wise to speak with the lady before courting her.

Enter
Coppélius

Hoffmann is finally roused from his trance by another strange inventor, Coppélius, who comes in with a great bag of scientific apparatus, including all varieties of spectacles. The young men purchase a pair which will show them the true nature of a woman's heart.

Enter
Spalanzani

Spalanzani returns, furious at the sight of Coppélius who is demanding more money for Olympia, since it is he who has furnished her eyes. Coppélius is put off with a note on the house of Elias, the Jew, and departs, suggesting that Spalanzani shall betroth Olympia to the wealthy young Hoffmann.

Exit
Coppélius

Enter
guests
Enter
Olympia
and
Cochenille

The arriving guests exclaim at the charming hospitality of the house. Spalanzani brings in his daughter Olympia, and presents her to the admiring throng. He instructs Cochenille to fetch a harp, and the young girl sings a sentimental little ballad to her father's accompaniment:

Moderato

p Voi - la la chan - son mig - non - - - - ne

Ah, there is the pret - ty song

Once or twice her voice starts to falter, but Cochenille hastens to touch a spring at her back and restore it. At length supper is announced and the guests retire, leaving Olympia alone with Hoffmann.

Exeunt guests, Spalanzani and Cochenille

"You are mine!" he exclaims, when she has answered a stiff little "Yes" to all his questions. "If only you would respond to my love!"

As he presses her hand, and releases another spring, Olympia rises abruptly, flutters about the room and disappears through the curtains.

Exit Olympia

Fearing that he has offended her, Hoffmann pursues her, in spite of the attempts of Nicklausse to bring him to his senses.

In a rage Coppélius returns. The Jew Elias has gone bankrupt; his note is valueless. He rushes into Olympia's cabinet with a cry of vengeance.

A waltz brings the guests back to dance. Olympia whirls Hoffmann about the room until he sinks exhausted and fainting on a sofa, breaking his magic glasses as he falls. At Spalanzani's orders Cochenille takes her away.

Enter Nicklausse
Exit Hoffmann
Enter Coppélius
Exit Coppélius
Enter guests
Enter Hoffmann
Enter and exit Olympia
Enter Spalanzani
Enter Coppélius

A terrific crash sounds from the neighboring cabinet.

"Heaven and earth," cries Spalanzani, rushing out, "she is broken!"

Coppélius reappears bursting into devilish laughter. The two inventors hurl curses at each other.

Hoffmann, who has hurried after them to the cabinet returns pale and terrified.

"An automaton," he murmurs, sinking to a chair, "only an automaton!"

Act II

SCENE: THE HOUSE OF GIULIETTA IN VENICE (25 Minutes)

IN her sumptuous palace overlooking the Grand Canal, the guests of the courtesan Giulietta recline at their ease. Gondolas glide beyond the lofty arcades of a portico. Lights glitter from chandeliers; a staircase is strewn with cushions; flowers bloom in every corner.

Guests and Hoffmann

The voices of Giulietta and Nicklausse rise from the background in the Barcarolle:

Giulietta and Nicklausse

Moderato

p Bel - le nuit, ò nuit d'a -mour, Sou - ris __ à nos iv - res - ses!
Love - ly night, o night of love, smile on __ our bliss se - rene! __

Enter
Schlemil
and
Pitichi-
naccio
Exeunt
guests,
Schlemil,
Pitichi-
naccio,
Giulietta
and
Nicklausse
Enter
Dapertutto

Hoffmann stands aside moodily as new guests arrive: Schlemil, the man without a shadow, and another admirer Pitichinaccio.

"Come, gentlemen, to the game!" cries Giulietta, and her guests repeat the invitation.

Nicklausse warns Hoffmann of the wiles of the courtesan. "I have horses saddled to take you away if necessary!" he explains, as they retire to the card tables.

The familiar motive of evil announces the arrival of the magician Dapertutto. He invokes the power of a magnificent diamond ring with which to bribe Giulietta:

Andante poco mosso

p

Scin - tille ____ di - a - mant. ____
Spar - kle ____ di - a - mond. ____

Enter
Giulietta
Exit
Dapertutto
Re-enter
guests,
Nicklausse,
Schlemil,
Pitichi-
naccio and
Dapertutto

"You have procured Schlemil's shadow for me," he says, when she returns to greet him. "Now get me the reflection of Hoffmann!"

He leaves her to ensnare the young poet, who proves an easy prey to her caresses.

The band of revelers return. Even Nicklausse cannot restore to his friend the reflection which he has lost in Giulietta's mirror. Hoffmann's raptures blend with the threats of Schlemil, the pleas of the wanton, and the mocking pity of Dapertutto and Pitichinaccio. There is nothing for Nicklausse but vain regret.

At length Hoffmann demands of Schlemil the key to Giulietta's chamber. It is refused. Dapertutto offers Hoffmann his sword. While the Barcarolle echoes from the distance, the poet mortally wounds his rival, seizes the key and rushes after the siren.

It is too late. She is already entering her gondola in the arms of Pitichinaccio.

Nicklausse drags Hoffmann away.

ACT III

SCENE: COUNCILOR CRESPEL'S HOUSE IN MUNICH (36 Minutes)

Antonia

AT her clavichord sits Antonia, a large portrait of her mother hanging on the wall behind her, and musical instruments standing about. The slanting rays of sunset stream in across a balcony through a large window on the left of the room. The young girl sings plaintively of her pet dove:

Andante

p

Elle a   fui   la   tour-te - rel - le, Elle a   fui loin de toi;
She has fled, the pret-ty dove,—— She has fled far from thee;

At once her father Crespel enters, filled with greatest anxiety: Enter Crespel

"My poor child, you promised me not to sing," he reminds her, saddened by the memory of his dead wife. She too had been a singer.

"It was my mother's voice," she protests, "living in me again."

"Ah, that is what tortures me!" As Antonia leaves the room, Exit Antonia repeating her promise, the old man comments on her feverish demeanor. Enter Franz

"Must I lose her as I lost her mother?" he muses. "It must be that ne'er-do-well Hoffmann who has roused her to this state." Then Exeunt Franz and Crespel calling the deaf old servant Franz, he tells him to admit nobody to the house. Enter Hoffmann and Nicklausse

A minute later, however, Hoffmann and Nicklausse make their appearance. The poet seats himself at the clavichord and sings:

Allegretto

C'est une chan-son d'a-mour qui s'en-vo-le triste ou fol-le,
'Tis a song of— love that flies off sad or joy-ful,

Soon Antonia joins him, adding her voice to his, in spite of her Enter Antonia father's command. The lovers rejoice in the prospect of their marriage. Exit Nicklausse

But the effort of singing proves too much for the delicate Antonia, Enter Crespel who is just about to collapse as her father reappears. Exit Antonia

"Dr. Miracle is here," announces Franz. Enter Franz

"That scoundrel!" cries Crespel. "He will kill my daughter as he did her mother."

The weird old physician advances with a horrible grin, jangling Enter Miracle his flasks and boxes.

"To please you I will give my patient absent treatment," he sneers.

Although Antonia has slipped out to her own room, the doctor makes a gesture toward her door which opens slowly. Then, drawing up a chair, he seems to hypnotize its invisible occupant with fantastic passes and grimaces.

In vain Crespel pushes him away; the diabolical physician returns Exeunt Miracle and Crespel through the wall. At length Miracle leaves them in peace, followed by the distracted councilor. Enter Antonia

"What did my father say?" asks Antonia, rejoining Hoffmann.

"Ask me nothing," he answers; "all will be well, I will come back Exit Hoffmann tomorrow.

Antonia is left alone. As she falls into a chair the hideous presence Enter Miracle of Dr. Miracle looms up behind her, tempting her to disregard her promise to her father and yield to her natural ambition.

"Who will save me!" sighs Antonia, glancing up at the portrait. "My mother?"

"Yes, you must obey her," advises Miracle.

The portrait lights up and becomes animated. The voice of Antonia's mother calls on her to sing.

Moderato

Chère en-fant que j'ap-pel-le comme au-tre fois, c'est ta mè-re, c'est elle;en-tends sa voix!—

Dear child whom I call as I used to do, 'Tis your mother 'tis she, lis-ten to her voice!

Spellbound the girl responds, while the old doctor takes up a violin and plays a mad accompaniment.

"My soul soars to the skies," cries Antonia, her notes hysterically rising higher and higher until she falls on the sofa, dying.

Crespel rushes in, followed by Nicklausse and Hoffmann.

"It is you that have killed her," he shouts to the poet, threatening him with a knife. Nicklausse holds him back.

Hoffmann demands that they call a doctor.

"Present!" announces Dr. Miracle, reappearing to take the pulse of his patient, and adds, "She is dead!"

"Antonia!" cries Hoffmann in despair.

EPILOGUE (9 Minutes)

"AND that is the history of my loves!" exclaims Hoffmann, again surrounded by his student friends in Luther's tavern.

Cries of "Stella, Stella!" sound from the neighboring theatre, where an unseen audience is according an ovation to the prima donna.

"What if the world does claim her?" mutters Lindorf. "She belongs to me."

"I understand your stories," exclaims Nicklausse, rising. "Olympia, Giulietta, Antonia—three natures in one single woman: Stella."

Hoffmann orders the punch to be lighted. The students betake themselves to their drinking.

An apparition of the Muse offers him the serenity of art in place of the sufferings of earthly passion. Hoffmann is moved to ecstasy by her appeal, but it is too late. By the time that Stella arrives to look for him, he lies in a drunken stupor on the table. She departs on the arm of Lindorf; the students continue their noisy drinking song.

[margin notes:]

Voice of mother (*off stage*)

Enter Crespel, Nicklausse and Hoffmann

Hoffmann, students, Lindorf, Nicklausse

Enter Stella Exeunt Stella and Lindorf

DELIBES

Léo Delibes was born at St. Germain du Val, Sarthe, on February 21, 1836, and entered the Paris *Conservatoire* at the age of twelve, studying under Adolphe Adam. He acquired practical stage experience as accompanist at the *Théâtre Lyrique*, utilizing his knowledge in a dozen operettas. Appointed to the post of second chorus master at the Paris *Opéra* he turned to the composition of ballets, his greatest success in this field being *Coppélia*.

In 1881, Delibes returned to the *Conservatoire* as professor of composition. Two years later he wrote his most important opera, *Lakmé*, and the next year was rewarded by admission to the French Academy. He died in Paris, January 16, 1891.

Delibes contributed to the operatic repertory a natural gift of melodiousness and vivacity developed with an elegance and polish that he achieved from constant practical experimentation.

LAKMÉ

Lakmé, a lyric drama in three acts was composed by Léo Delibes in 1883 and first performed on April 14 of the same year at the Opéra Comique *in Paris. Its libretto by Edmond Goudinet and Phillippe Gille was prepared from Pierre Loti's book* Le Mariage.

When Lakmé *came to this country it was given first in English, at the Academy of Music in 1886, and then in Italian with Adelina Patti, during a brief unofficial season at the Metropolitan in the*

307

Spring of 1890. It was brought to the regular repertory in 1892 in French with the original Paris heroine, Marie Van Zandt. In February, 1932, Lakmé *reappeared on the Metropolitan stage with Lily Pons in the title role.*

Characters, in order of appearance:
Hadji, servant of Nilakantha: *tenor*
Mallika, slave of Lakmé: *mezzo-soprano*
Nilakantha, a Brahman priest: *bass*
Lakmé, his daughter: *soprano*
Ellen, an English girl: *soprano*
Rose, her friend: *mezzo-soprano*
Gerald, an English officer, betrothed to Ellen: *tenor*
Mrs. Benson: *mezzo-soprano*
Frederic, an English officer: *baritone*
Hindu men and women, English officers and soldiers and sailors, Chinese merchants, dervishes, mountebanks, gypsies, bayaderes, etc.

Time: Nineteenth Century   *Place:* India

THE PRELUDE

An exotic theme later associated with the Brahman worship of the god Dourga is immediately followed by a restless figure which reappears to indicate the flighty natures of the English tourists. A third theme, the basis of the passionate love scene between Gerald and Lakmé in the second act, is introduced at greater length:

ACT I

SCENE: A RUINED TEMPLE IN AN INDIAN FOREST (50 Minutes)

THE first rays of the morning sun barely penetrate the thick verdure of an Indian forest, disclosing a tangle of flowering shrubs. Beyond them rise the ruins of a temple, half hidden in the trees. Traces of a garden can be distinguished, bound by a bamboo fence, which is pierced by a gate at the left. Far to the right a stream trickles through the underbrush.

Hadji and Mallika, Hindus Enter Nilakantha

The British occupation of India has driven the worshipers of Brahma from their accustomed temples to secret worship in the forest. Two Indian slaves, Hadji and Mallika, open the gate to admit a band of wary Hindus. The ancient priest Nilakantha emerges from the temple to welcome the faithful. As the voice of his daughter Lakmé is heard, chanting her devotions within, the people prostrate themselves, muttering their prayers. Lakmé enters and her father dismisses the congregation.

Enter
Lakmé
Exeunt
Hindus
Exeunt
Nilakantha
and Hadji

Then entrusting her to the slaves, the old man departs to brave the foreign displeasure and help his people prepare for their festival in the city.

Lakmé and Mallika mingle their voices in delight at the fragrance of the jasmine, the songs of the birds and the cool shade of the trees:

Andantino con moto

Sous le dôme é - pais
'Neath the leaf - y dome

They wander away, down the stream.

A burst of laughter tinkles through the stillness. Two English girls and their officious chaperon, Mrs. Benson, have been taking a morning stroll with two English officers, Gerald and Frederic. Adventure bound, the girls break down the bamboo, disregarding the scruples of Mrs. Benson, and the protests of Frederic, who recognizes the retreat as the temple of the vengeful fanatic, Nilakantha.

Exeunt
Lakmé and
Mallika
Enter
Rose,
Ellen, Mrs.
Benson,
Gerald and
Frederic

They chatter gaily, discussing the probable charms of the girl Lakmé who, as Frederic tells them, is considered a goddess—and comparing them with their own.

Rose finds some jewels in the grass which delight Ellen so much that she accepts the suggestion of her fiancé, Gerald, that he remain and copy their design.

Exeunt
Rose,
Ellen, Mrs.
Benson and
Frederic

Left alone, Gerald muses on the lovely being for whom the jewels must have been created.

"To touch them would be a profanation," he decides, and then, seeing that Lakmé is returning from the forest, hides himself in the shadows.

Enter
Lakmé

In spite of her fears for her father's safety, Lakmé is filled with a strange happiness which she cannot understand:

Andante

-Pour - quoi dans les· grands bois   ai - mé-je à m'é - ga - rer,   Pour y pleur · er?
O   why with -in the   for - est did I   love . to. stray,   on - ly to   weep?

Sending both slaves to watch over their master in the city, she is quite alone when she sees Gerald.

"You must go," she says breathlessly. "Do you not realize that to stay in this sacred spot means death?"

"Give me but a moment to drink in your beauty," he begs. "My own god will protect me: the god of spring and youth and love."

Allegro con moto

C'est le   dieu de la   jeun - es - se, c'est le   dieu du prin - temps
'Tis the   god— of youth that calls— us, 'tis the   god of the Spring.

Enter
Nilakantha
and slaves
Exit
Gerald

As their rapturous duet fades into stillness, Nilakantha and the slaves return. Gerald steals away unseen, but Hadji points out the broken fence to his indignant master.

"The intruder must die!" cries the old priest.

Act II

SCENE: A PUBLIC SQUARE IN A HINDU CITY (54 Minutes)

Merchants,
sailors,
tourists,
beggars,
thieves

THE noonday bazaar is thronged with a motley crowd. Hindu merchants crouch over their booths, offering rugs and perfumes to the strolling throng: sailors, tourists and the local populace. Chinese salesmen display jewels from their gleaming trays. Pickpockets filch stray treasures from the casual passer-by.

Enter Mrs.
Benson,
Frederic
and Rose
Exeunt
sailors and
merchants

Poor Mrs. Benson is frantic at the turmoil around her, but Frederic and Rose hurry to protect her from the rabble. From the pagoda that rises among the distant palm trees a bell rings out the hour of noon. The booths close for the day. The sailors hurry off to their mess.

The excitement of a new attraction holds the English visitors in the market place.

Enter
dancers

"Have you never heard of the bayaderes of India?" asks Frederic, motioning Rose and Mrs. Benson toward some seats. They eagerly applaud the varied exhibition of Indian and Persian divertissements which follow.

Enter
Nilakantha
and Lakmé

"Look at that old man with the young girl!" remarks Rose to her friends as the dancers conclude. "He frightens me."

"They are penitents, and go about reciting pious legends and gathering a few pennies," explains Frederic, who has not recognized the priest Nilakantha and his daughter entering in a disguise of rags.

Enter
Ellen and
Gerald

Ellen comes in joyously on the arm of Gerald. She forgives him for not bringing back the sketches of the jewelry, which he did not think it right to copy. They talk of a parade of the regiment, and

Frederic discusses a contemplated action against the natives. Both English couples wander away.

Exeunt Rose, Frederic, Ellen, Gerald and Mrs. Benson

Nilakantha rebukes his daughter for her mournful mood. "The gods are offended at the violation of their shrine, and wait for revenge," he explains. "Sing and be gay; perhaps the offender will look on you again with eyes of love and I shall know him."

Lakmé sings a ballad of the Pariah's daughter who with her magic bell cast an enchantment over Vishnu, the son of the divine Brahma:

As she repeats its bell-like refrain at her father's orders, she catches sight of Gerald in the gathering crowd. Half fainting with emotion, she falters to the arms of Gerald who has just returned. But as a detachment of British troops now march into the square, Frederic hurries his friend away to the post. The crowd follow after the soldiers.

Enter Gerald

Furtively Nilakantha summons a few of his devout Hindu supporters about him for a moment's converse.

"Separate the guilty one from his companions," are his orders. "I will let you know who he is, and mine will be the arm to strike. It is a sacred duty."

The old man leaves his daughter to the care of the slave Hadji who gladly offers her his help. Then he also retires and Lakmé is quite alone.

Exit Nilakantha

Gerald meanwhile hastens to her side.

"My gods are not the same as yours," says the girl of India, sadly dismissing her lover's impassioned declaration, which he sings to the theme of the prelude. Although unwilling to disclose her father's plans for his murder, she cannot wish for his death. She tells him of a little cabin hidden in the woods near the temple where he may withdraw from the world to her waiting arms.

He is torn between love and duty: his desire for the girl and his honor as an officer. His decision, however, is postponed by a

Enter
Brahmans
and
Nilakantha
Exit
Lakmé
Enter
Frederic

procession of Brahman worshipers, making their way to the temple of the goddess Dourga. Invoking her name in the solemn chant that was heard from the orchestra at the beginning of the prelude, they perform a sacred dance.

Frederic twits Gerald at his hurried departure from the ranks. "It was to admire the goddess that you left us, I suppose," he says, smiling. "I saw the Brahman's daughter here a minute ago."

"That was an idle fancy," exclaims Gerald, "and yet Lakmé is the one thought in my mind, the one bit of life in my heart."

Enter Mrs.
Benson,
Rose and
Ellen

Mrs. Benson and her charges find themselves caught in the crowd and jostled against their wills by the fanatical procession. The hymn rises to its climax. Nilakantha, summoning the conspirators about him, points out his victim. Then, as Gerald is screened from his friends by the flowing garments of the Hindus, the old priest plunges a dagger in his back.

Enter
Lakmé

Lakmé rushes to her lover, who has fainted from the wound. "They think that their vengeance is accomplished," she whispers, leaning over his body, "but now you belong utterly to me!"

Act III

SCENE: AN INDIAN FOREST (25 Minutes)

Lakmé
and Gerald

Softly intoning the pastoral theme of the woodland retreat, the orchestra prepares for the scene to come. With the help of her slave Hadji, Lakmé has brought the wounded Gerald to the little bamboo hut hidden deep in the tropical forest. Here she watches over him, singing a lullaby by the pallet of leaves where he lies stricken:

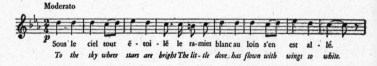

Moderato

Sous le ciel tout é-toi-lé le ra-mier blanc au loin s'en est al-lé.
To the sky where stars are bright The lit-tle dove has flown with wings so white.

Gradually he awakens, and recalls the events leading to their escape to the forest. The lovers blissfully contemplate the prospect of happiness before them. The voices that they hear softly in the distance, Lakmé tells Gerald, come from the sacred spring where lovers repair to pledge their vows. She too will bring a draught of the holy water, that they may drink to their unending love. Taking a vessel of ivory from the hut, she disappears in the forest.

Exit
Lakmé
Enter
Frederic

No sooner is she out of sight than Frederic, who has followed them by the broken ferns and traces of blood on the leaves, hurries to the spot.

"What are you doing here?" he asks, urgently. "You are needed with the regiment. The country is in revolt."

Since the call of duty does not penetrate Gerald's romantic reverie, Frederic reminds his friend of his English fiancée, of the feverish inconstancy of the Indian women, of the probability that a battle will be fought on the very next day.

Just as the wounded officer decides to return, he sees Lakmé, bringing back the mystical libation. Frederic departs, sure of his friend's resolve. When she looks at Gerald's face, Lakmé knows that he is no longer hers. In spite of his protestations, he is more concerned with the marching song of the English soldiers which echoes from the distance, than with her pleas.

Exit Frederic Enter Lakmé

Thus he does not see Lakmé wander off to pluck the deadly datura flower from a near-by branch, and raise its poisonous petals to her lips. Her gentle reminiscences of his tender words win him back to a new ardor, but it is too late. Together they drink the draught she has brought from the sacred spring; together their voices rise in rapture.

When Nilakantha, discovering their retreat, strides in upon them again, threatening the life of Gerald, Lakmé tells him of her sacrifice.

Enter Nilakantha

"We have drunk the holy pledge of love," she says, in a final ecstasy. "If the gods demand an expiation, let them call me!"

Gerald sobs that she is dying for his sake.

"She has risen to the splendor of eternal life!" cries the ancient priest.

MASSENET

JULES MASSENET, born in Montaud (Loire) in France, on May 12, 1842, entered the Paris *Conservatoire* at the age of 11, and ten years later won its *Grand Prix de Rome* with his cantata *David Rizzio*. Meanwhile he supported himself, and at the same time gained valuable stage experience, by playing the triangle and drum in Paris theatre orchestras.

After marrying a pupil to whom Liszt had introduced him in Rome, he returned to Paris where his operas and oratorios were produced with great popular acclaim. For eighteen years he taught as professor of composition at the Conservatory. He was elected a member of the French Academy and became a Commander of the Legion of Honor.

Encouraged by the success of *Manon* in 1884, he continued writing operas until his death in 1912.

He won the recognition of his contemporaries as a classic master for his facile style and exquisite instrumentation, though lacking marked vigor or strong artistic convictions.

MANON

MANON, *a lyric drama in five acts, was composed by Massenet, largely during the summer of 1882, at The Hague, in the old home of the Abbé Prevost, whose novel forms the basis of its libretto by Halévy and Gille.*

First produced at the Opéra Comique *in Paris, it reached the New York Academy of Music in an Italian version in 1885, and ten years later was presented in French at the Metropolitan, where it has held the stage off and on since 1909.*

The Cours-la-Reine *scene is usually omitted at the Metropolitan, the familiar Gavotte being transferred to the fourth Act in the Hotel Transylvanie.*

Characters, in order of appearance:

Guillot, Minister of Finance, an old beau: *baritone*
De Brétigny, a nobleman: *baritone*

Actresses $\left\{\begin{array}{l}\text{Poussette}\\\text{Javotte}\\\text{Rosette}\end{array}\right\}$ *soprano*

Innkeeper: *bass*
Lescaut, of the Royal Guards: *baritone*
Manon, his cousin: *soprano*
Le Chevalier des Grieux: *tenor*
Le Comte des Grieux, his father: *bass*
Porter, maidservant, croupier, sergeant, townspeople, guards, traveler, ladies of the Seminary, and card players

Time: 1721   *Place:* Amiens, Paris and Le Havre

ACT I

SCENE: THE COURTYARD OF AN INN AT AMIENS (37 Minutes)

THE curtain rises on the courtyard of the inn at Amiens. Through a gate at the back, visitors are arriving by coach. At the right is a small pavilion where guests may dine, built in the fanciful style of the eighteenth century; at the left the inn itself.

"Ho there, innkeeper!" calls Guillot, an old *roué*, shaking the white curls of his wig. "We wish to eat. Such inattention is not due people of quality!"

Guillot and Brétigny

"They must all be dead," joins in the younger nobleman Brétigny, in a rage.

Three pretty faces smile through the windows of the pavilion. Poussette, Javotte and Rosette add their voices to call for dinner.

Poussette, Javotte, Rosette in pavilion
Enter innkeeper and waiters

At length the innkeeper emerges, and following him a procession of waiters with covered pots. The company hails the prospect of dinner, and the men join the girls in the pavilion, leaving the innkeeper alone.

Exeunt Guillot, Brétigny
Exit innkeeper

"I have promised to hold a place in the coach for the Chevalier des Grieux," remarks the innkeeper. "Where can he be?"

As he returns to seek his client at the inn, a bell rings and a number of townspeople gather to watch for the coach.

Among them swaggers Lescaut, an officer of the guard, attended by a couple of guardsmen whom he sends off for a drink.

"I must wait for my cousin Manon," he explains to them; "I'll meet you a bit later."

The orchestra announces the arrival of the coach. The passengers descend, and fuss with their luggage. Finally Lescaut perceives a demure young girl emerging from the crowd. It must be Manon.

After a naïve kiss, she begs her cousin to forgive her chatter. This trip to the convent is her first journey, she explains. Her manner reflects her youth and innocence.

The crowd reassembles for the departure of the coach, and then draws away.

"Be a good girl, and I will collect your bags," says Lescaut, leaving her to her own devices.

Manon is alone. Her pretty face catches the eye of Guillot, looking for the waiter. He tells of his wealth and begs a word of love.

"If I didn't prefer to laugh, I surely would be angry," answers Manon, and the little dinner party in the pavilion calls him back with echoing merriment. Brétigny, who also appreciates Manon's charms, tries to protect her, but Guillot manages to whisper that his carriage will be there waiting, if she changes her mind.

Lescaut looks in for a moment, with a word of cousinly advice. Then he hurries off to his friends in the tavern.

Manon is left to amuse herself by watching the gay costumes of the actresses in the pavilion.

"I must leave these worldly thoughts at the convent door," she adds to herself; "still, what fun to amuse oneself all one's life!"

Suddenly she realizes that she is not alone. A young nobleman has entered the inn yard. The music hints his romantic nature. He is on his way home, and speaks of his father.

As he catches sight of her, his thoughts change:
"Is this a dream?" he asks. A solo violin plays the love theme:

Andante cantabile

Des Grieux addresses her respectfully:
"I seem to know your name——"
"My name is Manon. They are putting me in a convent."
"Never," he insists. "I will carry you away in my arms."
At that moment Guillot's coachman appears. Why not take his
carriage for themselves and ride off to Paris?

Allegro

Nous vi - vrons___ à Pa - ris, tous les deux, tous les deux,
We to Par - is will go, heart to heart, heart to heart,

Lescaut's voice in the distance and the laughter of the party in
the pavilion remind Manon of the significance of her decision. For
an instant she hesitates. Then off she hurries with her lover.

*Exeunt
Manon
and
des Grieux*

ACT II

SCENE: MANON'S APARTMENT IN PARIS (26 Minutes)

THE devotion of des Grieux is hinted by the development of his
impetuous theme in a brief orchestral prelude, and the curtain
rises. The runaway couple are seen in the dainty salon of their
Paris apartment.

*des Grieux
and Manon*

The Chevalier is writing a letter to his father, and Manon
watches over his shoulder. Together they read his description of
her charms.

He notices a strange bouquet of flowers on the table. "They
were thrown in through the window," she explains casually. "You
aren't jealous, are you?"

A servant announces the arrival of Lescaut and de Brétigny, who
has come disguised as a soldier in her cousin's regiment to persuade
Manon to elope with him. It is he who has sent the flowers.

*Enter
Lescaut
and
Brétigny*

Pompously Lescaut demands that des Grieux avenge the honor
of the house: "Do you agree to marry Manon? Yes, or no?"

The Chevalier shows him the letter in which he has asked his
father's permission for the marriage. They retire to the window to
read it.

De Brétigny draws Manon aside.

"Tonight your lover is to be abducted by his father's order," he whispers. "If you warn him, there will be nothing but misery for you both. I can offer you liberty and fortune. You will become the very queen of beauty!"

Exeunt
Lescaut
and
Brétigny
Exit
des Grieux

The intruders depart, and shortly after des Grieux follows them to post the letter. Manon is left alone to face her future. "Queen of beauty," she repeats, and the seductive words decide her: she will not warn the Chevalier. Sadly, she bids farewell to the little table where they have so often dined:

Enter
des Grieux

As she sobs out her last words, des Grieux returns, and sings of the vision he has just dreamed of a future with Manon:

Exit
des Grieux

A knock interrupts them. With a last vain impulse, Manon begs her lover to stay at her side. He goes. The noise of a struggle is heard without. "Ah, my poor Chevalier," sighs Manon.

ACT III

SCENE: SEMINARY OF ST. SULPICE (20 Minutes)

Ladies
of the
Seminary

THE pious ladies of the congregation of St. Sulpice gather for a moment in the paneled parlor to praise the sermon they have just heard by the Abbé des Grieux. Such eloquence does not suggest that the young preacher has but recently renounced a life of pleasure.

"What an admirable discourse!" they exclaim.

Enter
des Grieux
Exeunt
ladies
Enter Count

As the young man enters in his priestly vestments, the ladies withdraw. His father, the dignified count, soon appears.

"Is an alliance with Heaven better than an honest marriage?" the count demands. "Take some wife who is worthy of our name— that is where your duty lies."

"Nothing can keep me from my vows," answers the Abbé. Touched by his son's fervor, the count makes a generous offer of money, and then withdraws.

Exit
Count

Des Grieux cannot banish Manon from his thoughts. Her image haunts even his prayers:

No sooner has he left the sacristy than the porter ushers in Manon, gorgeously attired. She asks him to summon the Abbé. To the sound of distant chanting she flings herself on a *prie Dieu* and prays for pardon.

Des Grieux returns and orders her to leave.

"I have been guilty," she pleads. "Forgive me. Am I not still the Manon who loves you?"

As the love motive rises to a final climax, the Chevalier yields, and follows her out into the world.

Exit des Grieux
Enter Manon
Enter des Grieux

Exeunt Manon and des Grieux

Act IV

SCENE: THE HOTEL TRANSYLVANIE (20 Minutes)

A FASHIONABLE gambling house in Paris is thronged by pleasure seekers. At the gaming tables the players call their bets. Lescaut boasts of his success, while Poussette, Javotte, and Rosette sing jauntily of the joys of chance.

The ancient Guillot notices that des Grieux and Manon have entered. He is still jealous of the man who has won the girl he fancied. The Chevalier is ill at ease in these dubious surroundings.

"Do I no longer rule your heart?" asks Manon.

"I love you and I hate you," answers her lover, whose fortune has been squandered for her pleasure.

"If you still love me, try your hand at the cards," begs Manon. "We shall be rich again."

Guillot suggests a match, and Lescaut urges them on.

Manon, exhilarated by the gaiety of the scene, sings a sparkling gavotte in praise of the pleasures of youth:

Gamblers, croupiers, Lescaut, Guillot, Poussette Javotte, Rosette Enter Manon and des Grieux

Moderato e leggiero

p Pro - fi - tons bien de la jeun - es - se
Pro - fit then by the time of youth ——

Guillot and des Grieux settle down to their game. The Chevalier wins every hand.

Exit Guillot

"I withdraw," exclaims the exasperated old statesman at length. "With such an opponent, I would be a fool to go on." He calls the company together, formally accuses des Grieux of cheating, and stalks from the room.

Manon begs her lover to escape with her, but it is too late. Guillot returns with the police.

Enter Guillot, Count, and police

The Comte des Grieux makes a stately entrance and consents to the arrest of his son.

"But, Manon,—" pleads the Chevalier.

"The guard will take her where such women are sent."

ACT V

SCENE: THE ROAD TO HAVRE (16 Minutes)

Lescaut and des Grieux

ON the dusty highway to Havre, des Grieux has arranged with Lescaut to meet Manon on her way to exile.

She comes down the little path, faltering with weariness, and falls in the arms of des Grieux.

Exit Lescaut Enter Manon

"My only love," she says tenderly, "I do not know why I have caused you so much unhappiness. Forgive me."

"There is freedom for us ahead," insists des Grieux.

"I love you," she repeats softly; "this is our last farewell."

"Is this not my hand? Is this not my voice?" he sings to the melody of her plea in Saint Sulpice, in an effort to revive her. Her voice joins with his, and she dies in his arms.

"Manon" by J. Massenet. Permission granted by G. Schirmer, Inc., New York

THAÏS

THAÏS, *an opera in three acts and seven scenes, was composed by Massenet ten years after the success of* Manon—*its libretto being prepared by Louis Gallet. The work, although tragic in its conclusion and prevailing mood, is referred to on the title page as a "lyric comedy," perhaps because of the original ironic implications in the novel of Anatole France from which the text is derived.*

First produced at the Grand Opéra *in Paris in 1894, it was brought to New York with Mary Garden in the leading role in 1907, but did not enter the Metropolitan repertory until February 16, 1917, when the title role was sung for four seasons by Geraldine Farrar.*

Characters, in order of appearance:
Palemon, an old Cenobite monk: *bass*
Athanaël, a Cenobite: *baritone*
The Servitor of Nicias: *baritone*
Nicias, a Sybarite philosopher: *tenor*
Crobyle, a slave of Nicias: *soprano*
Myrtale, a slave of Nicias: *mezzo-soprano*
Thaïs, a courtesan and actress of Alexandria: *soprano*
"La Charmeuse," a dancer: *soprano*
Albine, an abbess: *mezzo-soprano*
Cenobite monks, histrions, comedians, and dancers, philosophers, friends of Nicias, populace and White Nuns.
Time: The end of the Fourth Century
Place: Alexandria and the Egyptian Desert

Act I

SCENE 1: THE HUTS OF THE CENOBITES ON THE BANKS OF THE NILE
(19 Minutes)

A few soft measures from the orchestra preface the first scene and continue an austere melody after the curtain rises. Near their desert huts twelve Cenobite monks are gathered at table for supper about their elder, Palemon.

Monks and Palemon

They ask a blessing on their meal of bread and honey, and then question each other: "Where is brother Athanaël?"

Enter Athanaël

Slowly, as if exhausted by fatigue or grief, the missing monk appears among them, and sinks heavily in his place.

He refuses food and drink. "My heart is full of bitterness," he explains mournfully. "I come from the wicked city which the woman Thaïs has converted to the infamous cult of Venus. It is true," he adds, perturbed, "as a youth I knew her once. But God preserved me from temptation and I found peace here in the desert. How glad I would be to win that fallen soul for the Lord!"

"It is better not to mingle with this evil generation," advises the old Palemon; "such is eternal wisdom!"

Exeunt monks and Palemon

The monks raise their voices in prayer and then retire for the night. Athanaël lies down on a mat in front of his hut.

Vision of Thaïs

Suddenly a mist seems to dissolve from the darkness and a distant vision unfolds of the theatre at Alexandria, crowded with people. Far off, the figure of Thaïs is seen, assuming the seductive postures of a courtesan. Remotely a thousand voices seem to shout her name.

The vision disappears; the day has dawned. Athanaël rises with a cry of shame, then prostrates himself in fervent prayer.

"Give me grace to save this woman from the bonds of the flesh!" he prays:

Allegro moderato

f Toi qui mis la pi-tié dans nos â - mes, Dieu bon, lou-ange à toi!
Thou who fil - lest our souls with com - pas - sion, O Lord, be praise to thee!

Enter monks and Palemon

Vainly Palemon reiterates his counsel. The monk rouses his companions to bid them farewell.

SCENE 2: THE TERRACE OF THE HOUSE OF NICIAS AT ALEXANDRIA
(25 Minutes)

Huge palm trees shade the luxurious palace of Nicias. Below spreads the rich city of Alexandria, and the sea beyond it. On the right the main portal is hung with an awning, behind which a banquet is being prepared.

Humbly the monk Athanaël approaches the house and asks the servitor to summon his master, Nicias. At first the impudent fellow tries to turn him away like a beggar. Finally he retreats to the house.

Athanaël turns to contemplate the view from the terrace.

"There is Alexandria," he exclaims, "the city where I was born in sin, the city I despise for its riches and beauty. May the angels of heaven purify its foul air!"

Hardly has he spoken his last words when merry laughter issues from the house, and Nicias comes forth, his arms about the shoulders of two beautiful slaves, Crobyle and Myrtale.

"What can I do for my old friend?" asks the young man, with a jest at Athanaël's unkempt appearance.

"I am here for a single day; I have come to save Thaïs, and lead her to God. Where can I find her?"

Nicias receives this news with a burst of laughter. "I have sold my last vineyard to purchase a week of her company; tonight she sups with me for the last time."

"Lend me a robe," begs the monk. "One must fight the powers of hell with their own weapons."

The slaves call for garments and perfumes, golden sandals and bracelets with which to dress Athanaël. Of his former habit, he insists on retaining his haircloth tunic. "He is as handsome as a god," conclude the minions, finishing their joyous task.

Guests of the evening throng the terrace, actors and dancers mingling with philosophers. "Beware of the terrible enemy," whispers Nicias to his friend; "here she comes."

The host draws Thaïs to a seat beside him; a dazzling figure decked in the richest apparel. For a moment they review the happiness of their short intimacy with wistful regret. Then she asks who is the fierce stranger.

"He is a philosopher, come to teach you holy doctrines," answers Nicias.

"What are they?" she inquires.

"Contempt of the flesh, love of suffering, strict penance," declares the monk, with quiet dignity.

Athanaël
and
servitor
Exit
servitor

Enter
Nicias and
Two slaves

Enter
guests,
actors,
dancers
and
philoso-
phers
Enter
Thaïs

Smiling at his severity, Thaïs addresses him, her words mingling tenderness with irony. "What do you know of the wisdom of a lover?" she asks. "Come, sit beside us, crown yourself with roses, and learn that nothing is real but love."

Qui-te fait si sé-vè—re, et pour-quoi dé-mens-tu la flam-me de tes yeux?
Whence doth come this se - ve - ri - ty, where-fore too, woulds't de-ny the flame that sears thine eyes?

Athanaël repulses these suggestions, which are warmly echoed by the entire company, gathered about Thaïs to witness the encounter.

"In your own palace I will yet bring you salvation!" he shouts, striding away in horror as she prepares again to assume the seductive poses of the vision.

ACT II

SCENE 1: ROOM IN THE HOUSE OF THAÏS (15 Minutes)

Thaïs

SURROUNDED by precious rugs from Byzantium, vases of exotic flowers, braziers of incense, and statues of her pagan deities, lies Thaïs, weary of the world, and surfeited with pleasure. She dismisses her companions, and taking up a mirror, vainly seeks reassurance that her beauty will endure:

Dis-moi que je suis belle et que je se-rai belle é-ter-nel-le-ment! É-ter-nel-le-ment!
Say I am love-ly, and say that I shall love-ly be to the end of time to the end of time!

Enter Athanaël

She looks up, to behold Athanaël standing silently on the threshold.

"Lord, cast a veil over her beauty," he prays, then turns to offer her the holy happiness which his faith has brought him.

When he speaks of eternal life, Thaïs is vaguely troubled. Sprinkling more incense in front of the statue of Venus, she chants a prayer to the goddess.

Athanaël, profoundly disturbed by her beauty, summons his ebbing resistance, tears off the borrowed robes, and cries out a curse on the living death that is hers.

"Do not let me die," pleads Thaïs, her former assurance completely broken. Throwing herself at his feet, she entreats him to have pity on her. Then, as the monk repeats his fervent promises, she confesses to a new joy that fills her soul.

In the distance sounds the voice of Nicias, begging for one more kiss.

"What does he know of love?" she asks, disdainfully. And yet, when the monk bids her dismiss the old lover, she cries that she must remain Thaïs the courtesan. Her vacant laughter breaks into passionate weeping as the curtain falls.

At this point a solo violin, supported by harps, intones the melody of the familiar Meditation, *intended to portray the spiritual transformation of Thaïs:*

SCENE 2: IN FRONT OF THE HOUSE OF THAÏS (33 Minutes)

On the steps of the portico of the house of Thaïs, the monk Athanaël lies sleeping in the moonlight. A lighted lamp reveals a small statuette of Eros near the entrance. Sounds of revelry come from another house, at the right, where Nicias is entertaining his guests by the gleam of many torches.

Athanaël

Thaïs enters softly, takes up the lamp to survey the portico, replaces it and comes down the steps to Athanaël.

Enter Thaïs

"Father," she says in a low voice, "your words have remained in my heart, and a great light has come to me. What must I do?"

"The dawn of peace is at hand," he answers. "I shall lead you to a convent where women dwell in blessed meditation, under the guidance of the sainted Albine. But first," he adds, "you must destroy every trace of your evil life, your riches and your shame."

She begs to keep the little ivory statute of Eros, a gift of Nicias, or at least to have it preserved in some monastery where, being an image of love, it may turn men to God. The monk rejects this suggestion with rage, and dashes the statue to the ground. Bent on destruction, they enter the house.

Exeunt Thaïs and Athanaël

Meanwhile a new and spirited rhythm heralds the arrival of Nicias and his guests. Intoxicated with his success at the gambling tables, the young host commands that dancers shall be brought while it is yet dark. Slaves brighten the scene with additional torches. A brilliant ballet follows with seven divertissements, each to a new measure. The climax is reached when a lovely girl, La Charmeuse, enlivens her graceful steps with flights of song, while the slaves Crobyle and Myrtale comment on her charms in an ecstatic duet.

Enter Nicias, guests and slaves
Ballet

Enter La Charmeuse

Enter
Athanaël

As the excitement reaches its zenith, Athanaël appears on the threshold of the house. He turns aside their greetings with severity. "Thaïs is no longer yours," he cries; "the ungodly Thaïs is no more. Behold her reborn!"

Enter
Thaïs and
slaves

Clad in rough woolen garb, a dark veil bound over her hair, Thaïs follows him from the house, surrounded by her slaves. They glance back fearfully at the smoke and flames which issue from its arches. The penitent and her confessor have consigned all the sinful luxury of her past life to the fire.

Nicias rushes forward to seize her. "Do not leave us," he pleads.

Staunchly the monk protects the new disciple. "Lay not your impious hands on the bride of God," he cries.

Enter
populace

The entire company now perceives the fire, and angrily laments the treasures to be lost. Athanaël and Thaïs stand calmly facing the threatening crowd. A stone is hurled at the monk. At length

Exeunt
Thaïs and
Athanaël

Nicias flings his newly won gold to the populace. For a moment their wrath is appeased. Then, as the palace falls to the ground, Thaïs departs with Athanaël.

ACT III

SCENE 1: THE OASIS (18 Minutes)

UNDER the burning sun of noon the women of the desert seek water at the oasis. Over the well great palms spread their shade in contrast to the blinding sands beyond, where the huts of the White Nuns gleam in the distance.

Thaïs and
Athanaël

Tortured with thirst, and weary from the long journey, Thaïs staggers bravely after the monk.

At first he roughly silences her complaints with remonstrances. "Mortify the flesh," he orders, "and expiate your sins." Then as she sinks, half fainting, his tone becomes kinder. "Perhaps I have prolonged your trial too much," he adds with compassion. "Let me bring you some cool water and fruit to refresh you."

Thaïs waits quietly for his return. Her soul is full of a divine peace. When he brings her the bowl of water, their voices join in a serene contentment:

Bai - gne d'eau mes mains et mes lev - res, don - ne ces fruits, don - ne ces fruits,
Bathe my hands and lips with this wa - ter, give me this fruit, give me this fruit,

From afar sound the prayers of the White Nuns, led by the venerable Albine.

As the procession winds its way to their presence, Athanaël approaches the abbess and entrusts Thaïs to her care. "We shall meet again in the celestial city," murmurs the penitent, reverently kissing his hands. Enter Nuns and Albine

With a cry of anguish, the monk watches her departure. "I shall see her no more, no more!"

SCENE 2: THE GARDEN OF THE CONVENT OF THE WHITE NUNS
(10 Minutes)

The white-robed nuns chant their somber office, kneeling in their garden beneath a great fig tree. In its shade lies the dying Thaïs. Nuns, Thaïs and Albine

"For three months she has watched and wept," exclaims Albine. "Penance has destroyed her body, but her sins are blotted out!" Then she turns to welcome Athanaël, who has appeared at the garden gate, pale and troubled, and now humbly stands before her. Enter Athanaël

The nuns withdraw. The monk drags himself toward the woman he loves. Exeunt Nuns and Albine

"Do you remember that shining journey, when you brought me here?" she asks faintly, while the music of the Meditation soars above her voice.

"I remember only your earthly beauty," answers Athanaël, but she cannot hear his words.

Rapturously she describes the angelic hosts which her dying eyes alone can see. In passionate despair, Athanaël cries out his love. It is too late, he cannot share her beatific vision.

"Thais" by J. Massenet. Copyright, 1907, by Heugel & Cie.

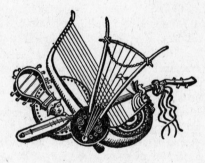

IX

Opera Invades the Countryside

EASTERN Europe, rich in peasant lore and traditional melodies, was allowing its wealth to lie neglected. Suddenly, in the mid-nineteenth century, when the Slavic nations became conscious of their political destiny, this portion of the continent turned to a revaluation of its culture. Inspired by what they found, the leading Slavic musicians cast off the influence of western art and embarked upon a new patriotic adventure.

In Bohemia, the national awakening came about gradually. Antonin Dvorák (1841-1904) and Bedrich Smetana preached the beauties of a music regenerated through the melodies of the folk. By taking peasant idioms and grafting them onto the architecture of accepted forms, both of these composers led the way to a strong Slavic nationalism in symphony and in opera. Italian vocal texts were abandoned in favor of the native language; and with his *Prodana Nevésta* (The Bartered Bride), Smetana ushered in a new era for the Bohemian theatre. All the standard forces of the opera house—chorus, ballet, and an orchestra of symphonic proportions—were utilized as background for a bright little comedy of peasant life.

In Russia, the rise of musical nationalism was much more violent. After preliminary steps by Alexander Dargomijszky and Michael Glinka, the leap from Italian opera to a glorification of Russian life and history was accomplished by Modest Moussorgsky in his two epics, *Boris Godunoff* and *Khovantchina*. In both of these operas, the motivating force was supplied by the chorus, who represented the Russian people at work, at play, and at revolution. Using a style that in no way derived from Wagner, Moussorgsky nevertheless stumbled upon the same principles which the German composer had developed: the use of leading motives and the symphonic importance of the orchestra. The similarity to Wagner ended there; the harmonies and barbaric rhythms of Moussorgsky grew out of the semi-oriental cast of Russian history.

Nikolai Rimsky-Korsakoff also followed the star of nationalism, but in a more conservative manner. In place of the stark realism of Moussorgsky, he brought fantasy and an occasional touch of satire to his treatment of historical themes. Alexander Borodin, another advocate of native culture, evoked the sumptuous orientalism of medieval Russia in his opera *Prince Igor* (1891), which is remembered for its brilliant ballets.

Of all the great Russian composers, only Peter Ilyitch Tchaikowsky (1840-1893) turned westward for his inspiration. His two operatic masterpieces, *Eugene Onegin* and *Pique Dame*, are almost completely occidental in feeling. But the urge which impelled the Russian lyric theatre toward national life has persisted even in our own decade with Shostakovich's peasant tragedy, *Lady Macbeth of Mzensk.*

SMETANA

THE birth of Bedrich Smetena on March 2, 1824, in the little town of Leitomischl, was celebrated by his father, a prosperous brewer, in a spirited dance, said to have been the first polka on record.

The elder Smetana did not, however, encourage his son's musical education, or even contribute to his support. With the help of Katharina Kolar, whom he later married, Smetana studied the piano in Prague under her master, Prokosch, and in 1848 started a piano school of his own.

Discouraged by the cool reception of his first compositions, Smetana accepted a conductorship in Gothenburg in 1856. Here his symphonic poems won him wide renown, and in 1861 he was invited to return to Prague, where he became leading conductor in the new National Opera House. Of his seven operas produced there, the second, *The Bartered Bride,* sufficed to establish his reputation throughout Europe.

In 1874 he resigned because of serious deafness, which was eventually followed by a mental ailment. Ten years later he died in an asylum.

Known as the father of Bohemian music, Smetana not only presented his native folk songs and dances in an effective, artistic form, but contributed a fluent melodic inspiration of his own.

THE BARTERED BRIDE

THE BARTERED BRIDE (DIE VERKAUFTE BRAUT) *is a comic opera in three acts, composed by Bedrich Smetana, the founder of the nationalist Bohemian school of music. With its original text by Karel Sabina, it was first presented in Prague on May 30, 1866, in the Czech language, under the title of* Prodana Nevésta.

In February, 1909, it started its career at the Metropolitan under the baton of Gustav Mahler with Emmy Destinn in the title role. Although it was sung in German, its authentic national flavor was assured by the fact that both these artists were Bohemian.

Characters, in order of appearance:

Hans, son of Micha by his first marriage: *tenor*
Marie, daughter of Kruschina and Kathinka: *soprano*
Kezal, the village marriage broker: *bass*
Kruschina, a prosperous peasant: *baritone*
Kathinka, his wife: *soprano*
Wenzel, son of Micha by his second marriage: *tenor*
Springer, head of a troupe of strolling players: *tenor*
Esmeralda, a dancer of the troupe: *soprano*
Muff, an Indian: *tenor*
Micha, a landowner: *bass*
Agnes, his second wife: *mezzo-soprano*
Villagers, children, members of the troupe of strolling players.

Time: A feast day, about 1850   *Place:* A Bohemian Village

332

OVERTURE

A vigorous fugato is built upon a theme to be repeated at the dramatic climax of the opera, the finale of the second act:

This is contrasted with a second sturdy theme which follows it on both occasions:

ACT I

SCENE: A SQUARE IN A BOHEMIAN VILLAGE (35 Minutes)

THE village inn is decorated in holiday mood, as the peasants throng out of church to enjoy the festivities of a local feast day. The sturdy wooden houses opposite are hung with wreaths and garlands; the girls have put fresh bows on their hair, and bright aprons over their colored skirts; the men have polished their high boots, and throw their caps in the air as one and all join in a merry chorus.

Peasants

Of all the maidens, only one is sad today: the lovely peasant girl Marie, for, as she tells her sweetheart Hans, she has been betrothed by her father against her will. He has ordered her to marry the son of Micha, the rich landowner who on this very day will introduce the promised bridegroom.

Marie and Hans

"It is only you I love," she protests, "and if you did not love me, there would be no sun left in the sky."

Hans too has his troubles. An unkind stepmother has forced him to leave his prosperous father's home and earn a living among strangers. They decide, however, in a romantic duet, that love will somehow cure all their woes:

Andante

Love re - moves all sor row.

Exeunt
Marie
and Hans
Enter
Kruschina,
Kathinka
and Kezal

Their departure is not noticed by Marie's parents, Kruschina and Kathinka, who are hurried across the square by the chattering marriage broker, Kezal. Shaking his fat umbrella to emphasize each word, he tells them to have complete confidence in him.

"Everything is all right, quite all right," he assures them. "Micha's son is very wealthy, a model of perfection; your daughter will fall in love with him at once. I never overlook a thing, just leave it all to me!"

Kathinka thinks it might be better to consult Marie; Kruschina wonders if Micha has not got a second son who might be a better match; but both are overruled. There is no answer to Kezal's pattering tongue.

Enter
Marie

Marie, however, returns, unswerving in her affection for Hans. "I have a sweetheart already," she says, to the melody of her former love duet, "and I have promised to marry him."

"But your father has signed a contract with Micha," announces Kezal, triumphantly. "His boy Wenzel is very shy; I'll bring him along soon. Meanwhile just trust me and I'll attend to Hans."

Exit Marie

Marie walks away miserably. There is no pleasure for her in the dancing that follows, though the entire town seems to have turned out in the square for a brilliant polka:

Moderato

Act II

SCENE: A ROOM IN THE INN (44 Minutes)

Hans,
peasant
boys and
Kezal

HANS and his friends make merry over their pots of ale at a table in the village inn. The young man proclaims that love is better than any drink.

"It all depends on whether you have money or not," insists Kezal, from the other side of the room.

The conversation is interrupted when a company of villagers

pour into the room to dance the furiant, a syncopated waltz measure, to a native melody of Bohemia:

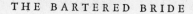

Once the dance is concluded and the room cleared, the booby Wenzel with red nose and stuttering tongue staggers through the door.

"My m-m-mamma made me come here to get married," he says with a foolish smile, "b-b-but if I find a wife all the p-p-people will make fun of me."

Marie realizes that this is her chance for freedom. She persuades Wenzel that the girl he is supposed to marry is in love with another man and would make his life miserable. As a substitute she invents the existence of a fictitious young lady who already adores him. He goes off with her happily, unaware that his new friend is Marie, the girl to whom his parents have betrothed him.

Exeunt
Wenzel
and Marie
Enter
Kezal
and Hans

Meanwhile the marriage broker has taken Hans in hand. "What you need is not love, which flies away overnight, but cold cash," he tells him. "Now I know a honey with plenty of money," and he enumerates the live stock and other wealth of a rich client.

"What's more if you give up Marie, I'll make it worth your while," Kezal continues. "I represent the son of Tobias Micha, and I'll pay you all of three hundred crowns if you relinquish her to him."

Hans thinks for a moment and then is seized with a bright idea. "Certainly I'll sign your contract," he declares, "provided it states clearly that Marie is to marry no one but the son of Tobias Micha,"—and he smiles to himself.

"I am catching the old fellow in his own trap," he says gleefully, as Kezal retreats in the belief that he has the best of the bargain. "He mustn't know that my love has never faltered, and that soon I will claim Marie for my own."

The marriage broker calls in the contracting parties, and the entire population throngs to witness the agreement. What is the

Enter
Kruschina,
Kathinka,
Marie and
villagers

general dismay when it is shown that Hans is signing away his beloved for three hundred crowns! As the orchestra resounds with the sturdy theme of the overture, the chorus hurls its reproaches on a man who would barter his bride.

Act III

SCENE: THE VILLAGE SQUARE, AS IN ACT 1 (39 Minutes)

Wenzel

WENZEL is still stupefied by the news that he is loved, and blubbers that life is too much for him.

Strolling
players
Springer
and
Esmeralda

A fanfare of trumpets and drums meanwhile heralds the arrival of a troupe of strolling players. In stentorian tones, their leader, Springer, announces that Esmeralda, queen of tightrope dancers, a wild Indian chief, and a ferocious brown bear will be the main attractions of the rehearsal and performance to follow.

Wenzel, who has found a point of vantage in the crowd, promptly picks out Esmeralda as the girl of his choice, and begs her to dance for him.

She has hardly started when bad news is brought. "Mr. Springer!" cries the Indian. "The man who plays the bear has drunk himself into a stupor, and there is no one to take his place. What can we do?"

Enter
Indian

The manager's eye lights on Wenzel, who is exactly the right height for the bear's costume. Perhaps Esmeralda can persuade him to act as substitute!

Exeunt
players
Enter
Micha,
Agnes and
Kezal

Wenzel is delighted to join any company in which Esmeralda is to be found. Eager to follow her, he twirls about in the dance she tries to teach him.

As the rehearsal is concluded, Micha and his wife Agnes arrive with the broker Kezal, who has prepared their son's contract of marriage to Marie.

Exeunt
Micha
Agnes and
Wenzel

"But I d-d-don't want to marry her," declares the booby. "I have met another girl who loves me." The rebellious son rushes away, pursued by his astonished parents.

Enter
Kruschina,
Kathinka,
Marie

Kruschina and Kathinka find themselves faced with exactly the same situation. Marie refuses to marry Wenzel.

"It's a shameful lie that Hans is no longer true to me," she declares. "Give me at least a little time to think about it."

Enter
Micha,
Agnes,
Wenzel

Micha and Agnes succeed in bringing Wenzel back to the marriage broker.

"But that is the girl who told me not to marry Marie," cries the booby, pointing at Marie herself. All four parents agree with Kezal that the situation may clear up if they do not rush things.

So Marie is left alone. "I cannot believe that Hans signed me away for money," she says sorrowfully; "how dreary the world seems without his love!"

Laughing at her tears, Hans rushes to her side. "I can explain everything in one moment," he announces cheerfully; but she is not convinced.

When the four parents return with the marriage broker, Hans is ready for them. "I do not need a father's home any longer," he tells the company, "for I have decided to have one of my own. I too am the son of Micha, and I hereby claim Marie for bride!"

At these words Marie runs to his arms, while everyone rejoices except the crestfallen Kezal.

There is a moment of confusion. Some village boys rush in with the news that the bear has broken loose and is coming to the square.

"I fooled you," cries the booby happily, pulling the bear skin off his head. "I am no bear—only Wenzel!"

"You know, Micha," says Kruschina, "I think that Hans is the best bridegroom for Marie after all."

"And you should thank the girl for bringing back your long-lost son," adds Kathinka.

Micha gives the happy pair his blessing, while the villagers exclaim that

> *"Wedding bells, far and wide,*
> *Celebrate the Bartered Bride!"*

Margin notes:
Exeunt Micha, Agnes, Wenzel, Kathinka, Kruschina and Kezal
Enter Hans

Enter Micha, Agnes, Kathinka, Kruschina and Kezal

Enter boys

Enter Wenzel

MOUSSORGSKY

MODEST MOUSSORGSKY was born in the village of Karevo, Russia, on March 16, 1839. Of a noble but impoverished family, he sought a career in the army. The experiment did not work out—the young officer thought more of musical composition than of military strategy. Obliged to earn a living, he became a government clerk, working at music during his spare time. In St. Petersburg he met other composers in a similar predicament: Borodin, a chemist; Rimsky-Korsakoff, a naval officer, and Cui, a critic. Mili Balakirev, their close friend, was the only professional musician of the group. These men, sharing a common viewpoint, were dubbed "The Five." They wanted Russian music to become a mirror of Russian existence, and not a slavish imitation of Western culture.

"The Five" regarded music mainly as a descriptive art. Moussorgsky used it as a means to portray the history and people of his native land in an idiom that was direct and national in feeling.

Unfortunately, Moussorgsky's technique was not always equal to his inspiration. For this reason, few of his larger works are performed today in their original form. The operas *Boris Godunoff* and *Khovantchina,* as well as the tone poem, "A Night on Bald Mountain," have been revised and re-orchestrated by Rimsky-Korsakoff.

Moussorgsky's life ended prematurely, on a note of bitterness and despair. Resigning his government clerkship, he almost starved in an attempt to support himself through musical activities. On March 16, 1881, the great composer died in the Nikolai Military

Hospital, St. Petersburg. His influence on the dramatic scope of modern music has been incalculable.

BORIS GODUNOFF

BORIS GODUNOFF, *a historical music drama now given in four acts, was first produced at St. Petersburg in 1874. Moussorgsky wrote his own text, basing the libretto upon Pushkin's historical drama of the same name, and upon Karamzin's* History of the Russian Empire. *The opera was twice revised by Rimsky-Korsakoff; in 1896 and 1908. It received its Metropolitan première on March 19, 1913, with Toscanini conducting and Adamo Didur as the Czar. Chaliapin's first assumption in New York of his most famous role was in December, 1921. After the season of 1928-29, the opera was dropped from the repertory and subsequently restored in March, 1939, with Ezio Pinza as Boris.*

Characters, in order of appearance:

Police official: *bass*
Tchelkaloff: *baritone*
Pimenn: *bass*
Grigori Otrepiev (the false Dmitri): *tenor*
Prince Schouïsky: *tenor*
Boris Godunoff: *bass-baritone*
The Innkeeper: *mezzo-soprano*
Varlaam ⎱ vagabond friars: ⎰ *bass*
Missaïl ⎰   ⎱ *tenor*
Xenia, daughter of Boris: *soprano*
Her nurse: *contralto*
Feodor, son of Boris: *mezzo-soprano*
A courtier: *tenor*
Marina Mnischek: *mezzo-soprano*
Rangoni, a Jesuit: *baritone*
Kroutschov, a noble: *tenor*
The simpleton: *tenor*
Lovitzki ⎱ Jesuits ⎰ *bass*
Tcherniakovski ⎰   ⎱ *bass*
Peasants, Pilgrims, Choir of Tchudov monastery,
Polish nobles and ladies, members of the Russian Duma

Time: Seventeenth Century   *Place:* Russia and Poland

The story takes place during the years 1598-1605. Boris Godunoff, brother-in-law of the weakling Czar Feodor, is Regent of Russia. He covets the crown. Only one person stands in his way:

the child Dmitri, rightful heir to the throne. Determined to rule, Boris orders the murder of Dmitri.

There is a short prelude to the opera, starting with a melody for English horn:

ACT I

SCENE 1: THE COURTYARD OF A MONASTERY (12 Minutes)

Peasants

THE courtyard of the monastery of Novodievich, near Moscow, is crowded with peasants. Czar Feodor has just died—his brother, Dmitri, has long since been murdered—and a successor must be chosen. As the people mill about in helpless indecision, groups of police enter the courtyard.

Enter police official

Lashing out with their knouts, they command the crowd to choose Boris by acclaim. The people protest, but their abject pleading drives the police to new fury. Godunoff is waiting in the cloister—he will make no move toward the throne without a sem-

Enter Tchelkaloff
Exit Tchelkaloff

blance of popular choice. In the midst of the tumult, Tchelkaloff, venerable clerk of the Duma, asks for silence. "Boris has declined the crown," he announces. "O people of Russia, pray for your misguided Regent!" As Tchelkaloff finishes, the landscape is lighted by rays of the setting sun. A chorus of pilgrims enters the mona-

Pilgrims

stery, and the peasants disperse.

SCENE 2: A CELL IN THE MONASTERY OF TCHUDOV (15 Minutes)

Pimenn

In a dimly lighted cell, the old monk Pimenn is recording the chronicles of Holy Russia:

Grigori

In the shadows of the cell, a young novice, Grigori Otrepiev, rises from troubled sleep. "Always the same dream!" he cries. "Always the same monastic walls in waking!"

"Softly!" answers Pimenn. "Great rulers have ended their days within these walls. Only now, with the usurper Godunoff on the throne, has the monarchy lost its ideals. I shall not live to record the misdeeds of Boris. That task is for you, Grigori."

The young monk looks intently at Pimenn. "How old," he asks, "would Czarevich Dmitri have been, if he were alive today?"

"Exactly your age," Pimenn replies.

Grigori is silent. A daring plan takes form in his mind. What if *he* were to impersonate the slain Czarevich:

Dawn penetrates the barred windows of the monastery. Pimenn slowly rises and Grigori accompanies him to the door. When the old monk has gone, the youth resolves to escape. "Boris!" he cries. "Here in this lonely cell is the avenger of a murdered child!"

Choir (invisible) Exit Pimenn

SCENE 3: A SQUARE BETWEEN THE CATHEDRALS OF THE ASSUMPTION AND THE ARCHANGEL (8 Minutes)

Boris' stratagem has worked. Urged by the people of Russia to ascend the throne, he appears before the Kremlin at Moscow, ready to be crowned. All the bells of the city peal their greetings; the deep-toned gongs

Peasants at Coronation

and the chimes:

"Make way for the Regent!" cries Prince Schouïsky, political ally of Godunoff. As Boris advances, the spectators in the huge square sing his praises:

Enter Schouïsky Enter Boris

Allegro moderato

Shine in glor-y, oh might-y mon-arch of Russ-ia, all hail!

Boris is filled with foreboding, even at this hour of triumph. Memories of the murdered Dmitri oppress his spirit. But he faces the jubilant crowd. "I invite you all," he proclaims, "noble and serf, to share in my coronation banquet." Then he enters the Cathedral of the Archangel, to pray. When Boris emerges, wearing the crown of Muscovy, the people joyously hail him as Czar.

ACT II

Grigori has cast his lot as pretender to the throne. Escaped from Tchudov, he is heading for Lithuania. En route, he joins company with two vagabond friars. The prelude to the second act is based in part upon the wild drinking song of one of these friars: The Town of Kazan,

Allegro con brio

and upon a whining tune with which the vagabonds proclaim their churchly mission:

Moderato

SCENE 1: AN INN NEAR THE LITHUANIAN BORDER (20 Minutes)

Innkeeper   THE tavern is deserted, save for the innkeeper who sits at her table singing:

Andantino

Once I caught a drake, oh a pret-ty drake.

Enter
Grigori,
Varlaam
and
Missäil

Grigori enters. With him are the friars, clamoring for drink. Varlaam, the noisier of the two, raises his glass and recounts the glorious siege of Kazan, where a Russian powder barrel blew twenty thousand Tartars to bits. At the end of his song, he notices that Grigori has not joined in the drinking. Somewhat slighted at this lack of attention, Varlaam lapses into a silly lullaby and sprawls across the table.

As both friars babble drunkenly, Grigori asks the innkeeper the shortest road to the frontier. He is about to slip away when, suddenly, a loud knock is heard at the door of the inn. The police enter, seeking the renegade monk. Since they cannot read the bill of arrest, they fail to recognize their quarry. "Perhaps I can help you," suggests Grigori. Pretending to scan the warrant, he describes minutely the face and dress of Varlaam.

Enter
police

The police pounce upon the old vagabond, who roughly throws them off. "I read badly," he exclaims, "but if it's a case of the gallows, I'll do my very best!" Seizing the warrant, Varlaam reads —at first with effort and then with increasing assurance—the description of Grigori Otrepiev, fugitive from Tchudov. Trembling with excitement, he turns to identify his young traveling companion, but Grigori has smashed the window pane, jumped to the ground below, and fled.

Varlaam
reading

Exit
Grigori
through
window

SCENE 2: THE CZAR'S APARTMENTS IN THE KREMLIN (32 Minutes)

Boris has reigned for six years. He has tried to be a worthy Czar, but famine grips the land, and unhappiness stalks his household. At the rise of the curtain Boris' daughter, Xenia, sings of her betrothed, buried in a foreign country:

Xenia

The girl is disconsolate. Not even the droll songs of her nurse or the lively games of her young brother, Czarevich Feodor, can cheer her. Boris enters the room. "Still grieving for your fiancé?" he asks tenderly of his beloved Xenia.

Nurse
Feodor

Enter
Boris

The girl has no answer for her father. As she withdraws with her nurse, the Czar turns indulgently to his heir, Feodor:

Exeunt
Xenia and
nurse

Ambition and its consequences pass through the mind of Boris. "I have attained the supreme power," he reflects. "Yet, I shall never be happy. My nobles plot against me, my country is laid waste by drought, my daughter is incurably melancholy."

Worst of all, the Czar is haunted by dreadful visions. Every night, the child Dmitri appears in his dreams. An unendurable sense of guilt is destroying his reason. Even in the sunlit chamber, with his son Feodor beside him, Boris sees the specter of the murdered Dmitri:

Boris' thoughts are broken off by a commotion in the corridor. "Go, Feodor," he orders, "and find out the cause of this disturbance." As the boy runs off, a courtier announces Prince Schouïsky. "Admit him," replies the Czar.

Exit
Feodor
Enter
Courtier
Exit Courtier
Re-enter
Feodor
Enter
Schouïsky

In less than a moment, Feodor has returned with an account of the noise in the corridor: "It was a quarrel between Xenia's nurse and a spoiled old parrot." At the end of the boy's story, Prince Schouïsky appears on the threshold. He is a stooped, cringing figure, distrusted by Boris, but indispensable to the regime:

"Your Majesty," Schouïsky begins haltingly, "there is a serious revolt in the provinces. The people have been roused by an impostor who calls himself Dmitri."

"Wait!" Boris exclaims. "Feodor, go to your room!" Exit
Feodor

When the two men are alone, the Czar cries out, "Can Dmitri have been raised from the dead?"

"No, Sire," Schouïsky answers. "I swear that his throat was cut before the Cathedral of Uglitch. For many days I stood guard and saw the festering wound."

"Enough!" shouts Boris. "Leave me!"

Schouïsky humbly withdraws. A clock begins to chime, persistently, ominously. Whirring fancies pulse through the brain of the Czar. Wherever he looks, he sees the specter of Dmitri—the childish body, the bloody shroud. Raving with fear, he sinks to the ground and prays for mercy.

Exit
Schouïsky

Boris

ACT III

The St. Petersburg opera management demanded a modicum of romantic interest for Boris Godunoff: *at least a heroine, and certainly a ballet. By way of acquiescence, Moussorgsky added the third act to his completed libretto.*

SCENE 1: MARINA'S BOUDOIR IN THE CASTLE OF SANDOMIR
(13 Minutes)

GRIGORI OTREPIEV'S adventures have led him to Lithuania and Poland, where the enemies of Boris have acclaimed him. Even to himself he is no longer Otrepiev—he is the Czarevich Dmitri, legitimate heir to the throne of Russia.

Marina Mnischek, a haughty Polish noblewoman, who has attracted the false Dmitri, sits idly at a dressing table in her boudoir. Dismissing her servile attendants, she dreams of wearing the crown of Russia. At her side hovers the Jesuit Rangoni, archintriguer. "You have a sacred duty to perform," he warns Marina. "Through your influence over Dmitri, the Russian Church must yield to Rome." Marina rebels at this counsel but finally submits to the dictates of the Jesuit.

Marina
and
attendants

Exeunt
attendants
Enter
Rangoni

SCENE 2: NIGHT IN THE GARDENS OF THE CASTLE (16 Minutes)

Enter the False Dmitri

Revelry fills the halls of Sandomir. The false Dmitri, in royal attire, enters the garden; he is to meet Marina at the fountain. As he waits, the guests emerge from the castle to the spirited strains of a polonaise:

Ballet of Polish nobles and ladies

Enter Marina

Hiding in the shrubbery, Dmitri sees Marina dancing with the Polish magnates. The pretender is baffled and hurt. But when the guests have gone, Marina comes to the fountain. She accepts Dmitri's love, on the condition that he share his throne with her. Dazzled by Marina's beauty and by her noble station, Dmitri embraces her:

Rangoni

Far off in the garden, Rangoni keeps watch, satisfied that his plans are succeeding.

ACT IV

SCENE 1: A CLEARING IN THE FOREST NEAR KROMY (16 Minutes)

Enter peasants and Kroutschov

RUSSIA is at revolution. The legend of the false Dmitri has inflamed the popular mind, and the people have renounced their Czar. A fierce, uncontrollable crowd surrounds a noble named Kroutschov who has been loyal to Boris, and drags him through the forest. Binding the boyar to a log, the serfs dance around him and mock at the change in his fortunes.

Enter simpleton

A simpleton crosses the scene, followed by the children of Kromy. He sits upon a stone and sings a doleful refrain. In the midst of the confusion, two familiar voices are heard in the forest, singing a prophecy of gloom and destruction:

Dark is the sun and dark the moon. All of the stars in the sky have set.

The vagabond friars, Varlaam and Missaïl, enter. Such is the force of circumstances that their prating is taken by the mob as inspired truth. Growing more and more unruly, the people shout a chorus of defiance to Boris and his ministers.

Still another incident excites the swirling crowd. Two itinerant Jesuits enter, singing the praises of the false Dmitri. Varlaam and Missaïl, sons of the Russian Church, propose that these adherents of Rome be strung to the highest tree. The mob, in an ugly mood, prepares to carry out their proposal. Only the arrival of the false Dmitri, riding in a procession through the forest, saves the unfortunate Jesuits:

Enter Varlaam and Missäil

Enter Lovitzki and Tcherniakovski

Enter Dmitri

. Arrogantly poised on horseback, Dmitri greets the crowd and pardons the kneeling Kroutschov. "I am Russia's ruler!" he proclaims. "Follow me to Moscow!"

The mob trails after him. Forsaken, the poor idiot remains behind, uttering the words, "Lament, you true believers, for darkness comes upon Russia."

Exeunt all except simpleton

SCENE 2: THE HALL OF THE DUMA (27 Minutes)

The Russian Duma has been called in extraordinary session, to combat the rebellion that rages through the land. The members are in their seats, awaiting the arrival of Boris, when Prince Schouïsky enters in great agitation. "Boris has gone mad!" he tells the Duma. Even as Schouïsky speaks, Boris appears at the door of the council chamber. "Back!" he cries. "Away! Child, you cannot haunt me!"

With effort, the Czar controls himself and mounts the throne. The holy monk Pimenn is awaiting an audience, and Boris consents to receive him. Slowly, Pimenn approaches the monarch and relates how one who was blind visited the Cathedral of Uglitch and there, at the grave of Dmitri, miraculously regained his sight.

"Stop!" shouts Boris. "I can bear it no longer." Clutching his heart, the Czar lurches from the throne and calls for his son.

Russian nobles Enter Schouïsky Enter Boris

Enter Pimenn

Enter
Feodor

"The end has come," he murmurs. "Oh, Feodor, rule wisely and well. Protect your sister Xenia. Obey the Church. Never inquire how your father came to power."

Choir

Outside in the square, the tolling of the funeral bell can be heard. In an adjoining chapel, a choir is celebrating the monarch's last rites:

Andante

Weep, oh all ye peo-ple weep!

Even in death, Boris will not acknowledge defeat. With his remaining strength, he ascends the throne and cries, "I still am Czar!" Then, pointing to his son, he whispers to the nobles, "Here is your ruler." The boy Feodor, scarcely conscious of his new rank, kneels despairingly beside the body of Boris Godunoff.

NOTE: *In the year 1605, Grigori Otrepiev invaded Moscow and seized the throne. Among other base deeds, he dishonored Princess Xenia and slew the Czarevich Feodor.*

RIMSKY-KORSAKOFF

Nikolai Rimsky-Korsakoff was born in the village of Tichvin in the Russian province of Novgorod, on March 18, 1844. Although he showed musical talent in early childhood, his parents decided on a naval career and sent him as a boy of twelve to the Naval Academy in St. Petersburg, as befitted their aristocratic station.

A few years later he met Balakirev, the leader of the Neo-Russian group of composers, who introduced him to the other members of the circle and supervised his musical education. In 1873 he resigned from the Navy, to give himself entirely to musical composition, but accepted the post of inspector of the marine bands, which he held for eleven years.

He followed Balakirev as conductor of the concerts of the Free Music School and also acted as his assistant in the Court Chapel. An expert in musical technique, Rimsky-Korsakoff dispensed his learning as a professor in the St. Petersburg Conservatory, and edited many works of his associates in the circle of "The Five," none of whom equaled him in instrumental mastery.

Like his colleagues in this group, he made use of Russian legend and history in most of his compositions, and all but two of his twelve operas. His glamorous tone color reflects the Oriental influences of the eastern part of Russia from which he came, and is well adapted to such fanciful texts as that of *Le Coq D'Or*.

By the time of his death, which took place on June 21, 1908, in Petrograd, his fame had extended throughout Europe and the United States.

LE COQ D'OR

LE COQ D'OR *was not performed in Russia during Rimsky-Korsakoff's lifetime because of the censorious attitude of the government toward any satire that might be thought aimed at the monarchy. Its première took place in a private theatre in Moscow in May, 1910, two years after his death.*

On March 6, 1918, it was first produced at the Metropolitan, in a pantomime arrangement devised in 1912 by Michael Fokine for the Russian Ballet. The singers were dressed in the uniform of choristers, and sat on each side of the stage, their voices being synchronized with the gestures of the dancers in costume on the stage.

This method of performance was used during four consecutive seasons, and the subsequent revivals of 1924 and 1928. On February 11, 1937, the work was presented with only one cast, as was originally intended by the composer, Lily Pons both impersonating and singing the role of the Queen.

The libretto of Le Coq D'Or (The Golden Cockerel) *was arranged by Vladimir Bielsky from the ironic poem of Alexander Pushkin.*

Characters, in order of appearance:

The Astrologer: *tenor*
King Dodon: *bass*
Prince Guidon: *tenor*
Prince Afron: *baritone*
General Polkan: *bass*
Voice of the golden cockerel: *soprano*
Amelfa, the royal housekeeper: *contralto*
Queen of Chemakha: *soprano*
Boyars, soldiers, slaves, populace

Time and *Place:* Legendary

PROLOGUE

Muted trumpets blazon forth the alarum of the golden cockerel:

This is instantly followed by a chromatic theme associated with the magical Queen of Chemakha, which is developed at some length by the strings:

Lento
pp

*Again the music changes. Bells tinkle the motive of the Astrol-
oger, who soon comes before the curtain in peaked cap and starry
mantle, stating that he is going to call to life the heroes of a fable
of long ago, which, though it may not be history, is at least highly
moral.*

Astrologer

Moderato assai
p

Par mon art   ca - ba - li - sti - que!
By   my   ca - ba - lis - tic sci - ence!

Act I

SCENE: A HALL IN THE PALACE (28 Minutes)

KING DODON has summoned his boyars to a royal Council. They
sit, grave bearded men, on benches surrounding their monarch, who
lolls in a gorgeous throne, decorated with peacock feathers. The
hall of state is large, and bright with green, blue, and yellow, which,
as can be guessed from his robes, is the King's favorite color. The
spring sunlight shines through the windows which look out on the
gay streets of a city in Southern Russia. On either side of the
throne sprawl the King's two sons, Afron and Guidon, while among
the Boyars the rough old commander-in-chief of the King's army,
General Polkan, sits in doddering dignity.

King,
General,
Princes
and
Boyars

"I have summoned you to ask for help," announces the King.
"All my life I have fought without a single hesitation. Now I am
old and tired and my foes are attacking me. Our armies have conquered in the North and South, but new enemies approach from
the sea. What shall I do about it?"

"Too bad the old fortune-teller is dead!" grumble the Boyars.
In the midst of the discussion the Astrologer steps down the
stairs to his own precise theme, and kneels before the monarch.

Enter
Astrologer

"Hail, proud King!" cries the old man. "I was advisor to your
father in my day, and I have brought you a gift to help you in your
trouble." He takes out of a bag a golden rooster. "This bird," he
continues, "should be placed on a spire. It will warn you of danger."

Golden
cockerel

The bird flaps its wings and sings

*"Cock-a-doodle-doodle-doo,
Sleep and I will watch for you."*

Exeunt
Astrologer,
Boyars,
Princes
and
General

Enter
Amelfa

The courtiers are thrilled by this miraculous assistance no less than the King, who orders the bird to be placed on a steeple, and promises the Astrologer that his slightest wish will be granted as a reward. The old man retires, followed by the courtiers.

Since relaxation is to be the rule of the day, the King's fat housekeeper Amelfa offers a toothsome repast of candy and fruit to her master. An ivory bed is carried in and the King falls into a carefree slumber. The guards sleepily repeat the song of the bird and then fall asleep at their posts.

Suddenly the bird sounds the alarm:

> *"Cock-a-doodle-doodle-doo*
> *Now beware of something new!"*

Enter
General,
Boyars
and
Princes
Exit
Amelfa

Trumpets echo from all sides, the crowd rushes to the palace in terror. Amelfa runs to hide. The general vows his allegiance. The young princes buckle on their armor; their father kisses them effusively. The sound of distant battle is heard.

The golden cockerel again insists that all is well, and the King returns to sleep, but no sooner has he dreamed a pleasant fantasy than the bird resumes his warning. Again the affrighted subjects rush in and eventually waken the yawning Dodon.

The grumbling monarch calls for his armor, and is lifted on his toy horse. After assuring himself that there is enough food to last the army for three years, he leads his people off to battle while they sing his praises with lusty shouts:

ACT II

SCENE: A MOUNTAIN GORGE (38 Minutes)

Dead
soldiers
Enter
troops

THE moon casts a dim light on a rocky gorge where Dodon's army has met with disaster. Barely visible in the dense mist, the bodies of stricken warriors lie among the bushes. The music of the march sounds in a minor key as some soldiers advance furtively two by two.

"What a terrible sight!" exclaims King Dodon, following them with General Polkan. "And here are my two sons, each killed by the other. There is nothing left for me but death!" and he bursts into tears.

Enter Dodon and General

His general rallies the troops. "We'll be glad to fight," they answer, "if we can find the enemy."

As the sun rises, the mists dissolve from the gorge. In their place stands a tent of brilliant brocade.

"The leader of the enemy must be there in hiding," cries Polkan. His terrified troops hurry off to safety.

From the tent emerges a beautiful young woman, accompanied by four slaves bearing musical instruments, and dressed in robes of scarlet and gold.

Enter Queen

Without a glance at the spellbound general and his monarch, she sings a hymn to the rising sun:

At its close she tells them that she is the Queen of Chemakha, and that she is about to conquer their city. Nevertheless she offers them wine which they drink with pleasure, while the remaining soldiers bear off their dead companions.

Exeunt soldiers with dead

To the chromatic theme of the prelude, she describes her crystal palace and snowy swans, and the blind obedience of her subjects. Yet she is sad, for she knows no master.

When the infatuated Dodon promises to thwart her to her heart's content, she is delighted, and suggests that they celebrate their new-found happiness in a gay dance. Protesting that he has forgotten his steps, Dodon acquiesces only when she threatens to take Polkan for partner instead. Tambourine in hand the Queen leads the way, "like a goldfish followed by a crab."

Faster and faster the King twirls about, while the Queen laughs at his clumsy steps.

Eventually he sinks exhausted on the ground. "If you like me," he says, panting and puffing with fatigue, "come and rule over my kingdom. You can eat and drink all day long and if you don't like Polkan, I'll cut off his head."

"Very well!" answers the Queen cheerfully. "How you do spoil me!"

Enter slaves

A procession of slaves file out from the tent, bearing mirrors and fans, rugs and jewels. The King's soldiers shout with joy at the prospect of the royal nuptials, and the cortege moves away.

ACT III

SCENE: OUTSIDE THE PALACE (18 Minutes)

RISING chords in the orchestra, followed by the cry of the golden cockerel, suggest the unrest that pervades the kingdom of Dodon.

Populace

The street in front of the palace is crowded with anxious people. Although the sun is shining brightly, a thunderstorm hangs heavy in the air.

Enter Amelfa Wedding procession

There is general relief when Amelfa comes out on the palace steps. "The King is bringing home a bride," she announces curtly. "Greet them as gaily as you can."

The wedding procession begins. Giants and dwarfs march in brilliant raiment. Men are disguised in the masks of animals. Slaves bear coffers of jewels. The people are delighted by the gay spectacle.

Enter King and Queen Enter Astrologer

At length the King and Queen drive up in their golden chariot. There is a moment of brief cheering. Suddenly the Astrologer appears on the portico of one of the houses.

"Who is that old man?" asks the Queen, uneasily.

A clap of thunder sounds from the distance.

"What favor can I do for you on this happy day?" asks the King cordially.

The Astrologer walks down through the crowd and approaches the royal chariot, never taking his eyes from the Queen.

"Mighty King," answers the old man, in the melody of the Prologue, "yesterday, you promised to fulfill my slightest wish. What I ask is the Queen of Chemakha."

"You are mad," answers the King. "Ask for anything else and you shall have it."

The Astrologer repeats his demand.

"I will not have any arguments," exclaims the King in a fury, and he taps the old man with his scepter. The Astrologer falls lifeless.

Astrologer dies

Shuddering chords again rise in the orchestra as clouds veil the sun, and thunder re-echoes in the sky.

The Queen bursts into laughter, but when the King tries to embrace her, she pushes him away with disdain. "You may well smile, you old rascal," she says, "but your own punishment is not far off." They ascend the steps of the palace.

The cry of the cockerel is heard from his perch:

Golden cockerel

> *"Cock-a-doodle-doo*
> *This will be the end of you!"*

Darting down above the heads of the terrified people, the bird swoops on the King with a mighty blow of his beak. Dodon drops dead.

Dodon dies

Another clap of thunder is followed by utter darkness, through which can be heard the tinkling laughter of the Queen. When light returns, both she and the bird have disappeared.

Exeunt Queen and cockerel

"The storm is past," shout the people, "but who will be our King?" They fall on their faces, weeping.

Epilogue

Again the Astrologer sings his fanciful tune in front of the curtain. "Noble spectators!" he cries, reassuringly. "Do not be too troubled by this tragic fairy story. The only people in it who were real were the Queen and myself!"

Astrologer

X

Opera Turns to Crime

THREE powerful influences: Bizet, Wagner and Verdi—hovered over Italy toward the close of the century.

The realistic features of French lyric opera reappeared with a new perspective in the equivalent Italian school, which reached fulfillment a few years later in the works of Giacomo Puccini (1858-1924). The French concentration on three voices was retained.

As far back as 1876 Ponchielli had shown in *La Gioconda* a touch of Wagnerian concern with the interdependence of music and drama.

It remained for his pupil, Mascagni, and Leoncavallo to compress the spacious vistas of Verdi into the span of a single hour. The courts of Aragon and Memphis were exchanged for a country village. Murders were committed afresh on the operatic stage, but with a new brutality. Opera turned to crime not as a solution of the melodrama, but as a means of proving that blood ran hot and red.

The success of Italian realism, or *verismo*, in opera was not entirely dependent on the melodramatic values of its subjects. It was refreshing to find on the stage everyday people whose actions were guaranteed to be true; yet the journalistic appeal was not the only clue to success. Nor were the simplified orchestration, the omission of subsidiary material, and the frequent use of unison singing in themselves accountable for its popularity. The typical Italian wealth of melody was the outstanding factor of the school, and since beautiful voices were always available, the broad cantabile arias that were allotted them drew instant approval from the audience.

The realism of Puccini horrified the critics of his time. Today it is not the tuberculosis of Mimi, the torture of Cavaradossi or the suicide of Butterfly that we remember, but the luscious melodies of the score, the passionate climaxes, and the ever spontaneous reflection of drama in music.

Puccini's technical skill did not fail him when he turned in middle life to *opera buffa*, and created the one-act realistic farce, *Gianni Schicchi*.

Another variation from the prevailing style of the time had been demonstrated by Umberto Giordano (1867-) in *Andrea Chenier*. Like Puccini's *La Bohème*, which was written in the same year (1896), it went to the streets of Paris for its setting, but returned to the grand opera dimensions of Ponchielli and Boito for its stature.

A mixture of German and Italian parentage endowed Ermanno Wolf-Ferrari (1876-) with an economy of means which he borrowed from the chamber music of Germany, and a concern for the commonplaces of the day which he caught from his Italian contemporaries and touched with a new delicacy.

Riccardo Zandonai (1883-) drew in similar manner from the musical sources of the modern French school.

Although blood and thunder were to haunt Italian opera for some time to come, a sharp reaction grew out of the horrors of the veristic composers. Italo Montemezzi preserved the realistic subtleties of modern psychology in his *L'Amore dei Tre Re* but his drama is tinted with romanticism, and its musical texture partakes of the alien impressionism of Debussy.

PONCHIELLI

Amilcare Ponchielli was born at Cremona on September 1,
1834. After studying at the Conservatory of Milan, he succeeded
in having his first opera, *I Promessi Sposi,* presented in his native
city (1856). Sixteen years later, this opera, in a revised version,
was performed at the *Teatro dal Verme,* Milan, with such marked
success that Ponchielli won a commission for a seven act ballet,
Le Due Gemelle, produced at *La Scala,* Milan, in 1873. His
masterpiece, *La Gioconda,* was given shortly afterward in the
same theatre.

Ponchielli represented a definite trend toward Wagnerism, with
his use of leading motives; at the same time, he relied extensively
on the elements of spectacle and color, as found in the *Mefistofele*
of his contemporary, Boito, and in the later works of Verdi. His
demands upon the resources of the lyric theatre were extensive.

Toward the end of his career Ponchielli became professor of
composition at the Milan Conservatory, a post which he filled with
great distinction until his death on January 16, 1886.

LA GIOCONDA

La Gioconda, *Ponchielli's opera in four acts with libretto by Tobio
Garrio (an acrostic for Arrigo Boito) was first produced at* La
Scala, *Milan, in 1876. Its Metropolitan première took place in
1883, with Christine Nilsson in the title role.*

Characters, in order of appearance:
Barnaba, a spy of the Inquisition: *baritone*
Gioconda, a ballad singer: *soprano*
La Cieca, Gioconda's blind mother: *contralto*
Zuane, a boatman: *bass*
Isepo, a public scribe: *tenor*
Enzo Grimaldo, a Genoese nobleman: *tenor*
Laura, wife of Alvise: *mezzo-soprano*
Alvise Badoero, a leader of the Inquisition: *bass*
A monk: *baritone*
A pilot: *baritone*
Two street singers; the voices of two gondoliers
Populace, sailors, ballet, chorus of boys, maskers

Time: Seventeenth Century   *Place:* Venice

ACT I: THE LION'S MOUTH
SCENE: COURTYARD OF THE DOGE'S PALACE (46 Minutes)

Populace, sailors, Barnaba

ON a brilliant afternoon in spring, a throng of sailors, shipwrights and working people of Venice has gathered in the courtyard of the ducal palace. In solitary contrast to the joyous crowd lurks a man of evil appearance. His hair is dark, his face a deathly white; and across his shoulder, as though in deference to the gaiety of the crowd, is slung a mandolin.

As the merriment in the courtyard reaches its height, the man steps forward and addresses the people. "The regatta is about to begin!" he proclaims. "Hark to the sound of the trumpets!"

Exeunt all but Barnaba

At once, the crowd rushes off to witness the races; their mentor gazes mockingly after them. He is Barnaba, spy of the Inquisition. Posing as an affable citizen of Venice, he mingles habitually with people along the canals, listening to their conversation and detecting enemies of the regime. Once he finds them out, he composes an accusation and drops it in the secret letter box of the Inquisition: the Lion's Mouth.

Enter Gioconda and Cieca

Now, as he lingers in the deserted gateway, he sees a victim approaching. It is Gioconda, the beautiful ballad singer who roams the streets of Venice in company with her blind mother, La Cieca. Barnaba has sworn to possess her; he will bring the same ruthlessness to bear in his conquest of the girl that he uses in affairs of state.

Hiding near the mighty staircase of the palace, he sees Gioconda help La Cieca to the steps of the neighboring cathedral. "Wait here near the shrine," the girl is saying. "O mother, I must go and seek my lover Enzo. When I find him, we shall return together."

"Farewell, daughter," the blind woman answers fondly.

Gioconda glances once more at La Cieca; then she crosses the courtyard to the main gate. Suddenly, she is stopped by Barnaba, who has come from his hiding place. "Stay here!" he exclaims. "You shall not escape me!"

With a cry of fright, Gioconda eludes him and rushes away. Her mother has heard the cry and rises from her place in alarm. "My daughter!" she calls. "Where are you? What has happened?" Groping pitifully, she tries to find Gioconda; her search in vain, she totters back to the steps of the church.

Exit Gioconda

Barnaba watches her intently—and conceives a villainous plan. Through the mother, he will win the daughter! Resolving to bring the old woman to her doom, he retreats behind the marble pillars as the populace returns to the courtyard. The regatta is over; the victor is borne triumphantly on the shoulders of the crowd. Everyone rejoices except the ill-natured loser of the race, Zuane. Standing apart from his companions, he sulks in silence.

Enter populace, sailors, Zuane and Isepo

The situation is ripe for Barnaba's cunning. "Zuane!" he calls, drawing near to the boatman. "I know why you lost the race!"

"My skiff was overweighted," Zuane angrily replies.

"Not at all! Your defeat was destined—it was the work of a sorceress!"

The superstitious boatman shudders. "What do you mean?"

"Behold!" whispers Barnaba. "Do you see the blind woman on the steps of the church? She is a witch! I heard her curse your rudder three times!"

As the spy continues to terrify the boatman, one of his satellites, Isepo, the public letter writer, approaches. He, too, falls under the spell of Barnaba's story. "La Cieca is a demon!" the spy declares. "She has no eyes—but she can see!"

Other members of the crowd have gathered around Zuane. When Barnaba's terrifying words are carried from mouth to mouth, a tremor runs through the crowd. "Away with the witch!" they shout. "Burn her! Destroy her!" Rushing upon the poor woman, who is telling the beads of her rosary, they drag her from the steps of the church.

The tumult can be heard in all the streets surrounding the palace. Drawn by the commotion, Gioconda returns. Encouraged by the presence of her lover Enzo, a sea captain, the girl runs to La Cieca's aid—and when the crowd becomes more threatening, Enzo shouts desperately for his crew of Dalmatian sailors to come and help him.

Enter Gioconda and Enzo

Exit
Enzo
Enter
Alvise
and
Laura

Enzo's call goes unheeded; no sailors appear, and the mob has started closing in on La Cieca. Suddenly a commanding voice issues from the vaulted balcony above the courtyard. It is Alvise Badoero, leader of the Inquisition. "This is rebellion!" he declares. "How dare the populace act as judges and executioners?"

Descending the great staircase of the Giants, he strides among the crowd until he reaches La Cieca. With Badoero is his wife—a masked woman, richly dressed. "O spare this blind creature!" she begs Alvise.

Enter
Enzo

Alvise hesitates as Barnaba whispers to him that La Cieca is a sorceress. In the midst of their parley, Enzo returns with his band of sailors, prepared to defend La Cieca against the hostile crowd. "Save her!" cries Alvise's wife, more insistently than before.

As the woman speaks, Enzo glances at her in wonder. What lies behind that velvet mask? The voice—the gestures—are familiar. They remind him of someone he loved in his native Genoa—Laura Adorno, who was taken from him and given in marriage to a Venetian noble.

The wife of Alvise glances swiftly at the stranger. Can this man in the garb of a Dalmatian be Enzo Grimaldo, to whom she once pledged her faith? Dismissing these memories, she turns to her husband and again intercedes for La Cieca. Much to Barnaba's anger, the blind beggar is released.

La Cieca has overheard the noble lady's plea for her freedom. "Angel of mercy!" she exclaims. "I cannot see you, but I give you my eternal gratitude. Accept my most precious gift—this rosary!"

Humbly, the wife of Alvise takes the rosary from the hand of La Cieca. And now Gioconda approaches her. "My lady," she asks, "will you tell me your name, that I may never forget you in my prayers?"

"Laura."

Enzo cannot repress his astonishment. As he gazes ardently at the noble Genoese, she returns his look; and the wily Barnaba, whose business it is to probe the hearts of human beings, notices the interchange of glances.

Alvise has been standing by impatiently. "Come, let us go into the cathedral!" he commands. Escorted by her husband, Laura enters the portico of St. Mark's.

Gioconda joyfully embraces Enzo and her mother; then she, too, crosses the sacred threshold with La Cieca. Only Enzo hesitates at the door—he is thinking of Laura.

Exeunt all except Enzo and Barnaba

"Enzo Grimaldo, Prince of Santafior!" calls a voice from across the courtyard. Enzo looks about in alarm—his disguise has been uncovered—and there, facing him, he sees the spy Barnaba.

"You are brave to walk abroad in Venice," the spy continues, "when you have been proscribed by our Doge! Is it for love of Laura?"

"I have pledged my faith to Gioconda!" Enzo declares.

"You think of her as a sister," laughs Barnaba. "It is Laura whom you love. Tonight, her husband attends the great council meeting at the palace—and Laura can flee with you on your ship!"

"Who are you?" Enzo asks suspiciously. "Why do you offer me your help?"

"I could destroy you at once," Barnaba answers, "but your death would not serve me. Gioconda loves you—she hates me. If she learns how false you are, I shall be able to make her mine!"

Enzo hesitates when he learns Barnaba's motives; but love overcomes him. "Very well!" he cries. "I shall await Laura on board my vessel tonight. And as for you, treacherous knave—a curse upon you!"

The Genoese prince rushes off. "A curse?" repeats Barnaba, looking after him. 'It may strike me—but Gioconda's idol shall be dashed to pieces!" Opening a door near the prisons of the palace, the spy calls to his accomplice Isepo, the public scribe. "Come here," he commands, "and write this letter for me to the secret chief of the Inquisition!"

Exit Enzo

Enter Isepo

As Barnaba starts dictating, Gioconda suddenly appears in the doorway of the church. At the sound of the villain's voice she crouches back in fear and listens to his words. "Your wife will elope with the sailor Enzo tonight," he bids Isepo write. "She will be on board his vessel." Stifling a sob, Gioconda returns to the church. She has not heard the name of Enzo's loved one; she does not know to whom Barnaba is sending the accusation; but her heart is crushed by the knowledge that Enzo is false.

Enter Gioconda Exit Gioconda

"Now go!" Barnaba orders Isepo. When the letter writer disappears, the spy gazes cynically about him at the mighty courtyard of the palace. He looks upward at the marble and gold of the fabulous structure. "O splendid monument!" he exclaims. "O palace with dismal torture chamber below, and the glittering chambers of the Doge above. I am your ear—I hear all plots

Exit Isepo

Exit
Barnaba
Enter
populace
and
ballet
against you! And now, accept this mark of my vigilance!" He furtively stuffs his written accusation against Enzo into one of the bronze lions' mouths—and disappears.

At once, the courtyard is filled with a happy, dancing throng. "Carnival!" they cry. "Let us dance the *furlana!*" Their revelry comes to an end; the voices of the worshipers within the cathedral can be heard in the square. As the crowd kneels in piety, a monk appears on the balcony of the church and exhorts them to pray.

Enter
monk
Enter
Gioconda
and Cieca
Amid the kneeling throng walk Gioconda and La Cieca. The girl is utterly miserable at Enzo's betrayal and longs only for death:

"Come, my daughter," urges La Cieca. "We shall console each other's grief!"

Hand in hand, the two women cross the courtyard and disappear through the gate, leaving the majestic palace of the Doge behind them.

ACT II: THE ROSARY

SCENE: ENZO'S SHIP IN THE VENETIAN LAGOON (35 Minutes)

Sailors
and chorus
of boys
ALL preparations have been made for Enzo's flight with Laura. His vessel is moored beside a deserted island in the Fusina lagoon; the sails are hoisted. As soon as Laura arrives and the moon sinks behind the clouds, the ship will raise anchor for Genoa.

As the sailors, midshipmen and boys bustle about the deck, putting everything in readiness, they notice a strange craft in the water below. Two men are rowing toward the ship—Barnaba and his accomplice, Isepo. "Who are you?" calls the Dalmatian pilot. "What do you want here?"

Enter
Barnaba
and Isepo
"We are fishermen," Barnaba answers, quickly taking count of the number of oars, the size of the galley, the amount of men on Enzo's vessel. "Go at once," he whispers to Isepo, "and place our scouts on the island!"

Exit
Isepo
Barnaba rows to shore, helps Isepo debark, and passes Enzo's galley again in his skiff. Still posing as a seaman, he sings a hearty fisherman's chant and makes his way unchallenged through the waters of the lagoon:

Exit
Barnaba

Ah!   Pesca   tor,   af - fon   da   l'es - ca.
Ah!   Fisher   man,   thy   bait   now   lo - wer!

Barnaba's song dies away; and Enzo comes on deck. As his men go below, he leans pensively at the rail, gazing at sky and sea:

Cie - lo   e   mar! —   l'e - te - reo   ve - lo   splen-de come un santo al - tar.
Hea - ven!   and   o - cean!   yon   e - the - real   veil   is   ra-diant   as   a   ho - ly shrine.

Enter
Enzo
Exeunt
sailors

"Will Laura come to me?" he wonders. "I cannot wait—my heart is beating wildly!"

Suddenly, Enzo sees Barnaba's craft approaching the ship. Within is Laura. Casting a rope over the side of his vessel, the captain secures the skiff and helps Laura ascend to the deck. Then Barnaba's craft pulls out toward Venice. "Good luck attend you!" the spy calls sneeringly.

Enter
Barnaba
and Laura

Exit
Barnaba

"I suspect that man!" whispers Laura. "He means us harm!"

"No matter!" Enzo answers. "He has saved you—and soon we shall leave Venice forever!"

"There is no time to lose!" Laura declares anxiously. "Be watchful!"

"We have nothing to fear on this deserted island," Enzo assures her. "Once the moon is hidden, we shall depart."

The lovers embrace passionately; going below to complete the final details of the voyage, Enzo bids Laura wait on deck.

Exit Enzo

For a moment, Laura pauses in bewilderment; the vastness of sea, sky and night overwhelm her. Then, perceiving a crude altar on the shore, she descends to the island and kneels in prayer.

Imperceptibly, a dim figure emerges from beneath the prow of the ship and moves toward the praying woman with drawn dagger. It is Gioconda. She does not recognize Laura unmasked—all she knows is that her rival kneels before her.

Enter
Gioconda

"Go! Flee with Enzo!" she cries bitterly. "The sails are hoisted, the rudder is ready. Go!"

As Laura rises in anxiety and shrinks from Gioconda, the ballad singer pursues her. "You fear me! You are unworthy of my Enzo!"

"I love him!" Laura declares. "I love him as the light of creation, and I would defy even death to be with him!"

Andante poco mosso

L'a - mo   co - me_il ful-gor del cre - a - to! co - me l'au - ra che av-vi-va_il re - spi - ro!

Him I love___ as the light of cre - a - tion, as the air   that new life and strength brings me!

Grasping Laura by the throat, Gioconda is about to stab the woman when a more exquisite form of revenge occurs to her. "Look!" she exclaims. "Do you see that boat approaching? It bears your husband. There is no escape for you now!"

Beside herself with fright, Laura lifts up the rosary—La Cieca's gift—and prays to the Holy Virgin. No sooner has Gioconda seen the rosary than she recognizes the savior of her mother. Every trace of hatred vanishes; she resolves to help her rival. "I have a boat near by," she whispers. "Hurry! You will arrive safely in Venice!" Removing her mask and giving it to Laura, she summons her steersman. Quickly, Laura steps into the skiff and is borne away.

Exit Laura

Enter Barnaba

She has left in good time—for Barnaba appears, ready to spring the trap he has prepared. Far off on the lagoon is a boat bearing the haughty Alvise, who has learned from the spy of his wife's infidelity. Barnaba eagerly beckons to his chief—and then, to his dismay, he finds that his prey has fled. "There, by the canal!" he shouts to Alvise. "Urge on the rowers! Try to overtake her!"

Exit Barnaba Enter Enzo

Fuming with rage, he rows onward in his skiff; Gioconda is left alone on the island. Hiding in the shadows, she sees Enzo return to the deck. "Laura!" he calls. "Laura, where are you?"

To his astonishment, the sailor hears the reproachful voice of Gioconda: "Your Laura has fled. She has gone back to her Alvise!"

"Be silent!" shouts Enzo. "I will follow her!"

"You will be slain!" Gioconda warns him. "Look out to sea; behold the Venetian galleys approaching. You must escape!"

Only now does Enzo realize that he has been trapped by Barnaba's treachery. Still thinking of Laura, he decides not to flee—he will stay and protect her. But the galleys are drawing nearer; Enzo's sailors mount the deck, crying out, "We are surrounded! All is lost!"

Enter sailors

"We'll burn our ship rather than surrender it!" Enzo proclaims. Seizing a blazing torch, he sets fire to the vessel. As the ship is gutted by flames, the sailors plunge into the water, hopeful of swimming to shore. "Farewell, my Laura!" shouts Enzo, leaping from the highest deck.

Gioconda crouches on the deserted island. "That name of Laura is ever on his lips!" she sobs. "But at least I may die with him!" As she rushes toward the blazing vessel, the ship collapses and sinks beneath the waves. In vain has Gioconda sought to perish.

ACT III: THE HOUSE OF GOLD

SCENE 1: A CHAMBER IN THE HOUSE OF GOLD (15 Minutes)

ALVISE BADOERO has not overtaken his wife on the flight back to Venice, but he knows beyond a doubt that she is guilty. To expiate her crime against his honor and good name, he has determined that she must die.

Pacing his chamber in steely anger, he sends for Laura. With a gesture of supreme irony, he has invited the most distinguished guests in the city to attend a ball at the House of Gold. In the midst of the festivities, he intends to carry out his revenge. And now as his wife enters the room, clad in an elaborate gown for the ball, Alvise bows sardonically. *Alvise*

Enter Laura

"You sent for me?" asks Laura, knowing nothing of her husband's plan, but feeling a vague sense of terror.

"You are to die!" Alvise answers. As he speaks, a lively song rises from the canal outside the windows of the palace:

Allegretto moderato

La ga - ia can - zo - ne fa l'e - co lan - guir
Our gay songs are end - ing, the soft e - choes die

"Here is a flask of poison," Alvise continues. "Do you hear that music outside? Your life must end before the last note has sounded!"

Thrusting the poison at his wife, he stalks from the chamber. As Laura glances fearfully at the phial, she hears a footstep behind her. It is Gioconda, who has stolen into the palace. "Do as I tell you!" the singer whispers, handing Laura a potion which will induce a sleep similar to death. "Drink it!" *Exit Alvise Enter Gioconda*

"I mistrust you," declares Laura. "You are my rival."

"Believe in me!" Gioconda urges. "My mother is in the palace chapel, praying for your soul. The song you hear on the water is sung by our friends who have brought us here. We are all trying to help you!"

With new resolution, Laura drains Gioconda's potion. The effects of the drug already upon her, she rushes into the adjoining *Exit Laura*

Exit
Gioconda
chamber, which the gloomy Alvise has set up as a tomb. Left alone, Gioconda quickly pours Alvise's poison into a phial that she carries; then she hides within an alcove, leaving the empty flask on a table.

Enter
Alvise
The song from the canal has ended; Alvise returns and sees the flask. "All is over," he mutters. Opening the door of the funeral chamber, he beholds Laura lying cold and rigid on her bier. Without a glimmer of compassion, the proud man turns away and strides from the room.

Exit
Alvise

Enter
Gioconda
Gioconda emerges from the alcove. "O mother," she cries despairingly, "for your sake—for the sake of your rosary—I have spared this woman, though she robbed me of my love!" Wretched and weeping, the ballad singer makes her way from the chamber.

SCENE 2: THE GRAND HALL (23 Minutes)

Alvise
and
maskers
Alvise stands in the brilliantly lighted reception hall of the House of Gold, receiving his guests. Courteous and affable, he betrays no trace of the tragedy he has just witnessed—nor does he offer any explanation for Laura's absence.

"You are welcome, O maskers," he declares. "This evening I have arranged a spectacle to please all of you—the Dance of the Hours." As the guests take their places, the lights in the great hall are lowered and a ballet troupe appears:

Enter
ballet

First come the hours of daybreak, with gray, somber costumes; then, the brightly attired hours of noon. A crimson glow fills the hall while the hours of evening take their place among the dancers, and finally, the purple hours of night bring the spectacle to a close.

Exit
ballet
Enter
Enzo,
Cieca and
Barnaba
The hall is again flooded with gleaming candlelight; the guests surround Alvise, congratulating him on the ballet. Suddenly, a scream is heard—and La Cieca, struggling helplessly, is dragged into the room by Barnaba.

"I caught her in the forbidden chambers!" the spy tells Alvise. "She was plotting some malice against you!"

"No!" La Cieca interrupts. "I meant no harm. I was only praying for the soul of my benefactress—she is dead!"

The guests listen in amazement; and slowly, the ringing of the death knell sounds through the palace. "Is it for Laura?" one of the masked nobles asks Barnaba.

"Yes!" Barnaba answers.

Alvise takes note of the stranger speaking to Barnaba; he observes the man's extreme dejection. "Who dares be downcast tonight," he demands, "if Alvise Badoero is gay?"

"I!" cries the guest, throwing aside his mask. "I, Enzo Grimaldo!"

"Hold him fast, Barnaba!" roars Alvise. "If he escapes, you shall answer with your life!"

Stunned by the news of Laura's death, Enzo pays no attention to his captors. "O Laura," he sobs, "you lie cold and motionless! There is nothing left for me!"

Già ti veg-go im-mo-ta e smor-ta,
I be-hold thee mo-tion-less, pal-lid,

Unobserved, Gioconda has entered the hall; approaching Barnaba stealthily, she whispers, "Bring Enzo safely to me at the Orfano canal and I will yield myself to you!"

Enter Gioconda

The spy gives his promise—but as Gioconda turns away, he envelops La Cieca with his cloak. "You were able to escape me yesterday," he mutters, "but never again!"

La Cieca is unable to cry out, for the most appalling confusion reigns within the hall. "All of you, draw near!" Alvise has cried. "My wife brought dishonor upon my name. Now behold her!" Tearing aside the velvet curtains of the funeral chamber, he reveals Laura outstretched upon her bier. Brandishing a dagger, Enzo hurls himself at Alvise; he is captured and led away. As Gioconda and the noble maskers stare with horror at the exultant Alvise, Barnaba silently leads the groping La Cieca from the hall.

Act IV: The Orfano Canal

SCENE: A RUINED PALACE ON THE ISLAND OF THE GUIDECCA
(32 Minutes)

It is night; in a lonely shelter on the Orfano Canal sits Gioconda. Wrapped in thoughts of death, she stares at a dagger before her and at the flask of poison that she has taken from Laura's chamber.

Gioconda

Soon, there is a knock at the creaking door of the ruined palace that serves Gioconda as a refuge. Two street singers have brought

Enter two
street
singers
Enter
Laura
Exit
Laura

their boat to the entrance gate on the canal; they bear the sleeping Laura, who is covered with a shroud.

"Put her on the bed behind the screen," Gioconda orders the men. "Hold everything in readiness tonight; we must help her to escape." And now Gioconda's commanding tone begins to waver. "O tell me," she pleads with the street singers, "did you not see my mother anywhere? I have searched every street in the city!"

Exeunt
two street
singers

The two men cannot help her; sadly, they depart. In despair, Gioconda gazes at the implements of death: the poison and the dagger. "Suicide!" she cries. "That is the only road left to me. My mother is lost; Enzo has forsaken me. What have I to live for?"

Enter
Enzo

Suddenly, she hears an approaching gondola—she looks up and sees Enzo in the doorway of the palace. Barnaba, true to his compact, has released him.

"Enzo!" she exclaims. "At last you are free!"

The sailor mournfully rebuffs her. "You will see me no more," he declares. "I am on my way to Laura's tomb."

"It is empty!" Gioconda shouts, hoping for death at the hands of Enzo. "I have removed the body!"

"You despoiler!" cries Enzo. "Where have you hidden her? Answer—or I'll kill you!"

Enter
Laura

He raises his dagger—and never lets it fall, for he hears Laura's voice from behind the screen. "Enzo!" she calls. Fully awakened, the woman rises to greet her lover. Instinctively, Gioconda buries her face in her cloak. "Let darkness hide their embrace from me!" she mutters.

In the distance is heard the song of the boatmen—the very melody that was sung outside Laura's window when Alvise handed her the poison. "It is the signal!" Gioconda exclaims. "Everything is ready. Now fly for your lives. Farewell forever!"

Exeunt
Enzo and
Laura

A gondola has drawn up before the ruined palace. Bestowing their heartfelt thanks upon Gioconda, Enzo and Laura take their places in the boat and depart. Gioconda, left behind, sobs with grief. Disordered thoughts crowd through her mind: suicide, her lost mother, the compact with Barnaba. Feeling that her last moments are upon her, she kneels before a crucifix and prays. The moon has disappeared in the clouds; the canal is plunged in

blackness—and Barnaba appears at the door. Unaware of his Enter
Barnaba
presence, Gioconda rises and makes ready to flee.

"What of our contract?" Barnaba shouts, entering the den and
barring her way.

"I shall keep the promise!" declares Gioconda, seeing no way of
escape. "But first let me adorn myself in splendor. Let me wear the
jewels in which I sing my songs!"

As Barnaba looks on, restraining his lust, Gioconda decks herself in theatrical robes and gems. Undetected by the villain, she
secretes a dagger in her cloak. Finally, she is ready. "I have
promised you, Barnaba, that you should have my body. Now take
it!" Raising the knife, she plunges it into her heart and falls dead.

The fiendish Barnaba bends over the body. "So you have
deceived me!" he screams. "Then hear me, and die forever damned:
last night I killed your mother!" With a cry of rage, the villain
rushes away.

MASCAGNI

PIETRO MASCAGNI was born in the city of Leghorn, Italy, on December 7, 1863. Since his father wanted him to become a lawyer, he was forced to study music in secret. It was only after much domestic friction that he was sent to the Conservatory of Milan to prepare for a musical career.

Once at Milan, Mascagni became irregular in his studies. Although he showed great promise in his work with the composer and teacher Ponchielli, he quickly tired of the usual exercises in counterpoint and fugue. Leaving the Conservatory, he joined a traveling opera company and later settled down to an obscure teaching position in a village near Foggia.

The young instructor was suddenly lifted into world fame by the première of *Cavalleria Rusticana*, which had taken first prize in the Sonzogno contest of 1889. *Iris,* less well known, was presented at the Metropolitan Opera House in 1907 and revived on two later occasions. In addition to many operas, Mascagni has also tried his hand at music for films and operetta. His most recent work is the historical pageant *Nerone*, produced at *La Scala* in 1935.

CAVALLERIA RUSTICANA
(*RUSTIC CHIVALRY*)

CAVALLERIA RUSTICANA, *a one-act melodrama of Sicilian village life, adapted from a story of Giovanni Verga, won for Mascagni first prize in the 1889 competition instituted by the publishing house of Sonzogno. It was produced at the* Costanzi Theatre, *Rome, in 1890 and reached the stage of the Metropolitan Opera House the following year. Because of its brevity,* Cavalleria Rusticana *has been coupled on the same bill with such widely divergent works as* Orfeo, Pagliacci, *or* Salome.

Characters, in order of appearance:

Santuzza: *soprano*
Mamma Lucia: *contralto*
Alfio, a carter: *baritone*
Turridu, son of Lucia: *tenor*
Lola, wife to Alfio: *mezzo-soprano*
Chorus of peasants

Time: Nineteenth Century

SCENE: A VILLAGE IN SICILY (73 Minutes)

Before the rise of the curtain, there is an extended prelude, containing the chief melodies of the opera. As the music reaches a climax, the voice of Turridu can be heard off stage in a serenade to his loved one, Lola:

Turridu
(*invisible*)

O Lo - la, bian - ca co - me fior di spi - no,——
O   Lo - la, with thy lips like crim - son ber - ries,——

His song dies away; the orchestra resumes its tragic introduction to the drama.

Enter chorus
Exit chorus
Enter Santuzza

I is Easter morning, and crowds of people throng the public square. Only one person in the entire village is unhappy on this festive day—the maiden, Santuzza. Waiting until the square is empty, she runs to the tavern opposite the church and knocks on the iron grille:

Enter Lucia

"Mamma Lucia!" she calls. "Where is your son Turridu?"

The door of the tavern opens, and the innkeeper emerges—a short, wizened peasant woman with a shawl drawn about her head. "What do you want with my son?" she demands.

"For the love of God," Santuzza exclaims, "have pity! Tell me where he's hiding!"

"He's gone to fetch some wine from Francofonte," Lucia answers laconically.

"No!" cries the maiden. "He was seen last night in the village!"

Lucia's composure is shaken by this information—she invites Santuzza to enter the tavern and tell her more. "I cannot cross your threshold!" the girl replies. "I am excommunicated!"

As the two women remain in the square, they hear the beating of a whip and the jingling of bells. It is the familiar sound of

Enter Alfio and chorus

Alfio, the carter, known to all the village for his jolly nature. Soon he approaches the tavern with a group of townspeople, even more jovial than usual—for on this holiday morning he is going home to Lola, the wife he adores:

Il ca - val - lo scal - pi - ta,   i so - na - gli squil - la - no,   schiocchi la fru-sta. Ehi là!
Proud-ly steps the stur - dy steed, Gay - ly ring the mer - ry bells, Crack! goes the whiplash! o - hi!

"Good day, Mamma Lucia," he calls. "Have you any more of that old wine?"

"Turridu is bringing some from the next town."

"Strange!" Alfio declares. "I saw him this morning near my house."

Before Lucia can answer, Santuzza signals her to be silent. To the maiden's intense relief, Alfio goes on his way. And now, through the open doors of the church comes the sound of the organ. Most of the villagers throng to mass, but a few remain outside in prayer where Santuzza, though banned from the church itself, leads them in an Easter hymn:

The hymn is ended—and as all the participants piously go inside to worship, Mamma Lucia lingers with Santuzza.

"Tell me," the old woman urges. "Santuzza, what is troubling you?"

Striving to master her emotion, the maiden confides in Lucia. "Well do you know," she begins, "that before Turridu went off to the wars, he was engaged to Lola. When he returned, she was wedded to Alfio. Just to forget her, Turridu sought another love. I gave him my virtue! But Lola was jealous; she still wanted him. And now, she has taken him from me!" The girl's voice breaks with grief:

Weeping bitterly, Santuzza implores Mamma Lucia to pray for her. The old woman, deeply moved, climbs the steps and enters the church. Santuzza is left alone—then she spies young Turridu jauntily crossing the square.

"Where are you going?" she calls.

"To see my mother," he replies coldly.

Overcome with misery, Santuzza tries to bar his way. "O Turridu," she pleads, "do you no longer love me? Is it only Lola you care for?"

Turridu evades the question—Santuzza renews her pleading—and suddenly a wanton voice is heard, singing of love and flowers. It is Lola!

Exit Alfio

Exit chorus

Exit Lucia Enter Turridu

Enter Lola

Fior di giag - gio - lo___ gli an-ge - li bel - li stan-no a mil-le in cie - lo___
My King of ro - ses!___ Ra - di - ant an -. gels stand in Heav'n in thou-sands—

With a smirking glance at her rival, Lola appears at the back of the square and walks toward the church. "Turridu," she remarks, "I'm going inside to services. Why don't you stay out here with poor Santuzza?" Turning to enter the building, the woman throws her lover a rose.

Exit Lola

And now Santuzza's grief is uncontrolled. "For the last time," she cries, "will you return to me, Turridu? Will you give me your love?"

No! Tu - rid - du, ri - ma - ni, ri - ma - ni an - co - ra,
No, Tu - rid - du, re - main, re - main! Do not leave me,

Exit Turridu

Savagely hurling her aside, Turridu enters the church. Santuzza lies upon the ground, dazed and wretched. Then a furious resolve takes hold of her. She will tell Alfio of the whole affair!

Enter Alfio

No sooner has Santuzza decided on this plan than Alfio appears. "God must have sent you!" she exclaims. "You shall see your wife coming out of church with Turridu!"

"What do you mean?" asks the carter.

"I mean that she has been faithless to you! She has given herself to him!"

At first, the slow-witted Alfio cannot believe Santuzza. Then, stirred to terrible anger, he vows revenge.

Exeunt Santuzza and Alfio

Realizing the hatred she has sown, Santuzza is overcome by remorse. But she is powerless to stop the raging Alfio—he has vowed to slay Turridu. As the carter goes off to perfect his plans, Santuzza, torn by a sense of guilt, runs after him.

The stage is empty; and while the organ from the church blends with the orchestra of the opera house, we hear the famous Intermezzo:

At last, the service has ended. As the people leave the church and cluster about the square, Turridu emerges with Lola. In recklessly gay mood, he invites his friends to drink with him at his mother's tavern.

Enter chorus, Turridu and Lola

Larghetto

Vi-va il vi - no spu -meg - gian - te, nel bic - chie - re scin - til - lan - te
Hail! the red wine rich - ly flow - ing, in the beak - er spark - ling, glow - ing

The villagers raise their glasses—and Alfio appears. "You are welcome!" cries Turridu, offering him a draught. "Come, join us!"

Enter Alfio

"Thank you," Alfio mutters, "but I'd rather not. I might be poisoned!"

Both men confront each other threateningly. While the villagers escort Lola homeward, Alfio challenges Turridu with the Sicilian sign of a duel: a bite on the ear. He stalks away; the crowd has dispersed, and Turridu is left in fear.

Exit Lola
Exeunt Alfio and chorus

"Mamma Lucia!" he calls, beating feverishly at the tavern door. "Mamma, I have something to tell you!"

As Lucia hurries from the inn and looks at him in bewilderment, Turridu exclaims, "O Mamma, I must go now. Give me your blessing! If I don't return, promise me that you'll take care of Santuzza—I have sworn to protect her!"

Enter Lucia

"What is it, my son?" cries Lucia. "What are you saying?"

But Turridu has run off. Excited voices are heard far back of the square. Filled with apprehension, Lucia makes her way toward the growing crowd and meets Santuzza. As both women huddle together, a scream pierces the air. One of the village girls come rushing toward them. "Turridu!" she cries. "Alfio has killed him!"

Exit Turridu
Enter Santuzza
Enter chorus

Shrieking wildly, Santuzza falls in front of the church. The grim tragedy of Easter day in a Sicilian village has come to an end.

LEONCAVALLO

RUGGIERO LEONCAVALLO was born on March 8, 1858, in the city of Naples, where he studied at the Conservatory. Embarking on a professional career was no easy matter for Leoncavallo; in order to earn the barest living, he was forced to perform as a café pianist, traveling in this capacity to England, Holland, France, Germany and Egypt.

Anxious to be launched as an opera composer, he submitted to the publishing house of Ricordi a libretto called *I Medici,* which was the first part of a projected trilogy: *Crepusculum.* The libretto was accepted, and the music completed within a year. Since no favorable action was taken on the score itself, Leoncavallo opened negotiations with the rival house of Sonzogno; and for this firm he composed his best known opera, *I Pagliacci,* based on his own libretto.

I Medici was finally produced and proved a failure—so much so, that the composer never finished the other two portions of the trilogy. *Zaza,* produced at Milan in 1900, was more favorably received, and when it was presented at the Metropolitan Opera House in 1920 with Geraldine Farrar in the title role, it aroused much enthusiasm; but it has not survived.

Among other works by Leoncavallo are *Der Roland,* a Hohenzollern saga, commissioned by Emperor Wilhelm II; a ballet, *La Vita d'una Marionetta,* and a symphonic poem, *Serafita.* The composer died at Montecatini, near Florence, on August 9, 1919.

I PAGLIACCI
(*THE STROLLING PLAYERS*)

I PAGLIACCI, *a two-act opera of the veristic school, written to the composer Leoncavallo's own libretto, was produced at the Teatro dal Verme, Milan, in May, 1892. It met with instantaneous success. One year later, Pagliacci was first performed at the Metropolitan Opera House, although its most spectacular American triumphs date from 1903, when Enrico Caruso assumed the role of Canio in New York.*

Characters, in order of appearance:

Tonio, a strolling player: *baritone*
Canio, master of the troupe: *tenor*
Nedda, his wife: *soprano*
Beppe, a player: *tenor*
Silvio, a villager: *baritone*
Chorus of villagers

Time: Nineteenth Century   *Place:* A Calabrian Village

THE PROLOGUE

A lively theme rises from the orchestra, representing the spirit of buffoonery—for the play is based on the lives of a band of strolling comedians:

Just as in the opera to follow, the externals of theatrical life soon yield to the tragic and personal disclosures behind the mask. But these are swept aside by the dominant spirit of buffoonery— and Tonio, the "heavy" of the troupe, slips through the curtains   Tonio and advances to the footlights.

"Ladies and gentlemen," he announces, "I am the Prologue. The author has not sent me, as of old, to tell you that the passions you are about to witness are make-believe. Oh, no! They are true —for actors, too, are human beings."

E vo - i, piut - to - sto che le no - stre po - ve - re gab -
And you must con. - sid - er, not so much our poor flim-sy cos -

ba - ne d'i -stri - o - ni, le no - str'a - ni - me con - si - de - ra - te.
tu - mer - y of ac - tors, ra - ther let our hearts speak to you for us.

"We are ready," he concludes. "Ring up the curtain!"

ACT I

SCENE: AFTERNOON IN THE VILLAGE OF MONTALTO, CALABRIA
(47 Minutes)

Chorus

WITH rapturous greetings from the townspeople, a donkey trots along the dusty road outside Montalto, drawing a cart full of strolling players. In the evening, there is to be a performance on the open air stage outside of town—the familiar figures of Harlequin, Columbine and Punchinello (Pagliaccio) will tread the boards. Now, the makeshift theatre has been set up—the players are arriving—and a mood of festivity fills the air.

Canio, Nedda, Tonio, Beppe

"Welcome!" the villagers shout. "Welcome, Pagliaccio!"

Canio, leader of the players, makes a sweeping bow. "We perform tonight at seven," he declares. "Come one and all—honor us with your presence!"

During the noisy greeting by the people, Tonio has been loitering near Canio's young wife, Nedda. He is a repulsive figure—maimed and twisted. Now he offers to help Nedda alight from the cart. "Look out!" snaps the jealous Canio, who has observed him. "I'll help her myself!"

Exit Tonio

Grumbling, Tonio disappears behind the traveling theatre—and a group of cordial villagers gather around Canio. "Come with us to the tavern!" they urge. "Let's have a drink!"

Exit Beppe

Canio gladly accepts. "Wait for me!" pleads Beppe, another member of the troupe. So far, all are accounted for except Nedda and Tonio.

The villagers tease Canio: "Is Tonio staying here to make love to your wife?"

At once, Canio becomes very grave. "It is better that no one try that game!" he answers. "Life and the stage are two very different things. Every night, in our little play, I come home as Pagliaccio, to find that my wife has been unfaithful—and on the stage, all I

can do is to rail comically at her and her lover. But if ever—oh,
if ever—it should happen in real life, what a different story that
would be!" Even at the thought, Canio is fired with jealousy:

The villagers, seeing they have touched a sore spot, try to
restore Canio to a more jovial mood. "Come," they laugh, "and let
us drink!" Kissing his wife farewell, Canio goes along to the
tavern with Beppe and his friends. Other townspeople pass by on
their way to church. Soon, there is no one at hand but Nedda
—and Tonio, lurking behind the improvised theatre.

Exeunt Canio and chorus

Nedda is melancholy. She muses on Canio's jealous outburst and
wonders, "Could he have read the secret in my eyes? Does he know
I have a lover?" Dismissing these thoughts, she looks into the
sky and sees a flock of birds overhead. The gayer side of her nature
asserts itself; and soon, Nedda finds herself calling to the birds
with a cry that her mother once taught her:

Drawn by Nedda's singing, Tonio creeps from the theatre. He
implores the woman to listen to him—he vows that he is desperately in love.

Enter Tonio

At first, Nedda scornfully banters with the clown. But when he
attempts to kiss her, she seizes a whip and strikes him in the face.

"By the Blessed Virgin," Tonio screams, "I swear that I will
have revenge on you, Nedda!"

Exit
Tonio

He limps away, muttering imprecations. Nedda is left alone—but not for long. Her lover, Silvio, has come from the village by a secret pathway:

Enter
Silvio

"Nedda!" he cries. "You will be leaving here tomorrow with your troupe—parted from me forever. O give up this husband of yours; abandon this life! Come, be mine!"

Nedda has never loved Canio, and now her sense of duty is overwhelmed by Silvio's pleading. "I will go with you," she sighs.

Enter
Tonio
Exit
Tonio

The lovers embrace—and are spied upon by Tonio, who gleefully hobbles off to the tavern to fetch his master. Unaware they are being watched, Nedda bids Silvio farewell. "Till tonight, then," she murmurs, "and forever I'll be yours!"

Enter
Canio and
Tonio
Exit
Silvio

Just as Nedda speaks these words, the jealous Canio appears upon the scene. Rushing forward, he pursues the fleeing villager, but can find no trace of him. Haggard and distraught, he returns and lays hold of his wife. "Your lover's name!" he demands. "Tell me his name!"

Enter
Beppe

As Nedda refuses, Canio draws a knife. At once, the watchful Beppe, who has followed him from the tavern, snatches the weapon. "Be careful!" Beppe cries. "Our audience will soon be here for the play!" The kindly clown draws Nedda away and escorts her into the theatre.

Exeunt
Nedda,
Beppe and
Tonio

Tonio lingers behind. "Don't worry," he whispers to Canio. "Her lover will soon return—I'll watch for him!" The wretch goes off, and Canio remains alone, staring at the stage on which he is soon to perform.

"Why must I pretend?" he sobs. "Why must I laugh as Pagliaccio, when I feel like weeping?" With heavy heart, he climbs the steps of the theatre, passes through the curtains, and disappears. The play must go on!

Act II

SCENE: EVENING IN MONTALTO (22 Minutes)

LONG wooden benches have been set up before the theatre; gaily lighted lanterns are strung overhead. And now, to the beating of Tonio's drum, the townspeople assemble to see the play. Among them is Silvio. Chorus

At last, after the villagers have shouted with impatience at the delay, the curtains of the miniature stage are opened. In childish delight, the audience applauds the crude setting: the interior of a little house with Nedda, dressed as Columbine, seated at table. Suddenly, the sounds of a guitar are heard. Behind the theatre, Harlequin, in the person of Beppe, is serenading his loved one: Nedda
Beppe
(*invisible*)

Allegretto

O—— Co-lom-bi-na_il te-ne-ro fi-do Ar-lec-chin è_a te vi-cin!——
O—— Col-um-bine, your Har-le-quin is here with you, Ten-der and true!——

Since Columbine is expecting another lover, she demurely ignores the serenade. And soon the other lover—the deformed Taddeo—appears at the door. Entering the room, Taddeo-Tonio makes passionate advances to Columbine. All of his protests of love bristle with double meaning as the heroine of the little play rebuffs him. "Oh, I know you are pure!" he asserts. "Purer than the snow itself. But why are you so cruel?" Enter
Tonio

The play unfolds: Harlequin enters, and forces Taddeo to surrender all claims to the affections of Columbine. As the two lovers sit down to supper, the clown departs—but soon he returns, panting with comic excitement. "Beware!" he calls. "Your husband Pagliaccio is coming home!" Enter
Beppe
Exit
Tonio
Re-enter
Tonio
Exeunt
Tonio and
Beppe

Taddeo disappears; Harlequin dives out the window. As part of the performance, Columbine gazes after him and murmurs, "Till tonight, then, and forever I'll be yours!" Suddenly, she looks back and sees her husband standing in the doorway—he has overheard!

And now the play ceases to be a play. Although dressed in the garb of Pagliaccio, Canio has forsaken the conventions of the stage. The doubly significant words of Columbine—"Till tonight!"—have unnerved him completely. For a while, he makes a brave effort to go on with his part. But finally, casting aside his clown's cap, he cries, "No! I am Pagliaccio no longer! I am the man who gave Nedda his love!" Enter
Canio

The villagers lean forward in apprehension. Canio has sunk into

a chair and buried his head in his arms. Sobs shake his voice as
he reproaches Nedda for her faithlessness:

Cantabile espressivo

Spe - rai, tan - to_il de - li - rio_ac - ce - ca - to m'a - ve - va,
I hoped ah! I was blind - ed in - deed in : my mad - ness:

Nervously, Nedda edges toward the audience and tries to go on
with the comedy. But Canio has risen—he advances relentlessly.
"Your lover's name!" he shouts. "Tell me, or I'll kill you!"

"No!" cries Nedda. "Never!"

Enter
Tonio and
Beppe The kindly Beppe has run onto the stage in an attempt to save
Nedda. It is no use—Tonio holds him back. Knife in hand, Pagli-
accio pursues his wife and strikes her dead.

Silvio The audience screams, and Silvio rushes forward. At once, Canio
plunges his dagger in the lover's breast. Turning to the horrified
villagers, he lets his weapon fall to the ground. "The comedy," he
gasps, "is finished!"

PUCCINI

GIACOMO PUCCINI was born in Lucca on December 23, 1858, of a family whose musical distinction had been a matter of record for four generations. Sent to the local conservatory by his mother, although he showed little musical aptitude in childhood, he became organist at a near-by church at the age of 17. A stipend from the Queen permitted him to study at the Milan Conservatory under Ponchielli.

Although tardy in developing his most notable successes, he composed a dozen important works in forty years, and was regarded by Verdi as the most talented of Italian dramatic composers of his time. Puccini died in 1924.

His style is marked by the felicitous display it affords the voice, without in any way diminishing intensity or menacing orchestral color. His musical inspiration is directly related to the dramatic values of his text. The popularity of his works, which in the first quarter of the century rivaled that of Verdi, is thus largely dependent on the dramatic gifts of his interpreters.

LA BOHÈME

LA BOHÈME *was composed by Giacomo Puccini a year after his successful* Manon Lescaut, *which it surpassed in acclaim. First produced in Turin, February 1, 1896, it reached England a year later, arrived in New York in 1898, and entered the Metropolitan repertory in December, 1901, where, with the exception of one season only, it has remained ever since, averaging almost six performances a year.*

Its librettists, Giuseppe Giacosa and Luigi Illica, based their text on Henri Murger's Scènes de la Vie de Bohème, a series of episodes which the author had drawn from his own experience as a struggling writer in Paris, in the '40's.

Characters, in order of appearance:

Marcello, a painter: *baritone*
Rodolfo, a poet: *tenor*
Colline, a philosopher: *bass*
Schaunard, a musician: *baritone*
Benoit, a landlord: *bass*
Mimi, an embroiderer: *soprano*
Parpignol, a toy vendor: *tenor*
Musetta, a grisette: *soprano*
Alcindoro, a councilor of state: *bass*
Customhouse sergeant: *bass*
Students, working girls, citizens, shopkeepers, street vendors, soldiers, waiters, boys and girls, etc.

Time: About 1830   *Place:* Paris

Act I

SCENE: IN THE ATTIC (35 Minutes)

A few vivacious measures, associated with the carefree Bohemians of the Latin Quarter, set the pace for the first scene:

Allegro vivace

The curtain rises briskly on a cheerless attic.

Marcello and Rodolfo

Marcello sits huddled in a muffler, painting "The Passage of the Red Sea" at his easel.

"This ocean makes me just as chilly as if it were pouring down my back," he observes, rising to examine his painting from further off, "and in revenge I am going to drown my Pharaoh!"

Rodolfo the poet, who has been staring at the snow through a skylight window, observes wistfully that smoke rises from every chimney but their own.

Allegro vivace

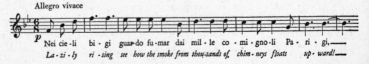

Nei cie-li bi-gi guar-do fu-mar dai mil-le co-mi-gno-li Pa-ri-gi,
La-zi-ly ri-sing see how the smoke from thou-sands of chim-neys floats up-ward!

"My fingers feel as cold as if they had been touching that ice-berg: Musetta's heart," says the painter. "There's only one thing to do," he concludes. "We'll burn up the chair, or, better still, The Red Sea!"

"Here, take the drama I've been writing," retorts Rodolfo; "it will burn well. Here's the first act!"

Both men warm their hands joyously at the blaze, and hardly see the arrival of their friend, the bearded Colline. As the pawn-shops are all closed for Christmas Eve, the philosopher has been unable to raise money on his packet of books, but the warmth of the meager fire softens his rage. **Enter Colline**

"Altogether too short!" he complains, as the flame dies out.

"Brevity is a good thing in plays," laughs Rodolfo, adding Act II to the fuel, and then stuffing in the rest of the manuscript.

"Down with the author!" cry Marcello and Colline as this too burns to ashes. But their tune changes when two boys bring in huge piles of provisions: wood, wine and tobacco, beef and a pasty. In their train triumphantly marches the musician, Schau-nard. **Enter Schaunard**

"But this is no place to feast on Christmas Eve," he insists, clearing the table, before his friends can sample all the dainties. "Let's drink here and then dine outside."

A double knock heralds the arrival of Benoit, the landlord, with his bill. The four friends ply him with wine until he grows tipsy. When he starts to relate his amorous adventures, they pretend to be horrified and thrust the old man out of the door. Then, dividing up the money, Marcello, Schaunard and Colline start off for the Café Momus, leaving Rodolfo to work on his new magazine. **Enter Benoit** **Exit Benoit**

Restlessly the poet tries to write, but throws away his pen in disgust. There is a timid knock, and the motive of Mimi rises from the orchestra: **Exeunt Marcello, Schaunard and Colline**

Lento

ppp

He hastens to open the door, and finds the girl standing modestly in apron and shawl. Out of breath from the stairs and exhausted by coughing, she shows him her candle which has blown out. **Enter Mimi**

Helping her to a chair, Rodolfo sprinkles water on her face, gives her a sip of wine, and lights her candle. At the door she turns back. The draught has again blown out the candle and she must have dropped her key. In giving her a second light, Rodolfo blows out both candles, so it is quite dark when they hunt for the key, and Mimi cannot see him find it and put it in his pocket. As his hand falls on hers, he clasps it tenderly:

Andantino affettuoso

Che ge - li - da ma - ni - na, se la la - sci ris - cal - dar.
Your ti - ny hand is fro - zen, let me warm it in - to life.

Then, with rising emotion, he tells her of his life as a poet, his poverty, and his dreams:

Andante lento

Ta - lot dal mio for - ziere
Bright eyes, as yours, be - lieve me.

At length he asks for her story.

"They call me Mimi," she answers, demurely, "though my name is Lucia. I embroider flowers of silk or linen, living quietly by myself. But when spring comes, I take a single rose and breathe its delicious perfume, for alas, there is no odor in the flowers that I can make!"

The voices of his friends drift up from the street below, calling Rodolfo. He opens the window and moonlight floods the attic. "We'll be with you in a few minutes," he tells them. "Keep two places for us at the Café."

Exeunt Mimi and Rodolfo

He turns back to Mimi enchanted by her beauty. Together their voices rise in praise of love, as, arm in arm, they walk out into the night.

Act II

SCENE: IN THE LATIN QUARTER (17 Minutes)

Crowd of students, street vendors, citizens Schaunard, Colline, Marcello

A MOTLEY crowd throngs the square outside the Café Momus. Hawkers announce their wares. Mothers pull their children after them, while guests frantically demand seats at the little tables in front of the restaurant.

Enter Mimi and Rodolfo

Schaunard is choosing a toy horn, and Colline is trying on a coat, when Rodolfo appears with Mimi. As the three friends go into the Café in search of a table, the lovers stroll about, Mimi with a charming pink bonnet which Rodolfo has bought her. The men return, table in hand; Rodolfo introduces his new companion with a flourish.

From the distance sounds the shrill voice of Parpignol, the toy vendor. His little cart is soon surrounded by eager children.

Parpignol and children

The Bohemians order supper, and Mimi boasts of her lover's good taste in the purchase of the bonnet.

"Bring me an order of poison," demands Marcello gloomily. He alone has heard the distant voice of his former faithless sweetheart Musetta. She makes a dashing entrance, flouncing in on the arm of the elderly councilor Alcindoro, decked in feathers and laces and ordering her admirer about like a dog; but Marcello pretends not to notice her. Annoyed by his indifference, she finally hurls down a plate. When that fails to attract his attention, she addresses him directly, preening herself on her irresistible charm:

Enter Musetta and Alcindoro

Alcindoro is unable to quiet her. Finally she tells him that her shoe pinches and sends him away for another pair. Marcello has again fallen a victim to her spell. The coast being clear, she throws herself into his arms to the delight and amusement of the others. A waiter brings the check, but the approaching sound of a military band distracts everyone's attention.

Exit Alcindoro

"The gentleman will pay," murmurs Musetta to the waiter; "add it to his account." They all march off after the soldiers to the beat of the drum. When Alcindoro returns, with his neat package of shoes, he finds nothing but an immense bill, and drops helplessly into a chair as the curtain falls.

Exeunt Marcello, Rodolfo, Schaunard, Colline, Musetta and Mimi Enter Alcindoro

Act III

SCENE: THE BARRIÈRE D'ENFER (24 Minutes)

THE tollgate at the entrance of the Orleans road into Paris has not yet opened for the day, and the customs officers huddle over their braziers in the snow. By the door of the tavern at the left hangs Marcello's Red Sea picture, now used as a signboard, with a new title: Port of Marseilles.

Customs officers

Blowing on their frostbitten fingers, a group of scavengers beg for admission to the city. A yawning official opens the gate, and then returns to his fire.

Scavengers

From within the tavern can be heard the echo of Musetta's waltz, followed by a gay refrain from invisible revelers.

Paris is waking up. First come the milk carts, then the farmers with eggs and poultry.

As Mimi's motive sounds gently from the orchestra, the girl comes in from the street on the right. She barely reaches the first snow-laden plane tree when she is seized with a fit of coughing.

"I am looking for an inn," she stammers to the official, who directs her to the door. A maidservant comes out. "Can you tell me where I may find the painter Marcello?" she asks her. "Tell him that Mimi is waiting for him."

In a moment Marcello hastens to greet her. "Yes, we have been here a month," he says. "Musetta teaches singing and I paint. Why don't you come in?"

"Oh, I can't," she answers timorously. "Rodolfo is in there. You must help me, Marcello. Rodolfo loves me and yet he avoids me. A single glance is enough to rouse his jealous rage. Help us to separate—it is the only way."

Bidding her hide behind one of the trees, Marcello summons Rodolfo from the tavern.

"I have decided to leave Mimi," announces the poet impetuously. "She is nothing but a heartless coquette. I love her, but it terrifies me. The girl is ill, probably dying of a terrible cough:"

U - na ter - ri - bil tos - se   l'es - il   pet - to   le   scuo - te.
By fierce in - ces - sant cough - ing   her fra - gile frame is   sha - ken,

At this confession, Mimi can no longer keep silent; Rodolfo discovers her. A raucous laugh from the tavern calls Marcello to the side of Musetta, leaving Mimi with the poet.

"I must go back alone to the little room that I deserted at the call of my lover," she exclaims sadly. "In the drawer of your table you will find my prayerbook and bracelet. I will send for them. But the little pink bonnet—that, you must keep in token of our love. Farewell!"

Ad - dio, sen - za ran - cor,
Fare - well, I wish you well!

Interrupting their idyll comes the noise of breaking dishes from

Trades-folk
Sergeant
Enter
Mimi

Enter
Marcello

Enter
Rodolfo

Exit
Marcello

the tavern. Musetta and Marcello are fighting again. Their shrill recriminations punctuate the gentle phrases of the lovers.

Musetta and Marcello

Mimi and Rodolfo cannot face separation, and cling to each other with a new faith. It will be enough for them to part when spring has come again.

Act IV

SCENE: IN THE ATTIC (28 Minutes)

THE vigorous phrases of the introduction anticipate a wintry scene in the attic, where Rodolfo and Marcello, again in bachelor quarters, gossip over their work.

Rodolfo and Marcello

Rodolfo has seen Musetta in velvet and riding in a coupé. Marcello reports that Mimi looks like a duchess in the carriage of her new protector, the Viscount. Together they regret their lost loves:

Schaunard and Colline bring in some rolls and a tiny salted herring.

Enter Schaunard and Colline

"Have a bit of salmon, Baron," suggests Rodolfo, in grand style.

"Or a nightingale's tongue for the Duke," echoes Marcello. With superb pretense, they serve an imaginary banquet. As their hilarity rises they cavort about the room. The mirth has reached fever heat when the door opens and Musetta appears in the greatest agitation.

Enter Musetta and Mimi

"Mimi is here," she cries; "she is ill." Schaunard and Colline drag the bed out from the wall, and Rodolfo hastens to guide her fainting steps towards it.

Musetta draws the three other men away from Rodolfo, who is embracing his beloved, and tells them that Mimi has deserted her old Viscount as she felt that the end was near and she wished to die in the arms of Rodolfo.

"I am so cold," sighs Mimi, rousing herself to greet the friends who hover over her in despair. There is no drop of wine, no grain of coffee in the house.

Exeunt
Musetta
and
Marcello

Musetta pulls off her earrings and tells Marcello to pawn them and bring a doctor. Then she hurries away to find a muff for Mimi's numb hands. Colline takes off the overcoat which has kept him warm for so many years and bids it a touching farewell:

Allegretto moderato e triste

pp

Vec - chia zi - mar - ta,   sen - ti,   io res - to al
Gar - ment an - tique and   rus - ty,   a last good -

pian,   tu a   scen-de- re il sa- cro mon-te or   de - vi
bye!   fare   well! fad - ed friend so tried and trust - y, ___

Exit
Colline
Exit
Schaunard

Then he too bears it to the pawnshop, Schaunard following him to fill the water bottle. The lovers are alone.

Wistfully Mimi reminds Rodolfo of her first visit, of the rose bonnet, and the gentleness with which he warmed her fingers.

Enter
Musetta,
Schaunard,
Colline,
Marcello

Just as the friends return with medicine, a sudden spasm of coughing seizes her again. Musetta brings the muff, which rouses the dying girl to childish delight.

"Love, do not weep," she whispers. "I am always with you. My hands are warm again; I can sleep now." Her eyes close.

Musetta mutters a prayer over the spirit lamp, where she is heating the medicine.

Rodolfo, still hopeful, stretches a cloak across the window to shield Mimi from the sunlight. "See how tranquil she is," he exclaims. Marcello, realizing that the girl is already dead, and unable to keep up the suspense, embraces his friend with a word of courage.

The orchestra, which has died away to one almost inaudible note, bursts out in an anguished fortissimo. Rodolfo flings himself on the bed, sobbing, "Mimi, Mimi."

TOSCA

Tosca, *a "melodrama" in three acts, was composed by Giacomo Puccini after the success of his* Manon Lescaut *and* La Bohème. *The text, prepared by his accustomed librettists, Giuseppe Giacosa and Luigi Illica, is based on the thrilling play of Victorien Sardou, which gains heightened excitement from the atmosphere of the music.*

Tosca was first performed at the Costanzi Theatre *in Rome, January 14, 1900, approximately a hundred years after the events of the opera are supposed to have taken place in that very city. A few months later it reached Buenos Aires and London, where Antonio Scotti. long associated with Metropolitan performances in the role of Baron Scarpia, first sang the part, with Milka Ternina as Tosca.*

These two artists also appeared in the first Metropolitan production of the opera on February 4, 1901, initiating a record for the work that extended uninterruptedly for thirty-one seasons. During this period Scotti played opposite some thirteen different Toscas including Eames, Fremstad, Farrar, and Jeritza.

Characters, in order of appearance:

Cesare Angelotti, former Consul of the Roman Republic: *bass*
A Sacristan of the Church of Sant' Andrea della Valle: *baritone*
Mario Cavaradossi, a painter: *tenor*

Floria Tosca, a singer: *soprano*
Baron Scarpia, Chief of Police in Rome: *baritone*
Spoletta, an agent of the police: *tenor*
Sciarrone, a police officer: *bass*
A shepherd boy: *contralto*
A jailer: *bass*
A cardinal, officers of justice, a scribe, an executioner, soldiers, police, men and women of the populace and the nobility.

Time: June, 1800   *Place:* Rome

Act I

SCENE: THE CHURCH OF SANT' ANDREA DELLA VALLE (44 Minutes)

Three portentous chords from the orchestra announce the motive of Baron Scarpia, the dreaded chief of the Roman police:

Andante molto sostenuto

THE curtain rises on the interior of the magnificent baroque church of Sant' Andrea della Valle. At the right a grille leads into the chapel of the Attavanti family. At the left on a rough dais stands a painter's easel, supporting a large picture covered with a cloth. Near it a shrine has been carved into the wall, with a marble basin of holy water beneath it.

Enter Angelotti

Breathless with fear and exhaustion, the escaped prisoner Angelotti staggers across the church, his prison garb torn and dishevelled.

"My sister said she would leave the key by the pillar," he murmurs, searching in every corner. "Ah, here it is, and here is the Attavanti Chapel!" he exclaims with relief. Then, peering timorously about him to be sure he has not been followed, he thrusts the key into the gate, opens it, and disappears.

Exit Angelotti

Enter Sacristan

A more cheerful theme now indicates the arrival of the Sacristan. Bustling about his duties, the old busybody discovers that the painter has not yet arrived. His brushes are dirty; a lunch basket near the easel is untouched.

Enter Cavaradossi

The Angelus bell summons the Sacristan to his knees. He is still mumbling a Latin prayer when the artist, Mario Cavaradossi, strides briskly in, and, going at once to his work, tears the cover off his picture. It is a Magdalen, with blue eyes and golden hair.

"I see you've painted that lady who comes here so often to pray!" exclaims the indiscreet Sacristan.

"Yes, I sketched her one morning on her knees," answers Cavara-dossi, busily plying his brush. Then, laying it aside, he adds, "The portrait is a strange blend of her golden coloring with the dusky beauty of my beloved, Floria Tosca."

Andante lento

Re - con - di - ta__ar - mo - ni - a di bel - lez - ze di - ver - se!
Strange har - mo - ny of con - trasts, thus de - li - cious - ly blend - ing!

His reference to the unknown model suggests that it is the Marchesa Attavanti, Angelotti's sister, who has inspired the portrait.

The Sacristan has meanwhile been busy cleaning brushes in a small basin, muttering that such ungodly folk as the painter and his friend should be burned by the Inquisition. At length he patters away, delighted by Cavaradossi's statement that he will not want the lunchbasket. The old man can find good use for it later himself!

Exit Sacristan

For a moment only the painter is left alone. Then, furtively peering from his retreat in the chapel, Angelotti recognizes his friend and rushes toward him. After an instant's hesitation, Cavara-dossi realizes that prison life has completely disguised his old companion of republican days. Hardly has he learned the details of Angelotti's escape, and closed the church door for his protection, when a familiar voice calls from the distance, "Mario! Mario!"

Enter Angelotti

"Quick," whispers the painter to his friend. "It is Tosca. She may be a great singer, but she is the most inquisitive of women. You must hide again until she goes. You look exhausted to death. . . . Here, take this basket; food and wine will help you."

Angelotti hastens back to the chapel and Cavaradossi turns to admit Tosca. Entering with an imperious gesture, and proudly tossing the plumes of her hat, the favorite songstress of Rome repels his advances.

Exit Angelotti Enter Tosca

"Why was the door closed? Who was in here talking to you?" she asks, irritably. The painter calms her as best he can, consumed with worry, meanwhile, for Angelotti. He shows so little concern for Tosca, that soon, tantalized by his indifference, she is begging him to meet her that night at the villa which is their accustomed trysting place.

Allegro moderato

Non la sos - pi - ri la nos - tra ca - set - ta.
Dost thou not long for our cot - tage se - clud - ed.

Although his eagerness now rises to the same rapturous pitch as her own, Cavaradossi is anxious to get rid of Tosca, as she is not slow to discover. Can it be that he plans another rendezvous with the model he has been painting? She looks carefully at the golden-haired portrait. "It is the Marchesa Attavanti!" she cries at last.

Cavaradossi admits that he has used the features of the woman he saw praying in the chapel. "But her eyes are far less beautiful than yours," he protests, leading Tosca away from the picture, "and there is no reason for you to be jealous." To a new melody he quiets her suspicions:

Andante mosso

Beneath the statue of the Virgin, the lovers seal their renewed confidence with a fond embrace. Then with a last hint that she would prefer the Magdalen's eyes to be painted black, like her own, Tosca departs.

Exit Tosca

Enter Angelotti

As soon as the coast is clear, Cavaradossi hurries to the chapel grating and beckons Angelotti to return.

"Tosca is so indiscreet I told her nothing," says the painter. "What are your plans?"

"My sister the Attavanti has left a woman's dress for me under the altar," says the fugitive. "In that disguise I can escape, perhaps, from the clutches of Scarpia!"

"You had better not wait till nightfall to get away from that monster," urges Cavaradossi. "From the chapel you will find a rough path across the fields to my villa. Here is the key. Hide there, and in case of danger run to the garden well. Halfway down, there is a passage connecting it with a secret cellar where you will be in perfect safety."

Exeunt Angelotti and Cavaradossi

Enter Sacristan and choristers

A cannon shot interrupts his words. "Your escape is discovered," exclaims the painter aghast. "I will come with you. We must go at once."

No sooner has Angelotti hurried through the chapel door with his friend than the Sacristan shuffles in breathless with news. "Bonaparte, that dog of an unbeliever, has been defeated!" he cries, calling acolytes and choristers to hear the tidings. "Tonight there will be torchlight processions and a gala performance, with Tosca singing a new cantata. Put on your vestments at once."

At the height of the confusion Baron Scarpia majestically strides through the church, his white wig contrasting with his saturnine face and inky cloak. A detachment of police are at his heels.

Enter
Scarpia,
Spoletta
and police

Dismissing the crowd with orders to make ready for the *Te Deum,* the Baron sends his assistant Spoletta to search the building. Then, turning to the Sacristan, he tells of the escaped prisoner and questions him as to possible clues.

Exeunt
choristers
Exit
Spoletta

Searching for a moment in the chapel, Scarpia finds a woman's fan. "This is the Attavanti crest!" he exclaims, looking closely at the object. "And this is the face of the Marchesa," he says, turning toward the easel to scrutinize the picture of the Magdalen.

A police officer brings out an empty lunch basket from the chapel. The Sacristan recognizes it as the one Cavaradossi had refused. Trembling with confusion, he does not hear Scarpia's comment:

"Angelotti has been here—it is he who has eaten the painter's provisions."

At that moment Tosca returns, full of agitation at not finding her lover at his easel. Scarpia, muttering to himself that the fan may help to rouse her jealousy and thus betray her into some confession regarding Cavaradossi, addresses her with formal courtesy.

Enter
Tosca
Exit
Sacristan

"Beautiful Tosca," he exclaims, offering her some holy water from the basin, "you who rouse men to Heaven with your exquisite voice, you have nothing in common with those wantons who meet their lovers in church and pose as Magdalens." He shows her the fan and asks what she knows of it.

Tosca recognizes the Attavanti arms and at once gives vent to her old fears. "I came here to tell Mario that I must sing at the celebration tonight and could not meet him, and this is what I learn!" she exclaims bitterly. Groups of humble petitioners flock into the church for the Te Deum.

Enter
members
of congre-
gation

Swearing to avenge herself on the lady of the picture, she weeps. Scarpia, well pleased at the success of his plans, but pretending to be full of compassion and reassurance, escorts her to the door. Then he summons Spoletta from behind a pillar, and drawing him aside from the crowd of rich and poor which now fills the church, tells him to follow Tosca closely, and report later at the Farnese Palace.

Exit
Tosca

Spoletta

The pealing of the organ proclaims that the ritual is about to

Swiss
guard

start. Cannon resound from the distance. The Swiss guard thrust back the multitude, making room for the procession to follow.

"Go, Tosca," cries Scarpia with the deepest irony. "I have fired your soul with suspicion; it will easily be turned into love."

Procession
of priests
and
Cardinal

The Cardinal, following the choristers and priests in his magnificent scarlet vestments, blesses the kneeling throng. The people utter their devotions in an undertone of Latin.

"I want to see that rebel on the scaffold," continues Scarpia in his malicious reverie, "but most of all I want to hold Tosca in my arms. For her alone I would renounce the hope of Heaven!" His voice takes up the sacred chant with pious fervor as the curtain falls, while his theme is three times blazoned from the orchestra.

Act II

SCENE: SCARPIA'S APARTMENTS IN THE FARNESE PALACE
(41 Minutes)

Scarpia

ALONE at his supper table in his rooms in the Farnese Palace, Scarpia looks at his watch with nervous agitation.

"Tosca is a good decoy," he mutters. "By this time my men should have arrested the two conspirators. At dawn they will be on the gallows!" Sounds of dancing float through the window at the left from the apartment below where Queen Caroline is entertaining. "They are waiting for Tosca to sing the cantata," muses Scarpia. He gives his lieutenant Sciarrone a note to summon her at the close of the performance. "A forcible conquest is more to my taste than a passive surrender," he adds to himself.

Enter
Spoletta

Spoletta arrives with news of his search for Angelotti. "We followed the lady to a villa," he reports nervously, while Scarpia proceeds with his supper. "Not a sign of the man we were looking for," continues the spy, "but we did catch the painter Cavaradossi and brought him here. I'm sure he knows where the other fellow is hidden."

Enter
Cavaradossi
and
officials

Scarpia sends for Cavaradossi, and bids Sciarrone also summon Roberti the executioner, an Exchequer judge and clerk. While the

Baron questions his prisoner, the music of the cantata echoes from the distance, the voice of Tosca soaring above the choir.

Scarpia's exaggerated courtesy provokes a series of insolent denials from Cavaradossi. He says he knows nothing of Angelotti, who is probably laughing at the police at this moment.

Infuriated by such impudence, and impatient at the music outside, Scarpia slams the window shut, and repeats his questions, which again Cavaradossi refuses to answer.

At this moment Tosca makes her appearance at the central door, in her gala robes, a coronet sparkling in her hair. She runs to embrace her lover, who warns her to say nothing of what she has seen at the villa. Enter
Tosca

"Mario Cavaradossi," declares Scarpia, "the judge is waiting to take your deposition." He points to a door opening to a room on the right and gives his instructions to the executioner. A new and insistent motive is heard in the orchestra, suggesting the grueling ordeal to follow:

The officials conduct the painter to the adjacent torture chamber, leaving Tosca and Scarpia alone. Exeunt
Cavaradossi
with
Spoletta
and officials

"Let us talk together like good friends," he says, politely offering her a chair. "Are you quite sure that there was no one at the villa?"

"Certainly not," replies Tosca with assumed composure. "If I wish to please you, must I tell you lies?"

"Only by being truthful can you spare your lover an hour of anguish," is his answer.

Tosca is horrified. She did not realize that Cavaradossi was to be tortured. "What is happening?" she asks anxiously.

"A fillet of steel is bound about his temples," answers Scarpia. "At each denial it is tightened, and hot blood spurts out."

A groan is heard from the next room.

Tosca manages to approach the door. "Are they hurting you still?" she calls piteously.

"No, no," is the answer. "You must have courage and keep silence."

Scarpia calls to the executioner to renew the torture and instructs Spoletta to open the door.

"I defy you," shouts Cavaradossi, from the next room.

Tosca is frantic. To Scarpia's repeated questions she answers as before, pleading meanwhile for mercy.

Then, as Cavaradossi's voice utters a prolonged cry of agony, she rises, and mutters in a stifled voice: "You will find Angelotti in a well in the garden."

"That will do, Roberti!" shouts Scarpia to his minions.

Enter
Cavaradossi
Spoletta
and
officials

They bring in the painter's limp body and place it on the sofa. Tosca showers it with caresses, and gradually brings her lover back to consciousness.

Scarpia calls Spoletta from his post with the other officials in the background. "Go to the well in the garden," he orders, raising his voice so that Cavaradossi may hear it.

"You have betrayed me," cries the painter to Tosca.

Enter
Sciarrone

At this moment Sciarrone brings in news that Napoleon has conquered at the battle of Marengo. Cavaradossi's misery turns into triumph: feverishly he cries that tyranny will be crushed by freedom:

Allegro concitato

L'al - ba vin - di - ce ap-par che fa gli em-pi tre-mar!
O may ven - geance a - wake and cause ty - rants to quake!

Exeunt
Cavaradossi
and
officials

Scarpia furiously orders his agents to drag the painter away. Again the Baron and Tosca are alone.

He resumes his courteous manner and offers her a glass of wine. "We must save your lover if we can," says the wily Scarpia, returning to his supper. "Let's talk it over."

"What is your price?" asks Tosca contemptuously.

"My influence is not to be bought for money," he answers. Then, rising from the table with growing excitement, he tells her that he has long admired her beauty, and that tonight her passionate nature has stirred him so deeply he has vowed to possess her.

Terrified, Tosca rushes to the window. "I would rather kill myself," she cries.

"You yourself are the price of Mario's freedom," he says coldly. "There is no use for you to appeal to the Queen, nor anyone else. I know that you hate me, but that makes me love you the more."

She draws back in horror from his embraces, but he pursues her about the room with such frenzy that she cries for help. A distant roll of drums interrupts them. He tells her that the condemned men are marching to the gallows. There is not much time to wait.

"I have done evil to no one," says Tosca, broken down by her grief. "Why does the Lord forsake me now?"

Andante lento appassionato

pp

Vis - si   d'ar - te,   vis - si   d'a - mo - re,
Love and   mu - sic: these have I   lived for,

She pleads with Scarpia for mercy. Once more he states his terms. Once more she repulses him.

Spoletta brings word that Angelotti has swallowed poison at his capture, and that Cavaradossi awaits Scarpia's decision. **Enter Spoletta**

"What is your answer?" the Baron asks of Tosca.

Weeping with shame, she nods in acquiescence, and buries her head in the sofa cushions.

"I cannot set Cavaradossi free at once," he tells her. "It must be thought that he is dead. But I will give orders to Spoletta for a mock execution." He turns to his underling. "You will see that the prisoner is shot as in the case of Palmieri," he orders emphatically, "a simulated execution." The police officer retires with a salute. **Exit Spoletta**

Tosca demands a safe-conduct for her lover and herself, to which the Baron agrees, seating himself at his desk to write the order. While he writes, she turns to the supper table for a glass of wine. Just as she raises it to her lips she perceives a sharp knife on the table. She hides it cautiously. When he finally rises to take her in his arms, she strikes him full in the breast.

He falls to the floor, dying with a prayer for mercy, but Tosca is obdurate. "He is dead," she says at last. "Now I can forgive him!" Without taking her eyes off his body, she washes her fingers in a glass of water, arranges her hair at the glass, plucks the passport from his stiffening fingers, sets candles at head and feet and places a crucifix on his breast. The theme of Scarpia whispers from the orchestra as she leaves, cautiously closing the door behind her.

ACT III

SCENE: THE PLATFORM OF THE CASTLE OF SANT' ANGELO
(27 Minutes)

THE battlements of the Castle of Sant' Angelo rise starkly about a parapet from which can be seen a wide vista of the city of Rome. It is a starlit night, and the distant dome of St. Peter's is clearly visible. A casemate on the left is furnished with a table, bench and stool. On the table a lamp is placed beside some writing materials. Another is fastened to the wall above a crucifix.

Shepherd
(*off stage*)
The sound of sheep bells echoes from the distance. Far off, a shepherd sings a simple ditty, followed by the stronger tone of matin chimes.

Enter
jailer,
sergeant
and
Cavaradossi
At length a jailer emerges from a trapdoor at the right, lights the lamps and hails the sentry who paces about the battlements. A sergeant conducts Cavaradossi to the jailer, who questions the prisoner briefly.

The painter begs his guard to take a letter to the woman he loves and offers him a ring as reward. Then he sits down to write, but his thoughts wander off to his last happy evening with Tosca:

"E lucevan
"When the stars
le stelle"
were brightly shining"

Enter
Spoletta
and Tosca
Exeunt
Spoletta,
jailer and
sergeant
Suddenly Tosca appears at the trapdoor, accompanied by Spoletta and the sergeant. Both men soon withdraw and, except for the distant sentry, the lovers are quite alone.

Joyously they read the words of the safe-conduct. Tosca tells Cavaradossi that she has killed Scarpia with her own hands.

He wonders that one so gentle could accomplish the grim task:

O dol - ci ma - ni man-su - e - te e pu - re,
O gen - tle hands, so pi - ti - ful and ten - der,

Together they lay their plans for the future. "You must go through a mock execution," she tells him, "and fall as if you were dead when the muskets are fired. Then we shall be free to seek a radiant future together."

Enter
firing
squad and
sergeant
Lost in rapture they are not aware of the arrival of the firing squad, although the sun has now risen and the sky is bright. The officer in charge leads Cavaradossi to the wall opposite the casemate where Tosca is watching.

The men take their positions and fire the fatal shot. "How well he acts!" exclaims Tosca as her lover falls prostrate. The sergeant inspects the body and then retreats with the guard, following Spoletta down the trap-door.

"Do not move yet," she whispers, as their tread echoes down the ladder. Then she approaches the body of her lover and uncovers it.

"Get up, Mario," she repeats, again and again. Then, seeing that he is actually dead, she shrieks her anguish to the heavens. Like herself, Scarpia has betrayed his promise with murder.

Distant shouts interrupt her lamentations. Sciarrone has brought the news of Scarpia's death and rushes in with Spoletta to seize the woman they suspect of the murder.

But Tosca is too quick for them. "Scarpia," she cries, "we shall meet on high!" Leaping to the edge of the parapet, she hurls herself over the battlement into space.

MADAMA BUTTERFLY

MADAMA BUTTERFLY *was originally composed by Giacomo Puccini as a one-act opera, and thus presented at* La Scala *in Milan on February 17, 1904. Its unfavorable reception led to its revision within the year into two acts, of which the two scenes of the second are now considered as Acts II and III. It reached Washington, D. C., in 1906, and on February 11, 1907, was first produced at the Metropolitan.*

The libretto was prepared by Puccini's customary librettists, Giuseppe Giacosa and Luigi Illica, after the play which David Belasco and John Luther Long had written on the latter's story.

Characters, in order of appearance:

B. F. Pinkerton, lieutenant, U. S. N.: *tenor*
Goro, a marriage broker: *tenor*
Suzuki, servant to Cio Cio San: *mezzo-soprano*
Sharpless, U. S. Consul: *baritone*
Madama Butterfly (Cio Cio San): *soprano*
Yakuside: *baritone*
The Imperial Commissioner: *bass*
The Uncle Priest: *bass*
Yamadori: *tenor*
Trouble (Cio Cio San's child)
Kate Pinkerton: *mezzo-soprano*
Cio Cio San's relations, friends, and servants

Time: The present day   *Place:* Nagasaki

Act I

SCENE: A JAPANESE HOUSE, TERRACE, AND GARDEN IN NAGASAKI
(47 Minutes)

AFTER a brief introduction suggesting the Oriental setting of the opera by its exotic rhythms, the curtain rises on a hill above the town of Nagasaki. From a flowering terrace on the right may be seen the bay and harbor. On the left stands a fragile dwelling which the marriage broker Goro is exhibiting to his client, Lieutenant Benjamin Franklin Pinkerton of the U. S. Navy.

Pinkerton, Goro

"But this is a house which a puff of wind could blow away," comments Pinkerton, who is seeking a dwelling for his Japanese bride-to-be, Cio Cio San.

"Everything is ready," announces the officious Goro. "Here are the servants," and he introduces Suzuki and two others. "The bride's relations will be here soon for the ceremony."

The voice of the American Consul, Sharpless, can be heard as he pants up the hill.

Suzuki
Exit
Suzuki
Enter
Sharpless
Exit
Goro

"I bought the house and the wife too for nine hundred and ninety-nine years," Pinkerton tells him, "but with the option to cancel both at a moment's notice," and he boasts of the easygoing gospel of the sailor:

Allegro sostenuto

Do - vun - que'al mon - do   Io Yan - kee va - ga bon - do
The whole world   o - ver,   on bus - i - ness and plea - sure,

Sharpless is shocked by the flippancy of the young officer and describes how the sincerity of Cio Cio San's voice had impressed him when he heard it at the Consulate.

"Surely it is only a deep devotion that can talk like that," he urges.

But Pinkerton's answer is to call for more whisky and toast his future American wife to the tune of the Star-Spangled Banner.

Goro breathlessly returns to announce the approach of Madame Butterfly (as Cio Cio San is called) and her friends. The men retire to watch their arrival:

Enter
Goro
Enter
Butterfly
and friends

Largo

Spi - ra sul ma re e sul - la   ter - ra.
A - cross the earth and o'er the   o - cean,

"I am the happiest girl in Japan, the happiest in all the world," sings Butterfly, while her friends comment rapturously on the view

The Americans question her on her background.

"My people were formerly wealthy, my mother is dreadfully poor, my father is dead, I have had to earn my living as a geisha I have one uncle, the priest; another, who's a little wanting. I an just fifteen." All this Butterfly relates with charming candor, an her friends confirm her responses.

Enter relatives, Commissioner, etc.

As the procession of relatives appear, concluding with th Imperial Commissioner and the official registrar, the American withdraw.

"What an odd collection!" exclaims Pinkerton at his assortmen of in-laws.

Sharpless warns him again: "The girl trusts you, be careful."

Butterfly introduces the various members of her family and trie to restrain the greediness with which they cluster about, herse refusing Pinkerton's sweetmeats. Instead she shows him the play things with which her sleeves are stuffed: handkerchiefs, a mirror a fan, and a sheathed knife which she tries to hide.

"It was sent to her father by the Mikado," whispers Goro t Pinkerton, "and he obeyed its invitation."

Her religious images Butterfly tosses aside—only yesterday sh stole secretly to the Mission and accepted the faith of the Amer cans.

The brief marriage ceremony is performed and toasts are drunk

A sudden interruption breaks up the celebrations. An old ma in a towering rage sends the company into a huddle of terror. It the uncle priest.

Enter Uncle Priest

"What were you doing at the Mission?" he asks furiously Butterfly, who stands apart from the rest, in dignified silence.

Exeunt Goro, Uncle Priest, Commissioner, relatives, friends and Sharpless

"She has renounced her true religion," he explains with a curse "You have renounced us all, and we renounce you!"

As Pinkerton orders the crowd away, their fury echoes vainl back to where he and his little wife are standing in the gathering twilight. In the security of his love, she can still be happy. The ver phrase of the uncle's curse is transmuted to the first theme of serene love duet:

Andantino calmo

Vie - ne la   se - ra ————
Even - ing is   fall - ing ————

Suzuki brings her snowy kimono to replace the ponderous cere

monial dress. Butterfly adorns herself, telling her lover of her
innocent fancies.

Exit
Suzuki

But as he urges his passion, she admits her hesitation in accepting a stranger from America, and pleads for his love.

"They say that in your country, if a man catches a butterfly, he
kills it with a needle." Once more in the orchestra sounds the theme
of the curse.

Without actually reassuring her, Pinkerton warms her with his
own fire, and together they sing their rapture as fireflies twinkle in
the garden and stars fill the sky.

Not - te se - re - na!   Guar - da: dor-me o - gni   co - sa!
Night doth en - fold   us   See the world   lies   sleep - ing!

Act II

SCENE: THE INTERIOR OF CIO CIO SAN'S HOUSE (46 Minutes)

AFTER a brief orchestral introduction in which the flutes again
suggest the intervals of the East, the curtain rises on the interior of
Butterfly's little house. With the sole companionship of her faithful
servant, she lives in strict seclusion, for three years have elapsed
with no word from Pinkerton. Suzuki is curled up, praying in front
of the image of Buddha. Butterfly stands motionless, taking no
part in the devotions.

Suzuki,
Butterfly

"The gods of Japan are lazy and idle," she insists, "and I am
afraid the American god does not know where we are living. How
long will it be before we starve, Suzuki?"

Her faith in her husband remains unshaken. Surely he has put
locks on the doors to protect his wife. Surely he will return, as he
said, when the robins are nesting. Trying to impose her confidence
on the skeptical maid, she describes the scene she has so often
pictured to herself of Pinkerton's return:

Un__ bel di ve - dre - mo   le - var - si un fil di fu - mo
One__ fine day we'll no - tice   a   thread   of smoke a - ris - ing

As she concludes, Goro and Sharpless pass the large window on
their way across the garden.

"Come," says the marriage broker, peeping in at intervals during
the conversation, "she's in here."

Enter
Goro and
Sharpless
Exit
Suzuki

Butterfly receives the Consul, and offers him American cigarettes and a rocking chair. She is overjoyed to hear that he has brought a letter from Pinkerton. Little does she suspect that it contains news of his American marriage. First he must tell her when the robins nest in America. Perhaps it is less often than in Japan. Her husband promised to return at that season, and she has watched the robins build their nests three times already.

Enter Yamadori

"Goro has brought half a dozen suitors," she adds, as the broker appears with one of them, the wealthy, if witless prince, Yamadori. With much pomp Yamadori urges his suit.

"But my hand belongs to someone else," answers Butterfly.

"For the wife, desertion gives the right of divorce," explains Goro.

"That may be Japanese law, but it is not true in my country, America," is her unwavering response.

Exeunt Goro and Yamadori

"Pinkerton's ship has been reported in the harbor," whispers Goro to the Consul, as Butterfly dismisses both suitor and broker, and waits for Sharpless to read the letter:

In - co - min - ciate.
Be - gin I beg you.

But Sharpless cannot bear to break the news of Pinkerton's treachery to his trusting wife. Instead he urges her to accept Yamadori.

Enter Trouble

She runs out of the room and brings back a yellow-haired baby. Sharpless is amazed. "Is this his child?" he demands.

"Did anyone ever see a little Japanese with blue eyes?" is her answer. "Today his name is Trouble, but soon he will be called Joy."

Exit Sharpless Enter Goro

Sharpless, realizing it is hopeless to bring Butterfly down to reality, retires, promising to inform Pinkerton that he has a son.

At this point Suzuki drags in the wretched marriage broker.

"An American baby born in such conditions would be treated as an outcast," he has told her.

Exit Goro Enter Suzuki

Butterfly runs to the shrine where the sacred dagger of her father's suicide is kept, and with it threatens Goro. He makes his escape.

At this moment the harbor cannon is heard. The women rush out to the terrace. It is Pinkerton's ship, the Abraham Lincoln.

Echoes of "One fine day" and the Star-Spangled Banner are followed in the orchestra by a reminiscence of the love duet.

Butterfly orders Suzuki to fill the house with flowers.

Get - tia - mo_a ma - ni   pie - ne   mam - mo - le_e tu - be - ro - se,
In   hand - fuls let us   scat - ter   vi - o - lets and white ros - es,

"Put a touch of red on my cheeks," adds Butterfly to her maid; "bring me my wedding garment."

Seating Suzuki and the baby in front of the window, where she has torn holes in the paper panes, Butterfly herself stands on watch. Distant muted voices, accompanied by pizzicato strings, hum the melody of Pinkerton's letter. As the curtain falls to this soft chant, only Butterfly is still awake.

Act III

SCENE: SAME AS ACT II (31 Minutes)

An extended musical interlude again suggests the exotic sounds of the Nagasaki harbor. The curtain rises on the same scene as before, Butterfly alone standing wakeful to watch the dawn, which breaks to the sound of bells.

Butterfly rouses herself and takes the baby off to bed. No sooner has she left the room, than a knock is heard. Suzuki hastens to admit Sharpless, and with him Pinkerton.

"Hush, do not disturb her," they caution.

"Who is that in the garden?" demands Suzuki, seeing a woman wandering about in foreign dress.

Pinkerton has brought his American wife, who is to care for Butterfly's child. The faithful maid can only groan, "Woe is me, woe is me!" and join her lamentations to the remorse of Pinkerton and the suggestions of the Consul.

As she leaves, Pinkerton bids farewell to the scene of his romance while Sharpless bewails the tragedy which he alone had foreseen.

Butterfly
Suzuki
Trouble
Exeunt
Butterfly and Trouble
Enter Sharpless, Pinkerton

Exit Suzuki

Ad - di - o   fio - ri - to_a - sil,   di le - ti - zia e d'a - mor,
Fare - well___ o hap - py home, fare - well   home of love,

The lieutenant departs, ignominiously. A minute later Kate Pinkerton comes in with Suzuki.

"Then you will tell her she may trust me with the child?" asks the American.

Suzuki promises.

Exit Pinkerton Enter Kate and Suzuki

Enter Butterfly

Butterfly calls from the room above. They try to prevent her, but she comes in and faces the three of them: her maid, Sharpless, and the stranger.

"Who is this woman that frightens me so?" she asks.

They tell her gently why Mrs. Pinkerton has come.

Exeunt Kate, Sharpless and Suzuki

"I will give him his son if he will come for him himself," answers Butterfly with dignity, as they all leave her alone.

She takes a white veil from the shrine and the sacred dagger from the wall, and softly reads the words engraved on the hilt:

"Die with honor, when it is impossible to live with honor."

Enter Trouble

Suddenly the child appears, pushed toward her through the door by Suzuki.

She bids him an anguished farewell:

Andante sostenuto

Q_a me, sce - so dal tro - no del - l'al!- to Pa - ra - di - so,
My son, sent to me from heav - en, straight from the throne of glo - ry

Then, blindfolding him with the veil, and thrusting the American flag in his little hands, she goes behind the screen. The dagger is heard, clattering to the ground. Butterfly staggers out, groping for the child, and falls beside him.

Enter Pinkerton, Sharpless and Suzuki

"Butterfly! Butterfly!" Pinkerton and Sharpless rush in. They are too late. The husband falls on his knees. The Consul picks up the child and kisses him.

GIANNI SCHICCHI

GIANNI SCHICCHI, *an opera in one act with libretto by Forzano,
was given its world première at the Metropolitan Opera House on
December 14, 1919, together with two other one-act operas of
Puccini:* Il Tabarro *and* Suor Angelica. *Of the entire trilogy, only
Gianni Schicchi has survived in popular favor. It was revived in
English during the season of 1936-37 with Lawrence Tibbett as
Gianni.*

Characters, in order of appearance:

Relatives of the deceased Buoso Donati
{
Zita: *mezzo-soprano*
Simone: *bass*
Rinuccio: *tenor*
Marco: *baritone*
Ciesca: *soprano*
Gherardo: *tenor*
Nella: *soprano*
Betto: *baritone*
Gherardino: *mezzo-soprano*
}
Gianni Schicchi: *baritone*
Lauretta, his daughter: *soprano*
Spinelloccio, a physician: *bass*
Nicolao, a notary: *bass*
Two witnesses: *basses*

Time: 1299   *Place:* Florence

SCENE: BUOSO DONATI'S BEDROOM (49 Minutes)

Relatives

IT is the year 1299 in the city of Florence. One of the town's most illustrious citizens—Buoso Donati—has just died. A group of devoted relatives are gathered in his chamber, extolling the virtues of the departed.

"I'll weep forever!" exclaims one of them.

"How about a will?" asks another. "Did he leave any?"

"I've heard it said," interrupts a third, "that he's left all his wealth to the monks of Santa Reparata."

A frantic search is begun for the dead man's final testament. "I've found it!" shouts young Rinuccio, nephew of Buoso. "And I'll share my inheritance with all of you—if you allow me to marry my beloved Lauretta, Gianni Schicchi's daughter."

"All right!" grumble the relatives, who despise the rustic origin of Schicchi and his daughter. "Let us have the will!"

Rinuccio beckons to his little cousin Gherardino. "Go," he whispers, "and ask Gianni Schicchi to come here with Lauretta!" As the child runs off, Rinuccio hands the precious document to his aunt Zita.

Zita has a hard time unrolling the parchment. Finally, after a titanic struggle with the seal, she succeeds. In their anxiety to see what is written, the relatives press closely together. "We wonder," they breathe, "who will inherit poor Buoso's mule and his villa and his sawmills at Signa."

As they read, their expressions change abruptly from hope to wild fury. "He's done it!" they scream. "He's left everything to the monks!" Pacing the room in dismay, they curse the dead man and all his works.

Again, Rinuccio takes the initiative. "There is only one person in all Florence who can advise us!" he declares.

"Who?"

"Gianni Schicchi! I have sent for him."

"That peasant!" the relatives exclaim spitefully. "He's only a lout from the backwoods!"

"You're wrong!" Rinuccio answers. "Gianni is clever and wise. What if he does come from the provinces? Other great men of Florence have made their way from humble beginnings!" The orchestra announces Gianni's theme:

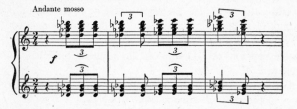

Suddenly, there is a knock at the door; the relatives resume their pose of mourning. Gianni Schicchi, long-nosed and shrewd, enters the chamber with his daughter Lauretta.

Enter Gianni and Lauretta

"Ah!" he sighs. "Such genuine bereavement! Still, you may as well cheer up. Even if Buoso has departed, there is always his money, you know."

"It's gone!" wails Zita. "And furthermore, let me tell you, Gianni Schicchi—my nephew Rinuccio will never wed your penniless daughter!"

Deeply annoyed, Gianni is on the point of leaving, when Rinuccio finally persuades him to stay. "Very well," the countryman consents. "Lauretta, run along now, and stay out on the balcony."

Exit Lauretta

When his daughter has left the room, Gianni looks keenly at the relatives: "Does anyone in town know that Buoso is dead?"

"No," they answer.

"Then no one must be told!" he commands. "Come, hide the body, remake the bed. If you send for a lawyer, I'll impersonate Buoso and dictate another will."

"Superb!" shout the relatives. "Gianni, you're a genius." Even sour old Zita joins in their tribute.

At that moment, Buoso's physician knocks on the door. "Let him come in!" Gianni commands. Hiding among the shadows, the wily peasant imitates the dead man's voice and sends the doctor away convinced that Buoso is recovering.

Enter Spinelloccio Exit Spinelloccio

"Now then," Gianni declares, donning the robe and nightcap of Buoso, "I suppose you all know that we are breaking the law. The criminal code of this city points out specifically that if anyone falsifies his name on a legal document—or if anyone aids in that falsification—he may have his right arm lopped off and be sent into exile."

Ad - dio, Fi - ren - ze, ad - dio, cie - lo di - vi - no,_____
Fare - well dear Flor - ence, dear cit - y of great charm _____

Enter
lawyer
and
witnesses
Cowed by this reminder, the relatives agree to let Gianni manage everything. He takes his place on the deathbed—and soon the lawyer arrives with two witnesses.

"I have sent for you," Gianni calls in a quavering voice, "to make my final will."

"But, Master Buoso," the lawyer protests. "Do you want your relatives in the room at such a time?"

"Oh, yes!" exclaims the pretended Buoso. "I should like to divide my money among them equally."

Exit
Rinuccio
The relatives glance at each other with expectancy. "Now he's coming to the mule and the villa and the sawmills!" they whisper.

"I leave my mule to my devoted friend, Gianni Schicchi," the dying man blandly announces.

The relatives dare not protest; they content themselves with grumbling.

"And my villa in town," the piping voice continues, "I leave to my friend Gianni Schicchi."

This is too much for Zita and her greedy troupe. "We'll not hear of it!" they cry. But as the occupant of the deathbed begins to make vague but threatening allusions to the amputation of a right arm, they subside.

"And I leave my sawmills at Signa—farewell, O dear right arm— to my friend, Gianni Schicchi."

Exeunt
lawyer
and
witnesses

Exeunt
relatives
and Gianni
The will is attested and sealed; lawyer and witnesses depart. And now the relatives advance on Schicchi with murderous intent. "Scoundrel!" they scream. "Traitor! Penniless impostor!"

"Get out of here!" he yells, throwing off the bedclothes. "This house is mine!" As the whole brood of parasites runs from one room to the other, robbing and pillaging, Gianni chases them with a stick and drives them down the stairs.

Enter
Lauretta
and
Rinuccio
Enter
Gianni
The doors that lead to the balcony are slowly opened, and as the city of Florence appears, bathed in sunlight, Rinuccio and Lauretta embrace.

Gianni, returned from pursuing the last of the relatives, looks at the lovers with satisfaction. Then he steps to the footlights and addresses the audience: "Ladies and gentlemen, I know my conduct has been questionable—but, if you have enjoyed yourselves this evening, I trust you will applaud the verdict of—NOT GUILTY!"

MONTEMEZZI

ITALO MONTEMEZZI was born in Vigasio, near Verona, Italy, on
May 31, 1875. Although sent to Milan by his family to study
engineering, he soon turned to music and was eventually admitted
to the Conservatory, in spite of inadequate elementary training.
Graduating in 1900, he worked for five years to complete his first
opera, *Giovanni Gallurese.*

With his third stage work, *L'Amore dei Tre Re,* he achieved
unquestioned fame, both within and beyond the borders of his
own country.

L'AMORE DEI TRE RE

*L'AMORE DEI TRE RE, or THE LOVE OF THREE KINGS, an opera in
three acts, was composed by Italo Montemezzi to a tragic poem
by the distinguished Italian playwright, Sem Benelli, author of
La Cena delle Beffe (The Jest).*

*First produced at La Scala in Milan on April 10, 1913, L'Amore
dei Tre Re was introduced to New York the next season, its Metropolitan première taking place on January 2, 1914, with Ferrari-
Fontana singing Avito as in the original performance.*

*Lucrezia Bori presented the part of Fiora to the Metropolitan and
continued to sing it for another season. The opera was revived in
March, 1918, and remained in the repertory for seven years. It has
subsequently reappeared at occasional intervals.*

*While composed with an uninterrupted melodic line in the
manner of Wagner, the music of Montemezzi does not make use of
thematic material to indicate definite individuals or objects, but to
heighten and illustrate the emotional intensity of the drama.*

Characters, in order of appearance:
Archibaldo, king of Altura: *bass*
Flaminio, a castle guard: *tenor*
Avito, a former prince of Altura: *tenor*
Fiora, wife of Manfredo: *soprano*
Manfredo, son of Archibaldo: *baritone*
A handmaiden: *soprano*
A young girl: *soprano*
A youth: *tenor*
An old woman: *mezzo-soprano*
Men and women of Altura

Time: Tenth Century, forty years
after a barbarian invasion
led by Archibaldo

Place: A Remote Castle
of Italy

Act I

SCENE: A HALL IN THE CASTLE (31 Minutes)

Crashing chords in the orchestra are followed by a rhythmic figure which reappears later to illustrate the vigorous barbaric horsemanship of Manfredo and his father:

As soon as the curtain rises, a quieter theme introduces the romantic nature of Manfredo's wife, Fiora, the gentle but passionate princess of Italy:

The spacious hall of a medieval castle is spanned by vaulting and lined with gleaming mosaics. Two low arches open on a terrace beyond which rise the Tuscan hills, dimly seen in the dark hour that precedes the dawn. A signal light shines faintly through the gloom.

Archibaldo and Flaminio

In flowing robes, the blind old Archibaldo, king of Altura, gropes his way into the hall from a doorway on the left, led by Flaminio, one of the castle guards. Weary from watching for the return of his son Manfredo, the King petulantly orders his servant hither and yon.

"What do you hear," he asks, "or are you dazed with slumber?

Who is it that sleeps in there?" He points to the door opposite.

"That is the room of your son's wife, Fiora," Flaminio answers patiently.

"She may well sleep," continues Archibaldo, while the melody of the prelude is repeated in the orchestra, "but when one is old like me, there is no sleep. Look again into the valley; I feel that Manfredo will return."

"Not if he goes on fighting my people in the mountains," insists his servant. "I know their courage: I was born among those hill-tops. That is why I gladly followed Princess Fiora when we gave her up to you for the sake of peace, though she was to have wedded our young Prince Avito."

The thoughts of the King also return to the past, when, as an ardent youth, he rode forth with his comrades to the conquest of Italy. The galloping theme of the prelude accompanies his glowing reminiscence of the advance of the invading army.

"If we had been the rightful children of this land," he concludes in a mighty climax, "she would teach us to conquer the world!"

Flaminio, who has no sympathy with the barbarian rulers, has heard the sound of a rustic flute in the distance, and uneasily leads his master away, putting out the lantern on the terrace, as the sky is already streaked with light. *Exeunt Archibaldo and Flaminio*

Wrapped in a mantle, the young Prince Avito emerges from Fiora's room, followed by the princess in a garment of ivory white. Her hair is dishevelled, and she clings passionately to Avito. *Enter Avito and Fiora*

"It is still night," he tells her, "but though the signal is early, it will soon be day, and we must part."

He shudders as he looks toward Archibaldo's door, but she assures him that in her love he will find peace.

Dam - mi le lab-bre e tan - ta ti da - ro di questa pace!
Give me thy lips and I will give thee of this peace!

Their passionate love scene is cut short by a second signal from the flute. The sky is growing light. Terrified by the fact that someone has extinguished the lantern, Avito hurries away by the terrace. *Exit Avito*

Archibaldo has meanwhile appeared at the door of his room, and

Enter
Archibaldo

calls persistently to Fiora, who vainly tries to escape in silence.

"I can hear you breathing," he mutters. "Whom were you talking to just now?"

"I was talking to myself," she answers. "I could not sleep, and so I came out on the terrace, thinking of Manfredo, my husband."

"Go!" he says scornfully. "Such lies from a mere child! Your words are as false as your heart. Go! If I laid hands on you, I would kill you!"

The sound of trumpets without announce the arrival of Manfredo. Archibaldo sends Flaminio to meet his master, then bitterly orders Fiora back to her room.

Enter
Flaminio
Exit
Flaminio
Exit
Fiora
Enter
Manfredo

Father and son embrace each other with warmth. "I have returned for a few days from the siege," announces the warrior. "The war will soon be over, and this brief homecoming is as dear to me as a long awaited reward. Surely Fiora will learn to love me. . . ."

Enter
Fiora

Passionately he turns to greet his wife, who appears at the door of her room, concealing the coldness of her heart with kind words of welcome.

"I came out on the terrace before dawn to look for you," she says, then turning to the old man, asks, "Is it not so, father?"

Archibaldo smothers his suspicions. Rather than hurt his son, he will assent to her deceptive tale.

Exeunt
Manfredo
and Fiora

"Fiora!" cries the joyful Manfredo. "Let me fold you in my arms, and I will carry you back to your ivory bed. You see, father," he continues, turning to Archibaldo as he leaves the room with his wife, "your son has found his happiness."

Left alone, the old King raises his hands to Heaven. "O Lord," he prays, "since thou hast taken my eyes, let me indeed be blind!"

Act II

SCENE: A TERRACE OF THE CASTLE (38 Minutes)

THE shifting clouds of a summer afternoon cast their shadows on a lofty circular terrace above the castle. From the top of the surrounding battlement, a staircase descends toward a bench that flanks the base of the wall. Distant trumpets sound a retreat.

Manfredo
and Fiora

Manfredo and Fiora approach the terrace from a door at the left. She is dressed in a richly embroidered garment.

"Tell me, Fiora," he begs her, "why are you so silent in the face of my grief at leaving you again?"

"I am sad only at your departure, my lord," she answers.

He begs her for some token that he may keep close to his heart.

"You wish my entire life!" she cries, the misery she has repressed for years suddenly bursting from her lips.

To the galloping theme of the prelude, Manfredo pictures his approaching journey down the valley. The tower where they stand now will be the last bit of home he will see.

"Oh, climb to the wall," he begs her, "and wave a greeting with your scarf. That is all I ask."

"And that shall be done," she answers, moved with sincere pity. **Exit Manfredo**

With a final embrace he rushes away, leaving her free at last. Shaking off the memory of his kiss, she ascends the steps and stands looking out over the wall, while a new agitated figure echoes from the orchestra:

Suddenly she hears the voice of Avito, calling her. Flaminio has lent him a guard's uniform, and he has made his way to her from the door on the right. **Enter Avito**

"I cannot see you any more," she tells him desperately. "My husband has won me at last; conquered me by compassion. You must leave me in peace."

At the sound of footsteps, Avito retires. A handmaiden brings a long white scarf from Manfredo. **Handmaiden**

Fiora mounts again to her post on the wall and wearily waves the scarf. Avito returns for a last farewell, and reaches up for the long wisp of white still clinging to her fingers, but she forbids him to touch it.

"There is nothing of you then, that belongs to me?" he asks sadly.

"Your life is mine," she answers, "but I have done evil to you." Again she waves the scarf.

"Come closer," she continues, "you may at least kiss the garment which I myself embroidered."

He seizes her mantle and covers it with kisses, and then, pleading with her to descend, receives her, half fainting in his arms. "Look up at me," he cries, rousing her to rapture by his own, "we are in Heaven!"

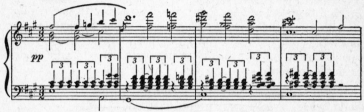

Enter Archibaldo and Flaminio

The rhapsody of the lovers is rudely shattered by the arrival of Archibaldo who has found his way to the terrace, followed by Flaminio.

Exit Avito

Avito draws his dagger and is about to rush upon the old man, when he is stopped by the guard. At the pleading gesture of Fiora, her lover departs.

"Who is there, Flaminio?" anxiously demands the King.

Exit Flaminio

"No one," stammers the servant, "but the Baron Manfredo has turned his horse and is riding homewards." Archibaldo dismisses him with an order to meet his master.

Left alone with Fiora, the old man again demands to know who has been with her. After repeated denials she rises as his groping fingers reach her where she cowers on the bench, crying: "He who has fled was my true lover, and when I think of him I know no fear, even of you."

Seizing her by the throat, Archibaldo reiterates his question.

"His name," she says at last in a clear voice, "is sweet death."

"If you die, I shall know how to track your lover," threatens the King, and raging at her falsehoods, chokes away her life.

Throbbing chords in the orchestra ebb to a gruesome silence. "Night is falling," muses Archibaldo, "I hear only the surging fury of my blood. And now soon Manfredo will return to his delight."

Enter Manfredo

"Fiora," calls his son, hastening to his side. "Where is she? I could no longer see her waving veil."

"I have slain her," answers the old man. "She was as impure as she was fair, betraying you in your own house."

"Then she was capable of love," says Manfredo wistfully, "though I was not the man. What was his name?"

"Alas I am blind and could not see him," answers Archibaldo. "Now lead my steps away; you must not see the marks of my fingers on her throat." Lifting the body of Fiora to his shoulders, the old King carries her out, following his son.

ACT III

SCENE: THE CRYPT IN THE CASTLE CHAPEL (18 Minutes)

BENEATH the dim mosaic arches of the chapel crypt lies Fiora on her bier of flowers. A group of veiled women are gathered at a distance, while men and youths stand with bare heads.

From the chapel above, the voices of the choir are heard chanting of the eternal life which shall some day be the lot of man.

"I have come with tears," says a young girl, "and found that the world is weeping with me."

An old woman reads a mute plea for revenge on the white face of Fiora. Other women take up the cry for vengeance. The tolling of bells warns them that they must depart. The old woman catches sight of Avito, who approaches from the stairs at the left. He stands motionless until all have gone out.

"We are alone," he exclaims, coming close to Fiora. "Speak to me—surely there is one breath left for me in those lips!" Weeping he throws himself desperately beside her, and presses his lips on hers.

"A miracle!" he cries at last, staggering in agony to his feet. "I too shall perish!" He totters to the door where Manfredo looms, standing like a shadowy apparition.

"We have caught you then," he says to Avito. "So you were the man she loved. It is well that you are dying. Not in vain did my father spread the poison on her lips. Only one thing I do not know. Tell me, did Fiora love you?"

"More than the life they took from her," is Avito's answer.

Manfredo helps him gently to the ground, then lifts his own hands to Heaven. "My God!" he cries, "why is there no hate in me?" Leaning over the bier, he too kisses the lips of Fiora and stands quivering beside her.

The ancient Archibaldo gropes his way toward them. "I heard a groan," he mutters. "I have found the robber."

"No, father," cries Manfredo in a dying voice. "You are wrong. It is I you have caught!"

"Ah, Manfredo!" answers the old man. "You too are beyond salvation with me in the shadows!"

Margin notes:
Men and women
Young girl
Old woman
Exeunt people
Enter Avito
Enter Manfredo
Enter Archibaldo

XI

Opera at the Crossroads

At the end of the nineteenth century, the shadow of Richard Wagner loomed like a mighty mountain over the field of opera. So thoroughly had this man influenced every phase of operatic endeavor, that even in death he threatened to eclipse all of his successors.

As an escape from "Wagnerism," with its implied lack of originality, most of the younger composers sought another medium. Engelbert Humperdinck, who applied Wagnerian principles to the children's opera *Hänsel und Gretel,* had sufficient skill to preserve his identity; and Richard Strauss, despite his close adherence to the Wagnerian pattern, has produced operas of striking individuality.

Two devices especially sacred to Wagner have been pushed by Strauss to their ultimate limits. One is the symphonic treatment of the orchestra, with an ever increasing number of men and instruments; the other is the bold, dramatic style of writing for voice with wide skips and difficult intervals. In the hands of a first-rate talent such as Strauss, this extension of Wagnerian technique has proven valuable and stimulating. When essayed by other, less gifted composers, it has sometimes led to a fatal conflict between singers and orchestra. Wagner has not proved fertile ground for further evolution. In general, his methods have either been followed literally, or used as a point of radical departure.

Claude Debussy chose the latter course. The system of leading motives was all that he adopted from Wagner; for the rest, he used his own devices: tenuous harmonies, delicate orchestration, and a plaintive type of song-speech known as *parlando*. This technique—labeled impressionism—found an admirable outlet in *Pelléas et Mélisande,* but has had little effect on the general evolution of opera—for Debussy's methods were too highly personal to invite development by other composers.

Between the extremes of Wagner and Debussy, a middle group has sprung up, assimilating what is best in both masters and adding to it an original contribution of talents. Modern Italian opera has evolved largely in this manner, particularly in the works of Ottorino Respighi (1879-1936) whose *La Campana Sommersa* (The Sunken Bell) was performed at the Metropolitan Opera House in 1929. Ildebrando Pizzetti (1880-) is another composer who has been content to fuse a distinguished personal idiom with a generous alloy of eclecticism. His *Fra Gherardo* was given at the Metropolitan in 1928 with Edward Johnson in the title role.

Besides the post-Wagnerian and the impressionistic varieties of opera, a third type has blossomed: the naturalistic. Begun by Gustave Charpentier with the working girl romance of *Louise,* it has since been led into the back alleys by Alban Berg (1885-1935) with the sordid background of *Wozzeck* (1921) and the Jack the Ripper conclusion of *Lulu* (1934). In each of these works, the singing voice is treated as an orchestral instrument, with supreme demands made upon its powers of pitch and volume.

A complexity of causes, attributable chiefly to the comparative youth of this country, the pressing economic expansion, and the flux of nationalities, may explain why the United States has not yet produced any lasting addition to the standard repertory. Among the more significant operas to the credit of American composers are *Peter Ibbetson* by Deems Taylor (1885-), which was given its première at the Metropolitan Opera House in 1931; *Four Saints in Three Acts* by Virgil Thomson (1896-), first presented in the Avery Memorial Theatre, Hartford (1934), by the Friends and Enemies of Modern Music; and *Porgy and Bess* by George Gershwin (1898-1937), a Theatre Guild production, given at the Alvin Theatre, New York, in 1935.

In regard to modern and particularly American opera, the question may be asked: why not more novelties at the Metropolitan? The answer can be stated briefly: New scores are constantly examined by the management, but unless they show definite promise of longevity, they are ruled out. In an organization with so large and so closely planned a budget as the Metropolitan Opera Association, the general manager cannot court financial disaster by presenting a work of doubtful appeal. When an American opera arrives that is equal to Metropolitan standards, it is produced. There is no such factor in modern opera production as a prejudice for or against American music. Everything depends upon the viability of the work itself.

Not only American opera, but lyric drama throughout the world today is in a period of suspension. Marching along the road begun by Peri and carried further by Gluck, Mozart, Beethoven, Gounod and Verdi, we can look back and see the lofty summit of Wagner behind us. Ahead, there is a mist. When it lifts, will another shining peak be revealed—or an abyss? No one can foretell. Opera is at the crossroads.

HUMPERDINCK

ENGELBERT HUMPERDINCK was born at Siegburg, near Bonn, Germany, on September 1, 1854, and was persuaded to desert architecture for music by his first piano teacher, Ferdinand Hiller. As winner of the Meyerbeer prize he visited France and Italy, where he met Richard Wagner, and was invited to Bayreuth. A close friend of the family, and instructor of Siegfried Wagner, Humperdinck assisted at the première of *Parsifal,* by ringing the Monsalvat bells. He also composed additional music which was used for rehearsal of the transformation scenes, but later eliminated.

As music critic and teacher, his influence extended as far as Barcelona, where he taught for two years, returning to occupy positions in Cologne and Frankfort.

Humperdinck's contribution to opera, as seen in *Hänsel und Gretel* and *Königskinder,* which was performed at the Metropolitan with Geraldine Farrar as the goose girl from 1910-1915, was the treatment of simple folk themes with a skilful contrapuntal sophistication which did not in any way detract from their freshness and charm. His musical settings of Shakespeare and other classics, written after 1900, when he became director of the *Akademische Meisterschule* in Berlin were less successful than his operas, but bear similar witness to his fine technical command. He died at Neustrelitz on September 27, 1921.

HÄNSEL UND GRETEL

HÄNSEL UND GRETEL, *a fairy opera in three scenes, was composed by Engelbert Humperdinck for his sister, Adelheid Wette, who had written a little play on Grimm's old nursery tale for her own children to act.*

First performed at Weimar, Germany, during Christmas week, 1893, it came to New York two years later, and was unsuccessfully performed in English at Daly's Theatre. Since November, 1905, when it was first produced at the Metropolitan under the direction of the composer, and repeated ten times, it has enjoyed nearly a hundred performances.

Characters, in order of appearance:

Gretel: *soprano*
Hänsel: *mezzo-soprano*
Gertrude, their mother: *mezzo-soprano*
Peter the broom maker, their father: *baritone*
The Sandman: *soprano*
The Dewman: *soprano*
The Witch: *mezzo-soprano*
The fourteen angels, children, wood voices

Time: The days of witches and fairies *Place:* A forest in Germany

THE OVERTURE

The overture opens with a melody used later as the Children's Prayer:

After extensive development, this is followed by other themes which reappear in the opera, and then is repeated tranquilly at the close.

ACT I

SCENE 1: AT HOME (30 Minutes)

Hänsel and Gretel

IN a forest hut, Hänsel is busy binding a broom for his father. His sister Gretel sits beside him, knitting a stocking and singing a little nursery rhyme about the geese that have to go barefoot because the cobbler can't make them shoes:

Hänsel adds a verse of his own.

"How I would like a pennysworth of bread and sugar," he sighs. "For a week there has been nothing but stale crusts."

"Hush, Hänsel," returns Gretel reprovingly. "What has mother said so often?

> *'When in direst need we stand,*
> *God will offer us His hand.'"*

Her voice repeats the first phrase of the Prayer.

Since Hänsel goes on grumbling, she takes a broom and chases him about the hut.

"If you will only behave, I will tell you a secret," she promises, and finally shows him a great jug of milk which a neighbor has brought them:

"Mother will surely make us a pudding when she gets home."

To express their joy, they break into a merry dance, Gretel leading, Hänsel trying clumsily to follow her:

Poco animato

Mit dem Füs-schen tapp, tapp, tapp;   mit den Händchen klapp,klapp,klapp;
With your foot you tap, tap; tap;   with your hands you clap, clap, clap;

At the height of the excitement Gertrude, their mother, flings open the door.

Enter Gertrude

"What on earth is going on?" she asks, angry that they have left their work. Running after them to administer a cuff, she knocks over the milkjug.

"What shall we have for supper now?" she wails. Hänsel's laughter provokes her still more. "Take this basket," she orders crossly, "and fill it with strawberries in the forest."

Exeunt Hänsel and Gretel

The children run away in terror. Gertrude sinks exhausted, and leaning her head on her arm, falls asleep over her prayers.

A rollicking voice drifts through the window. A minute later Peter the broom maker staggers into the hut, singing joyously:

Enter Peter

Commodo

Ral - la - la - la,   ral - la la - la,   Hun-ger ist der bes-te   Koch
Ral - la - la - la,   ral - la la - la,   hun-ger is the best of   cooks!

"That's a pretty song!" retorts Gertrude bitterly, wakened by the noise. "The cupboard is bare, and we have nothing to eat."

Peter merely laughs, and starts to empty his basket.

"What do I see?" exclaims his wife, helping him to unpack it. "Eggs, and beans, and coffee, and potatoes!" While the good things scatter over the floor, she dances with him for joy.

He tells her of his luck in town. Everybody bought one of his brooms for the holiday. "But where are the children?" he demands, his mug of beer halfway to his lips.

Gertrude tells him of the broken pitcher, and he laughs heartily. But when she informs him that she has sent Hänsel and Gretel into the Ilsenstein forest, he snatches a broomstick from the wall in alarm.

"Don't you know that a wicked old witch lives in that forest?" he asks, shuddering. "At midnight she rides out on her broomstick, hunting for children. By day she bakes them into cookies in her magic oven so that she can eat them." His voice reflects the terror of his words, as he and Gertrude vow to find the youngsters:

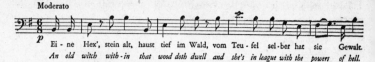

Ei - ne Hex', stein alt, haust tief im Wald, vom Teu - fel sel - ber hat sie Gewalt.
An old witch with - in that wood doth dwell and she's in league with the powers of hell.

A musical interlude entitled "The Witch's Ride" ushers in the second scene without intermission. First sounds the melody to which Peter has sung the words, "The broomstick."

Then come the wilder rhythms of The Witch's Ride,

and finally the serene harmonies of the Children's Prayer.

SCENE 2: IN THE WOODS (20 Minutes)

Gretel Under the trees of the great forest at sunset, Gretel sits weaving a garland of roses and singing an old nursery rhyme:

Ein Männ-lein steht im Wal - de ganz still und stumm,
There stands a lit - tle man in the wood a - lone,

Enter Hänsel Hänsel comes running in, his basket full of berries. Gretel tries to crown him with her garland.

"That is meant for a girl," he retorts, twining it in her hair. "You look like the Queen of the Woods," and he presents her with a bouquet.

A cuckoo calls softly through the forest, and the children try to imitate him. "Cuckoos steal eggs," explains the boy, and he starts nibbling the strawberries. Soon the children are quarreling over the basket, and devouring the contents.

"It's too late to pick any more berries," mourns Gretel, woefully. Her brother vainly searches for the path through the wood. The shadows deepen. Will-o'-the-wisps flicker in the bushes. Terrified,

Hänsel and Gretel call for help. Distant echoes frighten them the more.

At length a friendly little man dressed in gray approaches the children and quiets them with his gentle voice, sprinkling their eyes with sand from his bag with a gentle hissing noise:

As he disappears, brother and sister kneel together to repeat their Evening Prayer:

> *"When at night I go to sleep,*
> *Fourteen angels watch do keep."*

Huddling together, they sink down in the moss, arm in arm, while darkness falls about them.

Suddenly a brilliant light shines through the trees, unfolding a vision of fourteen angels. Down a celestial stair they descend silently and raise their hands in blessing over the children.

The Sandman's song gives way to the theme of the Children's Prayer which rises to a mighty climax from the trumpets and trombones and then dies away.

Act II

SCENE: THE GINGERBREAD HUT (36 Minutes)

The opening motive of the prelude is associated with the evil witch:

Then comes a flowing melody which we have heard in the Overture, and which suggests the coming of dawn in the forest:

A FILMY mist hangs over the wood where the children lie asleep, but gradually rises as the sturdy little Dewman marches in and sprinkles them with dew from a bluebell.

"I come with drops of cooling dew,
And in the sunlight waken you,"

he sings to the dawn music, and hurries away.

The children awake in the best of spirits. They warble like birds and frolic under the trees.

"I had a wonderful dream," declares Gretel, describing the angelic vision in the melody of the night before.

As the last traces of the mist have lifted, another surprise is in store. In the depths of the forest stands a marvelous gingerbread house, trimmed with candy, and surrounded by a fence of cookies.

Stunned at first, they approach it gleefully:

Allegretto

Wie duf - tet's von dor - ten, o schau nur die - se Pracht!__
What o - dor de - li - cious o say do I dream!__

They summon up courage to nibble a bit of cake from the wall when a shrill voice calls from within:

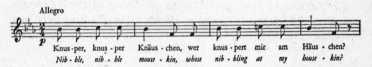

Allegro

Knus-per, knus-per Knäus-chen, wer knus-pert mir am Häus-chen?
Nib - ble, nib - ble mouse - kin, whose nib - bling at my house - kin?

Enter Witch

Since the warning is not repeated, they go on munching hungrily. Thus they do not see the wicked witch stealing up to them until she has thrown a rope about Hänsel's neck.

"Get out of my sight!" shouts Hänsel. "Let me go, I hate you!"

The witch screams with laughter and invites them to a feast in her house:

Poco allegretto

Kommt, klei - ne Mäus-lein, kommt in mein Häus - lein
Come, lit - tle mouse - y, come in to my house - y!

"What are you going to do to my brother?" puts in Gretel bravely.

"I'm going to fatten him up and give him a pleasant surprise."

The children do not trust her lying words and try to escape, but she halts them, waving her wand and muttering a magic spell:

Ho-kus po-kus, Hex-en-schuss!
Ho-cus, po-cus, witch-es' charm!

Triumphantly the witch thrusts Hänsel into a little cage and slams the door, leaving him alone with Gretel, while she goes into the house to find sweets for his breakfast.

Hänsel meanwhile shrewdly pretends to fall asleep, so the Witch mumbles on:

"I'll eat Gretel first, she's so nice and plump."

She heaps up a fresh fire under the oven near the cage, and then, mounting a broomstick, as a mysterious darkness descends over the wood, sweeps through the air to the music of The Witch's Ride, which has been heard in the interlude of Act I.

No sooner has she descended than daylight returns. She goes over to the cage.

"Show me your finger," she croaks.

Hänsel cleverly thrusts a bone through the bars of the cage.

"How thin you are!" she exclaims. "Gretel, bring some raisins and almonds!"

Returning with the goodies from the house, Gretel finds a juniper branch, just like the witch's wand. Perhaps she too can work a spell.

"Hocus pocus," she whispers, and Hänsel, magically released from his bonds, creeps out of his cage, and hides behind his sister.

The witch beckons Gretel to the oven. "Come here, child, and see if the gingerbread is ready. Just stand on tiptoe and look inside.

Gretel pretends not to understand. "Show me what you mean," she begs slyly.

As the witch leans inside the glowing oven, the children spring on her from behind, shove her in and lock the door. A great flame leaps from the chimney as the witch is baked into cake.

Exit Witch into oven

"Hurrah," cry the children, "the witch is dead!" and stuffing themselves with sugarplums they waltz gaily about, shouting:

Juch-hei! Nun ist die Hex-e tot, mau-se-tot, und aus die Noth!
Hur-rah! Now sing the witch is dead, real-ly dead, no more to dread!

A loud explosion interrupts them. The oven has blown up. When the dust has settled, the astonished brother and sister notice that the cookie fence has disappeared and in its place a score of children

Children come to life

stand stiffly in a row. Another wave of the magic wand, and Gretel summons them to life. Joyously they form a ring and dance about the pair singing:

Die Hex-e - rei ist nun vor - bei,
The — witch's might is bro - ken quite,

Enter Gertrude and Peter

To make their happiness complete, Peter and Gertrude hasten toward them with the warmest embraces. Two boys go to the ruins of the oven and fetch a huge cookie from the ashes. It is the witch herself, browned to a turn.

One and all join in a hymn of thanksgiving to the familiar words:

When in direst need we stand
God will offer us His hand.

CHARPENTIER

GUSTAVE CHARPENTIER was born in the village of Dieuze in Lorraine on June 25, 1860. After the Franco-Prussian War his family moved to Tourcoing near Lille, where the composer made his first musical studies.

Accepted by the Paris *Conservatoire* in 1881, he worked there with Massenet, and followed the example of his master by carrying off the *Grand Prix de Rome* in 1887. His winning composition was the cantata *Didon*. In 1912 he succeeded Massenet to the French Academy.

Charpentier's operas, *Louise* and *Julien*, depart from the prevailing romanticism of the nineteenth century lyric drama in France, and reflect both the realistic tendencies of the turn of the century, and their composer's consuming interest in the welfare of the working classes.

LOUISE

Both the text and music for Louise *are the work of its composer, Gustave Charpentier, who explained his use of the term a "musical romance," by his concern with the two chief elements of the romance or novel: description and dramatic action. The essential clash of the drama he placed between the heroine's love for her family and her longing for happiness and liberty. He attributed the triumph of the latter to a "mysterious auxiliary": the call of Paris itself, city of light and pleasure.*

Louise *was first produced at the* Opéra Comique *in Paris on February 2, 1900. In the following April on the same stage it served as the medium for the operatic debut of Mary Garden who replaced an indisposed prima donna in the third act. Miss Garden's success led to a continued association with the part which she introduced to New York in 1907. In January, 1921, Louise was added to the Metropolitan repertory, and ran for two seasons with Geraldine Farrar in the title role. Nine years later it was revived for four performances with Lucrezia Bori.*

Characters, in order of appearance:

Julien, a poet: *tenor*
Louise: *soprano*
The mother: *mezzo-soprano*
The father: *bass*
A young ragpicker: *soprano*
A coal picker: *contralto*
A noctambulist: *tenor*
A newspaper girl: *soprano*
A milk woman: *soprano*
A junk man: *bass*
A ragpicker: *baritone*
1st policeman: *tenor*
2nd policeman: *baritone*
A street arab: *soprano*
A street sweeper: *contralto*

A painter: *baritone* ⎤
A sculptor: *baritone* ⎮
The song writer: *baritone* ⎮
1st philosopher: *bass* ⎬ Bohemians
2nd philosopher: *bass* ⎮
A young poet: *tenor* ⎮
A student: *tenor* ⎦

A chair mender: *contralto*
An artichoke vendor: *soprano*
A bird food vendor: *soprano*
A carrot vendor: *tenor*
A water cress vendor: *contralto*
A green peas vendor: *tenor*

Blanche: *soprano* ⎤
Marguerite: *contralto* ⎬ sewing girls
Suzanne: *soprano* ⎮
Gertrude: *contralto* ⎦

Irma: *soprano* ⎫
Camille: *soprano* ⎪
Elsie: *soprano* ⎬ sewing girls
Madeleine: *mezzo-soprano* ⎭
An errand girl: *soprano*
The forewoman: *contralto*
An old clothes man: *tenor*
King of the Fools: *tenor*
Bohemians, dwellers of Montmartre, dancers

Time: About the year 1900   *Place:* Paris

Act I

SCENE: THE MANSARD ROOM OF A WORKINGMAN'S TENEMENT
(38 Minutes)

THE vigorous theme of Julien is announced by the orchestra and
repeated both in major and minor modes:

The evening light of April falls on the shabby table and chairs
of a workingman's home through a large window which opens on
a balcony. Beyond it a small neighboring terrace is framed by the
uneven roofs of the city.

Through the kitchen door on the right of the room, pots and
pans shine on their shelves. Near the front another door gives onto
the room of Louise's father and mother, while on the extreme left
next to the balcony is her own room.

Through the open window floats the voice of Julien the poet, who
has stationed himself on his balcony, and addresses his beloved.

First tiptoeing to the central entrance door of the apartment
and listening for footsteps, Louise approaches the balcony, reas-
sured that she is alone.

"In your last letter you told me to write your father again,"
pleads her lover. "You promised that if he refused you would run
away with me."

"I must have been mad," she answers earnestly. "I love you so
much—and yet I love them too. If I listen to them, it is death to
my heart; if I follow you, it is misery for them. In a moment my
mother will return. Tell me quickly how did you come to love me?"

"I saw you first in the dark, on the stairs," he confesses, "and
loved your fragile beauty. The next day was Easter; the whole city

Julien
(*off stage*)

Louise

celebrated with me when I saw you at your window like a Madonna."

"Oh, I had noticed you long before that," she puts in gaily, not Enter mother seeing that her mother has crept into the room and listens slyly to the conversation. "Once at the fete in Montmartre mother was annoyed by the way you smiled at me. Then, later, when I was drawing water in the courtyard, you showered me with rose petals. . . ."

"And once you came to your door," he continues, "and though we did not speak, our hearts told of our love."

Louise turns again to the door and, horrified, sees that her mother has listened to every word. The old woman clutches the girl by the arm and thrusts her into the kitchen. Then she brusquely orders Julien to be quiet, and when he defiantly resumes his serenading theme, slams the window shut.

When Louise comes back, trying to steady her nerves by putting away the provisions that her mother has brought from market, she has to listen to a cruel travesty on the words of her lover.

"If your father knew of this," shouts the old woman, after she has exhausted her powers of mimicry, "it would surely kill him."

"But why won't you let us get married?" cries the girl, beseechingly. "What have you against him? His gaiety? His poet's profession? His goodness and courage?"

"He's a shameless ne'er-do-well. You have nerve to boast of your lover."

"He is not my lover—yet," answers Louise firmly. "It would almost seem as if you wanted to drive us to it."

The sound of footsteps on the stairs puts an end to the discus-Enter father sion. The mother hurries into the kitchen to prepare for the father who comes in, dressed in humble working clothes, and sits down near the stove. Julien's letter is in his hand. Slowly he reads it, as the girl sets the table for supper; then, without a word, he draws her to him and kisses her tenderly. All three sit down to supper. The father serves the soup, and the three partake in silence. Then the mother carries the dishes away and brings in the meat.

The father philosophizes on the weary lot of the workingman. "Everyone has his place in the world. Happiness does not lie in wealth, but in the peace of home and loved ones." His theme reflects the serenity of his nature:

Lento

The old man takes up his pipe, and Louise hands her father the letter which he has laid aside. From the kitchen door she listens to her parents' discussion.

The father gently suggests further investigation of Julien's prospects and character. The mother is obdurate: if Julien is invited to the house, she will leave it. Finally, as the girl blurts a denial of her mother's accusations, the old woman strikes her.

The father intervenes. He pleads with his daughter that love has blinded her to the truth, that she lacks experience, that she must learn to forget Julien. From the next room echoes the mother's mockery of Julien's serenade.

"Take the paper," says the father kindly, "it will distract your mind to read me the news."

Sobbing, the girl starts to read: "The season is at its height, Paris is celebrating the spring. . . ."

ACT II

SCENE 1: AN OPEN CROSS WAY AT THE FOOT OF MONTMARTRE
(30 Minutes)

The awakening of a great city is depicted in the orchestral prelude by means of several themes, the first suggesting the underlying pulse of Paris;

the second evoking the romantic associations of its people;

the third typifying the constantly increasing activity of its streets.

THE mists of an early morning in April hang heavily over a dingy square at the foot of Montmartre. At the left, stone steps lead down to the streets below; at the right, a similar flight winds up toward the crest of the hill. Under a shed a frowsy milk woman is loading her pushcart. Near her a girl folds the morning papers for

Milk woman, newsgirl, ragpicker, coal gatherer, junkman

delivery. A young ragpicker examines the piles of rubbish at the right, sharing her booty with a coal gatherer, and a junk man.

"Just think, women are sleeping in silk at this very moment," sighs the girl.

"Your turn will come," hints the coal gatherer.

Enter noctambulist
Exit noctambulist

A strange figure in black hovers among the scavengers. It is the noctambulist, wandering in search of laughter and love.

"He is mad," remarks the newspaper girl at his fantastic declarations. The stranger runs off laughing, and collides with an old ragpicker.

Enter old ragpicker

"He ruined my daughter," sobs the old man, picking himself up.

"You can't hold your daughters in this town," puts in the junk man, "and you can't blame them if they prefer what they call heaven to the hell's life we lead."

Two policemen, street sweeper, urchin

The little ragpicker holds out her thin arms toward the first rays of the morning sun glinting from the roofs on the hill above. Two policemen saunter past on their early round. A street sweeper starts work with her broom. An urchin warms his hands at the milk woman's fire.

"Twenty years ago I had a carriage and a pair," boasts the street sweeper. "What a good time we had in that paradise!"

Exeunt scavengers and work-people
Enter Julien and Bohemians

"What was the address?" asks the urchin, pertly.

"Why Paris, of course!"

One by one the creatures of the night disappear.

A new rhythm pulses through the theme of the city as Julien beckons his Bohemian friends toward a house on the right.

"Louise's mother will leave her here at work," he tells them. "Then I'll be able to get her away with me."

"Too bad we didn't bring our instruments for a serenade," says the sculptor to the painter.

The song writer sings a ditty for the benefit of the various people who have come to their windows to see who is making the noise.

Exeunt Bohemians

Two philosophers note that everybody in Paris wants to be somebody else. Then they all leave Julien alone.

In the distance sound the familiar cries of the street vendors, selling rags and artichokes, carrots and bird seed, brooms, potatoes and green peas.

"It is the voice of Paris!" exults Julien. "Does it mean victory for our love?"

Sewing girls

Early arrivals among the sewing girls of the dressmaking establishment greet each other and disappear in the house on the right. Julien hides under the shed to watch them.

At length he sees Louise and her mother approaching. The old woman withdraws, peering distrustfully at the windows of the workrooms where she has left her daughter.

Julien hesitates, then boldly follows Louise and brings her back to the street with him. Reminding her of her promise to elope with him, he entreats her to cut loose from her parents. "If you love me, do not keep me waiting longer," he pleads.

She puts him off, throwing him a kiss as she goes back to work. "Tomorrow—perhaps later—I will come to you."

The old clothes man drags himself on his rounds, shouting his wares. Julien wanders dejectedly away. From the distance echo the morning cries of Paris.

SCENE 2: A SEWING ROOM IN A DRESSMAKING ESTABLISHMENT
(18 Minutes)

The whirring of sewing machines is suggested in the orchestral prelude, followed by the passionate theme of Julien's first declaration, which is again lost in the bustling motion as the curtain rises.

At tables littered high with silks and muslins sit some twenty girls, laughing, grumbling and gossiping. Two of them pin the pleats of a skirt to a form. A little apprentice is busy picking up pins.

A word from the forewoman brings silence for a moment.

The girls notice Louise, sitting pensively apart.

"She looks as if she had been crying," says one.

"She has a hard life," they agree. "Her mother beats her as if she were a child. Perhaps she is in love."

At this idea every girl tries to express her own views on the eternal subject.

"What thrills me," explains Irma, "is that mysterious voice of Paris, with its promises of pleasure."

A fanfare of horns from the street below calls them to the window. It is Julien come with his friends to serenade Louise. At first they applaud his lively song, although Louise herself is mortified by the conspicuousness of his attentions. Later, as his pleas become more passionate, the girls make fun of him, dancing gleefully about the room.

At length, desperate at their teasing, and worried that one of them may win Julien from her if she does not respond to his appeals, Louise takes her hat and hurries out of the door.

Margin notes:

Enter Louise and mother Exit mother

Exit Louise Old clothesman

Sewing girls, apprentice

Forewoman, Louise

Irma

Julien (*off stage*)

Exit Louise

The apprentice runs to the window. "They are going off together!" she cries, while the entire room breaks into laughter.

ACT III

SCENE: A SMALL GARDEN ON THE SLOPES OF MONTMARTRE
(45 Minutes)

The prelude opens with a theme to be associated with Julien's philosophy of personal liberty:

Then it continues with a single interval which opens Louise's joyous meditation.

Louise, Julien

SHE stands, lost in thought, leaning on the railing of the steps of the little house where Julien has brought her. In the garden, the poet sits reading a book by the fading light of dusk. Back of him a low wall pierced by a narrow gate is continued by a hedge, while beyond it extends a wide vista of the city of Paris, the Eiffel Tower rising among its many monuments. To the right, opposite the house, rises the scaffolding of the unfinished church of Sacré Coeur.

Smiling, Louise tells her lover of the new joy she has felt each day since first she gave herself to him:

De - puis le jour où je me suis don - né - e,
Since that first day when of my - self I gave you,

"You regret nothing?" he asks, and smiles to hear the old story of the persecutions of home. "Everyone has the right to be free," he declares; "every heart has the duty to love." The theme which opened the prelude reinforces his convictions.

Louise refuses to listen to his harsh criticisms of her parents, but he quiets her reproaches.

"It is for you, darling, that the city will make merry tonight," he tells her, "for you are the very symbol of the beauty that is Paris."

Together they repeat their hymn: "Paris, city of joy and love, be kind to us who love!" The theme of the city's romance is softly hinted. Lights prick up across the great scene below them. The boulevards spring into outline. Rockets burst in colored flares.

The rhapsody of the lovers rises to new heights. Transfigured by passion, Louise repeats Julien's first declaration of love with a new urgency. At length they disappear into the house.

Exeunt Julien and Louise Enter Bohemians

A moment of silence is interrupted by distant drums. They herald the arrival of a single gay Bohemian who leaps over the hedge, notices the light in an upper room of the little house, and beckons gaily to his companions. Others bring paper festoons and lanterns with which they decorate the garden, singing softly as they work.

Townspeople join the party. Beggars perch themselves in the scaffolding. A band marches in, followed by swarms of street urchins. A couple of comic policemen, mounted on toy horses, chase them back. The sewing girls have dressed themselves in gay dominoes. The noctambulist sports the motley of the King of the Fools.

Townspeople, beggars, policemen, sewing girls, King of the Fools

By the time that Louise and Julien appear on the steps of their house, the entire garden is filled with revelers, singing the glories of their Muse.

Enter Louise and Julien

The King of the Fools introduces to Louise a young dancer who waltzes as he sings of her charms. Then to the shouts of the multitude, he crowns Louise Queen of Bohemia. The sewing girls deck her with a festive mantle. In a gay procession the company defiles past her with waving banners.

Dancer

At length a rumor spreads dismay through the crowd. Louise's mother has made her way into their midst, unwanted. The old woman approaches them timidly, blinded by the lights. Gradually the revelers disperse.

Enter mother

"I do not come as an enemy," she says humbly to Julien, who has placed Louise behind him for safety. "But Louise's father is ill, she alone can save him. I beg of you to let her return. I promise she will come back to you."

Exeunt revelers

Julien gives his permission, so, with a last kiss, Louise follows her mother through the garden gate.

Exeunt Louise and mother

Act IV

SCENE: LOUISE'S HOME, AS IN ACT I (28 Minutes)

The peaceful theme of the father opens the prelude, followed by memories of Julien's love song and Louise's joyous meditation.

THOUGH it is late of a summer evening, Louise is still at work in her room, and her mother busy at washing in the kitchen. The old woman brings in a cup of tea to the father, seated reflectively at his table. She cannot interest him in the improvements which have brought new light to the window. Julien's balcony has been torn down.

Father, mother, Louise

"Yes, many things have disappeared," murmurs the old man, "and with them much happiness. There is joy in bringing up a child to the beauty of womanhood, but when some wretch steals her away and makes a stranger of her, nothing is left but discord and hatred."

The mother calls her daughter away from the balcony where she has wandered disconsolately. In vain the girl reminds her of the promise to let her return to her lover.

The father adds his plea that Louise become again the docile little girl she used to be. He recalls a lullaby of the good old days:

His tenderness has no more effect than the bitter reproaches of his wife. Louise can only repeat her lover's creed of liberty.

"It is not you who speak these words," says her father, but the girl continues, transfigured by the happy thoughts of her life with Julien. Distant voices echo the harmonies of the waltz. Feverishly she relives the scene of her coronation on the hill of Montmartre, while her parents can only wring their hands. Delirious with old memories she dances about the room unconscious of her surroundings. She must go back.

The futility of his attempts to stop her drives the old man into a fury equal to the mother's. He seizes a chair and aims it at his daughter. With a scream she dashes out of the door and down the stairs. Frantically he hobbles after her, but it is too late.

Exit Louise

Clutching the table he makes his way to the window, where the city lights are still blinking gaily. He raises his fist in a passionate imprecation:

"O Paris!" he cries, and the words sound like a curse.

DEBUSSY

CLAUDE DEBUSSY was born at St. Germain-en-Laye, near Paris, on August 22, 1862. His musical training was of a conventional order, with classes in harmony and composition at the Paris *Conservatoire*. It was from the poetic rather than the musical atmosphere around him that Debussy absorbed the tendencies that were to set his works apart.

After traveling to Russia in the employ of the wealthy Madame von Meck (famous for her correspondence with Tchaikowsky), Debussy returned to Paris. In 1884, he won the *Prix de Rome* with his cantata *L'Enfant Prodigue*.

Three years later, the composer met Stéphane Mallarmé and a group of French symbolist poets, under whose spell he brought to his music the calculated vagueness which has been its distinguishing feature.

Debussy's first important instrumental work, the *String Quartet*, was performed in 1893. The following year, his pastoral rhapsody, *Prélude à l'Après-Midi d'un Faune,* created a sensation by its freedom of form and of melody. The composer's other chief works for orchestra were the three *Nocturnes* (1900-1), *La Mer* (1903), *Iberia* (1906), and the *Images* (1909-10). *Pelléas et Mélisande* was his only opera.

Debussy died in Paris on March 26, 1918, after having exercised one of the most powerful influences on modern music.

PELLÉAS ET MÉLISANDE

PELLÉAS ET MÉLISANDE, *a lyric drama in five acts and twelve scenes, after the play of Maurice Maeterlinck, was first produced at the Paris Opéra Comique, April 30, 1902, with Jean Perier and Mary Garden in the title roles. André Messager conducted. Although performances of* Pelléas *were given in New York by other companies, it was not until March, 1925, that Debussy's opera reached the Metropolitan, with Edward Johnson and Lucrezia Bori as the tragic lovers.*

The music of Pelléas *is based upon the whole tone harmonies which Debussy brought to his symphonic and piano works. The many scenes of the opera are bridged by orchestral interludes.*

Characters, in order of appearance:

Golaud, grandson of King Arkel: *baritone*
Mélisande: *soprano*
Geneviève, mother of Golaud and Pelléas: *contralto*
Arkel, king of Allemonde: *bass*
Pelléas, half-brother of Golaud: *tenor*
Yniold, son of Golaud: *mezzo-soprano*
A physician: *bass*
Serving women, invisible chorus of sailors

Time: The Middle Ages   *Place:* The Kingdom of Allemonde

ACT I

SCENE 1: A FOREST (10 Minutes)

Before the rise of the curtain, a brief prelude introduces the atmospheric theme of the Forest:

This is followed by the motive of Golaud,

and by the wistful theme of Mélisande:

PRINCE GOLAUD, grandson of King Arkel of Allemonde, is wandering through a lonely wood. The wild beast that he hunts has eluded him, and he is hopelessly lost. "Am I never to leave this place?" he wonders.

Golaud

Suddenly, Golaud hears a sob. He looks up—and sees a maiden weeping beside a well. Her features are shadowy; her hair long and blonde.

Mélisande

"Why do you weep?" calls the prince.

Startled at the sound of a human voice in this solitude, the maiden leaps up to flee. It is only with difficulty that the kindly Golaud persuades her to stay.

"Has anyone harmed you?" he asks.

"Yes!" sobs the maiden. "Everyone!" She murmurs that she has run away. But to all further questions, she will answer nothing save that her name is Mélisande.

It is growing dark in the forest. "Come, Mélisande," urges Golaud. "The night will be chilly. I beg you to go with me."

"But where?" asks the maiden.

"How can I tell?" Golaud exclaims. "I too am lost!"

SCENE 2: A ROOM IN THE CASTLE (9 Minutes)

In the somber castle of Allemonde sits old Arkel, the king. The room is flooded with shadow. Only a pallid light falls from the high Gothic window, revealing the letter which Geneviève, the king's daughter-in-law, holds in her hand.

Arkel, Geneviève

"Here is what Golaud has sent us," she tells the king. Reading the missive aloud, Geneviève relates how her son already has married Mélisande. He fears to return home, because of the disapproval of King Arkel. And so he has written to his young half-brother, Pelléas: "If the king consents to receive my bride, then hang a lantern in the tower that overlooks the sea. I shall see it shine from my vessel in the harbor. If not, I shall go on and never return."

Folding the letter, Geneviève looks searchingly at the king. "What is your reply?" she asks.

Arkel sighs. "Golaud has always been so prudent and wise! Since the death of his wife, he has lived for naught else than his little son, Yniold. But now he seems to have forgotten it all!"

Enter Pelléas

The orchestra plays a timid, hesitant motive as Pelléas, grandson of the king, enters the room:

Hearing footsteps, old Arkel peers through the shadows that fill the chamber. "Is it you, Pelléas?" he calls.

"Yes, grandfather," answers the melancholy prince. "I have received still another letter—a note from my friend Marcellus. He is about to die. May I not set off to reach him before the hour of his passing?"

"You must wait!" Arkel declares. "Your own father is lying ill in the chamber above, hovering between life and death. Can you choose between your father and your friend?"

Exit Pelléas

Silently, Pelléas leaves the chamber, and soon the room is wrapped in darkness.

SCENE 3: BEFORE THE CASTLE (6 Minutes)

Mélisande and Geneviève

Mélisande has arrived at Allemonde—and now she stands on a terrace that commands a view of the sea.

"It is dark in the gardens!" she exclaims. "How many forests there are about the castle!"

Geneviève, who stands beside her, nods sympathetically. "You will soon grow accustomed to the darkness. Look to the other side, and you will get the light from the sea."

Enter Pelléas

As they speak, Pelléas appears on the terrace. It is the first time he has seen Mélisande. Averting his eyes, he gazes toward the sea and mutters, "We shall have a storm tonight."

Invisible chorus of sailors

In the distance are heard the voices of sailors—a ship is leaving the harbor. "It is the vessel that brought me," murmurs Mélisande. Now there is no escape. She must stay on in the dismal castle!

Exit Geneviève

Twilight has fallen. "I must go below," Geneviève explains, "to see my little grandchild Yniold." As she departs, Pelléas and Mélisande watch the beacons in the harbor. With a feeling of unrest, they stare at the gathering storm. Then they prepare to descend.

"Give me your hand," says Pelléas. "I shall guide you down the path."

"My hands are full of flowers!" Mélisande exclaims.

"Then I will hold you by the arm." As they descend, the young prince turns sadly to Mélisande. "Perhaps I shall leave tomorrow."

"Oh!" sobs Mélisande. "Why must you go?"

ACT II

SCENE 1: A FOUNTAIN IN THE PARK (6 Minutes)

PELLÉAS has stayed on at Allemonde. His friendship with Mélisande has grown stronger. And now he accompanies her on an excursion to a well near the castle, which once had the miraculous power of restoring sight to the blind.

Pelléas and Mélisande

As they enter, the orchestra plays a joyous theme that runs throughout the scene:

The day is warm and splendid; the marble basin beside the well shines in the sunlight. And yet, neither Pelléas nor Mélisande is happy.

"It is lonely here!" whispers Mélisande.

"Yes, one might hear the water sleep." Glancing jealously at the young bride, Pelléas demands, "Did *he* find you beside a well?"

"He did," Mélisande answers, "but I cannot remember." She leans over the marble basin and stares into the depths below. Moved by a strange impulse, she takes from her finger the ring that Golaud has given her, and tosses it in the air.

"Take care!" warns Pelléas. "Do not throw it so high!"

Like a wilful child, Mélisande persists at her play. But suddenly, she drops the ring into the well and cries, "I have lost it! What shall I tell Golaud?"

"Tell him the truth!" Pelléas declares.

As they go out, and the curtain falls, the connecting interlude is based upon the joyous motive with which the scene began. But

*this music soon yields to the theme of Golaud, which appears in a
new and ominous harmonization:*

SCENE 2: A ROOM IN THE CASTLE (11 Minutes)

Golaud
and
Mélisande

Golaud has been wounded on a hunt. At the stroke of twelve—
the very moment when Mélisande lost the ring—the prince's steed
had bolted and dashed into a tree. Rider and horse fell to the
ground. Now he is propped up in bed, and Mélisande stays beside
him. She seems so wretched that Golaud tries to comfort her as
best he can.

"Here," he says tenderly, "give me your hands. I could crush
them as if they were flowers!" But as he caresses the young bride's
fingers, he starts up in dismay. "Where is the ring I gave you?"

"I dropped it at the shore," Mélisande falters, "when I went to
gather shells for Yniold."

Golaud looks gravely at his wife. "You must recover it at once!"
he declares. "I would rather lose all else I possess!"

"But I am so afraid!" moans Mélisande. "I dare not go alone to
the shore at night!"

"Ask Pelléas to go with you," Golaud orders. "I shall not rest
until I recover the ring."

Weeping bitterly, Mélisande sets out on her quest. "Oh!" she
sobs, "how unhappy I am!"

*The following interlude conveys all the terror of night about the
castle. Distant trumpet calls add to the eeriness of the effect:*

SCENE 3: BEFORE A GROTTO (4 Minutes)

Pelléas and
Mélisande

In the darkness, Pelléas and Mélisande grope their way to the
grotto which opens on the sea.

"You must be able to describe the place where you lost the ring," Pelléas remarks, "in case Golaud should ask you."

Suddenly, the moon emerges from the clouds, throwing a flood of light on the entrance to the grotto. Three white-haired figures are huddled within.

"Ah!" screams Mélisande in fright. "Let us go!"

"Hush!" Pelléas cautions. "They are paupers who have come here to sleep. We ought not waken them."

"Let us go!" pleads Mélisande. "We shall come back another day!"

Silently, they return to the castle of Allemonde.

Act III

SCENE 1: A TOWER OF THE CASTLE (13 Minutes)

LATE at night, Mélisande stands at her tower window. She has unbound her hair—and as she combs it out, she sings a childish melody:

Mélisande

Mes longs che - veux des - cen - dent jus - qu'au seuil de la tour;
My long, long hair it reach - es to the foot of the tower;

Soon Pelléas appears on a pathway below. He begs Mélisande to lean forward. She agrees, and her long hair streams to the foot of the wall. Pelléas grasps it.

Enter
Pelléas

"I hold you!" he cries. "You shall not escape!"

As Pelléas murmurs his love in notes and rhythms that closely resemble speech—(parlando)—the orchestra plays a languorous melody:

Mélisande grows increasingly anxious. And now she hears approaching footsteps. "Pelléas!" she calls. "Let me go! I think it is Golaud!"

Enter
Golaud

Pelléas tries quickly to release Mélisande—but her tresses are caught in the branches. It is not long before Golaud comes up the pathway.

"What are you doing here?" he demands of Pelléas. "And you, Mélisande—it is almost midnight! What children you are, both of you!" Laughing nervously, Golaud continues on his way, leaving the lovers in embarrassed silence.

SCENE 2: THE VAULTS OF THE CASTLE (3 Minutes)

Pelléas and
Golaud

Pelléas has never before visited the cavernous cellars of Allemonde. Now, accompanied by Golaud, he creeps through the vaults.

"Stoop over!" demands Golaud. "Can you see the abyss, Pelléas?"

Greatly disturbed, Pelléas notices the lantern trembling in his brother's hand. Thoughts of sudden death flood his mind. "Come!" he cries. "It is stifling in here. Let us go out!"

During a short connecting interlude, the orchestra provides the sensation of rising from the depths into the sunlight. At first, only slowly moving figures are heard—but with the advent of a brilliant series of arpeggios on the harps, the mood changes to one of relief after the forbidding episode in the cavern.

SCENE 3: A TERRACE AT THE ENTRANCE OF THE VAULTS (3 Minutes)

Pelléas and
Golaud

With a cry of joy, Pelléas emerges from the dank cellars. "Ah, I can breathe again!" he exclaims. "How good it is to behold the daylight! Look, Golaud—there are the children, going to bathe at the shore. And I can see my mother with Mélisande in the tower."

Golaud has been listening gloomily. Now he speaks: "I overheard all that happened last night at the tower. It is not the first time that I have sensed a bond between you and Mélisande. I am not angry—but in the future you must avoid her. She is about to become a mother."

Glancing pointedly at Pelléas, Golaud turns away.

SCENE 4: BEFORE THE CASTLE (10 Minutes)

Golaud
and Yniold

Try as he may, Golaud cannot conquer his suspicions. Is it possible that Pelléas has betrayed him? In order to find out more conclusively, he calls his little son Yniold, who sees all that is going on about the castle, and questions the boy:

The child babbles vaguely and says nothing of import. Suddenly, Golaud looks up from the bench where they are resting and notices a light in Mélisande's chamber. "Come, Yniold," he urges. "I will hoist you on my shoulders, and you shall tell me exactly what you see inside the room."

"Oh!" cries the child, peeping within. "I see uncle Pelléas!"

"What is he doing?" Golaud demands. "Tell me!"

"He is staring at the lamplight," Yniold answers.

"More! Tell me more!" shouts the wretched Golaud.

"Father, you are hurting me! Let me down!"

"Come!" mutters the prince. In terrible agitation, he seizes the child and strides away.

Act IV

SCENE 1: A ROOM IN THE CASTLE (16 Minutes)

THE father of Pelléas, long ailing, is on his way to recovery. All about the castle, life has been renewed. Even Geneviève, the sad wife, has wept tears of joy at hearing her husband speak again.

And now Pelléas, unable to endure the pangs of repression, is about to set off on a long journey. Meeting Mélisande in a corridor of the castle, he tells her of his decision—and asks to see her for the last time at the well of the blind men. _{Pelléas and Mélisande}

Someone is approaching; Pelléas steals quickly away. And soon, the old King Arkel crosses the corridor. "Come, Mélisande," he calls. "Now that the father of Pelléas is saved, we can be joyful. I have been watching you—and you have suffered too long!" _{Exit Pelléas Enter Arkel}

With gentle affection, Arkel draws the young bride toward him. "Sometimes," he declares, "an old man must kiss the brow of a maid or the cheek of a child to keep his trust in the freshness of life!"

Suddenly, Golaud enters the room. There is blood on his brow— he has been making his way through a hedgerow of thorns. "Pelléas leaves tonight!" he announces gruffly. _{Enter Golaud}

When Mélisande offers to tend his wounds, Golaud rebuffs her furiously. But as she tries to flee, he forces her to the ground. "On your knees!" he commands. "Now follow me!" Clutching her violently by the hair, he drags her the length of the chamber. "Absalom!" he roars, thinking of the tresses caught fast in the tree beside the tower. "Absalom!"

With all the failing strength that he can summon, Arkel restrains his grandson. And abruptly, Golaud changes his mood. "You shall do whatever you choose," he says coldly to Mélisande. **Exit Golaud** "I will not stop you. And then—" He turns and leaves the chamber.

"I am so unhappy!" sobs Mélisande.

Arkel embraces her compassionately. "If I were God," he solemnly asserts, "I would have pity on the hearts of men!"

During the following interlude, the Golaud motive grows in power until it assumes the proportions of an elemental force seeking to destroy the lovers. Then, as an unnatural silence descends upon the orchestra, the curtain rises.

SCENE 2: A FOUNTAIN IN THE PARK (14 Minutes)

Pelléas As one who is fleeing from disaster, Pelléas has decided to leave Mélisande forever. It is with fear that he awaits her at the well of the blind. "Perhaps I ought not to see her," he thinks. "But then—I would be sacrificing my final memory!"

Enter Mélisande At last, Mélisande appears. Many things have delayed her: Golaud has had a nightmare; her own dress has been caught on a doornail of the castle. And now she steps out of the moonlight into the shadows.

"Do you not know," Pelléas asks, striving in vain to master the pounding of his heart, "why I have asked you to come here tonight? Do you not know what I have to tell you?"

"No," answers Mélisande.

"I love you!"

In a voice that is vibrant with emotion, Mélisande answers, "I love you as well!"

A harsh, grating sound is heard in the distance. The castle gates are closing—the chains have fallen! Desperately, Pelléas takes Mélisande in his arms. "They have barred our way!" he cries. "We cannot turn back now!"

In the ecstasy of the moment, the lovers forget their peril. But soon, Mélisande hears stealthy footsteps. "Ah!" she whispers. "I can see Golaud! He is hiding behind a tree!"

"Then run for your life!" Pelléas begs her. "I will stay here and hold him off."

Mélisande refuses. In a frenzy of despair, she embraces Pelléas— and at once, Golaud rushes from his hiding place. Sword in hand, he reaches the fountain and strikes Pelléas dead.

Enter Golaud

Turning from the body of her lover, Mélisande flees into the forest. "Alas, I am only a coward!" she whimpers. Golaud follows her in silence.

ACT V

SCENE: A ROOM IN THE CASTLE (26 Minutes)

There is a short prelude to the final act, based on a theme of stark simplicity:

In a chamber that overlooks the sea, Mélisande is lying on a great bed. Near her are the old King Arkel and a physician. Slumped in a corner of the room, his face averted, is Golaud.

Physician, Arkel, Golaud, Mélisande

"O prince," the physician declares, "it is not from a paltry sword wound that Mélisande will die. The guilt is not yours!"

Plunged in grief, Golaud ignores the physician's consoling words. "I have slain!" he mutters. "Slain without cause."

But soon, Mélisande opens her eyes. "The window!" she calls faintly. "Leave it ajar—let me have some air from the sea."

Timidly, Golaud approaches his bride. "Mélisande!" he exclaims. "Is it you, Golaud? You have grown so thin and old!"

The unhappy prince turns to Arkel and the physician. "May I be alone with her?" he pleads. "It will not be for long. There is something I want to know."

Golaud's plea is granted—the two men withdraw. And now, with tortured voice and eyes, Golaud asks Mélisande the question that has been gnawing at his very existence. "Tell me!" he cries. "Did you love Pelléas with a love that is forbidden?"

Exeunt Arkel and physician

"No," answers Mèlisande. "We were not guilty."

"I must have the truth!" Golaud shouts despairingly. "I cannot go to my grave like one who is blind!"

Re-enter Arkel and physician

"The truth?" Mélisande murmurs. She falls back—the life spark seems to have left her. And in alarm, Golaud summons the physician.

With soft, kindly words, King Arkel tries to revive the failing princess. "Will you look at your child?" he asks. "Your little daughter? She is here."

Arkel holds the melancholy infant in his arms. "I am sorry for her," gasps Mélisande, gazing blankly at the child:

Enter serving women

Unbidden, the serving women of the castle have entered the room. "What are they doing here?" Golaud demands uneasily. His fear is increased when the women kneel in silence.

"They have come in proper time," whispers the physician. "Mélisande is gone."

"So quickly!" Arkel exclaims. Filled with pity, the old king leads Golaud from the room. "Come!" he declares. "It is better not to stay here. Your child must not remain in this chamber—it is her turn to live on now, and replace her mother!"

As the curtain slowly falls, the music grows ever softer until the distant song of a trumpet, scarcely murmured, can be heard—and then no more.

S T R A U S S

RICHARD STRAUSS was born in Munich on June 11, 1864, of a well-to-do musical family. Attracting a good deal of attention with his early compositions, he decided to leave the University of Munich in 1883 and devote himself entirely to music as a career.

At first, rather than attempt the questionable economic status of a composer, Strauss sought recognition as a conductor. In later years, he was able to devote far more time to his creative efforts, with an almost unprecedented income accruing from royalties and first performance rights on his works.

As conductor, Strauss held posts with the opera at Munich and Weimar, as well as guest appearances at Bayreuth and Dresden. For a time, he led the Berlin Philharmonic, and during the five years immediately following the First World War, he was director of the Vienna State Opera. Recently, his public appearances have been less frequent.

Strauss' fame as a composer was originally secured by his symphonic works. In the daring use of bold harmonies, virtuoso orchestration and the employment of pretentious "programs" for his music, he aroused much comment.

Fresh from his symphonic triumphs, Strauss entered the field of opera with *Guntram,* a work strongly reminiscent of Wagner. There followed *Feuersnot,* and then Strauss' first great operatic success: *Salome.* With *Elektra* and *Rosenkavalier* he became known as an opera composer of the first order. Among his later works only *Die Aegyptische Helena* and his revision of Gluck's *Iphigénie en Tauride* have been presented at the Metropolitan.

SALOME

SALOME, *a music drama in one act, received its première at Dresden in December, 1905. The opera's libretto was translated literally by Hedwig Lachmann from the play of Oscar Wilde. In December, 1907* Salome *reached the Metropolitan, where it occasioned quite a stir. Not even the artistry of Olive Fremstad in the title role could convince a conservative element among the audience that* Salome *was not fundamentally degrading. And thus, except for occasional performances of Strauss' opera by visiting companies, New York was without* Salome *until 1933, when the one-act music drama was restored to the Metropolitan repertory at the request of the public.*

Characters, in order of appearance:
Narraboth, a young Syrian captain: *tenor*
A page of Herodias: *contralto*
Two soldiers ⎫
A Cappadocian ⎭ *basses*
Jochanaan (John the Baptist): *baritone*
Salome: *soprano*
A slave: *soprano*
Herod, Tetrarch of Judea: *tenor*
Herodias, his consort: *mezzo-soprano*
Five Jews: 4 *tenors;* 1 *bass*
Two Nazarenes: *tenor* and *bass*
An executioner: *mute*

Time: 30 A.D.   *Place:* Judea

SCENE: A GREAT TERRACE IN THE PALACE OF HEROD (87 Minutes)

The orchestra plays a three bar theme—the Salome motive— which immediately creates an atmosphere of decadent orientalism, and the curtain rises:

IN the light of a pale, unearthly moon that rides through the clouds, the young officer Narraboth lingers on the terrace of Herod's palace. Staring into the banquet hall, where the princess Salome sits at table, he is filled with longing:

Narraboth

"How fair she is tonight!" he exclaims in rapture. Two soldiers and a Cappadocian keep watch in brooding silence. And next to Narraboth stands a page of the queen Herodias.

Soldiers, Cappadocian Page

"You look at Salome too much!" warns the page. "Something terrible will happen!"

Suddenly, a stentorian voice rises from the depths of a cistern on the terrace. "After me," proclaims the invisible orator, "will come another who is greater than I. When He comes, the eyes of the blind shall see—the ears of the deaf shall be opened!"

Jochanaan (invisible)

"Who is speaking?" the Cappadocian asks the soldiers.

"A holy man from the desert," they reply. "His name is Jochanaan."

Trembling with excitement, Narraboth breaks in upon their talk. "The princess is leaving the table!" he cries. "She is coming this way!"

And soon Salome appears on the terrace, youthful and perverse, glittering in her sumptuous robes.

Enter Salome

At this moment, the motive of Lust emerges from the orchestra:

"I cannot stay inside!" mutters the princess. "How my step-father, the Tetrarch, keeps looking at me!"

As she breathes the night air, Salome sighs with relief. But her disordered fancy is attracted by a strange voice—the prophet Jochanaan, preaching the doctrine of Christ from the bottom of his cistern.

Imperiously, Salome turns to the soldiers. "Let this man be brought forth!" she commands.

"We dare not," the soldiers answer. "It is forbidden!"

Determined to achieve her wish, Salome glances seductively at the young captain of the guard. "*You* will do this for me, Narraboth," she urges. "And tomorrow, when I pass in my litter, perhaps I shall smile at you."

Enter
Jochanaan

In vain does Narraboth try to resist. Breaking the Tetrarch's command, he gives orders for the prophet to be led from his cell. The heavy locks which surround the cistern are opened; and slowly, Jochanaan climbs from the darkness of his prison to the moonlit terrace.

Two leading motives are associated with the prophet. The first, mystic in character, has often been called the theme of Prophecy.

The second motive, more vigorous and forthright, is simply known as the theme of Jochanaan:

In the humble dress of a penitent, the prophet stands on the rim of the cistern. His face is white—his hair dark and tangled. Staring through space he feels Salome's gaze resting upon him. "Who is this woman?" he demands.

"I am Salome," the princess replies, "daughter of Herodias."

"Go back!" shouts the prophet. "Your mother has filled the earth with her shame!"

Salome listens eagerly to the prophet's words. "Speak again, Jochanaan!" she implores. "Your voice is music in my ears!"

The young captain of the guard, insane with jealousy and longing, begs the princess to return to the banquet hall. But Salome ignores him. "Jochanaan!" she exclaims. "It is your body that I desire!"

"Enough!" cries Jochanaan. "I will not hear you!"

Salome renews her onslaught: "I desire not your body, but your hair. It is like a cluster of grapes on the wine trees of Edom." Her ecstasy rises through the orchestra:

Again the prophet cries out against the temptress. And again, Salome pursues him with relentless passion. "Jochanaan!" she screams. "I must kiss your lips!"

Unable to endure his misery, young Narraboth stabs himself and falls between Salome and the prophet. But the princess is intent upon her desire:

Death of Narraboth

"Daughter of sin," admonishes the prophet, "you have one chance of salvation. Go seek Him on the lake of Galilee and ask to be forgiven."

With a fixed stare, Salome chants despairingly, "Your lips, Jochanaan! I must kiss your lips!"

"Never!" gasps Jochanaan. "Never! O Salome, you are accursed!"

The prophet strides back into his cistern—the grating is lowered, the chains are locked. Salome creeps about the rim and peers into the darkness below. A look of wild joy crosses her face—she will achieve her desire!

Hearing people approach from the banquet hall, Salome crouches near the cistern. Soon Herod, Tetrarch of Judea, staggers to the

Exit Jochanaan

Enter Herod, Herodias and Jews

terrace, besotted with wine. With him come his painted wife, Herodias, and her retinue of male favorites.

"Where is Salome?" cries the Tetrarch. "Why has she not returned to the banquet?"

"You must not look at my daughter!" Herodias exclaims. "You are always seeking her out!"

Coldly disregarding his wife's command, Herod lets his eyes rove in search of Salome. And suddenly, he sees the dead body of Narraboth. Recoiling in fright, the superstitious ruler fancies he hears the beating of wings.

"You are ill," mocks Herodias. "We shall go inside the palace."

"I am not ill," Herod retorts irritably. He has perceived Salome beside the cistern—and he invites her to drink wine with him.

As Salome refuses, a mighty voice soars from below. It is Jochanaan, predicting the end of all evil.

Jochanaan
(*invisible*)

"Bid him be silent!" shrieks Herodias, fearfully. "Why do you not hand him over to the Jews?"

"I have already told you," Herod answers, "that he is a holy man who has seen God."

Jews

Instantly, there is an uproar among Herod's Jewish attendants. "No one has seen God," they declare, "since the time of the prophet Elias!"

Enter
Nazarenes

"That is not so!" assert two Nazarenes, disciples of Jesus. "The Messiah Himself is on earth, working miracles in Galilee. He has even raised the dead."

"Raised the dead?" whispers Herod in craven fear. "That must not be. I forbid it!"

As the sound of Jochanaan's voice rises in a new torrent of wrath from the cistern, Herodias turns savagely on the monarch. *"Bid him be silent!"* she screams.

Herod does not listen to her. His attention has wandered to his stepdaughter. "Dance for me, Salome!" he pleads.

"Tetrarch," demands the princess, "will you grant me any reward I desire?"

"Anything!" Herod exclaims.

Exacting a solemn promise from the monarch, Salome arrays herself for the dance. In a frenzy of anticipation, Herod rises from his throne. Once more, he hears the beating of vast wings. Burning fever grips his drunken brain—and throwing off the garland of roses that crowns his brow, he reels backward in exhaustion.

"I am ready," calls Salome.

To the accompaniment of wild, percussive rhythms, the princess whirls about the terrace, casting aside, one by one, her filmy garments. For a moment, she pauses before the cistern where Jochanaan is imprisoned. Then, flinging away her final veil, she throws herself at the feet of Herod.

"Glorious!" cries the monarch. "O princess, claim your reward!"

"I desire," Salome answers, "that they bring me—on a silver platter—the head of Jochanaan!"

Herod is stunned. "No!" he pleads. "Anything but that. I will give you my precious jewels—my white peacocks—even the veil of the Temple!"

Shrieking with rage at this blasphemy, the Jews leave the palace. "I wish the head of Jochanaan!" Salome persists. "You have sworn an oath, Tetrarch!"

Herod brokenly assents. With an evil smile, Herodias draws the death ring from her husband's finger and passes it to the executioner, who descends into the cistern, his scimitar poised on his shoulder—and a harrowing silence hangs upon the scene.

"Why does he not strike?" screams Salome. "Send more soldiers! Bring me the head of Jochanaan!"

The executioner's arm rises from the cistern. In his hand is a silver platter containing the head of the prophet. "Ah!" exclaims the princess in delirious joy. "You would not suffer me to kiss your lips, Jochanaan. Now you are dead—and I who live, will fulfill my desire!"

Herod glances at his wife in terror. "Come!" he mutters. "Let us go into the palace!" Calling to his slaves, he bids them extinguish the torches.

It is dark on the terrace. The voice of Salome rises in faint, sated accents: "Ah, Jochanaan, I have kissed your mouth. There was a bitter taste on your lips. Was it the taste of blood—or perchance of love?"

Even in her weariness, the princess is triumphant. A note of ecstasy rings through her voice as she proclaims, "But what of bitterness? And what of love? Jochanaan, *I have kissed your lips!*"

The moon soars through the clouds, revealing Salome in a ghastly embrace with the head. "Kill that woman!" screams Herod.

At once the soldiers of Judea surround the princess and crush her to death beneath their shields.

ELEKTRA

ELEKTRA, *a tragedy in one act, was the initial result of Strauss'
long collaboration with the writer, Hugo von Hofmannsthal—an
association which was later to give rise to* Rosenkavalier *and*
Ariadne auf Naxos. *Like nearly all of Strauss' operas,* Elektra
*received its world première at Dresden. The date was January 25,
1909. It was performed for the first time at the Metropolitan Opera
House in December, 1932, with Gertrude Kappel in the title role.*

Characters, in order of appearance:

Five serving maids: 1 *alto,* 2 *mezzo-sopranos,* and 2 *sopranos*
The overseer: *soprano*
Elektra, daughter of Agamemnon: *soprano*
Chrysothemis, her sister: *soprano*
Klytemnestra: *mezzo-soprano*
Her confidante: *soprano*
Her trainbearer: *soprano*
A young servant: *tenor*
An old servant: *bass*
Orestes, brother of Elektra: *baritone*
His preceptor: *bass*
Aegisthus: *tenor*

Time: The Homeric Era

Place: Mycenae

SCENE: THE REAR OF THE PALACE OF AGAMEMNON AT MYCENAE
(98 Minutes)

As the curtains sweep upward, the orchestra proclaims the theme of Agamemnon:

AN atmosphere of grim foreboding hovers over the palace yard as five serving maids and their overseer crouch beside a well. "Where is Elektra?" one of them mutters. "It is the hour when she howls the name of her father and the walls ring with her cries."

[margin: Five maids and overseer]

Suddenly, Elektra, daughter of Agamemnon, appears in a gallery of the palace like a wild, hunted animal. She is despised by most of the servants—hated by her family. Ever present in her mind is the cowardly murder of her father by his queen, Klytemnestra, and the queen's paramour, Aegisthus. Thirsting for vengeance, Elektra has abandoned her quarters in the palace and gone to live in the stable yard. Her garments are ragged and filthy—her hair wild and disordered. And now, when she spies the serving maids watching her, she springs back and disappears, a living embodiment of hatred.

[margin: Enter Elektra]

[margin: Exit Elektra]

"Did you see her?" the women exclaim. "Oh, how she looks at us! She must be a demon!" As they gossip bitterly, one of them—a young and impressionable girl—raises her voice in defense of Elektra. "There is no one in the world so royal!" the maiden declares. "Elektra is the daughter of a king!"

Lashing the girl brutally, the overseer drives her toward the dingy servants' quarters. The other women follow. As dusk turns slowly to night, the courtyard is empty. Nothing can be heard except the falling of the lash and the pitiable cries of the young servant.

And now Elektra emerges from her place of concealment. With deepest solemnity, she addresses the spirit of her father:

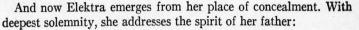

"It is the hour when they killed you," she moans. "Your bride and her lover struck you in the bath, till the water turned red with foaming blood. They dragged you headlong from the room before your eyes were closed. And thus you shall return—with staring eyes and a circlet of wounds for your crown. O father, let me see you once again!"

As Elektra kneels upon the ground, weeping convulsively, a lyric theme rises from the orchestra—Agamemnon's Children:

"Agamemnon!" she shouts. "Your day will come! Your murderers will be slain—and sacrifices made beside your tomb." Elektra's thoughts turn from sorrow to vengeance. "And we," she concludes, in a transfigured vision, "we—your two daughters and your son Orestes—will come to your grave and dance in triumph!"

The palace door has opened and Elektra's trance is abruptly shattered. There, on the threshold, stands her sister Chrysothemis. At the sight of her, Elektra turns fiercely away.

But Chrysothemis advances. "They are plotting against you!"

she whispers. "The queen and Aegisthus mean to throw you into a dark tower."

"So be it!" snarls Elektra. "All we can do is wait for death to overtake both of them!"

"I cannot wait!" her sister declares. "I want to live—to leave this palace behind me forever!" Young and fair, Chrysothemis cries out despairingly:

Kin - der will ich ha - ben   be - vor mein Leib ver - welkt!
Child - ren will I cher - ish   be - fore my bo - dy fades!

"O Elektra," she begs, "give up your plans for veangeance! Then both of us can be free!"

As the prophetess of hatred rears angrily at her sister, strange noises fill the air: the groaning of beasts—the cracking of whips. Attendants bearing lighted torches run feverishly along the gallery of the palace. The queen is approaching! She has had a terrible nightmare, and is on her way to make sacrifices to the gods.

"I cannot stay!" declares Chrysothemis. Trembling, she makes her escape into another wing of the building. And now, amid a procession of slaves, Klytemnestra—sallow and bloated beneath her weight of jewels—appears on the balcony.

Exit Chry-
sothemis
Enter
Klytem-
nestra
and her
attendant

"Ha!" she exclaims. "Behold my daughter's glance! She would like to kill me!"

But the queen's anger soon vanishes. Fearful and lonely, she determines to speak to Elektra, even though her attendants warn her of the danger.

"Begone!" she orders. "I must talk with her!"

Exeunt
attendants

Left to herself, Klytemnestra descends into the gloomy courtyard. "Tell me!" she begs her daughter. "Do you know of any remedy for dreams? I am haunted in waking and sleeping; my suffering is endless!"

"There is a remedy," Elektra answers cryptically, "when the right blood shall flow!"

"Whose blood?" persists the queen.

"A woman's!"

"Is she a virgin or has she mated?"

"Mated—indeed!" laughs Elektra.

"And who shall officiate at the sacrifice?"

"A man!"

"Answer quickly—I must know! Is he one of our own?"

Elektra counters with a question. "Will you allow my brother Orestes to return to our house, mother?"

At once, the queen glances savagely at her daughter. "I have forbidden his name to be mentioned!"

"Because you are afraid!" retorts Elektra. "You dream of him night and day—you know *he will return!*"

Klytemnestra openly admits that she dreads the thought of retribution—the coming of her son Orestes, whom she exiled years before. "But I am safe!" she declares. "Three armed sentries guard my door. And as for you—I'll find a means to make you speak. You shall tell me what sacrifice to offer the gods. My dreams must be ended—*I must sleep!*"

The time has come for Elektra to throw aside all pretense. "You are the sacrifice!" she screams. "Orestes and I will enter your chamber. We will drive you down the stairs, to the vaults of the palace. And there, in the darkness, before the shadow of my father, the ax will fall!"

Speechless with fright, Klytemnestra crumples before her daughter's accusing gaze. She sinks to the ground, gasping for breath. But at this moment, her trainbearer comes running from the palace, bearing news. As she whispers to Klytemnestra, a look of incredulity appears on the face of the queen. Then transformed into a triumphant Fury, Klytemnestra raises herself and shakes her fist menacingly at Elektra. "Torches!" she cries. "Torches!"

In a short time, the courtyard is filled with attendants waving lighted brands. While they escort the queen into the palace, Elektra looks after them in amazement. "What can they have told her?" she wonders.

Immediately, she learns the terrible news. Chrysothemis rushes toward her with the cry, "Orestes is dead! Two men have just arrived with the story!"

"No!" Elektra shudders. "It cannot be true!" Finally, convinced beyond a doubt, she huddles in despair on the palace steps; all sorts of plans revolve in her disordered mind. At length, she grasps her sister with a new fervor. "If Orestes is dead, we must act alone!"

Enter
trainbearer

Enter
attendants
Exeunt
Klytem-
nestra,
trainbearer
and
attendants

Enter
Chry-
sothemis

Refusing to share in the murderous adventure, Chrysothemis flees within the palace. "Be accursed!" Elektra calls after her. In a violent resolve to avenge her father, she starts digging for the ax with which he was slain. Years before, she had buried it in this courtyard. Now, she breaks off her task in alarm as a stranger passes through the gate.

Exit
Chry-
sothemis

Enter
Orestes

"What are you doing here?" she demands.

"I have come with a companion to tell the queen of Orestes' death," the stranger replies. "We are waiting to be admitted to her presence."

In reality, the stranger is Orestes:

He has come with his preceptor to murder the queen—and the tale of his own death is only a ruse to gain access to the palace. At first neither he nor Elektra recognizes the other; the passing of years has wrought many changes in the children of Agamemnon. It is only by his sister's grief at the false news he bears that Orestes finally knows her. "Elektra!" he cries.

The spark of recognition slowly grows within the princess until it becomes a flaming brand. "Orestes!" With a shout of joy, Elektra collapses. "You have come at last! Our work shall soon be ended!"

An elderly man—the preceptor of Orestes—hastily enters the yard and warns Elektra to be silent. Soon, a lighted torch gleams in the entrance of the palace. Klytemnestra's confidante has come to escort the two strangers to the queen. As they enter, Elektra stands motionless. Then she runs up and down before the gallery, like a wild beast.

Enter
Preceptor
Exeunt
Orestes
and
Preceptor

"The ax!" she cries. "I have forgotten to give it to them!" Suddenly, a horrible shriek rings through the palace. It is Klytemnestra, in her death agony! "Strike again!" shouts Elektra. And at the second shriek, the princess bursts into insane laughter.

Hearing the disturbance, Chrysothemis and the maids have rushed into the courtyard—but they scatter in fear as the tyrannical Aegisthus, the queen's lover, returns from the hunt. "Where are the servants?" he cries. "Will no one light me to the door?"

Enter and
exeunt
Chry-
sothemis
and maids,
Enter
Aegisthus

With mock deference, Elektra appears on the threshold. "O prince," she murmurs, "may I atone for my past misdeeds, and guide you within?"

Glancingly suspiciously at Elektra, Aegisthus enters the palace. The great doors swing closed—and a moment later, the tyrant struggles to escape from the gallery. "Murder!" he cries. "They are killing me!" As the hands of Orestes and the preceptor close ever tighter about his throat, Aegisthus shrieks despairingly, "Does no one hear me?"

"Agamemnon hears you!" shouts Elektra, as the paramour is slain.

By this time, the courtyard is ablaze with light. The adherents of Orestes have conquered the palace. Chrysothemis runs to embrace her sister.

"We are with the gods!" Elektra exclaims. "Our task is fulfilled!" With firm, ecstatic steps, she begins an unknown dance. Faster and faster she whirls, celebrating the consummation of her vengeance.

"Elektra!" pleads her sister. "Come with me!"

"Be silent and dance!" is the reply. At the height of her triumph, Elektra spins dizzily and falls. Her mission has been accomplished—life has left her.

Terrified, Chrysothemis bends over her sister's body. Then, running up the steps of the palace, she beats frantically on the great doors, imploring the aid of her brother. "Orestes!" she cries. "Orestes!"

The motive of Agamemnon's son fills the theatre with an overwhelming flood of sound, and the curtain falls.

DER ROSENKAVALIER

Der Rosenkavalier, *translated either as* The Rose-Bearer *or* The Knight of the Rose, *is a comedy for music, written by the distinguished playwright Hugo von Hofmannsthal for its composer, Richard Strauss. First produced in Dresden, January 26, 1911, it was presented at the Metropolitan on December 9, 1913, and has frequently been revived.*

Characters, in order of appearance:

Octavian, Count Rofrano: *mezzo-soprano*
The Marschallin, Princess von Werdenberg: *soprano*
Mohammed, a young negro boy
Major-domo to the Marschallin: *tenor*
Baron Ochs von Lerchenau: *bass*
Notary: *bass*
A milliner: *soprano*
Animal vendor: *tenor*
Valzacchi, an intriguer: *tenor*
Annina, companion of Valzacchi: *contralto*
Three noble orphans: *sopranos and alto*
A singer: *tenor*
Hairdresser
Leopold, footman to the Baron
Von Faninal, a wealthy parvenu: *baritone*
Marianne, duenna of Sophie: *soprano*

Major-domo to Faninal: *tenor*
Sophie, Faninal's daughter: *soprano*
Innkeeper: *tenor*
Commissioner of Police: *bass*
Footmen, maids, couriers, waiters, children, watchmen

Time: The reign of Maria Theresa of Austria,   *Place:* Vienna
about 1745

Introduction

The brief orchestral introduction opens with a spirited theme associated with the ardent young hero, Octavian:

It is soon followed by a motive referring to the Marschallin:

After its climax, the prelude slackens until a broad melody is heard suggesting the love of the Marschallin and her young suitor, additionally characterized by the spirit of resignation which is the keynote of her nature.

Act I

Scene: The Marschallin's Bedroom (56 Minutes)

Marschallin, Octavian   In her great baroque boudoir, the Princess of Werdenberg is lying in the embraces of her lover Octavian. She has hardly arisen from the magnificent bed in a niche at the left of the chamber. A screen beside it does not quite conceal the young man's coat; on a sofa lies his sword. Early morning sunlight streams in from a large window at the right, while in the orchestra trills the song of birds.

"No one knows how perfect you are but I myself!" exclaims the young man passionately. Furious that the entering daylight threatens his intimacy, he dashes to the window to pull the curtains.

The Princess, who has responded to his declarations with tenderness, laughs gently at his impatience. In the distance a bell rings twice.

"Quick, hide yourself, and the sword too, foolish boy," she orders, while a little negro servant in a huge yellow turban marches through her private door in the center of the room and sets her breakfast tray on a table leaving promptly with a deep obeisance to his mistress.

Enter Mohammed

Exit Mohammed

"It's a lucky chance that your husband the Field Marshal is still hunting boar in Croatia," boasts Octavian. "The longer he stays away, the happier I will be."

The Marschallin has had a disturbing dream of her husband's return. Octavian's jealousy flares up, but turns to alarm as a fracas can be heard growing louder beyond the door. Can it be the Field Marshal returning?

"Quick, hide among the bed curtains," whispers the Marschallin.

A gruff coarse voice outside gives her a clue.

Exit Octavian

"It is my old cousin from the country, Baron Ochs von Lerchenau," she decides, with a sigh of relief; "I quite forgot to read his last letter."

Octavian has meanwhile dressed himself in the skirt, kerchief, and mobcap of the Marschallin's chambermaid and reappears curtseying with a roguish speech in the dialect of the peasantry.

Enter Octavian disguised as Mariandel

A brief kiss from his amused mistress, and Octavian turns, almost running into the huge bloated figure of the Baron, who staggers through the narrow doorway to the accompaniment of his own theme:

Enter Baron and the Marschallin's footmen

The old man chucks Octavian under the chin, taking him for a pretty girl. Finally the footmen remind him of the presence of the Marschallin, and he turns to greet her, while Octavian busies himself near the bed.

The Baron cannot take his eyes off the alleged serving maid. Gradually, however, the purpose of his visit comes to light:

"Your Highness may have learned from my letter," he announces, "that I have decided to take a wife, a girl of fifteen, fresh from the convent, the daughter of the wealthy Herr Faninal, recently ennobled."

Octavian tries to slip away with the breakfast tray, but is prevented by the Baron, who evinces an enormous appetite, both for the chocolate, and for the chambermaid.

"Here, Mariandel," calls the Marschallin to her lover, choosing a name at random, "bring it back and wait on his lordship."

The old reprobate contrives to ask Octavian for a rendezvous, and in the next breath begs his cousin's help in finding a fitting ambassador to carry the silver rose to his future bride in token of their betrothal.

Enter Major-domo

The Major-domo comes in to announce that the usual petitioners await an audience with the Marschallin. Ochs profits by the interruption to make further advances to the supposed Mariandel, but the servant girl rebuffs him with exemplary virtue.

Exit Major-domo

As the Major-domo retires, the old libertine describes his conquests at length, and boldly concludes with a request to add Mariandel to his future suite.

Though she turns down this suggestion, it awakens in the Princess a new idea:

"Mariandel, fetch the miniature in the jeweled medallion! Here," she says, showing a portrait of Octavian to Ochs, "how would you like this young man, a distant cousin of mine, to carry the silver rose to your betrothed?"

Exit Mariandel (Octavian in disguise)

The Baron remarks the resemblance to Mariandel, which the Marschallin infers is due to the possibility of their being brother and sister. This leads to a confession: he too has in his employ a son of his caprice, his footman, Leopold. Again he addresses the maid, who departs, slamming the door in his face.

Enter lackeys, notary, cooks and orphans

Her ladyship retires behind the screen, while a procession of petitioners streams from the official door of the bedroom at the right. Lackeys carry out the toilet table from the wall. A notary busies himself with his books, the cooks scan their menu.

Three noble orphan girls in deepest mourning are led in by their widowed mother and shrilly beseech the Princess for help.

Milliner

The milliner, opening her boxes, presents her most dashing hats for inspection, under fantastic names.

Animal vendor, Valzacchi and Annina

An animal vendor exhibits his lap dogs, monkey and parrots. The Marschallin emerges from behind the screen. Greeted with reverence by the entire company, she first introduces her attorney to the Baron, who leads him aside in conference. Then she gives a purse to the orphans and dismisses the loquacious Italian scandalmonger Valzacchi, who with his companion Annina, has offered to serve her in matters of intrigue.

Exeunt orphans
Enter hairdresser

The orphans babble their gratitude and depart.

The hairdresser advances to the toilet table where the Marschallin has seated herself. His assistant offers him curling irons. Together they work at her ladyship's coiffure.

The flute player has taken up his post, and accompanies the Italian tenor in a sentimental aria:

Enter flute player and singer

Tempo di menuetto

Di ri - go —— ri_ar - ma - to il se - no

Meanwhile a shabby bodyguard gathers about the Baron who continues his discussion with the attorney, insisting that an ample dowry shall be turned over to him.

"You have made me look middle-aged," complains the Marschallin to her hairdresser, then asks her Major-domo to dismiss the company.

Exeunt hair-dressers, animal vendor, singer, flute player, milliner, cooks, notary and lackeys, etc.
Exeunt Valzacchi, Annina
Exit Baron's suite

Valzacchi and Annina steal over to Baron Ochs, and offer their help as spies.

"To prove your skill, find out what you can about Mariandel," he instructs them, and they join his retinue. He then accepts the Marschallin's offer of her young cousin as bearer of the rose. Taking the casket from his doltish footman, Leopold, he leaves it with her and ceremoniously withdraws.

The Princess is left alone. She takes a mirror in her hand.

"I remember a girl who was whisked off from a convent to the altar," she remarks wistfully. "Where is she now? Soon they will say: 'There goes the old princess!' And yet I feel the same. What is the meaning of it all? Only that *how* we face our life—makes all the difference!"

Octavian rushes in, dressed in his riding habit.

Enter Octavian

"Dearest, be kind and gentle with me," begs the Marschallin, calming the fire of his embraces, "not like the others."

Fervently he tries to silence her remonstrance.

"All things must pass, like dreams," she continues. "Time flows on till suddenly we are aware of its passage—and yet what use is there to fear it?"

He cannot understand her words. Is she dismissing him? His ardor cannot reach her philosophic mood. He goes.

Exit Octavian

"And not a single kiss!" reflects the Marschallin. She summons lackeys to call him back, but they report that he has galloped off like the wind. Then she rings for the little black boy and gives him the leather jewel case. "Tell Count Octavian it is the silver rose," she bids him; "he will understand."

Act II

SCENE: A RECEPTION HALL IN THE HOUSE OF HERR VON FANINAL
(43 Minutes)

A brief orchestral prelude at once introduces the theme of Herr von Faninal:

It is followed by the Betrothal theme, which heralds the rise of the curtain.

A SENSE of excitement and anticipation pervades the garish salon on which the curtain rises.

Faninal,
Sophie
Marianne

"This is a solemn day, a great day, a festive day," stammers Faninal to his gentle young daughter, Sophie. He cannot hide his nervous satisfaction at the fine marriage that has been arranged for her.

"The new carriage is waiting at the door," interrupts Marianne, the duenna.

Major-
domo

"Time to start!" prompts the Major-domo. "Etiquette prescribes that the father must be absent when the messenger brings the silver rose."

Exeunt
Faninal,
Major-
domo

As Faninal bustles off, Sophie gives way to a naïve but spiritual exaltation. "In this sacred hour, I give thanks to my Creator for leading me to the honorable estate of matrimony," she declares.

The aged Marianne is meanwhile standing by the great side window, babbling of the crowd in the street and the coaches that bring the Baron's messenger. Cries of "Count Rofrano" sound from without.

Enter
Faninal's
suite,
Octavian
and his
suite

A swarm of lackeys open the center doors, where Octavian's footmen stand in their master's livery of green and silver, flanked by grotesque soldiers and couriers. Octavian enters bareheaded, gleaming in snowy damask. Taking the silver rose from the case held by a footman, he descends the steps toward Sophie with a courtly grace, though somewhat disconcerted by her beauty and youth. She takes the rose from his hands:

Chords from the flutes, harps, celesta and three solo violins suggest the metallic luster of the silver rose:

After the first conventional exchanges Sophie breaks into rapture: "It seems like a flower from Heaven, one of the roses of Paradise. Where can I have felt such joy before?"

These very words Octavian repeats with a new awe akin to love:

Octavian's footman has meanwhile handed the jewel case to Marianne who takes the rose from Sophie and puts it away. Faninal's servants retire with Octavian's suite. The young couple are left alone with the duenna. *Exeunt both suites*

To a graceful waltz rhythm Sophie chatters all she has learned of Octavian's titles and relations. "You can laugh at me if you choose," she concludes archly, "for I have never met a young gentleman that I have liked half so well before."

The door at the back is now thrown open and Faninal ceremoniously escorts the Baron, surrounded by his motley following of shabby servants. *Enter Faninal, Baron and their suites*

"He acts like a dealer, inspecting a colt," murmurs Sophie to herself, "and his face is all pockmarked." The Baron, meanwhile, is far more interested in Octavian's resemblance to the maid Mariandel, whose charms he has not forgotten.

The Major-domo of the house dismisses the servants, two of whom serve wine to the guests. *Exeunt all retainers*

First impressing Sophie with his superiority, the Baron proceeds to woo her with boorish coarseness.

Faninal rubs his hands at the picture of two aristocrats in his parlor at once, but Octavian, infuriated at the brutal manners of Sophie's suitor, can hardly keep his hands off his sword.

"Tender as a pullet," gloats the Baron, forcing the young girl to his lap. "Mine is the luck of all the Lerchenaus."

At length Sophie can bear it no longer and cries, "Hands off! What do you think you are?" at which the callous old man relates the pleasures of their future life together to the strains of a sentimental waltz:

Tempo di valse

Exeunt
Ochs and
Faninal

As soon as he is aware that the Marschallin's attorney has appeared, Baron Ochs leads him off with Faninal and his lawyers, insisting that his bourgeois father-in-law-to-be keep three paces behind him.

Again Octavian and Sophie are left alone with Marianne.

The young cavalier's theme soars up at his first words: "Will you marry that thing, my cousin?"

"Not for the world," she answers passionately.

Exit
Marianne

The Major-domo rushes in, distracted. The Lerchenau servants, besotted with Faninal's good wines, are making free with the servant girls of the house. Marianne must go with him to quiet the tumult, which has actually invaded the reception hall. She leaves the young couple to themselves.

"You must help me now," pleads Sophie.

"First you must help yourself," he answers kindly. "To save us both you must be the woman you are." She responds to his first kisses with tenderness.

Enter
Valzacchi,
Annina

Enter the
Baron

As they rapturously embrace, the two Italian spies, Valzacchi and Annina, creep from two great fireplaces and seize the young lovers, calling loudly for the Baron.

"Ecco," they exclaim, relinquishing their victims to face the incoming dignitary.

"It is my duty to inform you," begins Octavian, with pride, "that this young lady—"

"You do not waste your time," interrupts the Baron, pointedly. "I like your spirit!"

"This young lady—" continues Octavian, desperately, "will have none of you."

The Baron tries to lead Sophie off to the notaries in spite of him.

"You are a cheat, a clown, a boor," continues her new lover hotly, "as my sword will teach you."

In vain the Baron whistles for his servants, who retreat before Octavian's sword, and only rush forward after the young man has succeeded in wounding Ochs above his elbow.

Enter
Baron's
suite

"Murder!" roars the Baron. "A doctor! Linen! Call the watch!" The room is filled by the retinues of both houses, who continue their brawl until Faninal takes matters in hand. Marianne hurries for linen and sponges, which she applies to the wounded Baron, who is placed groaning on a couple of chairs.

Enter
Faninal's
suite

Enter
Faninal

Faninal first directs his rage at Octavian, who courteously apologizes, but his paternal fury rises higher as Sophie quietly informs him that she will not marry the Baron.

"You'll marry him," he swears, "or I'll send you back to the convent for the rest of your life."

"Careful, darling," whispers Octavian from the center doorway, making his exit while Marianne leads Sophie away.

Exeunt
Octavian,
Marianne
and
Sophie

The Baron's own theme reminds Faninal that he must attend to his wounded guest. He orders wine and then hurries off, nursing his resentment against his daughter's rebellion.

Exeunt
Faninal
and suite

After a couple of drinks the Baron sends away his servants to prepare his bed. Then, in a mellower mood, he hums over the waltz of his happy future.

Exeunt
Baron's
servants
Enter
Annina

The spy Annina, finding him alone, issues from her hiding place with a letter in her hand: an assignation from the Marschallin's chambermaid. At his request she reads it to him.

"Do you remember Mariandel?" the letter concludes. "She waits for an answer."

The Baron is entranced at his good luck. There will be time later to pay Annina for her pains. She clenches her fist at his niggardliness, but he hums on softly to a sentimental waltz.

Act III

SCENE: A PRIVATE ROOM AT AN INN (43 Minutes)

THE curtain rises on a dingy room in a questionable inn. In a niche on the left, heavy curtains barely conceal a bed. Nearer the front a fire is burning in a mean fireplace. In the center a table, laid for two, is lighted by a many-branched candlestick. On the right a window faces on the street, but above the door in the center another small blind window lets in no light. A similar window pierces the left wall.

In a silent pantomime, Valzacchi is seen, putting the last touches

Valzacchi,

Annina
Exit
Annina
on the disguise that Annina has assumed as a respectable widow. The conspirators do not seem surprised when a head suddenly pops out from the left window and as suddenly withdraws.

Octavian
(*disguised as Mariandel*)
Enter
suspicious
characters
A decently dressed old woman now ushers in Octavian, his servant's skirt and blouse concealing his riding boots and breeches. He throws a purse to Valzacchi, who with Annina has recently entered his employ, and then departs. Five suspicious-looking men tiptoe in and are quickly concealed by Valzacchi behind various secret doors, while flurries of the sentimental waltz suggest that the Baron will arrive at any moment. Another waltz echoes from a band in the distance. At a given signal, Valzacchi rehearses his hirelings in their entrances from the trapdoor, and then orders candles to be lighted on the mantel, the table, and various wall sconces.

Enter
Baron
Ochs
At length he opens both wings of the center door and respectfully bows in Baron Ochs, leading Octavian by one arm.

"Has your lordship further wishes?" asks the obsequious landlord.

Impatient at the unnecessary extravagance, the Baron takes a napkin from the table and extinguishes most of the candles. "And what is that music? I ordered none," he says angrily, as the waltz rises from the orchestra. "Send the servants away. My man can wait on us himself."

Exeunt
Valzacchi
and
servants
After repeated signals, Ochs gets rid of his servant and presses a glass of wine on Octavian, who coyly refuses it.

Feigning terror at the Baron's advances, Octavian pretends to run away.

The likeness of the supposed Mariandel to the bearer of the rose now worries the Baron, and it is Octavian's turn to quiet his fears. One of Valzacchi's apparitions pops prematurely from his trapdoor, but again the Baron is persuaded there is nothing to worry about.

As the body servant opens the door, the strains of the Baron's waltz-dream float in, and Octavian pretends to weep with emotion, giving way to the most maudlin hysteria.

"Your dress must be too tight," says the Baron, cosily. "It is warm here," and he takes off his own wig.

At this moment a series of heads appear at every door and window. The Baron gives a frightened bellow.

Enter
Annina,
Valzacchi
and
children
Annina in her widow's weeds, followed by Valzacchi, leads in four children who claim the Baron as their father. "This is the man who has deserted me!" she cries.

"Have you sent for Faninal yet?" whispers Octavian to Valzacchi.

"He'll be here in a moment," is the answer.

Loud cries from the street preface the arrival of the police, led by the Commissary.

The Baron approaches the officer with confidence, but is speedily rebuffed, as Valzacchi refuses to identify him as the Baron von Lerchenau.

"Who is the girl?" asks the Commissary.

Only one explanation occurs to the confused Baron: "She is my affianced bride, young Mistress Faninal."

No sooner has he uttered the name than Faninal himself appears, eager to agree that the Baron is in fact his son-in-law. His pride, however, changes to fury when he realizes that Ochs has called the wench Mariandel by the name of his Sophie. His footmen rush to support his trembling form, and his daughter, who has accompanied him in a carriage, comes in to help him away to a quieter room.

As the Baron continues his frantic explanations, Octavian calls the Commissary aside, leading him toward the recessed bed, where he disappears for a moment. From the curtains are thrown various articles of woman's dress. With difficulty the two police agents hold the Baron back, but just as Octavian's head appears between the curtains, the landlord announces: "The Princess of Werdenberg."

With a superb exposition of her original theme, the Marschallin makes her entrance, flanked by a retinue of servants, her train carried by the little negro page.

The complexities of the situation are soon disentangled. Sophie comes out with a message from her father to the Baron. If ever he approaches the Faninal house again, he will have himself to thank for the consequences.

The Marschallin at length dismisses the Baron with a gay challenge to his breeding in accepting circumstances as they are. He must renounce the marriage with Sophie. The Commissary goes off, satisfied with her explanation that the whole affair has been a farce, a mere Viennese masquerade. The Marschallin is left alone with Sophie and Octavian.

"So it was all a farce," repeats Sophie, mournfully, as she guesses that the Marschallin has some hold over Octavian of which she is not aware.

The older woman addresses the younger for the first time: "You

---

Margin notes:

Innkeeper and waiters

Enter Commissary and police

Enter Faninal

Enter Sophie
Exeunt Faninal and Sophie

Enter Marschallin, negro page and suite
Enter Sophie

Exit Baron
Exeunt Commissary, Annina, Valzacchi and Innkeeper

learned to love quickly," she says. "Your pale cheeks tell the story."

"I do not understand," answers Sophie. "If I am pale it is because of my father's sudden illness. I must go to him."

"Stay, child," insists the Marschallin. "I shall bid your father ride home in my carriage, and as for you, my cousin, Count Octavain, will know the cure."

"How good you are, Marie Therese," murmurs the cavalier.

"I made a vow to love unselfishly, and to cherish the woman to whom he would some day turn," explains the Marschallin, opening the great trio for the three women's voices.

Moderato e molto sostenuto

Hab' mir's ge - lobt　ihn lieb＿＿＿　zu ha - ben.
I made a vow to love＿＿＿ him right - ly,

"I feel like one at worship," cries Sophie to Octavian, "and yet the only thing I fully understand is that I love you."

"I cannot tell what has come to pass," says Octavian to Sophie, "and yet I know nothing but my love for you."

Exit Mar- schallin　Unnoticed, the great lady goes off to be of service to Faninal. The two young people, clasped in each other's arms, sing of the miracle that has happened:

Andante tranquillo

Ist ein Traum, kann nicht wirklich sein＿＿ dass　wir zwei　bei ei - nan- der sein!
'Tis a dream, tell me　is it true＿＿ that　you love me and I love you!

Faninal's footmen appear with candles, to usher out their master and the Marschallin to her carriage. The lovers make obeisance to them, and then resume their rapturous duet.

Exeunt Sophie and Octavian

Negro page

Sophie sinks into Octavian's arms, dropping her handkerchief as he leads her off. A moment later the little negro servant trips in with a candle, looks for the handkerchief, picks it up with a gesture of triumph, and trips out again.

XII

The Mechanics of Opera Production

It takes over seven hundred people and two corporations to produce opera at the Metropolitan.

Opera is presented by the Metropolitan Opera Association, Inc., formed in 1932 and presided over by twenty-five directors under the leadership of Paul D. Cravath, President; Cornelius N. Bliss, Chairman, and George A. Sloan as Chairman of the Executive Committee.

The building is provided rent free by the Metropolitan Opera and Real Estate Company, a corporation which purchased the house in 1892 after a disastrous fire, rebuilt the auditorium, and retained the thirty-five parterre boxes in lieu of rent.

The management is headed by Edward Johnson and his two associates, Edward Ziegler, and Earle R. Lewis who also serves as box office treasurer. Directly under them is the company, which varies from year to year, but usually includes over thirty sopranos, a dozen contraltos and mezzos, a score of tenors, almost as many baritones and a dozen bassos.

Listed also as members of the company are six conductors, a dozen assistant conductors, who officiate at rehearsals, two chorus masters, three stage directors, a ballet master and librarian.

In spite of the foreign names of many of these individuals, there are more citizens of the United States in the company than from the rest of the world put together, though a total of twenty different countries is represented.

Associated with the company, the two largest groups of music

483

makers are the orchestra and chorus, each of which varies with the assignments of the various operas, but approximates a hundred people. The stage band is also a variable list, but may comprise as many as twenty men.

It takes more than music, however, to make opera; and the roster of men and women grouped under sixteen different technical departments actually outnumbers the singers and players.

Since the singing voice enjoys a shorter life than the skill of mind and muscle, it is natural that the staff averages a longer record at the Metropolitan than the singers. Many of the department heads have held their positions since the turn of the century, while the longest vocal career in the present company is just under thirty years.

Visible on the stage as specified by the various operas of the repertory are the forty-four men and women of the ballet. Crowd scenes may require as many as one hundred supers, who are hired as occasion demands.

Before the curtain rises, an army of stage hands tacks down the floor cloth, sets up the scenery, and adjusts the flies and drops, while a regiment of property men disposes of furniture, flowers, weapons and other gear at the direction of the Master of Properties. Electricians are grouped under their Chief, and scene painters take orders from the Scenic Artist.

Scenery and costumes are also designed by outstanding artists whom the Metropolitan secures for occasional new productions.

In their respective offices in the upper floors of the Opera House, the Costumer, and Wigs and Make-up man plan and execute the trains and tresses of the company and chorus. The Musical Secretary juggles the repertory into the five evenings of the week with additional matinees and special performances to fit the needs of the season. He then passes on the rehearsal requirements to the Rehearsal Department, which notifies the artists of their daily assignments.

The Construction Carpenter and his staff build the solid pieces of scenery, securing materials, as do the other offices, through a special Technical Department.

In the front of the House the Superintendent of the Building is in charge of the ushers, cleaning women and maids. At the Box Office ten people are busy day and night, selling tickets through the window, answering telephone calls, filling mail orders, etc. Deep in the cellars, the Chief Engineer and his staff keep the building warm.

Another score of men and women work at their desks all day. The Treasurer heads financial affairs. The Secretary is the link between the Management and its vast army of correspondents. The Advertising Department arranges for the printing of posters, the insertion of newspaper notices, and the correction of programs. The Publicity Department distributes press seats, arranges for interviews with artists and pastes up the vast clipping books in which all printed criticisms are enshrined.

These sixteen departments are all called into new forms of service when the company goes on tour. In addition to several weeks in the spring, when the Metropolitan takes some dozen productions on the road, there are frequent performances during the winter season in Philadelphia, Hartford, and other cities.

On these occasions special lightweight scenery and properties must be assembled and transported, thousands of costumes and accessories packed in hampers, and hundreds of boxes filled with electrical equipment and properties, not to mention the special transportation facilities necessary to move the principals, orchestra and chorus to their new scene of action.

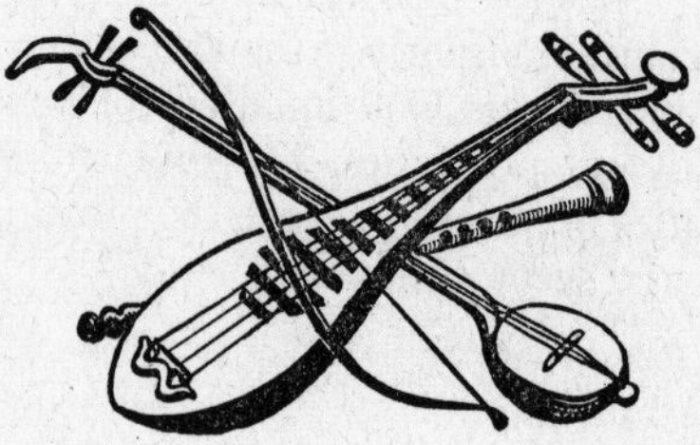

XIII

Metropolitan Summary

THE opening of the Metropolitan Opera House on October 22, 1883, was celebrated by a performance of Gounod's *Faust*. From the first season two essential traditions were unmistakably present. The new house was designed to provide for over a hundred boxes: a far less exclusive number than the nine that existed in the old Academy of Music, which since 1854 had been the seat of opera in New York City. Another notable feature was the variety characterizing the choice of repertory which during the first season included nine Italian, eight French and two German works. Democracy in the audience and variety on the stage: these traditions have endured at the Metropolitan for over half a century, through the administrations of eight executive directors.

Many times, however, have changing conditions forced the Metropolitan to alter its financial set-up. The expenses of the first season proved so heavy that Henry E. Abbey, who had leased the house as an independent producer, was unwilling to continue without a substantial guarantee. Artists of sufficient renown to compete with the list provided by Col. Mapleson at the Academy brought the costs of opera production to a prohibitive figure.

Next season, accordingly, the directors turned to Dr. Leopold Damrosch, who initiated a period of opera in German by German artists. In the early days of this era, which extended from 1884 to 1891, the repertory was principally German, but with the wane of Italian opera at the Academy, and the increasing demand for variety at the Metropolitan, the emphasis on German works was broadened to include a wider range. Finally, in 1890, the management of the house was returned to Abbey, who delegated most of his authority to Maurice Grau.

In the hands of Grau, the Metropolitan echoed with applause for his famous "ideal casts." The company boasted such glorious names as Jean and Edouard de Reszke, Nordica, Eames, Calvé, Sembrich, Ternina, Plançon, Maurel, Melba, Scotti, Gadski and a host of others. Upon Grau's retirement because of illness in 1903, Heinrich Conried took over the directorship. His regime brought into the company Caruso, Farrar and Fremstad. Felix Mottl and Gustav Mahler appeared as conductors; *Parsifal, Salome* and *Madama Butterfly* were given for the first time.

Conried too was forced to resign because of ill health; his successors were Giulio Gatti-Casazza and Andreas Dippel, with Arturo Toscanini, Mahler and Alfred Hertz in charge of the performances. For two seasons authority was divided; then Gatti became sole director in 1910. With Toscanini as an able and devoted co-worker, Gatti made the next five seasons of his directorship the high level of rounded excellence in the presentation of opera in the modern era. Toscanini resigned from the Metropolitan in the spring of 1915. The following twenty years under the direction of Gatti were marked by difficulties created by the World War during which the performance of most German scores and the German language were banned from the house. The Gatti regime was highlighted too by the prosperity of the '20's; the brilliant careers of Jeritza, Chaliapin and Bori following the death of Caruso; the advent of Talley, Tibbett, Grace Moore and Lily Pons; the establishment of the Metropolitan Opera Association; the first Metropolitan opera to be broadcast by radio on Christmas, 1931; the public appeal for funds in 1933 and 1934; the intervention of the Juilliard Foundation, and finally, the appearance of Kirsten Flagstad.

With the retirement of Gatti-Casazza, the brief control of Herbert Witherspoon and the accession of Edward Johnson, the season of 1935 introduced a new chapter in the Metropolitan's history. It was featured by a revival of *Fidelio* for Mme. Flagstad, the participation of the Metropolitan Opera Guild, and also by a noticeable increase in public interest. At the end of the season Lucrezia Bori closed a distinguished career by retiring from public activity. Early in May, 1936, a new venture was launched: performances of opera at popular prices and opportunities for young American singers to gain operatic experience. The experiment was repeated in the spring of 1937.

The briefest history of the Metropolitan would be incomplete without a record of the world premières of Puccini's *La Fanciulla del West*, and Humperdinck's *Königskinder* (both in December, 1911), of Giordano's *Madame Sans Gêne* (1914), Deems Taylor's *The King's Henchman* (1927), and *Peter Ibbetson* (1930), Gruenberg's *Emperor Jones* (1932), and Damrosch's *The Man Without a Country* (1936), all of which outlasted their initial season.

The Metropolitan was the scene of the first performances in America of *Lucia di Lammermoor* (1883), *La Gioconda* (1883), *Die Meistersinger* (1886), *Tristan und Isolde* (1886), *Siegfried* (1887), *Walküre* (1888), *Götterdämmerung* (1888), *Das Rheingold* (1889), *Werther* (1894), *Tosca* (1901), *Parsifal* (1903), *Salome* (1907), *Ariane et Barbe-Bleue* (1912), *Boris Godunoff* (1913), *Der Rosenkavalier* (1913), *L'Amore dei Tre Re* (1914), *Prince Igor* (1915), *Iphigenia in Tauris* (1916), *Le Coq d'Or* (1918), *Oberon* (1918), *Gianni Schicchi* (1918), *Die Tote Stadt* (1921), *Snegourotchka* (1922), *La Vida Breve*, *Le Rossignol* (1926), *Turandot* (1926), *Die Aegyptische Helena* and *La Campana Sommersa* (1928), *La Rondine* (1928), *Jonny Spielt Auf* and *Fra Gherardo* (1929), *Sadko* and *The Fair at Sorochintzy* (1930), *Schwanda* (1931) and *Simon Boccanegra* (1932).

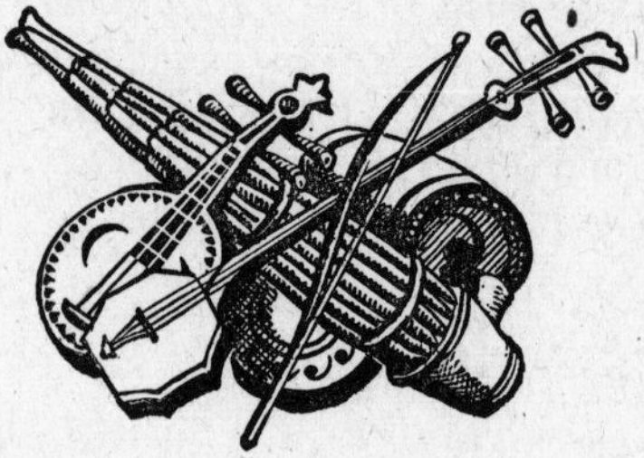

Bibliography

BOOKS ABOUT OPERA

ABRAHAM, GERALD: *A Hundred Years of Music*. N. Y.: Alfred A. Knopf, 1938. $4.00.

ABRAHAM, GERALD: *Masters of Russian Music*. N. Y.: Alfred A. Knopf, 1936. $3.75.

ANNESLEY, CHARLES: *The Standard Operaglass*. N. Y.: Tudor Press, 1920. $1.29.

BERNSTEIN, ALLEN MILTON: *The Do-Re-Mi of the Nibelung Ring*. N. Y.: Greenberg, 1928, reprinted 1937. $1.50.

BURCH, GLADYS and RIPPENGER, HELMUT: *The Music Quiz*. N. Y.: Stackpole Sons, 1938. $1.25.

DILLER, ANGELA: *The Story of Lohengrin*. N. Y.: G. Schirmer, 1932. $.75.

DILLER, ANGELA: *The Story of Siegfried*. N. Y.: G. Schirmer, 1931. $.60.

GILMAN, LAWRENCE: *Wagner's Operas*. N. Y.: Farrar & Rinehart, 1937. $2.50.

GRABBE, PAUL and NORDOFF, PAUL: *Minute Stories of the Opera*. N. Y.: Grosset & Dunlap, 1932. $1.00.

HEINZ, ALBERT: *The Mastersingers of Nuremberg*. N. Y.: G. Schirmer, 1890. $1.00.

HUTCHESON, ERNEST G.: *Elektra*. N. Y.: G. Schirmer, 1910, Cloth. $1.00. Paper, $.75.

KOBBÉ, GUSTAV: *The Complete Opera Book*. N. Y.: Putnam, 1919-35. $5.00.

KOBBÉ, GUSTAV: *Wagner's Music Dramas (Analyzed)*. N. Y.: G. Schirmer, 1904. $1.25.

KREHBIEL, HENRY EDWARD: *Book of Operas.* One vol. edition. N. Y.: Macmillan, 1937. $1.49.

LAVIGNAC, ALBERT: *The Music Dramas of Richard Wagner.* N. Y.: Dodd, Mead, 1905. $3.00.

MARTENS, FREDERICK H.: *1001 Nights of Opera.* N. Y.: Appleton, 1926. $3.50.

MELITZ, L. L.: *The Opera-Goers' Complete Guide.* N. Y.: Dodd, Mead, 1908-24. $2.50.

METROPOLITAN OPERA GUILD, SPONSOR:

Aïda, adapted by Robert Lawrence. N. Y.: Grosset & Dunlap, 1938. $.50.

Carmen, adapted by Robert Lawrence. N. Y.: Grosset & Dunlap, 1938. $.50.

Götterdämmerung, adapted by Robert Lawrence. N. Y.: Grosset & Dunlap, 1939. $.50.

Hänsel and Gretel, adapted by Robert Lawrence. N. Y.: Grosset & Dunlap, 1938. $.50.

Lohengrin, adapted by Robert Lawrence. N. Y.: Grosset & Dunlap, 1938. $.50.

Das Rheingold, adapted by Robert Lawrence. N. Y.: Grosset & Dunlap, 1939, $.50.

Siegfried, adapted by Robert Lawrence. N. Y.: Grosset & Dunlap, 1939. $.50.

Walküre, adapted by Robert Lawrence. N. Y.: Grosset & Dunlap, 1939. $.50.

Music Libraries. London: Grafton & Co., 1938. $5.25.

McSPADDEN, J. W.: *Opera Synopses.* N. Y.: Crowell, 1911-15-21. $2.50.

NEWMAN, ERNEST: *Stories of Great Operas,* 3 vols. N. Y.: Alfred A. Knopf, 1928-30. $3.50 each. Or in one volume reprint edition: Garden City: Garden City Publishing Co. $1.47.

SANBORN, PITTS: *Metropolitan Book of the Opera.* N. Y.: Simon & Schuster, 1937. $3.00.

STREATFEILD, R. A.: *The Opera.* N. Y.: E. P. Dutton, 1925. $2.50.

THOMPSON, OSCAR: *The International Encyclopedia of Music and Musicians.* N. Y.: Dodd, Mead, 1938. $12.50.

UPTON, G. P.: *The Standard Operas.* Chicago: McClurg & Co., 1886-1907. $3.00.

UPTON, G. P. and BOROWSKI: *Standard Opera and Concert Guide.* N. Y.: Blue Ribbon Publishing Co., 1936. $1.49.

Victor Book of the Opera. Camden, N. J.: RCA Manufacturing Co., 1939. $2.00.

WATKINS, MARY F.: *First Aid to the Opera-Goer.* N. Y.: Stokes, 1924. $1.50.

WEBER, HENRIETTE: *The Prize Song. Stories of Famous Operas.* N. Y.: Oxford University Press, 1935. $3.00.

BOOKS ABOUT COMPOSERS

ABRAHAM, GERALD and CALVOCORESSI: *Masters of Russian Music.* N. Y.: Alfred A. Knopf, 1936. $3.75.

BEKKER, PAUL: *The Changing Opera.* Trans. from the German by Arthur Mendel. N. Y.: W. W. Norton, 1935. $3.50.

DAVENPORT, MARCIA: *Mozart.* N. Y.: Charles Scribner's Sons, 1932. $3.50.

DE BOVET, M. A.: *Charles Gounod, His Life and Works.* London: Low, Marston, 1891.

DOLE, NATHAN HASKEL: *A Score of Famous Composers.* N. Y.: Thomas Y. Crowell Co., 1891-1929. $3.75.

ELSON, ARTHUR: *Modern Composers of Europe.* Boston: L. C. Page & Company, 1905. $3.00.

ENGEL, CARL: *Alla Breve.* N. Y.: G. Schirmer, 1921. $2.00.

HANSL, EVA and KAUFMANN, HELEN: *Minute Sketches of Great Composers.* N. Y.: Grosset & Dunlap, 1932. $2.50.

HENDERSON, WM. J.: *Richard Wagner, His Life and His Dramas.* N. Y.: Putnam, 1902. $4.00.

JELL, GEORGE C.: *Master Builders of Opera.* N. Y.: Charles Scribner's Sons, 1933. $2.50.

KOBBÉ, GUSTAV: *Wagner's Life and Work.* N. Y.: G. Schirmer, 1896.

MASON, DANIEL GREGORY: *Beethoven and His Forerunners.* N. Y.: Macmillan Co., 1904. $2.00.

NEWMAN, ERNEST: *Life of Richard Wagner.* N. Y.: Alfred A. Knopf, 1933. Vol. I and II, each. $5.00.

RIMSKY-KORSAKOFF, NIKOLAI: *My Musical Life.* Trans. from the Russian by J. E. Joffe. N. Y.: Alfred A. Knopf, 1923. $1.29.

SCHWIMMER, FRANCISKA: *Great Musicians as Children.* N. Y.: Doubleday, Doran & Co., 1929. $2.00.

SELIGMAN, VINCENT: *Puccini Among Friends*. N. Y.: Macmillan Co., 1938. $4.00.

SITWELL, SACHEVERELL: *Mozart*. Davies 3/6 in print in England only.

SPECHT, R.: *Giacomo Puccini*. Trans. by Phillips. N. Y.: Alfred A. Knopf, 1933. $3.75.

THAYER, ALEXANDER WHEELOCK: *Life of Beethoven*. Trans. from the German by H. E. Krehbiel. N. Y.: The Beethoven Association, 1921. $20.00.

TOYE, FRANCIS: *Giuseppe Verdi*. N. Y.: Alfred A. Knopf, 1931. $3.75.

TOYE, FRANCIS: *Rossini, A Study in Tragic-Comedy*. N. Y.: Alfred A. Knopf, 1934. $3.75.

TURNER, W. J.: *Mozart—The Man and His Works*. Alfred A. Knopf, 1938. $4.00.

WAGNER, RICHARD: *My Life* (authorized trans.). N. Y.: Dodd, Mead & Co., 1931. $5.00. Reprint edition, Tudor Publishing Co. $1.89.

BOOKS ABOUT ARTISTS

CARUSO, DOROTHY B. and GODDARD, T. B.: *Wings of Song—The Story of Caruso*. N. Y.: Minton Balch, 1928. $3.50.

EAMES, EMMA: *Some Memories and Reflections*. N. Y.: D. Appleton, 1927. $5.00.

FARRAR, GERALDINE: *Such Sweet Compulsion*. N. Y.: Greystone Press, 1938. $3.00.

GILMAN, LAWRENCE: *Toscanini and Great Music*. N. Y.: Farrar & Rinehart, 1938. $2.50.

HOMER, SIDNEY: *My Wife and I*. N. Y.: The Macmillan Co., 1939. $3.50.

KLEIN, HERMANN: *Great Women Singers of My Time*. N. Y.: E. P. Dutton, 1931. $3.50.

LAWTON, MARY: *Schumann-Heink, Last of the Titans*. N. Y.: The Macmillan Co., 1928. $3.50.

LEHMANN, LOTTE: *Midway in My Song*. Indianapolis: Bobbs Merrill, 1938. $3.00.

MELBA, NELLIE: *Melodies and Memories.* N. Y.: Doubleday Doran, 1925. $5.00.

TETRAZZINI, LUISA: *My Life of Song.* N. Y.: Dorrance, 1921. $4.00.

THOMPSON, OSCAR: *The American Singer: One Hundred Years of Success in Opera.* N. Y.: Dial Press, 1937. $2.75.

BOOKS ABOUT THE METROPOLITAN

HEYLBUT, ROSE and GERBER, AIMÉ: *Backstage at the Opera.* N. Y.: Thomas Y. Crowell Co., 1937. $3.00.

KOLODIN, IRVING: *The Metropolitan Opera, 1883-1935.* N. Y.: Oxford University Press, 1936. $3.75.

Opera Cavalcade, The Story of the Metropolitan. N. Y.: Metropolitan Opera Guild, 1938. $1.25.

TAUBMAN, H. HOWARD: *Opera Front and Back.* N. Y.: Charles Scribner's Sons, 1938. $3.75.

LIBRETTOS

The official Metropolitan librettos may be obtained, with an English translation, at prices varying from forty to seventy cents, including postage, from Mr. Charles Allen, Libretto Department, Metropolitan Opera House, New York City.

A special Libretto Service is offered to members of The Metropolitan Opera Guild, whereby official librettos of operas to be broadcast from the Metropolitan Opera House will be mailed to applicants in advance. For further details, apply to The Metropolitan Opera Guild, Inc., 654 Madison Avenue, New York, New York.

MUSICAL DICTIONARIES AND ENCYCLOPEDIAS

Baker's Biographical Dictionary of Musicians, 4th ed. N. Y.: G. Schirmer, 1939. $2.00.

Grove's Dictionary of Music and Musicians, 3rd ed. 6 vols. N. Y.: Macmillan Company, 1938-39. $18.00.

SEARCHINGER, CESAR: *Art of Music,* Vol. 9 (*The Opera*). N. Y.: National Society of Music, 1915-17. Although the work is out of print, it may be found in many libraries, and has proved of sufficient value to be listed in this volume.

THOMPSON, OSCAR: *The International Encyclopedia of Music and Musicians.* N. Y.: Dodd, Mead, 1938. $12.50.

Alphabetical List of Operas